Second-Generation Holocaust Literature

To Aidan,

Many thanks for the use of your haunting photograph. It really expresses the tone of the book well.

E. M. Hlothh.

Studies in German Literature, Linguistics, and Culture

Second-Generation Holocaust Literature

Legacies of Survival and Perpetration

Erin McGlothlin

CAMDEN HOUSE

Copyright © 2006 Erin McGlothlin

All Rights Reserved. Except as permitted under current legislation,
no part of this work may be photocopied, stored in a retrieval system,
published, performed in public, adapted, broadcast, transmitted,
recorded, or reproduced in any form or by any means,
without the prior permission of the copyright owner.

First published 2006
by Camden House

Camden House is an imprint of Boydell & Brewer Inc.
668 Mt. Hope Avenue, Rochester, NY 14620, USA
www.camden-house.com
and of Boydell & Brewer Limited
PO Box 9, Woodbridge, Suffolk IP12 3DF, UK
www.boydellandbrewer.com

ISBN: 1–57113–352–6

Library of Congress Cataloging-in-Publication Data

McGlothlin, Erin Heather.
    Second-generation holocaust literature: legacies of survival and
perpetration / Erin McGlothlin.
        p. cm. — (Studies in German literature, linguistics, and culture)
    Includes bibliographical references and index.
    ISBN 1–57113–352–6 (hardcover: alk. paper)
    1. German literature — 20th century — History and criticism.
2. Holocaust, Jewish (1939–1945), in literature. 3. Children of Holocaust
survivors, Writings of. 4. Children of Nazis, Writings of.   I. Title.
II. Series: Studies in German literature, linguistics, and culture
(Unnumbered)

PT405.M3877 2007
830.9'358 — dc22

2006016730

Illustration credits — 1 and 3: From MAUS II: A SURVIVOR'S TALE/AND HERE MY TROUBLE BEGAN by Art Spiegelman, copyright © 1986, 1989, 1990, 1991 by Art Spiegelman. Used by permission of Pantheon Books, a division of Random House, Inc.; 2: From MAUS I: A SURVIVOR'S TALE/MY FATHER BLEEDS HISTORY by Art Spiegelman. Copyright © 1973, 1980, 1982, 1984, 1985, 1986 by Art Spiegelman. Used by permission of Pantheon Books, a division of Random House, Inc. UK permissions pending from the Wylie Agency.

A catalogue record for this title is available from the British Library.

This publication is printed on acid-free paper.
Printed in the United States of America.

*In memory of my father,
Charles Holton McGlothlin (1929–1996)*

Contents

Acknowledgments ix

Introduction: Rupture and Repair:
Marking the Legacy of the Second Generation 1

Part I. The Legacy of Survival

1: "A Tale Repeated Over and Over Again":
Polyidentity and Narrative Paralysis in
Thane Rosenbaum's *Elijah Visible* 43

2: "In Auschwitz We Didn't Wear Watches":
Marking Time in Art Spiegelman's *Maus* 66

3: "Because We Need Traces":
Robert Schindel's *Gebürtig* and the Crisis
of the Second-Generation Witness 91

4: Documenting Absence in Patrick Modiano's
Dora Bruder and Katja Behrens's
"Arthur Mayer, or The Silence" 125

Part II. The Legacy of Perpetration

5: "Under a False Name": Peter Schneider's
Vati and the Misnomer of Genre 143

6: My Mother Wears a Hitler Mustache:
Marking the Mother in Niklas Frank and
Joshua Sobol's *Der Vater* 174

7: The Future of *Väterliteratur:* Bernhard
   Schlink's *Der Vorleser* and Uwe Timm's
   Am Beispiel meines Bruders   199

Conclusion: The "Glass Wall":
   Marked by an Invisible Divide   228

Works Cited   233

Index   247

Acknowledgments

I AM INDEBTED TO several institutions that supported me at the various stages of this book. To the faculty of the Department of Germanic Languages and Literatures at the University of Virginia I am grateful for their support of my research and for helping me conceive and define this project. My colleagues in the Department of Germanic Languages and Literatures at Washington University in St. Louis, along with the administration there, provided the financial assistance and time necessary to expand and refine the manuscript, and were additionally generous with advice and mentoring. I would also like to thank the Washington University Center for the Humanities and the Visiting Scholars Program at the United States Holocaust Memorial Museum's Center for Advanced Holocaust Studies for their financial support of the final stages of the publication process.

It is a pleasure to acknowledge the contribution of the following people who have played a role in the development of this manuscript: Renate Voris, Jeffrey Grossman, Benjamin Bennett, Allan Megill, Walter Grünzweig, Dan Bar-On, Janette Hudson, Joshua Kavaloski, Catherine Keane, Lynne Tatlock, Pamela Barmash, and the participants of the 2003 Seminar on Literature and the Holocaust at the Center for Advanced Holocaust Studies, especially Geoffrey Hartman, Sara Horowitz, and Elizabeth Baer. In particular, I would like to give my most heartfelt thanks to my close friend and colleague Dorothe Bach, who over the years has been my best and most reliable reader. I am also grateful to Elizabeth Dick, Theodore Jackson, Anna Leeper, and Tracy N. Graves, who assisted me with translation, editing, and indexing. Jim Walker at Camden House has been the most helpful editor I could have wished for; he made the entire process enjoyable with his generous guidance and wisdom.

Finally, I would like to recognize my friends in St. Louis and elsewhere for their unfailing confidence in my ability to make this book happen. I also wish to thank my brother Drew and sister Cara for their love and support. To Bruce Ponman I give loving thanks for his belief in me and his patience during the entire process. And last, but certainly not least, I wish to acknowledge my mother, Velma, for her encouragement, her tireless efforts to help me achieve my goals, and her generous love. She remains a role model for me.

E. McG.
May 2006

Introduction:
Rupture and Repair: Marking the Legacy of the Second Generation

For what crime did he have to atone? He didn't know. What did he have to conceal, to mask, to erase? What secret lay unconscious in him that, with the least modification in his life, would surface like a corpse — a corpse that a murderer had been tempted to drown in a lake. It was his special fate to play a bit part in a play he hadn't written, a play performed years before his birth, with its own actors and audience. And once the curtain was down, he had to remain on the stage with the others, like him, born after the performance, or during, or before, remembering the play they had seen or acted in, as torturer or as victim. Was he waiting for the curtain to go up again?
— Henri Raczymow, *Writing the Book of Esther*

Stigmata of the Unknown

In *The War After: Living with the Holocaust* (1996), Anne Karpf writes of growing up as the child of Holocaust survivors in postwar England, an experience that, as she discovers as an adult, has profoundly shaped her identity and her understanding of the world around her. For much of her childhood, youth, and early adulthood she is plagued by excessive fear of potential danger to her family, anxiety about breaking her close but at times stifling bond with her parents, and unfocused rage at having been bequeathed such a difficult and often incomprehensible history of family trauma. She struggles with what she sees as two contradictory pressures: on the one hand, she wishes to respect her parents' legacy of the Holocaust, which she believes requires her to preserve her "undifferentiated" (105), "unicellular" (102) relationship with them, fulfill a self-imposed mission to somehow redeem their experience by becoming successful and happy, and suppress her own negative emotions. On the other hand, she desires to break the symbiotic bond with them and discover her own path in life, unimpeded by a family trauma that has deeply affected her but that she has not personally experienced. Her sense of self is built not on her own lived experience but rather on a largely unknown event that preceded her birth: "It seemed then as if I hadn't lived the central experience of my life — at its heart, at mine, was an absence" (146). Her difficulty in claiming an independent identity is thus compounded by the uncanny feeling that she is forever cut off from the meaning of a past event that grounds her present life.

Karpf's dilemma becomes acute when she falls in love with a non-Jewish man, a situation that is directly at odds with her parents' attempts to preserve the family's link to Jewish tradition. Eventually, her struggle with these competing claims manifests itself physically as a severe rash:

> I tried repeatedly to reconcile these warring views until, eventually, it all extruded through my hands, unerring somatic proof (the body being an incorrigible punster) that I couldn't in fact handle it. Beads of moisture appeared, trapped beneath the skin, on the palm of one hand, and with them came a compelling urge to scratch. Then I started to claw at my left hand with the nails of my right until blood ran. This mania of scratching continued until the whole surface of the hand turned raging, stinging scarlet and there came, despite the wound (or perhaps because of it), a sense of release, followed almost immediately by guilt.
>
> This sequence was repeated many times until the palm was florid with yellow and green crests of pus. The other hand also became infected. They seemed like self-inflicted stigmata, visible and so particularly shaming. (98)

Karpf's struggle to make sense of an unlived event that has molded her life and to integrate her two irreconcilable desires, namely, to connect to the legacy of her parents' Holocaust memory and to search for a viable identity of her own apart from this memory, erupts into a full-blown somatic disorder. Her body becomes the battlefield onto which the conflict is displaced, and her frantic scratching becomes an evocative expression of her inner turmoil. Her hands, the parts first afflicted by the disorder (later it spreads to her entire body), enact the dual nature of her dilemma; just as each hand takes on the roles of both perpetrator and victim (each aggressively scratching the other in turn, each displaying the wound caused by the other), she herself is an actor with two contradictory roles in an ambivalent drama of aggression and victimization. On the one hand, she expresses intense feelings of guilt about her love for a non-Jew, perceiving her independence as both the cause of rupture in a family that has already been devastated by the Holocaust and a betrayal of Jewish tradition. In this scenario, she casts herself as her parents' tormentor, one who renews the suffering and sorrow they experienced in the Shoah. On the other hand, she feels closely tied to her parents' traumatic experiences and marks herself as the inheritor of a legacy of suffering and loss that she can barely comprehend. She performs the roles of both perpetrator and victim, categories that are defined as diametrically opposite and thus resist integration. Karpf's schizoid identifications with the extreme poles of violence and trauma mark her troubled relationship to family memory and history, erupting continually into a conflict in which she declares war against herself. Her body becomes the arena in which this engagement is staged, and the psychic conflict that turns into a physical malady leaves the trace of this struggle in the form of the wound. Karpf is thus marked by her difficult relationship to the Holocaust; her own body becomes a secondary site of the ongoing traumatic effects of the Holocaust, an event that no longer poses a real physical threat to its victims. She designates her wounds stigmata, a term that bears powerful connotations, evoking both the Christian notion of martyrdom and suffering in the figure of Jesus, whose wounds of crucifixion are resembled by Karpf's own hands, and the marks of shame that in ancient Greece were cut or burned into the body, signifying that the bearer was a member of a marginalized group, either a slave or a criminal. Stigmata are thus used to identify both sufferer and malefactor, or, translated into the language of the Holocaust, both victim and perpetrator. For this reason, Karpf's choice of the designation stigmata for her wounds is fitting, for it expresses her schizoid identification with both roles and her precarious relationship to her parents' Holocaust past. Furthermore, her lesions are particularly striking because they are hauntingly reminiscent of the marks branded into her mother's skin at Auschwitz, the legendary tattooed number that represented the Nazis' radical objectification and dehumanization of Jewish prisoners: "After years of my scratching, a close friend asked whether the place on my inside forearm that I was repeatedly injuring wasn't the same place, indeed the very same arm, where my mother's concentration camp number was inked" (106). However, unlike her mother's markings, which were made against her mother's will and signify her mother's immediate experience and survival of the Holocaust, Karpf's stigmata are self-inflicted. Significantly, it is Karpf herself who inscribes a stigma into her own body, branding herself in a public way and linking her own identity with her parents' Holocaust past. However, her physical marks remain signifiers without referent, for, unlike the tattooed numbers of her mother, they do not refer directly to any Holocaust experience. In this way, Karpf violently and masochistically transforms her body into a site marked by a Holocaust trauma that she cannot directly access, a locus of remembrance that has no recourse to lived memory. Furthermore, her literal marking of the body, in which her struggle with her parents' past manifests itself physically, is echoed by her writing, in which she attempts to inscribe into narrative an experience that is not her own. Her book, which attempts to integrate her parents' experience in the Holocaust with her own legacy of that experience, thus also represents an act of marking, one in which the text, much like her body, takes on the trace of her struggle with the past.

Karpf's perception of being marked by the Holocaust experience of her parents is evocatively echoed by a writer whose legacy comes from the diametrically opposite experience of Holocaust survival, that of Holocaust perpetration. Irene Anhalt, the daughter of an SS officer, describes a markedly similar relationship to the legacy of the Holocaust, albeit it from a different perspective, in a short narrative entitled "Abschied von meinem Vater" ("Farewell to My Father"). In this letter to her deceased father, which she wrote in the late 1980s, Anhalt attempts to understand the effects his involvement in the Nazi regime and participation in Nazi crimes have had both on her childhood and on her current relationship to Germany's legacy of genocide and violence. At one point in this necessarily one-sided dialogue, she describes a particularly striking postwar scene in which she, still a child, waits for her father, about whom she knows very little, to return from a Soviet prisoner-of-war camp:

> More and more often now I sat down on the damp stones that led from the courtyard to the cellar, and scratched swastikas into the dry skin of my shins. The left leg, the one that had been shot, which still dragged a little when I walked, I scratched especially deeply. I placed the crosses so close together it seemed as though they were taking each other by the hand, and all the while I whispered the forbidden names, Hitler, Stalin, Goebbels, Goering. I did not stop until both legs were smeared with blood. ("Farewell," 36)[1]

The child, herself scarred by the violence of Germany's brutal war (her foot was wounded by shrapnel while she and her mother fled westward in front of the Soviet army in 1945), performs, much like the adult Karpf, an act of self-mutilation, marking herself with a different sort of stigma — the swastika, the powerfully evocative emblem of the vanquished National Socialist dictatorship. Anhalt's carving of the swastika into her already marked body takes on a ritualistic quality as she chants the names of the Nazi leaders, the criminals whose names have become forbidden for the child to utter in postwar Germany, a period marked by sudden social amnesia with regard to Nazi crimes. Her fervid whispering functions as an incantation that is meant to conjure up her father's past, an experience that, despite the silence surrounding it, she knows is significant, but of which she is ignorant. By invoking the unspoken and unexperienced Nazi past, the child attempts to somehow understand and claim it for herself. At the same time, in her inscription of her body with the symbolic iconography of National Socialism, she tries to insert herself into her father's world of Nazi ideology. With her act of self-

---

[1] "Immer häufiger setzte ich mich auf die feuchten Steine, die vom Hof in den Keller führten, und ritzte mir Hakenkreuze in die trockene Haut meiner Schienbeine. Das linke Bein, das Durchschossene, das ich noch immer etwas nachzog beim Gehen, ritzte ich besonders tief ein. Ich setzte die Kreuze so dicht nebeneinander, daß es aussah, als würden sie sich bei den Händen fassen, dabei flüsterte ich die verbotenen Namen Hitler, Stalin, Goebbels, Göring. Erst wenn beide Beine blutverschmiert waren, hörte ich auf" (Anhalt, "Abschied," 42).

mutilation, she thus transforms herself into a site of engagement with the Nazi past, marking her own body as the property of both father and Fatherland. Like Karpf with her frantic scratching, Anhalt performs the roles of both perpetrator and victim with her ritualistic carving of stigmata. On the one hand, with her sadistic-masochistic cutting, she reproduces the violent perpetration of the Nazis and figures herself as complicit in Nazi crimes. At the same time, however, she herself suffers from this violence and thus is marked as a victim of Nazi inscription as well. For Anhalt, as for Karpf, the child's struggle to know the Holocaust and Nazi past of the parents is played out on the body, which becomes marked by an event it has never experienced. In this way, with the inscription of their stigmata, both women perform acts of remembrance that have no referent in their own memory. Anhalt's letter to her absent father, like Karpf's book, documents her attempt to come to grips with an unlived past that powerfully affects her life in the present.

"Phantom Pains": The Gap between Experience and Effect

Karpf and Anhalt are two writers who, in very different ways and from entirely different perspectives, share a common problem: both feel marked by the continued presence of the Holocaust past. Neither has any direct experience with the events of the Shoah, yet both have a secondary link to the Nazi design to exterminate European Jewry through their parents, who were directly involved in radically different ways: Anhalt's father as a perpetrator of the crimes and Karpf's parents as victims of them. Although their parents' respective relationships to the Holocaust differ intrinsically as a result of the very different roles they played (or were forced to play) in it, Karpf and Anhalt share the structurally similar (if qualitatively different) feeling of being marked by an extreme experience of trauma and violence that neither woman has personally lived through. The trope of the stigma, which appears in both women's writings, is particularly fitting for their respective relationships to the past, for according to the Greek origin of the word, stigmata function as a common designation for both slaves and criminals, two radically different groups. These two types of bearers of stigmata stand at the extreme poles of the experience of violence, perpetration, and victimization: the slave, as one who has been forcibly robbed of self-determination and turned into an object, and the criminal, as one who has violated the law and transgressed against codified social mores. The critical difference between the two groups is the element of agency: the slave possesses no agency and is therefore innocent, while the criminal willfully abuses his agency (and perhaps even robs another of agency) and is therefore guilty. Significantly, however, with the stigmata, both groups are branded as other and thus marginalized socially. Their respective experiences are designated with the common mark because, by virtue of their proximity to violence and violation, they are not easily integrated into social structures. As the Israeli psychologist Dan Bar-On discusses in his book, *The Indescribable and the Undiscussable: Reconstructing Human Discourse after Trauma* (1999), both poles of the experience of violence resist incorporation into conventional discourse: the trauma of the victim on account of its indescribability, and the violation and brutality of the perpetrator by virtue of its undiscussability.[2] The two radically different experiences of victimization and perpetration, as signified by the stigmata, are linked together by their otherness and their inability to be adequately transmitted by linguistic and narrative conventions. Anhalt and Karpf thus, in a sense, share a common situation, for they possess stigmata of the non-integratable experience of Holocaust violence, although in

---

[2] Trauma studies have given us a vocabulary to describe not only the trauma of the Holocaust survivor, but, more recently, the ways in which the children of survivors have been traumatized as well. Thus we have a good deal of insight into how the experience of violence affects both the victim and subsequent generations. However, the question of what violence does to the violator has yet to be answered and a vocabulary describing the long-term psychic effects of violation has yet to be developed, making it difficult to describe the legacy of the children of perpetrators. Some researchers use the word "trauma" in their general discussions of the psychic disturbances in the children of both perpetrators and survivors (Bergmann and Jucovy, Bar-On ["An Encounter"], Eckstaedt, Rosenthal, Auerhahn and Laub), but there is understandably a good deal of hesitation to use the word to refer directly to the experiences of the children of perpetrators. Yael Danieli, editor of the *International Handbook of Multigenerational Legacies of Trauma* (1998), implies the existence of trauma in the children of perpetrators by her inclusion of an essay on the children of Nazis. The author of that essay, Gertrud Hardtmann, includes a section entitled "Nazi Children's Trauma," but unfortunately she neither develops a definition of second-generation perpetrator trauma nor attempts to explain how the trauma of Nazi children differs from that of the children of survivors. Dan Bar-On's distinction in *The Indescribable and the Undiscussable* between a trauma that is indescribable (one that is too painful to put into language) and a history that is undiscussable (one that has been effaced from normalized discourse) is as yet perhaps the most perceptive discernment between the two groups. On a less psychoanalytic note, another way of distinguishing the two groups is suggested by Eva Hoffman, who prefers to reserve the word trauma for the survivors of persecution and their offspring: "For tragedy, of course, involves a conflict — agon — between opposing principles and agents. Trauma is produced by persecution of subjects to whom all agency and principle have been denied" (*After Such Knowledge*, 41). Hoffman implies here that perpetrators (and, by extension, their offspring) thus cannot be designated victims of trauma, however they were affected psychically by their acts of violation, but rather they, as agents of historical conflict, should be seen in the context of the tragic.

each case the signifier of otherness points to a different referent: in Karpf's case, the shame of the stigma is grounded in the experience of the victim, whereas Anhalt's mark of shame comes from the experience of the perpetrator. Significantly, however, unlike the slave or criminal of ancient times, whose stigmata refer to their own lived experiences of violence, Karpf and Anhalt possess stigmata for which there are no referents in their own lives. For, importantly, Karpf is not a victim of the Holocaust, and Anhalt is not a perpetrator. Their marks are not the physical signifiers of their own personal experience, but rather are the inherited traces of their parents' history of trauma and violation, a history that for the two women is both known (in the sense that they know of the event) and at the same time profoundly unknown (in the sense that their knowledge does not derive from personal experience).[3]

Karpf's and Anhalt's respective narratives belong to a larger body of literature by writers who, as a result of their parents' experiences, feel similarly marked by the unlived Holocaust past. For this group of writers, which liter-

---

[3] Dori Laub and Nanette C. Auerhahn, in their extensive work on traumatic memory, have developed a typology of traumatic knowledge not only among the survivors of trauma but in the second generation as well. As they explain, in the case of traumatic events, one is always caught between the extreme poles of knowledge and amnestic ignorance: "We all hover at different distances between knowing and not knowing about trauma, caught between the compulsion to complete the process of knowing and the inability or fear of doing so. It is the nature of trauma to elude our knowledge, because of both defence and deficit" (Laub and Auerhahn, 288). With regard to the second generation, the crisis of knowledge derives precisely from the fact that the children did not experience the traumatic event themselves: "Survivors' children, with their empathic capacity and relative distance from the experience, may serve as an easier medium for knowledge to evolve and memories to emerge, with associations and imagery (Auerhahn and Prelinger, 1983). But theirs is a displaced knowledge — at the centre there is a 'hole' (Fresco, 1984; Cohen, 1985), an event that defies representation and instead is experienced as an absence" (Laub and Auerhahn, 289). Although Auerhahn and Laub do not discuss in detail the problem of knowing for the perpetrators of trauma, they do acknowledge that it is relevant to perpetrator psychology: "Of course, it is not just survivors who can live in a twilight state between knowing and not knowing" (Auerhahn and Laub, 25). One could extend their analysis of the forms of knowing to the legacy of violation and the defenses against knowing in the perpetrator family, in which the crimes are often alluded to but never openly acknowledged or admitted. In her recent book, *After Such Knowledge: Memory, History and the Legacy of the Holocaust* (2004), Eva Hoffman connects the second-generation problem of knowledge to Freud's notion of the uncanny: "This is exactly the crux of the second generation's difficulty: that it has inherited not experience, but its shadows. The uncanny, in Freud's formulation, is the sensation of something that is both very alien and deeply familiar, something that only the unconscious knows. If so, then the second generation has grown up with the uncanny" (66).

ary critics beginning with Alan Berger have termed the *second generation,* the Holocaust figures as an intimate companion during childhood and adult life; they experience the aftermath and the legacy of National Socialist crimes intimately and personally in what Eric Santner calls the "primal scene of socialization" (35) — that of the family. The children of the victims and perpetrators alike grew up with the simultaneous presence and absence of Holocaust memory in their everyday family lives, and thus feel profoundly stamped by its legacy. Just as the identity of their parents is defined largely with reference to their experiences of those dark years between 1933 and 1945 (specifically, with regard to whether they created the darkness or were overcome by it), so too the children construct their own identity in relation to the Holocaust. According to Eva Hoffman, the daughter of survivors, "For me, in the beginning was the war, and the Holocaust was the ontological basis of my universe" (*After Such Knowledge,* 278).

The present study examines texts that fall under the rubric of second-generation writing, meaning that they are either written by the children of Holocaust perpetrators or survivors, or that they are written from the perspective of these children (a distinction that will be made clear later). One of the most prominent aspects of these texts, I argue, is the distinct sense of being marked by an unlived narrative, of carrying the trace of the Holocaust past within the present. For Nadine Fresco, the daughter of survivors, the mark of the legacy of survival is a stigma of suffering and shame, handed down intergenerationally from survivor-parent to child:

> On arrival in Paris, the deportees who returned from the camps were sent to the Hôtel Lutétia. And each of them, merely by his return, emphasized the absence of someone else who had not come back [. . .] Like a chain of remorse and reproach, in which each individual drew on the back of the one in front of him the mark of shame drawn at the same moment on his own back by the one behind him. And at the end of the chain was the child. (425)

In Fresco's powerful image, the survivor, whose very existence becomes a signifier for the multitudes who did not survive, transfers the signification of absence down the line to the second generation. In this way, the legacy of Holocaust survival is inscribed into the back of the child, a mark that is sensed intensely but nevertheless remains unknown and inaccessible. It exists as an empty sign, a signifier for which there is no content to be discovered: "It was an impossible mourning, 'wounds of the memory' of parents frozen in silence, behind their dry eyes (Schneider, 1980). They transmitted only the wound to their children, to whom memory had been refused and who grew up in the compact void of the unspeakable" (Fresco, 419). The children of survivors inherit their parents' wounds, or more precisely, they inherit not the wound itself (the direct experience of trauma and physical damage), but the mere mark of the wound, the signifier for an experience not personally experienced, "the scar without the wound" (Sicher, *Breaking Crystal*, 27).

For the children of perpetrators, whom Eva Hoffman terms "that contrapuntal 'second generation'" (*After Such Knowledge*, 118), the Nazi past is likewise inscribed into the present as a trace that cannot be assimilated into postwar German normality, a force that disrupts the drive toward the amnestic displacement of the perpetration of the Holocaust. According to Almuth Massing, the whitewashed landscape of postwar Germany disguises but cannot erase the stain of brutality and murder:

> Buildings, streets, and square show hardly a trace of all this since the war, nor do they evoke memories of the fascist scenes that were staged there. The Adolf-Hitlerplatz is called Albaniplatz once more. Its expanse of gray asphalt is given over to traffic. History has been smoothed over as well. And yet in the souls of men, it lives on. This violent relationship with the past has left its mark. ("Effects," 95)[4]

Unlike Fresco's image of the unseen inscription of survival into the back of the child, here the mark of the past does not figure as an emblem worn on the body. Rather, it festers inside as an internal lesion that, likewise unseen, prohibits the easy digestion of history, despite the external whitewashing of the traces of violence and the restoration of normality. The offspring of perpetrators inherit the history of their parents' unacknowledged crimes, a legacy of violence and violation whose effects are felt as a stain upon their souls.

The writers of the second generation thus possess the mark of a history they did not themselves experience, a visceral feeling that something critical distinguishes them from their contemporaries. Nadine Fresco describes this sense of being marked by an unlived past as one in which the body displays the symptoms of a trauma it never experienced: "The amputated are left only with phantom pains, but who can say that the pain felt in a hand that one no longer has is not pain. These latter-day Jews are like people who have had a hand amputated that they never had. It is a phantom pain, in which amnesia takes the place of memory" (421). Fresco employs the metaphor of the phantom pains of a limb that never existed to describe the complex relationship of the children of survivors to their parents' experience in the Holocaust, but the image is evocative of the situation of the children of perpetra-

---

[4] "Bauwerke, Straßen und Plätze lassen nach dem Krieg kaum Spuren erkennen noch erwecken sie Erinnerungen an ihr faschistisches Szenarium. Der Adolf-Hitler-Platz heißt wieder Albaniplatz. Sein grauer Asphalt schafft begehbare Fläche. Geschichte ist eingeebnet. Doch in den Seelen der Menschen ist sie nicht ausgelöscht. Dieser gewaltsame Umgang mit Vergangenheit hinterließ Folgen" (Massing, "Auswirkungen," 71).

tors as well, for it illustrates a crisis of signification that characterizes both groups' writing about the past. Just as the pains cannot be traced to their cause, the trauma of the second generation is essentially divorced from the Holocaust experience that engendered it. The signifier remains, but it is unable to locate its referent, resulting in a truncated relationship between experience and effect. For the children of survivors, this experience is one of unintegrated trauma and rupture in familial continuity; for the children of perpetrators it is the family's unintegratable history of violation and brutality. The event that has marked the second generation of both legacies is inaccessible, yet the mark of that experience remains and, like the phantom pain, continues to haunt its bearer. Fresco's image of the amputated hand is a particularly fitting metaphor for the task of the second-generation writer, who speaks from this condition of a priori loss and yet writes through the amputation, holding the pen with a phantom hand that through the work of writing is fashioned into a functioning limb. By taking up the pen, the children of both survivors and perpetrators, despite the very different legacies they inherit and the different ways they respond to these legacies, begin to reconnect to an unknown experience that has indelibly marked their lives.

The writers of the second generation, as evidenced by Anhalt and Karpf, attempt to negotiate the crisis of signification and their severed relationship to the Holocaust through the process of imaginative writing, in which they attempt to explore through language an event that they do not personally know but that they nevertheless sense by its absence. Their imagination of the Holocaust past of the parents becomes a way for them to reconnect to the referent of the mark and thus to try to establish a link between experience and effect. In this way, the writers not only investigate the reference point of their invisible inscriptions, but they in turn actively inscribe as well, marking the ways in which the Holocaust has impacted them. In its often obsessive engagement with the Holocaust past, the second generation seeks to artistically restore some of the holes that riddle the memory of the catastrophe, to imagine an event of which one cannot be epistemologically certain, to tell "the story to remember what the survivors themselves have forgotten" (Sicher, *Breaking Crystal,* 32). In short, the second generation engages in what Marianne Hirsch calls the work of *postmemory,* which she defines as "the response of the second generation to the trauma of the first" ("Surviving Images," 8). For Hirsch the hallmarks of postmemory are the epistemological and experiential distance from the traumatic events themselves as well as the repeated attempts on the part of the second generation to bridge this divide through imagination and representation:

> The term "postmemory" is meant to convey its temporal and qualitative difference from survivor memory, its secondary, or second-generation memory quality, its basis in displacement, its vicariousness

and belatedness. Postmemory is a powerful form of memory precisely because its connection to its object or source is mediated not through recollection but through representation, projection and creation — often based on silence rather than speech, on the invisible rather than the visible. That is not, of course, to say that survivor memory itself is unmediated, but that it is more directly — chronologically — connected to the past. ("Surviving Images," 9)

Postmemory, according to Hirsch, is not a matter of writing a history of the Holocaust, of recovering the facts in order to fill in the epistemological gaps. Rather than concerning itself primarily with certainty and historical truth, postmemorial writing employs narrative to acknowledge the impossibility of fully grasping what happened, even as it ventures to construct a story about the Holocaust. In this way, the writing of the second generation gives expression to the chronic condition of what Henri Raczymow, the son of survivors, terms "memory shot through with holes" ("Memory Shot Through With Holes," 98) and at the same time tells a story of the disaster, however fragmented, faulty, and incomplete. In the space of narrative, the writers explore their imagination of the events of the Holocaust and their own sense of coming "after" it. Second-generation writing acknowledges and attempts to transcend its inability to know and fully remember the Holocaust and thus it performs a crucial double move: it both records the personal and historical rupture caused by the Nazi genocide of European Jews and, at the same time, attempts to effect a measure of rehabilitation through imagination, a creative repair of a history torn asunder in which the signifier is once again joined to a referent, if only provisionally.[5] Raczymow uses the metaphor of sewing to describe this twofold gesture: "The memory has burst, as a balloon bursts, but we spend our time sewing it back up. Sewing is an old tradition among us. In fact, sewing scraps together is every writer's task, a hypothetically endless task, an impossible task" ("Memory Shot Through With Holes," 103). Nava Semel, also the child of survivors, likewise sees writing as a process that simultaneously opens up the scarred-over wounds of history and stitches them back together again: "Writing tears them off and sews them at the same time" (69). The metaphor of sewing is particularly apt for the project of second-generation writing, not only because, as Raczymow claims, it defers the drive toward totality with its inherent incomplete-

---

[5] Alan Berger, in his study *Children of Job: American Second-Generation Witnesses to the Holocaust*, connects this idea of repair among the children of survivors to Jewish theological tradition with the concept of *tikkun*, an imperative toward perfection of the world. Berger distinguishes between two types of repair: *tikkun atzmi*, or mending of the self, which he associates with the tradition of Jewish particularism; and *tikkun olam*, or repair of the world, which he links to Jewish universalism.

ness, its gaps between the stitches, but because the act of sewing is itself also a form of marking, a repair that, with the stitch, leaves visible traces.

Narratives of Crisis

Second-generation literature thus becomes the arena in which the creative imagining, the rupture and repair of the Holocaust past take place, the garment that the writer simultaneously rends and mends. Like the bodies of Anhalt and Karpf, which are marked by a bitter struggle with the Holocaust past, narrative itself is marked by the second-generation writer's attempt to imagine, represent, and come to terms with the presence of an unknown past. The stigmatization of the second-generation body is displaced onto the body of the text, where the crisis of signification marks the text's poetics. In much second-generation writing, stigmatization and anxiety about signification are performed not only at the text's thematic level, but in its narrative organization as well. According to Geoffrey Hartman, this is often the case with narratives that attempt to know and come to terms with traumatic events, for the processes of repression involved in trauma and its legacy prohibit the representation of the event directly:

> The theory holds that the knowledge of trauma, or the knowledge which comes from that source, is composed of two contradictory elements. One is the traumatic event, registered rather than experienced. It seems to have bypassed perception and consciousness and falls directly into the psyche. The other is a kind of memory of the event, in the form of a perpetual troping of it by the bypassed or severely split (dissociated) psyche. On the level of poetics, literal and figurative may correspond to these two types of cognition. ("On Traumatic Knowledge and Literary Studies," 537)

For Hartman, the text's tropological processes reveal the fractured condition of signification caused by the traumatic event, in which the referent of the traumatic event can not be accessed and all that remains is the signifier of the traumatic symptom. In terms of marking, this means that the text often cannot explicitly refer to its own stigmatized content, but rather can only perform this stigmatization figuratively in the way that it produces that content. The crisis of signification in the second generation resounds in the text's narrative structure, where the struggle to construct, absorb, displace, defer, repress, reproduce, reject, conceal, and uncover the legacy of the Holocaust leaves its own mark. The second generation's attempt to imagine its parents' past results in a narrative crisis in which narrative voice fractures, protagonists multiply in a compulsion to repeat, temporality is suspended, and generic conventions are transgressed or radically reshaped. These narrative transgressions are not merely gestures of experimentation; rather, they are textual wounds that struggle to solve the crisis of signification and to heal. By examining these narrative scars, we glimpse the extent to which not only the writer but the literary text itself is marked by the continuing aftershocks of the Shoah. For this reason, the manner in which the second-generation text tells the story of its struggle with its Holocaust legacy *itself* tells a story of that legacy. The text's poetics become the site at which the events of the Holocaust are registered and their legacy is inscribed. The writing of the second generation functions as a residue of this marking of Holocaust legacy, which leaves its traces in the process of writing rather than revealing the full presence of the event.

Gazing into a Common Chasm: Legacies of Survival and Perpetration

Because my study centers on texts written quite consciously from the position of the second generation — that is, from the perspective of the children of those who directly experienced or perpetrated the Holocaust — I employ the term *second-generation Holocaust literature*. My use of the designation *second generation* is based on the commonly used definition developed by the literary critics Alan Berger and Efraim Sicher, who have borrowed the term from psychological and journalistic studies of the children of survivors by Martin S. Bergmann and Milton E. Jucovy, Dan Bar-On (*Fear and Hope, Legacy of Silence,* "An Encounter"), Aaron Hass, Robert M. Prince, Helen Epstein, and others. Berger defines the term fairly narrowly, reserving it for writers who are actually "offspring of Jewish Holocaust survivors" (1).[6] Sicher retains Berger's term but expands it to include other Jewish writers of the same generation who are writing from the perspective of "after":

> Some might argue that only children of survivors have the right to speak for the victims; what then, one might ask, of adopted children, children of refugees, or the generation contemporaneous with children of survivors who may share many of their psychological, ideological, and theological concerns? [. . .] I start out from the broadest possible view of the "second generation," following George Steiner's self-definition as "a kind of survivor," and I incorporate all who write "after" in order to survey a wide — but not exhaustive — range of themes

---

[6] In Berger's most recent work on the second generation, the anthology *Second Generation Voices,* which was coedited with Naomi Berger, he broadens his inquiry to include the descendents of Holocaust perpetrators, which the Bergers term "another second generation" (1). Significantly, in expanding their definition the Bergers retain the biographical component that requires that both sides of the second generation be the actual offspring of perpetrators and survivors.

and issues in the context of both the particular problems of the generation of the children of survivors and the broader issue of writing identity after Auschwitz. (*Breaking Crystal,* 7)

Sicher employs the term *second-generation Holocaust literature* to describe not only the texts written by the children of survivors but, more generally, to include writings that explore the legacy of survival, whether or not the writer's family had direct experience of the Holocaust. I take Sicher's framework as my departure for this usage, for the texts I include in this study are written by both writers whose families experienced the Holocaust and those whose families were not involved in the Holocaust but who nevertheless take on the perspective of the second generation and access that experience imaginatively.[7] Furthermore, I expand Sicher's definition, which views second-generation literature about the Holocaust as necessarily a literature that addresses the memory of survival, to include texts written from the point of view of the children of perpetrators, a group of texts sometimes known in German as *Väterliteratur,* or the *literature of the fathers.* Despite the fact that the term has been employed in the field of psychology for at least two decades to include both groups (Bergmann and Jucovy, Bar-On [*Fear and Hope, Legacy of Silence,* "An Encounter"], Eckstaedt, Rosenthal), the field of literary studies has largely avoided considering both the children of perpetrators and the children of survivors under the common designation second generation (Sigrid Weigel is a notable exception). Although the ways in which the Holocaust was experienced by the parents and therefore the legacy transmitted to the children are quite different for the two groups, the general positions of the children to their parents' pasts are quite similar: both groups feel marked by the Holocaust, an event that is ever present in their lives but not personally experienced, and both struggle to understand their own place in the world in light of their link to the traumatic past. There is much that argues for comparing the two groups, as Eric Santner suggests when he employs the term second generation to designate the children of perpetrators, noting the "remarkable similarities" found in both groups (35). Furthermore, as scholars such as Dan Diner point out, rather than separated by the legacy the Holocaust, the offspring of survivors and perpetrators are profoundly conjoined in "a kind of communality of opposites" ("Negative

---

[7] Critics have suggested various designations for writers who have no personal experience of the Holocaust but attempt to access the experience imaginatively: Geoffrey Hartman calls them "witnesses by adoption" (*The Longest Shadow,* 8), Norma Rosen employs the term "witnesses-through-the-imagination" (51) and Froma Zeitlin proposes "vicarious witnesses." Marianne Hirsch goes one further than Hartman in describing her theory of postmemory "as retrospective witnessing by adoption" ("Surviving Images," 10).

Symbiosis," 251)[8] tied to the memory of the Shoah. Despite the gulf that separates the legacy of perpetration from the legacy of survival and the qualitative differences in their perspectives, the children of survivors and the children of perpetrators are like two sides of the same coin, for they both must confront the aftermath of an event that they have not experienced. Both groups stand at the opposite edges of the chasm of the Shoah and gaze transfixed into the depths.[9]

Although the respective fields of literary criticism and psychology possess quite different goals and focus on different aspects of the phenomenon of the second generation, the suitability of the procedure by which psychology

---

[8] "eine Art gegensätzlicher Gemeinsamkeit" (Diner, "Negative Symbiose," 185).

[9] Angela Kühner warns that one must be careful when employing the concept of trauma to avoid "the problem of drawing a parallel between the side of the victims and that of the perpetrators" ("das [. . .] Problem der Parallelisierung von Täter- und Opferseite"), for the trauma of the children of survivors is of a radically different order than the "heavy burden" ("schwere Last") experienced by the children of perpetrators (77). However, Kühner agrees that, despite the inherent incomparability of their disparate legacies, the two groups are in fact linked by their respective perspectives on a common experience: "The same event that traumatized the collective of victims is often of central importance for the identity and collective memory of the side of the perpetrators" ("Das gleiche Ereignis, das das Opferkollektiv traumatisiert hat, ist häufig auch für die Identität und das kollektive Gedächtnis der Täterseite von zentraler Bedeutung" [77]). Following Dan Diner, Kühner argues that the second generation's intensely personal relationship to the Holocaust, whether stemming from the legacy of perpetration or that of survival, distinguishes it from the more general (German or Jewish) public that has no intimate link to the event: "It is one thing to experience days of remembrance, films, books, and memorials with the consciousness that 'it could have happened to me, it happened to my ancestors,' and quite another to be fully aware that one's own ancestors belonged to the perpetrators or the victims. For this reason, there is simultaneously a deep-reaching difference (gap) between the descendents of the perpetrators and those of the victims and, according to Diner, a 'communality of opposites' that is inevitably shaped by the same event. Every attempt at public commemoration or public debate is faced with the challenge of doing justice to this tense relationship between difference and commonality" ("Es ist etwas völlig anderes, ob jemand Gedenktage, Filme, Bücher, Gedenkstätten in dem Bewusstsein erlebt 'es hätte mir passieren können,' es ist meinen Vorfahren passiert, oder ob jemand dies im Bewusstsein erlebt, dass die eigenen Vorfahren zu den Tätern oder Mitläufern gehörten. Zwischen den Nachkommen der Täter- und Opferseite gibt es deshalb gleichzeitig eine tief greifende Verschiedenheit (Kluft) und die von Diner beschriebene 'gegensätzliche Gemeinsamkeit,' die in der unausweichlichen Prägung durch das gleiche Ereignis liegt. Jeder Versuch des öffentlichen Gedenkens und der öffentlichen Auseinandersetzung steht vor der Herausforderung, diesem Spannungsverhältnis zwischen Verschiedenheit und Gemeinsamkeit gerecht zu werden" [108]).

approaches memory one generation after the Holocaust suggests that the same can be done in literary studies. One might ask why there have been very few attempts to look at the literature of both groups in conjunction with one another.[10] For despite the profound difference in point of reference for the two types of literature and the problem of bringing them together without relativizing either the suffering of the victims and survivors or the guilt of the perpetrators, their uncannily similar expressions of being marked by a devastating event merit their juxtaposition, if not comparison. Without conflating the two groups or claiming reconciliation between them, this book affirms this position by bringing second-generation literature and *Väterliteratur* together to investigate how individual second-generation texts imagine the Holocaust and mediate its legacy.

Defining the Signifiers:
Second-Generation Literature and *Väterliteratur*

Before I proceed to an analysis of the significance of various connotations of marking as well as a description of the texts under investigation in this study, I believe it is useful to examine briefly the terms *second-generation literature* and *Väterliteratur*. As stated above, I choose *second-generation literature* to designate both literature from the perspective of survivors' children and that from the point of view of the children of Nazi perpetrators, although I refer to *Väterliteratur* in chapters 5, 6, and 7 in my discussion of specific texts that have been attributed to that genre.

---

[10] Alan L. Berger and Naomi Berger have recently published an anthology of autobiographical writings of the two groups entitled *Second Generation Voices: Reflections by Children of Holocaust Survivors and Perpetrators*. Although the Bergers break new ground by including the work of both children of survivors and children of perpetrators in the same volume, their project does not aim at a textual analysis of this literature, for it is presented primarily as a window into the socio-psychology of the second generation and not as literature *per se*. Furthermore, the Bergers' extensive experience with the work of the children of survivors and unfamiliarity with the writings of the children of perpetrators result in a significant imbalance in favor of the legacy of survival. Fewer than a third of the contributions focus on the legacy of perpetration, and all of these, with the exception of an article by Gottfried H. Wagner, were originally written in English by Germans who now reside in the United States. This near-exclusive focus on literature written in English perhaps accounts for the Bergers' unfamiliarity with the large body of German-language *Väterliteratur* ("Why has there not been an outpouring of literature of second-generation perpetrators akin to that written by second-generation Holocaust witnesses? Perhaps the contributions in this part will stimulate others to respond" [257]) and their mistaken claim that responses by the German second generation emerged only in the late 1980s (8).

The term *second generation*, developed in psychological studies of the children of survivors and then applied to literature written by them, is generally accepted as a useful designation by a number of critics who have written on post-Holocaust literature, including Berger, Sicher, Hirsch, Hartman, James Young, and others. Berger, the first critic to write a book-length analysis of the literature of the second generation, identifies the term with biblical history and the (dis)continuity of Jewish cultural and religious identity (as indicated by the title of his book, *Children of Job*) and employs it consciously to link the events of the Holocaust to previous catastrophes in Jewish history:

> Like the second children of Job, these second-generation witnesses attest to an event that they never lived through but that ineluctably shapes their lives. Further, like the transmission of earlier transformative events in Jewish history such as the story of the Exodus, and the destructions of the Temple, the telling of the Holocaust story must be passed *l'dor va'dor*, from generation to generation. (1)

For Berger, the term signals both the discontinuity and massive destruction wrought by the Shoah, requiring that history "restart" with a first and therefore a second generation, and the continuity of Jewish history that is passed down between the generations despite the catastrophes that threaten to destroy it. Although Sicher and others assume Berger's designation for the literature of survivors' children, however, Berger's overt association of the term with Jewish history is often downplayed or dropped from the content altogether, and what remains is the largely unexplored term itself. *Second-generation literature* is mostly used self-evidently in literary criticism to designate a group of texts that signal the rupture in history caused by the Holocaust and the attempt to effect some sort of regeneration.

For Sigrid Weigel, however, the term is anything but self-evident, for it implies a particular conception of the Holocaust's place within (or without) history as well as an association of that history with what she terms "a familial, genealogical concept of time."[11] The Holocaust is figured by the term *second generation* both as a unique catastrophe that is extracted out of the continuity of history and as an original event that propagates both history and familial continuity. In Weigel's view, the term *second generation* contains a similar paradox to the one that governs the notion of the unique character of the Holocaust: if the Holocaust is indeed a completely unique event, a catastrophe without precedent or comparison, then it must stand outside the continuity of history. Yet if the Holocaust does not belong to history, then how can one try to explain its causes, to integrate it into its own time, to

---

[11] "eine familiale, genealogische Zeitvorstellung" (Weigel, "Télescopage im Unbewussten," 270).

represent it with language, which according to James Young, "tends to mend perceived breaking points in history" (*Writing and Rewriting the Holocaust*, 97)? The concept *second generation* is thus practically a "catch-all" term that in its emotive and textual power aligns itself with biblical, even mythical notions of inherited guilt and punishment, chosenness, and regeneration, while at the same time insisting on its rupture from any tradition that might provide a model for its own self-understanding. Furthermore, as Weigel points out, conventional deployments of the term assume a rigid distinction between the first generation, that of the direct participants, whether survivors or perpetrators, and the generation that follows, which has no direct experience of the event. Such a gross division of Holocaust experience into generations of full experience or complete non-experience ignores the interlinking (*Verschachtelung*) of various age groups who were involved to a lesser degree (for example, as exiles who left Germany after the 1938 *Kristallnacht* pogroms or as members of the Hitler Youth and League of German Girls) but nevertheless were profoundly affected by their experiences ("'Generation' as a Symbolic Form," 272).[12]

I discuss the genre of *Väterliteratur* in detail in chapters 5, 6, and 7; however, I believe it is critical to examine the term here as a designation as well. Like second-generation literature, *Väterliteratur* relies on the concept of history as a discourse experienced in the family. However, in contrast to the term *second generation*, which stresses the idea of genealogical regeneration and inheritance between generations and beyond, *Väterliteratur* posits the engagement with the Holocaust past as a one-time conflict within the family. According to Eric Santner, the German postwar family is the primary

---

[12] Eva Hoffman further points out that, at least on the side of the legacy of survival (and, one could argue, with the legacy of perpetration as well), the term "second generation" implies a homogeneous character to what in reality is a very diverse group: "If a 'generation' is defined by shared historical experience and certain attitudes or beliefs that follow from it, then the 'second generation' is surely a very tenuous instance of it. We have grown up, in the postwar Jewish dispersion, in different countries and cultures, under very different circumstances and within different political systems" (*After Such Knowledge*, 28). However, as Hoffman continues, despite the lack of uniformity in social terms, there is much commonality on a more figurative level: "Perhaps the character of this grouping can best be defined (to use a term borrowed from a certain idea of the nation) as an 'imagined community' — that is, a community based not so much on geography or circumstance as on sets of meanings, symbols, and even literary fictions that it has in common and that enable its members to recognize and converse with each other with a sense of mutual belonging" (*After Such Knowledge*, 28). With regard to the legacy of perpetration, Harold Marcuse has developed a detailed system of seven "age cohorts" that parses the rough and often misleading designations of the first, second, and third generations in Germany.

arena in which the second generation inherits its connection to Germany's Nazi past and perpetration of the Holocaust: "legacies — or perhaps more accurately: the ghosts, the revenant objects — of the Nazi period are transmitted to the second and third generations at the sites of the primal scene of socialization, that is, within the context of a certain psychopathology of the postwar family" (35). By designating the second generation's struggle with family history *Väterliteratur*, critics align the engagement with the past with an Oedipal conception of family conflict, focusing exclusively on the relationship between father and child. In this case, the father is seen as the representative of the history in the family, the parent that transmits the memory of the Third Reich to the child. However, although numerous critics employ the term (see chapter 5), only a few call into question certain of its ideological associations. Even those who, like Gisela Moffit and Susan Figge, question many of the assumptions made about the genre, particularly the notion that the conflict is reserved for the father-son relationship and that the daughter has no place in this paradigm, accept the term's privileging of the father as the figure around whom postwar Germans' memory of the Holocaust revolves. The *literature of the fathers* is thus a term that, rather than concentrating on contemporary Germany's connection to its Holocaust past as the primary object of inquiry, sees the past only as it is manifested in the authoritarian figure of the father and furthermore uses the Holocaust as the arena in which the seemingly more important generational conflict is played out. In the critical understanding of the term *Väterliteratur*, the memory of Holocaust perpetration is displaced by family conflict and thus risks disappearing in a euphemism that erases the magnitude of the event by reducing it to a mere battle between father and child, in which the child is figured as the father's victim and thus appropriates the role of the historical victims of the Holocaust. The zeal with which critics have adopted the term *Väterliteratur* can be seen as a linguistic repetition of the very element that they criticize in the texts, namely the displacement of the perpetration of the Holocaust onto the postwar authoritarian family, for I contend that the term *Väterliteratur* evocatively echoes its absent, effaced counterpart, *Täterliteratur* (literature of the perpetrators). In the transformation of *Täterliteratur* into *Väterliteratur*, the focus on Germany's historical crimes in the Holocaust gives way to a concentration on the mundane, transhistorical struggle between the generations.

 This book employs the two terms *Väterliteratur* and *second-generation Holocaust literature* in order to situate itself within the respective discourses that surround these textual groupings. My intention is that, by having exposed the problematic associations of each term, I can use them functionally without accepting them uncritically. As I have stated, I employ the term *second-generation literature* to designate both texts written from the perspective of the legacy of survival and texts that address the legacy of perpetration.

I choose the term to designate both groups for two reasons. First, I require a term that fits both types of texts, and though laden with biblical interpretation that ties it more to Jewish experience, *second generation* is ambiguous enough to be applied to both groups of literature, while *Väterliteratur* narrowly defines those texts that concentrate only on the father, a problem that, as I explain in chapters 6 and 7, already has plagued attempts to use it in the discourse on perpetrator memory. Furthermore, structurally speaking, both groups exist on the same level; they both write from the position of the aftermath and thus belong loosely to the same generation. Second, the precedent of designating both groups with the same term exists in the field of psychology and, more recently, in the discipline of literary studies. My study thus participates in and is integrated into the larger discourses that govern post-Holocaust literature, and, by employing the term *second-generation Holocaust literature* can thus utilize the common language that governs these discussions.

Tropes of Marking in the Second Generation

The trope of marking, as I claim, is operative in the literature of the children of both survivors and perpetrators, expressing the second generation's particular perspective with regard to the Holocaust. Yet, as might be expected, the figure of stigmatization does not function in all second-generation texts in the same way. Rather, the trope of marking emerges in each text as a complex operation that employs a number of discourses associated with difference, guilt, Holocaust trauma, and mourning.

In particular, the literature of the legacy of survival self-consciously employs a poetics of marking that often alludes to the survivors' own historical experience of stigmatization in the Holocaust, in which the Nazis identified Jewish populations and marked them as outsiders within their respective communities. By invoking and appropriating the iconic signifiers[13] of stigmatization in the Holocaust, second-generation writers explore German

---

[13] In his recent study, *Committed to Memory: Cultural Mediations of the Holocaust* (2003), Oren Baruch Stier takes a close look at what he calls Holocaust icons, such as the cattle car and the Auschwitz tattoo, which he describes as "symbolic, often visual, pointers that are themselves derived directly from the events to which they refer" (25). According to Stier, these "material icons" (31) are "embodied, invested with a surfeit of signification" (33) and thus function as receptacles of multiple, often competing, Holocaust narratives. Stier's primary focus of investigation with regard to Holocaust icons is the way they are utilized in "memorial-museological environments" (33), although he does include a short discussion of the ways in which visual icons are appropriated by literary narratives, such as Art Spiegelman's *Maus* and Emily Prager's 1991 novel *Eve's Tattoo*.

definitions of Jewish difference that were a prerequisite to the identification, isolation, and destruction of the Jews and express their sense of being marked secondarily by the legacy of the Holocaust. The Nazis used various methods to mark Jews in both Nazi Germany and occupied countries, beginning with more figurative measures, such as the stamping of identity cards with the letter "J" to denote their bearers as Jewish (and therefore stateless) and the compulsory designation of all German Jews with the middle names Sarah and Israel, and moving on to more immediately visual identification, such as the requirement that Jews wear armbands and badges displaying the Star of David in order to designate them as scapegoats and sequester them from non-Jewish populations. This gradual transition from figurative marking to literal marking (a process that mirrors the Nazis' tendency toward the radical literalization of the metaphor, in which Jews were labeled vermin and then eventually annihilated with pesticide) culminated in the practice of marking Jews as other onto their very flesh, with the numbers that were tattooed onto arms of prisoners at Auschwitz-Birkenau. According to Primo Levi, this method of branding prisoners took the notion of marking to the extreme in that it effectively effaced the identity of the victim and reconstituted him as a pure object, the property of the Third Reich:

> The operation was not very painful and lasted no more than a minute, but it was traumatic. Its symbolic meaning was clear to everyone: this is an indelible mark, you will never leave here; this is the mark with which slaves are branded and cattle sent to the slaughter, and that is what you have become. You no longer have a name; this is your new name. The violence of the tattoo was gratuitous, an end in itself, pure offense: were the three canvas numbers sewed to pants, jackets, and winter coat not enough? No, they were not enough: something more was needed, a non-verbal message, so that the innocent would feel his sentence written on his flesh. It was also a return to barbarism, all the more perturbing for Orthodox Jews: in fact, precisely in order to distinguish Jews from the barbarians, the tattoo is forbidden by Mosaic law (Leviticus 19:28). (119)

The violation of the tattoo, as Levi points out, was offensive in its radical negation of selfhood by marking the body as no longer belonging to itself. Thus, the fate planned for the prisoner by the captors was not announced as a mere figurative intention, but rather was inscribed concretely into the flesh. In this way, the "symbolic meaning" of the tattoo was underscored by its permanent quality, which even the body and its continual process of organic renewal could not efface. With the tattoo, the body was thus inalterably marked by history. Because of this permanence, the Auschwitz tattoo, the Nazi method of marking that has far outlasted the Nazi regime, remains one of the most visceral signifiers of the Holocaust past in the post-Holocaust imagination, for the survivors carried it with them out of the camps and into their postwar lives. Perhaps this is one reason why the image of the tattoo in particular looms over many narratives written by the children of survivors, as is evident in Karpf's struggle with the rash on her arm, her psychosomatic echo of her mother's branding. The children of Auschwitz survivors grew up seeing the tattoo, the shameful visual reminder of victimhood and suffering that marked the parent as different, and just as it was indelibly imprinted into the parent's flesh, it was stamped into the consciousness of the second generation as well.

A number of second-generation narratives address images of the marked parent and the tattoo as signifier for the unknown Holocaust past. In David Grossman's *See Under: Love* (1989), Momik, the young son of Holocaust survivors, attempts to understand his own legacy by deciphering the hidden numerical logic represented by the tattoo, as if this decoding might finally unlock the secrets of the unknown past:

> Then Momik tried to figure out the secret code on Grandfather's arm. He'd tried this before with Papa's and Bella's and Aunt Idka's code numbers, but he didn't get anywhere that time either. The numbers drove him crazy because they weren't written in ink and they couldn't be washed off with water or spit. Momik tried everything to wash Grandfather's arm, but the numbers stayed fixed, which gave Momik an idea that maybe the number wasn't written from the outside but from the inside, and that convinced him more than ever that there was somebody there inside Grandfather, and the others too maybe, which is how they call out for help, and Momik racked his brains to understand what it could be, and he wrote down Grandfather's number in his spy notebook next to Papa's and Bella's and Idka's, and did all kinds of calculations, and then luckily in school they learned about gematria and the numerical values of the alphabet which naturally Momik was the first in his class to understand, and when he got home he tried to turn the numbers into letters in different ways, but all he got was a bunch of strange words he didn't understand, and still Momik would not give up. (18–19)

Momik suspects that the numbers on the arms of the adults around him are somehow incomprehensible signs for the realm of what he calls "Over There," a traumatic place that is entirely unknown to him but that figures prominently in the adults' emotional world and thus also in Momik's own imagination. In an effort to decipher the signs of this dominion and release the adults from the grip of its power, he attempts to locate a referent for the signifier by translating the numbers into an understandable idiom. In this way, he would thus "crack" the code to the adults' private language of suffering and trauma.

In some second-generation narratives, the children of survivors go so far as to assume the Auschwitz number in an attempt to know, through their own bodies, the experience of the parents, and thus to write themselves into that experience. This assumption of the tattoo can take place either figuratively, as with Nava Semel ("I pull the nonexistent sleeve to the nonexistent number with an overly dramatic gesture" [68]) or literally, as Dora Apel, in her work on second-generation Holocaust art, relates: "In an act of surrogate witnessing, some members of the postwar generation have gone so far as to have actual numbers tattooed on their bodies" (165). This assumption of the tattoo can be interpreted in a number of different ways. First, it can be seen as an expression of difference, in which the child assumes a familiar symbol in order to make manifest her own feeling of stigmatization. In addition, one could view the appropriation of the tattoo as an attempt to take on the trappings of victimhood, to characterize one's self as an outsider and a victim. Or, as Nadine Fresco suggests, quoting a statement by an unnamed child of survivors, it represents the child's nostalgia for something she has never experienced — the desire to understand, in the flesh so to speak, the event that has cast a long shadow over her life: "'Even now, when I see someone with a number engraved on his arm, what I feel more than anything else is an almost incommunicable feeling, made up for the most part of jealousy [. . .] I shall never be one of them, still less one of those who did not come back. What they lived through was a drama that is not mine'" (421). Dora Apel suggests a fourth interpretation, in which the child consciously commits to a sense of solidarity with her family and Jewish tradition (186). Whatever the individual motivation behind the assumption of the Auschwitz tattoo, the second generation accesses and makes use of it and other Holocaust iconography in an attempt to mark itself into the legacy of the Shoah.

In employing Holocaust iconography, the children of survivors also refer to Jewish mourning tradition in their endeavor to explore and express their marked identities. As I argue above, second-generation narratives attempt to negotiate their crisis of signification in a twofold way: they both reenact the rupture caused by the Holocaust and venture to effect its repair, a process of marking embodied in the metaphor of sewing. The first part of this dual act of marking involves the ritual of mourning for one's parents, for one's lost family, for the future that never was. In Jewish tradition, the state of mourning is marked by *keri'ah,* the ritual act of tearing one's clothing when a family member dies. In this practice, the mourner, forbidden by the Torah to express his grief by making cuts or marks upon the self, rends a garment instead and then wears this garment during the period of mourning known as *Shivah* as an evocative expression of the personal and familial rupture caused by the death of a loved one. For the second generation, however, the process of mourning is a complicated one, for they feel compelled to mourn the deaths of family members they have never known, whose deaths precede their own lives. In the case of most second-generation writers, there are no death certificates, dates of death, or graves to mark the murder of their relatives, and therefore these deaths fall largely outside the Jewish calendar of ritual mourning. The second generation must thus access Jewish mourning ritual in an alternative way in order to mark and remember its family legacy. Narrative becomes the space where the anonymous deaths are marked and mourned, taking "the place of graves for those who had no graves" (Raczymow, "Memory Shot Through With Holes," 101). The literal act of *keri'ah,* the physical marking of the loss of a family member and the eloquent expression of the severed state of the soul in mourning, is taken up and transformed by second-generation writing into a figurative counterpart to the tearing of the mourner's garment. Second-generation literature thus mourns the dead with its own metaphorical rendering of *keri'ah,* the marking of memory in the evocation of rupture. At the same time, by using their writing to express the fracture caused by the Holocaust, second-generation writers forge a link to Jewish mourning ritual, reinscribing their murdered family into both personal and Jewish memory and effecting a sort of repair of their torn legacy.

A tropology of marking exists in the literature of perpetration as well, one that also expresses the concept of being marked by an unknown history. However, in this literature the sense of stigmatization is articulated quite differently than it is in the writings of the children of survivors. In narratives by both the children of perpetrators and the children of survivors, there is an overwhelming perception of being tied to an immense and opaque history, one that is powerfully present in their contemporary lives but largely unknown. In second-generation perpetrator narratives, however, the sense of stigmatization is figured not as the trace of bodily suffering and the act of mourning, as with the legacy of survival. Rather, in the legacy of perpetration the Holocaust past is perceived as a tremendous burden of almost biblical proportions that the children of Nazis have no choice but to bear, one that is laden with both the real and imagined crimes of their parents and the additional sense of being somehow tainted by their parents' violent past. Above all, this burden and feeling of being marked by history are tied to concepts of guilt that, as Sigrid Weigel points out ("'Generation' as a Symbolic Form," 269), are not related first and foremost to the actual historical events of the Holocaust itself. Rather, for the second generation on the side of the perpetrators, guilt is more directly connected with the parents' own refusal to admit responsibility for their complicity in the genocide of the Jews, a phenomenon Ralph Giordano identifies as "die zweite Schuld" ("the second guilt"). The parents' rejection of guilt, which takes the form of amnesia, is thus passed down to the children, who inherit it as their own burden to bear, an instance in which "the sins of the fathers" are visited upon the children (Exodus 20:5). This notion of inherited guilt is characterized as a mythical legacy, a quasi-biblical condition that threatens to displace consideration of the historical crimes themselves. The guilt inherited by the second generation is often figured as form of original sin, or, in German, *Erbsünde*, which means literally "inherited sin." By associating the second generation's relationship to the Holocaust past as one of original sin, the legacy of the parents' crimes is rewritten as an allegorical narrative in which the innocent children, representing the plight of all mankind, are born into a world that is already fallen and must immediately assume responsibility for and somehow make good the catastrophe that precedes their birth. They are born into a state of disgrace that marks their identity from the first moments of their lives, hence the title of Peter Sichrovsky's 1987 book of interviews with the children of Nazi families, *Schuldig geboren* (*Born Guilty*). Rudolf, one of Sichrovsky's subjects and the son of German perpetrators who escaped to South America under assumed identities, characterizes the guilt he claims as his birthright as a burden of mythic magnitude:

> First of all I must tell you that I'm haunted by guilt. And people who are guilty are punished, if not here and now then in another place. My turn is sure to come. There's no escape. But you'll learn nothing from me. Not a word. What they did will remain a secret. No one will find out. Their deeds, or rather, their misdeeds, shall not be mentioned anywhere. Not a single word, except the guilt now rests on my shoulders. My parents, they're already roasting in hell. They died a long time ago; it's over for them, this life. But they left me behind. Born in guilt, left behind in guilt. (*Born Guilty*, 39)[14]

Rudolf assumes the burden of his parents' guilt, a responsibility he declines to share with his interlocutor, refusing even to evoke the crimes his parents have committed. By agreeing to shoulder the enormity of this unnamed guilt, Rudolf figures himself as a scapegoat, forced, like Aaron's goat, to wander out alone into the desert, bearing the blame for the crimes of others. In this way, he resolves his own crisis of signification by assuming responsibility for the missing referent of his parents' crimes.

---

[14] "Die Schuld verfolgt mich, wissen Sie. Und wer schuldig ist, wird auch bestraft. Wenn nicht hier und jetzt, dann zu einer anderen Zeit an einem anderen Ort. Mich wird sie auch noch erreichen. Ich entkomme ihr nicht. Aber erfahren werden Sie nichts von mir. Nichts, kein Wort. Was sie getan haben, bleibt ein Geheimnis, niemand soll es erfahren. Ihre Taten oder besser Untaten sollen nie irgendwo erwähnt werden. Kein Wort. Nur, auf mir liegt heute die Schuld. Meine Eltern, die kochen schon in der Hölle. Die sind längst tot, haben es hinter sich, dieses Leben. Und mich ließen sie zurück. Schuldig geboren, schuldig zurückgelassen" (Sichrovsky, *Schuldig geboren*, 50).

Along with the tropes of original sin, inherited guilt, and scapegoating, second-generation perpetrator narratives take up a further allusion to biblical guilt and marking, that of the mark of Cain. Cain, guilty of the crime of fratricide for murdering Abel, is condemned by God to wander the earth as a fugitive (Genesis 4:8–16). In response to Cain's fear of being hunted and killed for his crime by his fellow humans, God proclaims that anyone who would kill Cain be punished seven times over, and in order that Cain might be recognized, God places a mark upon him. Cain is thus doubly marked — as both perpetrator and as the protected charge of the Lord. The mark of Cain has customarily been seen "as a brand or stigma meant to identify, humiliate and punish the criminal Cain" (Mellinkoff, 1), a physical marking that, similar in function to the Greek stigma, is meant to distinguish him visually from the rest of mankind. Thus the notion of Cain's mark is one in which the perpetrator is unable to escape recognition for his crime; he must live its legacy constantly, for he signifies it with his very body. At the same time, however, by virtue of this very mark, he is able to evade punishment for his misdeed. He lives in a suspended state, for his crime is neither overlooked nor absolved; nor is he able to do penance, be forgiven, and carry on with his life. Stigmatized in this way, the criminal thus signifies a guilt that cannot be resolved and a criminal past that is perpetually present, neither entirely forgotten nor forgiven. With regard to the second generation, the Holocaust past functions in the much the same manner as the mark of Cain — as an unresolved force that, despite continual attempts by postwar German society to forget and move past it, remains an ever-present problem that binds the children of perpetrators to their parents' crimes. However, unlike Cain's mark, which calls attention to his own crime, the metaphorical mark borne by members of the second generation is a signifier for crimes they did not themselves commit. Thus, like the children of survivors, the children of perpetrators carry a mark that finds no referent in personal experience. Importantly, however, the mark functions differently for each group: for the children of survivors it is "the scar without the wound" (Sicher, *Breaking Crystal*, 27), whereas for the children of perpetrators it is a brand of perpetually present guilt that eludes resolution.

The mark of Cain, the sign of an unresolved criminal past, is bequeathed to the children of perpetrators along with the parents' guilt; however, in this case, it does not, as with Cain, take the form of an external stigma that immediately distinguishes these children visually. Rather, their inherited mark is figured as hereditary, an internal genetic flaw that is passed down from perpetrator parent to child, an identification that signifies how the child is bound to the parent's criminal legacy. The children are thus tied to the Holocaust by virtue of their very blood. Sichrovsky's interview subject Rudolf characterizes this blood tie between the generations as a biological transfer of evil, in which the children are genetically marked by their parents' actions:

> I must not have any children. This line must come to an end with me. What should I tell the little ones about Grandpa? I lived with my parents too long, who knows what evil I carry within me? It mustn't be handed down. It's over, our proud noble lineage. If anyone should ask, the "von" [from] in my name at most means "from where." But soon there'll be nobody to ask. (*Born Guilty*, 46)[15]

Rudolf views himself as inherently tainted by his parents' Nazi past, both physically and in terms of signification, and he vows to take drastic measures to prevent the further contamination of future generations. In order to free himself of the Prussian, militaristic associations of his noble name (which he refuses to reveal here), he empties it of meaning by altering it into an interrogative that erases both his lineage and his family's transgressions. Moreover, he figures his body as a repository of the genetic material of evil that he fears might be passed on to subsequent generations, and he is therefore determined to end the family line, vowing to never have children. Although he refuses to allow his own marked identity to be reproduced, however, by characterizing his parents' legacy as a biological one, in which the evil of Nazism is passed to the child at birth, he ends up reproducing Nazi discourse on race and eugenics, which construct moral characteristics as genetic traits that distinguish the races from each other. In his appropriation of Nazi language to express his sense of being genetically marked by his parents' past, he marks himself as the linguistic inheritor of Nazi ideology and thus insists on a break with his parents' past and at the same time forges a link to it.

As we have seen, both the children of survivors and the children of perpetrators express their perception of being marked by their parents' experience of the Holocaust, employing tropes that speak to their very different experiences of victimization and guilt. Significantly, however, neither the writing of the children of survivors nor that of the children of perpetrators relegates itself exclusively to tropes of marking from either side of the victim/perpetrator dichotomy. As I establish in my opening discussion of the narratives of Irene Anhalt and Anne Karpf, writers from both sides of Holo-

---

[15] "Ich darf keine Kinder haben. Dieses Geschlecht muß mit mir aussterben. Was hätte ich den Kindern über den lieben Großvater erzählen sollen? Auf mich fällt die Rache, und das ist gut so. Zu lange habe ich mit meinem Eltern gelebt, wer weiß, was alles in mir steckt? Es soll nicht weitergegeben werden. Aus, vorbei ist es mit dem stolzen Adel. Das 'von' in meinem Namen kann nur noch 'von wo' heißen. Wenn Sie später einmal fragen. Befragen werden Sie bald keinen mehr können" (Sichrovsky, *Schuldig geboren*, 57).

caust experience each access metaphors of perpetration and victimization. Karpf, for example, marks herself as both perpetrator and victim not only in her self-mutilating ritual of scratching, but also in relation to her parents, with whom she interchangeably takes on both roles. As she points out, she feels equally marked by both sides of the dichotomy:

> I had two recurring fantasies. In one I was like a jelly which hadn't set: if you took away the mold I just dribbled away. The jelly mold seemed to embody the rigid, prescriptive side of me — the unyielding bully who kept me in check, myself as Nazi. But without it I felt utterly uncontained, as though I wouldn't cohere. The other fantasy was of being in a vast, dark vat, on to whose sides I was clinging for dear life. If I let go, I would surely drown. (107)

In Karpf's fantasies, she is figured as a perpetrator, even a Nazi, with regard to her parents, for her attempts to claim a life apart from theirs seem to her to reenact the brutalization they experienced in the Holocaust. Yet, at the same time, she marks herself as a victim who, barely able to survive her precarious existence, continues to suffer the aftereffects of the Holocaust. Her tortuous practice of scratching becomes a ritual in which she simultaneously performs both roles and thus attempts to resolve her ambivalent relationship to her parents and their past. Such identification with the positions of both victim and perpetrator is common in narratives by the children of survivors, for, as Dina Wardi has shown in her study on the relationships between survivors and their children, the second generation is often charged with the impossible tasks of filling the void caused by the Holocaust, reestablishing lost family, and giving meaning to the parents' past suffering. In such an environment, the assertion of desires that run counter to the parents' plans for their child's life often seems tantamount to renewing the parents' suffering. In this family reenactment of Holocaust trauma, the child is thus figured as a perpetrator, the one who threatens to destroy the façade of postwar prosperity and uncover the ongoing anguish that lies behind it.

The children of perpetrators also access tropes of marking from the other side of the radical divide of Holocaust experience, that of victimization. As Michael Schneider, Ernestine Schlant, Sigrid Weigel ("'Generation' as Symbolic Form"), and others have argued, the appropriation of or identification with the role of the victim is prevalent in the genre of *Väterliteratur*, in which the ostensible exploration of the public, fascist past of the father reveals itself to be a private indictment of him for his authoritarian offenses against the child. By utilizing the father's Nazi past as a discursive arena in which generational aggression and familial conflict are played out, the texts of *Väterliteratur* often construct a scenario in which the child marks himself as the "real" victim of the father's crimes, thus appropriating and displacing the experience of the historical victims of the Holocaust. As Stefan, another of Sichrovsky's interviewees, claims:

> I was the Jew in my family. Father, Mother, Grandmother — all of them conspired to perpetuate the terror in the family. And I was their target. No, they weren't out to kill me, because that would have been too easy. They just wanted to make me suffer, like tearing the wings off a fly and watching it writhe in agony, trying to escape [. . .]
>
> There's all that talk about you Jews being the victims of the war. But for those of you who survived, the suffering ended with Hitler's death. But for us, the children of the Nazis, it didn't end. When their world collapsed in ruin and ashes, the heroes of the Third Reich staked out another battleground — the family [. . .]
>
> I'm not responsible for what my father did. I wasn't born then and have nothing to do with it. And I don't feel responsible for it [. . .] I am an entirely different person, perhaps even his exact opposite. I think of myself as being in the other camp, someone who is suffering under him just as all those others during the Third Reich. Today his brutality and aggressiveness threaten *me*, not those others against whom he keeps on ranting, but that's only talk. (*Born Guilty*, 137–40)[16]

Stefan's statements are perhaps a more extreme expression of the appropriation of the status of victim than is found in the majority of the texts of *Väterliteratur*, but in their extremity they are instructive. Unlike Rudolf, who takes on the mark of inherited guilt, Stefan rejects any connection to his father's crimes. Rather, he distances himself as far away from his father's violation as possible by placing himself at the "exact opposite" end of the perpetrator-victim spectrum. He then fashions himself as his father's latest prey, even going so far as to consciously displace the historical victims of the

---

[16] "Ich war der Jude in meiner Familie. Der Vater, die Mutter, die Großmutter, alle haben sie den Terror in der Familie weitergeführt. Und mich hatten sie im Auge. Ganz klein machen wollten sie mich, nicht umbringen, nein, dann wäre ja alles vorbei gewesen. So wie man einer Fliege nur einen Flügel ausreißt und dann beobachtet, wie sie verzweifelt versucht zu fliehen [. . .] Man redet immer soviel von euch Juden als den eigentlichen Opfern des Krieges. Aber für die, die überlebt haben, war er vorbei, als Hitler sich umbrachte. Nur für uns, die Kinder der Nazis, ging er weiter. Das Schlachtfeld Familie entdeckten die Helden des Dritten Reiches, als ihr eigenes in Schutt und Asche fiel [. . .] Ich kann nichts dafür, was mein Vater getan hat. Ich war damals nicht auf der Welt und habe auch nichts damit zu tun. Ich fühl' mich auch nicht dafür verantwortlich [. . .] Ich bin ein völlig anderer Mensch, vielleicht sogar das exakte Gegenteil. Ich fühl mich auf der anderen Seite als einer, der genauso unter ihm leidet, wie all jene im Dritten Reich. Seine Brutalität und Aggressivität ist heute vor allem für mich gefährlich und nicht für die anderen, über die er zwar ununterbrochen wettert, aber eben nur redet" (Sichrovsky, *Schuldig geboren*, 151–54).

Holocaust ("for them it's over" [*Born Guilty*, 140][17]) and claim for himself the status of one of the "real victims" (*Born Guilty*, 145).[18] Furthermore, he not only identifies himself as his father's newest victim, but also goes so far to take on the badge of "the Jew," a label that signifies to him the epitome of victimhood and suffering. Stefan's use of the definite article points to his tendency toward essentialism and highlights his strategy of evacuating the category of victim in order to claim for himself a victimhood that transcends the historical specificity of the Holocaust. In this way, he not only transforms himself into a martyr, a figure akin to Christ who must suffer for the sins of others; he effectively acquits his father of his Holocaust crimes (as he claims, "the Jews now are better off than anybody else" [*Born Guilty*, 145],[19] so the crimes could not have been that significant) and re-indicts him for the more serious crime of familial violence.

The trope of marking thus operates in second-generation writing in a variety of complex ways, utilizing various iconographic symbols and discourses relating to the Holocaust in order to confront and possibly resolve the crisis of signification. In each case, second-generation texts, whether written from the perspective of the legacy of perpetration or that of survival, access badges, stigmata, and brands that signify Holocaust memory in an attempt to find a language to express the writers' sense of rupture, as well as to build a bridge over the division between the parents' experience of trauma and violation and its effect on the children. In some instances, such as the expression of mourning on the part of the children of survivors or the assumption of the role of scapegoat by the children of perpetrators, the poetics of marking articulate poignantly the writers' relationship to their troubled family histories. In others, particularly Stefan's appropriation of Jewish identity, but also Karpf's self-designation as a Nazi, second-generation attempts to resolve the troubled past and restore the ruptured sign can also move in problematic directions, resulting in the denial of historical accuracy, the re-enactment of violence and trauma, and the reification of rigid categories of victim and perpetrator.

Second-Generation Texts

This study considers ten texts published between 1987 and 2003 that can be (or have been) designated *second-generation literature* or *Väterliteratur*. I have divided my analysis into two parts to correspond to the respective lega-

---

[17] "Für die ist doch die Sache gelaufen" (Sichrovsky, *Schuldig geboren*, 154).

[18] "die eigentlich Betroffenen" (Sichrovsky, *Schuldig geboren*, 160).

[19] "Heute geht es den Juden besser als allen anderen" (Sichrovsky, *Schuldig geboren*, 160).

cies of survival and perpetration. Part 1 investigates five second-generation texts by Jewish writers from various national backgrounds that thematize the vicarious experience of the Holocaust from the perspective of survival. Part 2 analyzes narratives by four German writers that focus on the legacy of perpetration in the postwar German family.

Part 1 begins with an examination of *Elijah Visible*, a 1996 collection of short stories by Thane Rosenbaum, the son of Holocaust survivors. A lawyer turned writer and literary editor of the journal *Tikkun*, Rosenbaum received the 1996 Edgar Lewis Wallant Award for *Elijah Visible*. With the publication of his later novels *Second Hand Smoke* (2000) and *The Golems of Gotham* (2003), he has emerged as one of the most prominent American writers of the second generation. All of the nine stories in *Elijah Visible* focus specifically on the second-generation experience of their protagonist, Adam Posner, who is profoundly affected by his parents' history and must struggle to find a place within their traumatic legacy and in a post-Holocaust America in which he has little connection to Jewish religious tradition. However, as the reader eventually comes to learn, the similarity among the stories ends with the name Adam Posner and his second-generation identity, for in each story, he is a manifestly different person of a different age, with a different profession, even with different parents. My analysis of Rosenbaum's stories focuses on these problems of character identity and vocal unity. As I demonstrate, the polyidentity of the protagonist in each story is an expression of dissociation and repetition compulsion, traumatic symptoms he has inherited as a part of his Holocaust legacy. These traumatic symptoms in turn become disorders within the narrative itself, where they are manifested as a narrative paralysis, causing the text to fail in its project of narrative renewal.

In the second chapter, I turn my discussion to Art Spiegelman's two-part graphic novel *Maus*, the story of Spiegelman's attempt to record and represent his parents' experiences in the Holocaust, as narrated by his father. Since the publication of the first volume in 1986 and the second in 1991 (which won, among other prizes, the National Book Critics Circle Award and the Pulitzer Prize), *Maus* has become one of the most celebrated and widely read literary works about the Holocaust and without question the most prominent text to emerge from the second generation. *Maus* has come to represent the position and problems of the children of survivors in general, and for this reason it is often regarded as the second-generation novel par excellence. Spiegelman's text has thus played a major part in shaping our understanding of the relationship of children of Holocaust survivors to their parents' history and the limitations and possibilities of second-generation art and literature. In this chapter, I take a close look at how Spiegelman's novel attempts to represent the Holocaust past from its mediated position in the present. In particular, I examine how the interaction between image and verbal narration in Spiegelman's *Maus* marks its anxiety about the ambiguity of temporality, which is most evident in the disjointed relationship between the three narrative levels and the rigid temporal planes of past and present. As I contend, although the gesture of narrating the father's past is a move to solidify his experience and turn it into the *then* of history and keep it from the *now* of the present, Spiegelman's text acknowledges the impossibility of this move to neatly and decisively distinguish the traumatic past from the present of living.

Chapter 3 examines the role of the second-generation witness in *Gebürtig* (1992),[20] the acclaimed novel by the Austrian-Jewish writer Robert Schindel that in 2002 was made into a German-language film directed by Schindel and Lukas Stepanik. Although Schindel writes squarely from the perspective of the second generation, he is himself a child survivor. Born in 1944 in Austria to parents who were active in the communist resistance movement, Schindel was placed in a Viennese orphanage run by the National Socialists when his parents were captured and deported to Auschwitz. His father was murdered in Dachau in March 1945, but his mother survived Auschwitz and Ravensbrück and was reunited with Schindel in 1945. Schindel is best known in Austria for his lyric poetry and, more recently, as a public intellectual who speaks openly about the often fraught relationship between Jewish and non-Jewish Austrians. Although Schindel's poetry addresses both his autobiographical experience and the larger theme of the murder of the European Jews, it was with *Gebürtig*, his second novel, winner of the 1993 Erich-Fried-Preis, that he became known as a second-generation writer. *Gebürtig* is an epic tour de force, with dozens of characters, three major and several minor narrative strands, a novel-within-the-novel, and a complicated temporal structure that glides between the past and the present. Uniting the diverse stories and characters is the novel's focus on the ways in which the legacy of the Holocaust continues to affect the personal relationships between Jewish Austrians and their non-Jewish Austrian (and German) contemporaries. In other words, the novel presents loaded encounters between what Eva Hoffman terms two "contrapuntal" second-generational groups: the children of perpetrators and the children of survivors. As I discuss in that chapter, this theme of oppositional legacies makes itself known in the heterogeneous narrativity of the novel, which is organized according to provisional dualities that I term counterparts. One pair of counterparts includes the main character Danny and his brother Sascha, the enigmatic

---

[20] The English translation of Schindel's *Gebürtig*, by Michael Roloff, appeared in 1995 under the title *Born-Where*. In my opinion, however, Roloff's translation contains a number of significant errors. I have therefore chosen to use Roloff's work as a reference, but to translate citations of *Gebürtig* myself (with help from my erstwhile research assistant, Elizabeth Dick). Page numbers from *Gebürtig* listed here thus refer to the original German text.

twin sons of a woman who survived the Holocaust. Sascha, as Danny's alter ego, fulfills the role of the passive observer to Danny's acting character. My reading of the narrative pair reveals the problematic split between living and writing in the second generation, which results in a narrative crisis that resounds throughout the novel.

Chapter 4, the last chapter in part 1, examines two further second-generation works: Katja Behrens's 1993 German story "Arthur Mayer oder Das Schweigen" ("Arthur Mayer, or The Silence") and Patrick Modiano's 1997 French novella *Dora Bruder* (this titled is shared by the 1999 English translation). Behrens, a prominent contemporary German-Jewish writer, was born in Berlin in 1942, and from 1943 to 1945 she was hidden, along with her mother and grandmother, in Austria. Like Robert Schindel, she thus survived the Nazi plan of extermination; however, as with Schindel, she writes not from the position of the survivor, but from the mediated perspective of the second generation. Modiano is also the child of a parent who escaped the fate intended by the Nazis; his father, an Egyptian Jew, lived in occupied Paris illegally as a black marketeer and continually evaded police attempts to capture him. Modiano is one of the most acclaimed writers in contemporary France and, with his debut novel *La Place de l'Étoile* (1968), was one of the first to focus his literary efforts on the period of the Nazi occupation, including the themes of French collaboration and the deportation of the Jews to concentration and death camps in the east. Both *Dora Bruder* and "Arthur Mayer oder Das Schweigen" are autobiographical texts that explore the traces of the Holocaust past in the present, and the narrators in both stories undertake this project by attempting to reconstruct the history of particular persons who were caught up in the Nazi machine. However, unlike in *Maus,* in which Spiegelman produces a second-generation account of his father's experience, Behrens and Modiano piece together the histories not of their parents, but of unknown persons who perished in the Holocaust. Modiano attempts to document the life of a young Jewish girl who ran away from a convent and lived precariously in the streets of Nazi-occupied Paris in 1942. In a similar way, Behrens's narrative tries to piece together the life and death of a prominent Jewish doctor whose family, prior to its deportation, had lived for generations in a small German town. In this chapter, I analyze and compare Behrens's and Modiano's projects of reconstructing the missing individual (who, in both books, functions as a metonymy for the erasure of whole populations) and their respective narrative strategies of textual documentation. What results in the case of both writers is a type of writing that combines both literary and encyclopedic genres in an attempt to textualize the absence of the Holocaust in contemporary European life.

I begin the second part of the book, which focuses on the legacy of the Holocaust from the perspective of the descendants of perpetrators, with analyses of two texts that have frequently been associated with *Väterliteratur*. In chapter 5, I discuss the development of the genre, examining in particular the dominant critical perspective that accepts only texts that are self-evidently autobiographical and that moreover displays hostility toward fictional attempts to work through the past. I then turn the discussion to Peter Schneider's 1987 story *Vati*, a text that fictionalizes the postwar encounter between a figure that resembles Josef Mengele, living under an assumed identity in South America, and his grown son, who travels to meet him for the first time since his early childhood. Schneider, one of the most prolific writers in contemporary Germany, is one of the two authors in this study (the other is Bernhard Schlink) whose biography does not tie them directly (that is, through the immediate family) to the legacy of perpetration. Although he is a member of the rebellious generation of 1968 and thus has identified with its attempt to uncover the crimes committed by the parent generation in the Third Reich, Schneider's own father was neither a member of the Nazi party nor a soldier and thus was not an active perpetrator. With *Vati*, Schneider imaginatively accesses the perspective of the child of a perpetrator and thus appears to identify his fictional text with the project of *Väterliteratur*, a genre conventionally reserved for autobiographical works, a gesture that has aroused vehement criticism from the German literary establishment. As I demonstrate through a careful reading of the text's metaphors of marking and tropes of signification, although *Vati* endeavors thematically to align itself with *Väterliteratur*, on an aesthetic level it calls into question the genre's project of coming to terms with the fathers' crimes.

In chapter 6, I continue my investigation of *Väterliteratur*, questioning in particular the genre's exclusive concentration on the struggle between father and son. The focus of this chapter is Niklas Frank's 1987 autobiographical novel *Der Vater* (*In the Shadow of the Reich*, 1991) and the 1995 play of the same name by Frank and the acclaimed Israeli playwright Joshua Sobol. Niklas Frank, a well-known journalist who wrote for the German magazine *Stern*, is the son of Hans Frank, a high-ranking member of the Nazi party and the General Governor of occupied Poland, who was hanged at Nuremburg. His book, which was first serialized in *Stern* under the title "Mein Vater, der Nazi-Mörder" (My Father, the Nazi Murderer), caused a good deal of controversy in the German press on account of the extreme bitterness and hatred with which he depicts his father; Henryk Broder writes that the book was understood by the German public as tantamount to "a declaration of war on national identity."[21] Both the title and the violent German public reaction to *Der Vater* would seem to make it a prototypical narrative of *Väterliteratur*, but as I maintain in my reading of the text, it is

---

[21] "eine Kriegserklärung an die nationale Identität" (Broder, 167).

imprinted first and foremost not by the criminal father, but by the mother, who, as a mouthpiece for Hitler himself, transmits the legacy of Nazism to the child. As I demonstrate, the role of the mother in the second-generation memory of fascism and National Socialism, a powerful undercurrent in the book that runs beneath the more obvious reckoning with the father, is manifested more evidently in Sobol and Frank's play, where it is staged as the primary site of engagement between the child and the Nazi past.

In the seventh chapter, I address two more recent German texts that emerge from the tradition of *Väterliteratur* and at the same time complicate the notion that the legacy of the Holocaust past in Germany is transmitted primarily from parent to child. Berhard Schlink's 1995 fictional text *Der Vorleser* (*The Reader*, 1997) and Uwe Timm's 2003 autobiographical work *Am Beispiel meines Bruders* (*In My Brother's Shadow*, 2005) are both works that, like Modiano's *Dora Bruder* and Behrens's "Arthur Mayer oder Das Schweigen," represent alternative modes of second-generation engagement with the past. However, whereas Modiano and Behrens choose to focus their investigation into the Holocaust past on unknown persons, Timm and Schlink center their stories on the effects of Germany's legacy of genocide on intimate relationships between the generations. Timm's text, which received considerable acclaim from the German literary media, keeps its investigation within the family but moves past the oppositional focus on the parents (who, though not committed Nazis themselves, were at times supporters of the regime) to meditate on the life of his brother, who becomes for Timm the primary representative of Germany's culpability in the war. At the age of eighteen, his brother volunteered for the Waffen SS and died in battle on the eastern front in 1943, leaving behind a diary and letters in which he recorded his impressions of the war. Timm reads and attempts to interpret his brother's thoughts and feelings about his role in the war, and at the same time juxtaposes this image of his brother and the family myth that has developed about him, which, in Timm's opinion, downplay or even deny altogether his brother's status as a perpetrator, with texts that focus on the actual historical conditions of war and genocide in Eastern Europe and Russia. My reading of *Am Beispiel meines Bruders* demonstrates how, with its concentration on not only Timm's brother, but also his father, the text continues the tradition of *Väterliteratur*. At the same time, Timm avoids the bitter reckoning with the parents found in conventional father texts and concentrates instead on the ways in which the violent and euphemistic language of the Nazi period was employed in the German postwar family to maintain narratives of victimization and suffering. While Timm's text retains the conventional focus on the family as the site of the second-generation struggle to assume and comprehend Germany's legacy of genocide, *Der Vorleser* figures the relationship between the perpetrator generation and that of the second generation as one of erotic attachment. Schlink's novel tells the story of

Michael Berg, who, as a teenager in the 1950s, is drawn into a sexual relationship with Hanna Schmitz, a thirty-six year old woman who had been an SS guard in a concentration camp, a fact that Michael learns only years later when she is put on trial for her crimes. Thus, although the novel unfolds in the decades after the Holocaust and does not portray the years of atrocity themselves, its narrative force is directed toward Hanna's past as a perpetrator. *Der Vorleser* has achieved enormous international success and garnered considerable attention from its status as a rare literary treatment of the Holocaust that focuses intensively on the private life of a perpetrator. Critics have responded with both warm praise and vehement criticism to the novel's foregrounding of an intergenerational love story, but have generally agreed that, despite its shift in focus from the father to the female lover, *Der Vorleser* aligns itself with the project of *Väterliteratur*. The narrator in Schlink's text encourages such a reading by claiming his narrative to be representative of the German second generation. However, as I argue, the narrator's conflation of his own idiosyncratic experience with that of the student generation functions as a narrative trick to disguise his own singular failure to acknowledge Hanna's crimes.

I choose these texts for three reasons. First, and perhaps most important, all ten texts prominently stage the problem of Holocaust memory in ways that mark the second generation. In each of the two parts of this study, my analysis begins with works in which the action revolves around a character or characters whose parent or parents were actively involved in the events of the Holocaust, whether as perpetrators (*Vati*, the novel and play *Der Vater*), as victims/survivors (*Elijah Visible*, *Maus*), or, in the case of *Gebürtig*, as both perpetrators and survivors. In all six of these texts, the transmission of Holocaust legacy occurs through the channels of the parent-child relationship, and the child is called on to negotiate the parents' past within the context of his own contemporary life. In the last chapters of each part, I then turn to works that complicate the model of parent-child conveyance of the Holocaust past. In these texts, the second-generation narrators direct their inquiry into the past not to their parents but either to persons completely unknown to them ("Arthur Mayer," *Dora Bruder*) or to persons with whom they are intimately connected (*Am Beispiel meines Bruders*, *Der Vorleser*). Second, I choose these texts not because of any overt thematic similarities or differences between them (other than, of course, their adherence to my definition of second-generation literature), meaning that I would try to argue a particular point by finding works that fit into a pre-determined paradigm, but rather because in each case the text addresses the problems of stigmatization and the imagination of the past in a particularly interesting or provocative way. Instead of working from the outside in by looking for texts that support certain pre-established notions about second-generation literature and then interpreting them in accordance with a set framework, I work from the inside out: I allow each text to speak to me about its own marked engagement with the legacy of the Holocaust and I then choose those whose imagining of the Holocaust tells, in my opinion, a story that merits further exploration. Finally, in order to explore the role of narrative in the production of postmemory and the ways in which the text's structure relates to how the text marks the Holocaust, I include texts composed in a variety of genres. Some very disparate genres are represented here: the novel and the novella (*Gebürtig, Am Beispiel meines Bruders, Der Vorleser, Der Vater, Dora Bruder*) a single short story ("Arthur Mayer") and a collection of short stories (*Elijah Visible*), a play (*Der Vater*), a graphic novel (*Maus*) and a particularly German form akin to the novella, an *Erzählung* (*Vati*). Although a sample of only ten works cannot provide us with a complete and comprehensive knowledge of all the methods and processes used by second-generation texts, the variety of genres and narrative forms explored in this study can render a mosaic-like image of the multiple ways in which the Holocaust is imagined and marked in the second generation.

The texts I have chosen have differing relationships to their own production and to the past that they attempt to imagine and represent. Although, as the premises for my study state, the texts are written from the perspective of the second generation, each has a different degree of reference to the writer's own experience with Holocaust memory in the family. Some of the texts make claims to autobiographical reference and at the same time acknowledge their own literary license, and others present themselves as fictional while simultaneously alleging apparent connections to the authors' own experiences. For example, several of the works, including *Maus, Der Vater, Am Beispiel meines Bruders, Dora Bruder,* and "Arthur Mayer," present themselves as autobiographical texts; the stories they relate are more (in the case of *Maus* and *Am Beispiel meines Bruders*) or less (the play *Der Vater*) based on the experience of the writers and either their parents, or, as in "Arthur Mayer" and *Dora Bruder,* other real people who perished in the Holocaust. At the same time, however, all of these texts raise questions about their claim to truth by utilizing representational devices that function as *Verfremdungseffekte* (alienation effects): *Maus,* through the form of the animal fable, the play *Der Vater,* through its own self-conscious, theatrical staging, *Am Beispiel meines Bruders,* through its juxtaposition of contradictory discourses, and *Dora Bruder* and "Arthur Mayer," through their self-conscious use of encyclopedic and cartographic organization.

Gebürtig and *Elijah Visible,* on the other hand, present themselves as fictional texts, but as critics (Kaukoreit, Berger) have pointed out, their stories fall under the rubric of autobiographical fiction, since in each case the plot maintains a loose referent in the author's own experiences with the trauma of his parents' history. *Vati* and *Der Vorleser* are fictional texts written by authors whose parents were neither survivors nor perpetrators, yet their authors were both active members of the '68 generation and have identified more generally with the second-generation project of confronting the perpetrator generation. Furthermore, as Colin Riordan points out, *Vati* is a fictionalized retelling of an actual encounter between Josef Mengele and his son (as reported in the German magazine *Bunte Illustrierte*) and can be designated as either fictionalized biography or biographical fiction. Thus, in each of the books, some measure of reference to an extra-textual reality of the Holocaust past is asserted and at the same time made problematic. Such a blurring between fiction and autobiography might even be expected in the case of these texts, for on the one hand, in imagining an event that was not experienced, the text is forced to resort to fictional detail in order to fill in the blanks. On the other hand, a purely fictional account butts up against the historical reality of the Holocaust, the certainty that what happened can never be a purely textual experience without reference to real pain and suffering. As Efraim Sicher and Sara Horowitz demonstrate, second-generation literature, forced to move back and forth between each of the poles of fiction and autobiography, "pushes against generic boundaries" (Horowitz, 277) and exposes them to be, at least in the case of the Holocaust, inadequate and misleading distinctions.

In addition to varying relationships to the historical reality of their authors, the texts each depict a different relationship to the Holocaust. The common factor that links each of the texts, however, is the point of reference in the contemporary lives of the children of those involved in the Holocaust. In all the texts, the primary scene of narration is not the Holocaust past of the parents, but the present lives of the children, the arena in which the legacy of the past makes its mark. The texts differ with regard to their willingness to actually imagine the Holocaust directly. Four of the works, *Maus, Der Vater* (both novel and play), and *Dora Bruder,* do attempt to directly represent the Holocaust past of either the narrators' parents or (in the case of Modiano's text) an unknown person. However, no text presents the Holocaust story as the only narrative occurrence, alternating between representations of past experiences (Vladek Spiegelman's ordeals in the ghettos and camps, Hans Frank's role as the *Generalgouverneur* of Poland, Dora Bruder's imagined wanderings through Paris) and the author's commentary and imagination in the present. Significantly, in none of the texts is the Holocaust past conjured in realistic representations. Rather, as noted above, these works highlight the mediated character of the process of imagining an unexperienced past by depicting the Holocaust in a stylized, highly artificial rendering. *Maus, Der Vater,* and *Dora Bruder* approach the Holocaust and attempt to represent it, but, through the use of the *Verfremdungseffekt,* deny any claim to absolute accuracy in their depiction of what happened (although Art Spiegelman's careful documentary research certainly aimed to provide as much factual evidence as possible). In the other texts, on the other hand, there are no sustained representations of the Holocaust past and the focus remains largely on the present lives of the second-generation characters. In each case, the Holocaust is felt as a legacy in the present, a residue of memory that can only be marked by its absence. In *Elijah Visible* and *Vati*, the parents' pasts are opaque to both the characters and the reader; the only clues to the existence of trauma or perpetration are occasional hints given by the narrators. In *Der Vorleser, Am Beispiel meines Bruders,* and "Arthur Mayer," the narrators self-consciously attempt to reconstruct the wartime experiences of, on the one hand, a lover and a brother who were members of the SS, and on the other, an unknown Jewish doctor who perished in Auschwitz, but their efforts are thwarted by a postwar German society that resists any attempt to violate the carefully controlled silence about the Nazi past. In *Gebürtig*, the Holocaust is mediated through the characters' oblique references to the ways in which Austria's involvement in the Holocaust shapes present-day relations between Jews and non-Jews. In the case of these six texts, in contrast to *Maus, Dora Bruder,* and *Der Vater,* the Holocaust as an event takes the form of an unimaginable force that, though largely unrepresented, casts a heavy shadow over the present.

In each of the ten texts discussed here, there is an incident in which the protagonist finds himself marked viscerally, almost physically, by the Holocaust past of his parents. My examination of each of these texts thus includes a brief discussion of these images of stigmatization. In Peter Schneider's *Vati*, for example, the narrator claims to be marked by "an inscription on my forehead that everyone but me could decipher,"[22] a signifier of his father's criminal past, of which only he is ignorant. In Art Spiegelman's *Maus,* Artie, the witness who records his father's story, is marked by the visual text as both sympathetic witness and aggressive perpetrator. However, as I have stated, my main focus is not these incidents of thematic marking, however evocative they are, but rather the texts' narrative performance of stigmatization. For this reason, my analysis of each of the texts concentrates chiefly on the ways in which the narratives themselves overcome their crisis of signification and mark the protagonists' engagement with their parents' past.

---

[22] "eine Schrift auf der Stirn, die jeder außer mir selber entziffern konnte" (Schneider, *Vati,* 12).

Part I. The Legacy of Survival

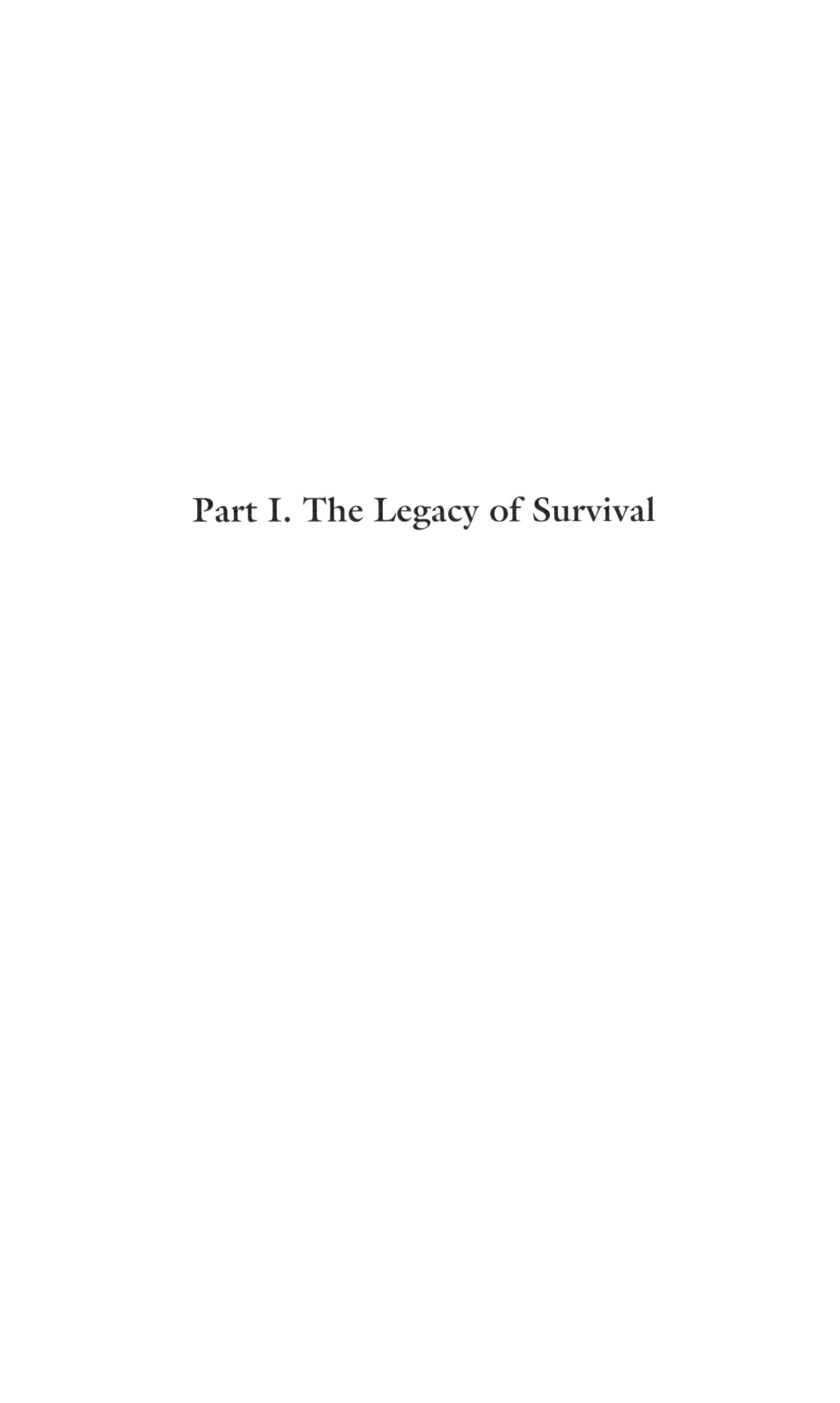

1: "A Tale Repeated Over and Over Again": Polyidentity and Narrative Paralysis in Thane Rosenbaum's *Elijah Visible*

Born after the war, because of the war, sometimes to replace a child who died in the war, the Jews I am speaking of here feel their existence as a sort of exile, not from a place in the present or future, but from a time, now gone forever, which would have been that of identity itself.
— Nadine Fresco, "Remembering the Unknown"

Canvases of Trauma and Grief

IN "ROMANCING THE *YOHRZEIT* LIGHT," the second short story in Thane Rosenbaum's collection *Elijah Visible,* Adam Posner, a New York painter, seeks a viable medium through which he can articulate his grief over the death of his mother, a Holocaust survivor. His sense of obligation to honor his mother becomes even more difficult because of his history of rebellion against the religious traditions that were important to her. His radical break with Judaism has long since erased any familiarity with Jewish mourning ritual: "Adam didn't know the prayers; the kaddish remained a mystery, like a foreign language. The Hebrew vowels and consonants just wouldn't come. He may have once known them, but no longer" (23). Unable to mark his mother's death in the language of Jewish tradition, he turns to the one language he masters — that of art. Through his creative work he attempts to translate his overwhelming grief into concrete expression:

> After Esther's death, Adam had lapsed into an ungovernable depression. The world around him seemed more dark and lifeless than usual. His art began to reflect these feelings, becoming even more spasmodic; the angry expressionistic images choking the canvas, and each other. The canvases themselves took on more monstrous apocalyptic shapes and physical dimensions [. . .] And the representational images, well . . . they depicted burnings, famines, sicknesses, nightmares — devastations of one sort or another. The urban litter that he normally assimilated into his paintings took on a more raw and violent form [. . .] Crack vials, used condoms, a doll missing its arms, a discarded pair of underwear. (23)

Although Adam paints to give expression to his congested ability to mourn, his art becomes the point of convergence for emotions that far transcend the primary experience of grief, functioning as a lightning rod for violent events that are outside his own personal experience. In channeling his grief for his mother through his art, Adam becomes the conduit not only for his own sense of loss, but for her trauma as well. Moreover, he reenacts this unknown trauma in the process of painting, where he turns his canvases into massive wounds by repeatedly inflicting violence on them. His mother's legacy thus manifests itself in his paintings in two ways: as an original traumatic event and as its aftermath in the traces of trauma. Some of his canvases become representations of an original experience of disaster in which the violence is not only depicted, but reproduced as well: "the angry expressionistic images choking the canvas, and each other." Other paintings contain only the residues of the trauma caused by these events of devastation, deposits of "urban litter" without clear reference to the connection between traumatic event and traumatic effect. Dismembered objects and remnants of violent subjugation and physical suffering, such as the mutilated doll and the abandoned underwear, function as signifiers for events not known but only imagined. The paintings are vicariously traumatized bodies in a landscape of apocalyptic disaster and biblical destruction, yet they are only able to signify the traumatic effect itself, not the violent incident that precipitated the trauma. In this way Adam's paintings function as metaphors for Adam himself, who becomes, to use the critic Froma Zeitlin's term, a "vicarious witness" of trauma, the conflux of unknown Holocaust experiences that, having outlasted his mother, haunt him in her stead.

Adam's Polyidentity

In all of the short stories in *Elijah Visible*, the Holocaust as an event is mediated solely by its trace in the postwar and contemporary lives of its survivors and their children. The Shoah itself makes no explicit appearance in the book; as a historical event it remains on the periphery, continually alluded to but not represented. The stories take place in the familiar private and public arenas of postwar American and Jewish-American life: a typical kindergarten class, a Passover seder, a meeting between childhood friends in a busy airport. However, although all of the stories revolve around events not overtly concerned with the Holocaust, each story eventually reveals itself to be the scene of an ongoing, obsessive imagining and re-experiencing of traumatic memories associated with the Holocaust that unfolds in tension with the fragmentation and assimilation of Jewish communities and identities in the context of postwar American prosperity and consumerism.

    The stories of the collection are linked by what appears to be a common protagonist — a character by the name of Adam Posner, the American-born son of Holocaust survivors. However, despite a nominal identity, Adam Posner takes on a completely different manifestation in each of the stories. In each story, Adam possesses new indicators of identity that are markedly different from those in the other tales; in turn, he is a different age (both child and adult), lives in a different place, has different parents, practices a different profession. One can attribute these differences to neither narrative development nor a multiplicity of perspectives on one unified character. If they are linked to one another within and between the stories, their common bond resists the conventions of narrative continuity and identity.

Several critics have briefly mentioned the problem of the multiple Adams and its possible meaning in the text, and all agree that the function of the narrative technique is significant for the ways in which the Holocaust is remembered in the stories. According to Marcie Hershman, the character of Adam Posner highlights the complex situation of the American child of survivors:

> As with so many in contemporary America his [Adam Posner's] is a sense-of-self in flux, yet as a child of survivors, his identity, conversely, is rooted.
>
> The collection's ingenious structure mimics the pull between inheritance and impermanence, as story after story slightly rearranges the reader's assumption of who Adam is [. . .] Rather than create a sense of discontinuity, the shifts become a matter of fascination: Look how different, the author seems to [be] saying, the individual caught in a web of history can be. (242)

According to this view, Adam is but one individual with multiple functions and stories whose relationship to history inhibits both a multiplicity of "characters" and a singular notion of identity. For Hershman, it is not Adam's connection to the Holocaust that causes his multiple identity, but rather the character's multiplicity appears as an effect of the instability of contemporary life. His link to the Holocaust, on the other hand, appears as the healing force that binds the self together and gives it a semblance of identity. In this way, the Holocaust legacy inherited by Adam functions both positively and negatively, for although it provides a stable ground for identity in a world that continually undermines notions of a fixed self, it also traps him in a static, unchanging world in which no transcendence is possible.

Efraim Sicher also stresses the role the Holocaust plays for the multiple character of Adam, who in Sicher's opinion represents the multiplicity of possible attitudes that a member of the second generation might possess vis-à-vis the past:

> Each story tells of a different Adam Posner, a different Adam of the new age. Each speaks to an alternate response to trauma and memory ranging, on the one hand, from a totalizing paranoiac obsession, ascrib-

ing all of life to the trauma of the past, [. . .] to the other extreme, denial and amnesia [. . .], the insistence that life must be lived without the burden of the past. ("In the Shadow of History," 178)

According to Sicher, Adam is a conglomerate of possible responses to inherited or vicarious Holocaust trauma. In each story, he provides another variation of the task of living in the shadow of the Holocaust past and the difficulty of fulfilling his function as the "uncorrupted hope" (Rosenbaum, *Elijah Visible,* 115) for the future, the one who must live out the uncompleted lives of relatives who were murdered in the Holocaust. Sicher suggests that the existence of the multiple Adams points to the complexity of Holocaust trauma and mourning, for just as the enormity of the crime itself eludes any single explanation or representation of the event, there is no single response to it in the second generation. Sicher views this diversity as a negative aspect of the second generation's relationship to the past, for in his opinion, the very multiplicity works against the process of working through the past and preserving Holocaust memory: "In all these stories, the trauma of the parents' Holocaust experience is a crippling inheritance, especially when memory is silenced, while in America's plurality of ethnic identities and memories remembrance risks becoming a meaningless ritual" ("In the Shadow of History," 179).

A third explanation for the existence of the many Adams is put forth by Janet Burstein, who views the collection of stories as the process of mourning that gradually moves toward mastery of the traumatic past, a task that she calls "an essential cultural function" (188) specific to the second generation. Each Adam thus represents a different station on the journey toward overcoming trauma, and the Adam in the later stories is, for Burstein, clearly closer to having worked through the past than the Adams of the first stories: "But his own traumatic memories are obscure at the beginning of this collection. They are clarified only as the stories track Adam — in different personae — toward fuller perception of them" (189). Adam moves from the overwhelmed victim of the return of the repressed in the first story, to mute rage in "Act of Defiance," to his "wiser" (189) search for Jewish tradition in the title story. By the end of the collection, Adam has progressed from denial and repression to a more reflective position with regard to his parents' suffering: "Clearly, he has begun the work of separating his own losses from those of his parents. The collection ends with a story that bears the fruit of this increasingly critical detachment" (190). In contrast to Sicher, Burstein views the Adams as occupying a different stage in the single linear development of the process of healing.

For Hershman, Sicher, and Burstein, the question of the nominal identity of the Adam characters in *Elijah Visible* revolves around the extremes of multiplicity and identity. Either the Adams can be read as differing manifestations of a single identity, or he is necessarily multiplied into the infinite and mutually exclusive possibilities of the second generation. My reading of the stories moves between these two extremes. Rather than relegating Adam(s) to either multiplicity or identity, I contend that his relationship to the Shoah lends him a polyidentity, one that is both fluid and fixed. By moving between the poles of identity and plurality, the stories in *Elijah Visible* perform the double move I have identified as a feature of second-generation literature: they record the rupture caused by the Holocaust and at the same time try to repair this rift and to restore continuity to a world that still suffers from the wounds of the Holocaust.

Rupture and Continuity

Despite his nominal identity, Rosenbaum's Adam Posner is a character who is in no way identical to himself. He possesses the unifying signifier, but there is no single self to which the nominal designation can point. Behind the coherence of the name lies a rupture in the notion of identity that reflects James Young's "traumatic breach" (*Writing and Rewriting the Holocaust*, 98) in history and Jewish identity left by the Holocaust. Adam is the fractured product of the Shoah, a conglomeration of multiple pieces that cannot be retrofitted together to make a whole. Although each Adam is, in essence, the same in every story (in each case he is the only child of Holocaust survivors), he becomes fragmented into a collection of unrelated stories that cannot be integrated into a single, identical narrative. Like his parents, the survivors who experienced the Holocaust, he is broken and incomplete, for the impact of the traumatic memory he has inherited from them necessarily precludes a whole, continuous sense of self. The Adam of each story lives a sort of schizophrenic existence in which he is necessarily cut off from himself and must confront and imagine the memory of his parents' past alone and in an incomplete state. In his fractured condition, he has no access to the other pieces of his identity, yet his function is to fill the emotional void left by the Holocaust and to testify to his parents' traumatic survival. In short, he is what Dina Wardi terms a "memorial candle," the second-generation keeper of Holocaust memory who possesses no real identity in the family apart from the Holocaust.

The stories of *Elijah Visible* not only record the breach caused by the Holocaust, but attempt to repair it as well, by restoring continuity, by reconstituting that which was lost, by reimagining the past. This second part of the double move of recording and repairing rupture is effected by precisely the same narrative element that operates in the first part, that is, by the polyidentity of Adam Posner. For as much as the various Adams seem separate from and independent of one another, they are linked together by their experiences as "children of the Holocaust" (Wardi), who are nurtured by the centrality of the Shoah in their parents' lives. Although the parents differ in each story, ranging from patently absent in the daily life of their son ("Lost, in a Sense," "Bingo by the Bungalow") to obsessed with his education and development ("The Little Blue Snowman"), they all are so strongly affected by the trauma of their experiences that they are unable to parent him outside the shadow of the Holocaust or to provide a childhood for him that is unaffected by their own traumatic memories. Adam, for his part, suffers a great deal under the weight of his parents' Holocaust experiences and harbors fantasies of escaping his legacy as the child of survivors. In "Lost, in a Sense" he claims,

> I had often thought that I had been adopted, or wished that I had been. Left on that mythical doorstep, wrapped in swaddling clothes, a rueful note attached to the basket, mistakenly taken by the wrong parents at the hospital. Confusion at the maternity ward; the Holocaust survivors' baby wound up with parents of unconflicted pasts, and me, away I went to the land of remorse and apocalyptic preparation. I wanted, at times fervently, to link myself with the fictional parents who had abandoned me at the door of these misery-struck immigrants. I would have forgiven them had they come back — had they ever even existed. (174)

In this fantasy of his own origins, Adam rewrites his birth as the story of Moses, both inserting himself and his own experiences into Jewish textual tradition and positing the Bible as the countertext to his parents' Holocaust story, a legacy of continuity that offers him an identity apart from the Holocaust. Adam longs for a different family, one not "ravished by nightmare and divided by darkness" (170); one that will provide him with the "sense of place" (171) and "safe sanctuary" (170) he so desires. However, despite the efforts of his imagination, he is not able to access a family that is free of the burdens of traumatic memory. His extended family, in every case, has been almost completely obliterated by the Holocaust, and his parents appear as broken, shattered beings who barely recognize their son's presence. As Adam describes it, "It was a fatherless upbringing, and yet there was a father" (43). Adam's parents are barely up to the task of parenting him, of supporting his emotional needs and providing him with an upbringing appropriate to the situation. They are unable to act and make decisions apart from their traumatic experiences of the loss of family and their own survival: "Unless the circumstances called for nuclear war or the avoidance of another Holocaust, they were unfit parents" (170). However, in *Elijah Visible,* an alternative family emerges for Adam in lieu of his own parents, one that is rooted in the memory of the traumatic past itself. In every story, the parents recede into the background, living ghosts who are themselves haunted, and it is the Holocaust instead that emerges as Adam's true parent. In this way,

Adam's different manifestations are linked by this common parentage. The Adams themselves are related to one another in this odd sort of family; even though they are, in every case, the only children in their respective immediate families (meaning that they are the only non-survivors in a family that has little extension), they become brothers to one another intertextually. The isolation they feel within their own families is thus eased by the extended kinship provided by the narrative link between the stories.

In addition to their nominal and narrative connections, the Adams are related to each other in a further crucial way: they share the same language. In every story, a crucial moment occurs in which the narrator (sometimes Adam, at other times an unnamed narrator who uses Adam's voice in indirect discourse) divulges the parents' crucial connection to the Holocaust. Although this moment occurs at different times and in varying contexts within the narratives, the language used to express this disclosure is remarkably similar, for in each case it is a variation of the opening theme introduced in "Cattle Car Complex": "Adam's parents had been in the camps" (5).[1] This repeated recital of similar language becomes a common invocation of the memory of the Holocaust, a moment in each of the stories in which the reader is informed that it is not only Adam's name (a seemingly arbitrary signifier) that links the diverse stories, but a latent experience as well. The language employed to disclose the legacy of his parents' past is shared by all the Adams and thus becomes "a common language" (10, 21); in its evocation of Holocaust memory this means of communication connects them to one another and helps strengthen the link established nominally and textually between them. The "common language" becomes the means by which they find the connection and recognition they miss within their own families.

In "The Rabbi Double-Faults," Adam, here a teenager, responds to this sense of connection when he meets Rabbi Joseph Rose, the twin brother of his congregation's rabbi, Sheldon Vered. Rabbi Vered, like Adam's parents, "was one of them. A survivor too" (141), but Rabbi Rose immigrated to

---

[1] "Romancing the Yohrzeit Light": "I didn't survive the camps so you could walk around looking and acting like a camp guard" (20); "The Pants in the Family": "His patient had survived the camps. Her husband had the same curriculum vitae" (41); "An Act of Defiance": "He [Uncle Haskell] had crawled out of Auschwitz [. . .] Yet another in a long series of mangled family portraits, constructed by me, for me. The same was done with my parents" (58); "Elijah Visible": "the Posner family had survived the Holocaust" (90); "Bingo by the Bungalow": "It was a summer loony bin of refugees [. . .] Each a survivor from one camp or another: Bergen-Belsen, Maidanek, Treblinka, Auschwitz" (107–8); "The Rabbi Double-Faults": "My parents were in the camps too" (144); "Lost, in a Sense": "my parents, who were old and beaten, and defeated by the Holocaust" (169); "The Little Blue Snowman of Washington Heights": "The parents had been in the camps in Poland" (197).

Palestine before the war, and thus escaped the death and suffering experienced by his parents and siblings. Like Adam, Rabbi Rose has no experience of the events of the Holocaust, and this unexperienced past links the two together:

> "So this is the young prodigy," his brother said, extending his hand for a warm, friendly shake. "I am your rabbi's brother. Please call me Joseph."
> "I know who you are," I said. "I heard your sermon yesterday. I'm Adam." And then reflexively, as though guided by my mother's needy, desperate soul, I added, "My parents were in the camps too." Spoken as some secret password, a sacramental wink that just might confer immediate acceptance into the brotherhood of those related to survivors of the Holocaust. (144)

Adam has more in common with the Israeli Rabbi Rose than with his own parents and conversely, Rabbi Rose is more akin to Adam than to his own brother. Experience of the Holocaust separates the two families; on the one side, Rabbi Vered and Adam's parents are bound together by their survival, and on the other, Adam and Rabbi Rose (and, by extension, the other Adams as well) are linked by their common ground on the outside fringes of an event they never directly experienced. As Rabbi Vered says to Adam and Rabbi Rose, "Maybe the two of you should play together. You have come to America [to] find a brother, Joseph; maybe you have found one in Adam" (144). Adam uses a "secret password," a "common language" based on reference to "the camps" as a sort of familial code that will allow him to occupy his place within this "brotherhood of those related to survivors of the Holocaust," the kinship of those who never experienced the event directly. Significantly, this "common language" only occurs thematically between himself and Rabbi Rose and intertextually between himself and his fellow Adam-brothers. He does not share this language with his own parents, although it is Adam's relationship with his mother that sparks the mention of the password, "as though guided by my mother's needy, desperate soul." The communication between survivors and non-survivors is hindered by the gulf of experience that separates them:

> A crack in the silence had revealed itself, and I was determined to bust clear through the other side. Or, failing that, at least slip by unnoticed. I wanted to know more about what had happened to him during the war. It was always such an impenetrable secret — my parents, speaking in code, changing the passwords repeatedly, keeping me off the scent. (48)

In contrast to his linguistic link to Rabbi Rose and the other Adams through the "secret password" they all share as "brothers," Adam is cut off from the language of his parents' experiences, which he describes as "def[ying] translation" (64). Furthermore, he is all but severed from the language of Jewish tradition as well, and is forced to mimic this language in "a seance of incomprehensible words, the mother tongue of orphans in the Diaspora, pig Latin for nonkosher Jews" (89). The "common language" Adam finds is thus not one inherited from either his parents or Jewish tradition, although, as we have seen with his imagination of himself as Moses, he continually attempts to write himself into this tradition, even if this imagining casts him as a Moses in post-Holocaust times. The "common language" is one that he shares primarily with the other Adams and that therefore occurs only intertextually between the stories.

The regenerated and rejuvenated sense of family that emerges in and between the stories of *Elijah Visible* is thus not to be found in the isolated and damaged nuclear units that in each case consist of Adam and his parents. Adam explicitly rejects this notion of a family, one in which he alone must carry the weight of his parents' Holocaust past and bear witness to the destruction of their families. For Adam, this role of "memorial candle," in which he is expected to be "their uncorrupted hope, the promise of a life unburdened by nightmare and guilt" (115) and the substitute for family who were killed the Holocaust, does not provide the repair of community and restoration of continuity he seeks. Rather, the text reinstates an alternate extended family of sorts, one that rewrites the family histories of loss and suffering. By establishing a textual brotherhood of Adams, one that paradoxically enacts a rejuvenation of the lost Holocaust family out of Holocaust trauma, the text attempts to restore the loss recorded on the level of each individual Adam and his family. However, continuity and closure do not become effects or byproducts of the text. Rather, the text attempts to knit back together that which was torn asunder in the Shoah, even in those moments when it is clear that closure is to be continually deferred. The drive toward continuity is thus a matter of textual practice and not textual effect.

Trauma and Second-Generation Memory

The textual problematic of the protagonist's polyidentity in *Elijah Visible* can be seen as an expression of the second generation's attempt to confront and repair family history. This engagement with the Holocaust past does not merely take place on the level of the stories' narrative content but is embedded in the very narrative structure of the text, where the engagement is enacted textually. The text's structure therefore becomes an additional arena in which Holocaust memory makes its mark, one in which the legacy of the Shoah is felt more strongly than on the plot level. This linkage between legacy and narrative is particularly critical when we turn to the role of trauma in Rosenbaum's text. As I contend, Adam's polyidentity is an instance of textual trauma, one in which narrative structure serves as the expression of the second generation's traumatic imagining of the Holocaust.

Before I discuss the features of trauma in the second generation and their specific function in *Elijah Visible*, I believe it is useful to briefly define trauma and to identify some of its more pertinent characteristics. According to *Webster's*, *trauma*, which is derived from the Greek *trauma*, meaning "wound," can be either a "body injury produced by violence or any [. . .] extrinsic agent" or "a startling experience which has a lasting effect on mental life" (1507). The notion of trauma is thus based on both an original event and the lasting wounds produced by this event. Freud develops a theory of traumatic experience in *Jenseits des Lustprinzips* (1920; *Beyond the Pleasure Principle*), where he discusses the persistent effects of catastrophic events on the individual, which are revealed in dreams, unconscious repetitive symptoms, and linguistic devices (such as repression and displacement), that attempt to ward off the memory of the original experience. For Freud, trauma makes itself known in the patient by its unsummoned, recurring presence long after the traumatic event is over. Modern clinical psychology has elaborated on Freud's definition of trauma and combined it with clinical experience into a diagnosable disorder known as *Post-Traumatic Stress Disorder* (PTSD), a condition occurring in a person who has experienced, witnessed, or been confronted with events that involved actual or threatened death or injury. PTSD is characterized by a period of latency and forgetting, in which the person is no longer conscious of the continued presence of the event. The person may suffer from a variety of repetitive symptoms, including flashbacks, waking nightmares, and dissociative states, which are often mobilized by a "triggering event," a situation that resembles or symbolizes aspects of the traumatic occurrence (Calhoun and Resick, 49). The effects of this disorder are most persistent and severe when the originating event is of human origin and not an act of nature (*Diagnostic and Statistical Manual-IV-TR* 309.81). PTSD is a psychological concept that has emerged from clinical studies of survivors of large-scale traumas such as the Holocaust, and it is often used to describe the persistent effects of the Holocaust in the lives of both survivors and their children.

Cathy Caruth, who has written extensively on trauma and its role in literary texts, derives her definition from Freud's notion of trauma, which figures the experience of trauma as one of latent memory, and combines it with modern psychological definitions. According to Caruth, trauma makes itself known through the unconscious, repeated acts of the survivor, which haunt him ritually and repetitively but shed little light on the original event. One critical aspect of trauma for Caruth is its original inaccessibility, for the impact of trauma lies not in its demonstrative effect or the forgetting of said effect, but in the "inherent latency within the experience itself" (*Unclaimed Experience*, 17), in the very deferral of the experience in the first place.

Caruth identifies a second critical aspect in the concept of trauma in her discussion of Freud's example of Tasso's story of Tancred. Freud uses the example of Tancred's double wounding of his lover Clorinda to demonstrate the passive and unwitting repetition of traumatic experience. For Caruth, however, it is not only the repetition that is central to the trauma but the fact that Tancred's trauma is so closely connected to that of Clorinda:

> For while the story of Tancred, the repeated thrusts of his unwitting sword and the suffering he recognizes through the voice he hears, represents the experience of an individual traumatized by his own past — the repetition of his own trauma as it shapes his life — the wound that speaks is not precisely Tancred's own but the wound, the trauma, of another [. . .] But we can also read the address of the voice here, not as the story of the individual in relation to the events of his own past, but as the story of the way in which one's own trauma is tied up with the trauma of another, the way in which trauma may lead, therefore, to the encounter with another, through the very possibility and surprise of listening to another's wound. (*Unclaimed Experience*, 8)

Trauma, according to Caruth, is not only the story of the individual and his own traumatic experience, but the ways in which trauma is induced by the perception of another's wound, by the existence of another's traumatic story. She reads Freud's example of Tancred as a parable for psychoanalysis itself and the ways in which it is called upon to listen to the traumatized voice of another.[2] Trauma is thus not only the repetition of the individual's own suffering but can also be the repeated testimony to the suffering of another as well.

Discussions of trauma in the second generation frequently refer to trauma theory developed in studies of Holocaust survivors, drawing connections between the traumatic experience of survivors and that of their children, but pointing out one crucial difference: the Holocaust trauma felt by the second generation is not directly experienced but rather inherited as a legacy. Rather than suffering the traumatic events of its own experience, the second generation endures an unresolved trauma that is passed down by the survivors. In her work on postmemorial trauma, Marianne Hirsch takes up two aspects of trauma that are critical for Caruth, namely its latency and the critical connection between trauma and witnessing, and connects them explicitly to the experience of the second generation. According to Hirsch, not

---

[2] Sigrid Weigel points out a critical problem with Caruth's use of the Tancred tale in her discussion of trauma: Caruth, in concentrating on Tancred's listening to Clorinda's vocal wound, figures him as a survivor and effectively explicitly ignores his guilt as a perpetrator ("The Symptomatology of a Universalized Concept of Trauma," 89).

only is it appropriate to speak of the presence of trauma in the second generation, it is precisely within the second generation that the narrative of trauma manifests itself fully:

> Thus postmemory characterizes the experience of those who, like me, have grown up dominated by narratives that preceded their birth, whose own belated stories are displaced by the powerful stories of the previous generation, shaped by monumental traumatic events that resist understanding and integration [. . .]
>
> The notion of postmemory derives from the recognition of the belated nature of traumatic memory itself. If indeed one of the signs of trauma is its delayed recognition, if trauma is recognizable only through its after-effects, then it is not surprising that it is transmitted across generations. Perhaps it is *only* in subsequent generations that trauma can be witnessed and worked through, by those who were not there to live it but who received its effects, belatedly, through the narratives, actions and symptoms of the previous generation. ("Surviving Images," 12)

According to Hirsch, because trauma makes itself known belatedly, the second generation inherits the survivors' traumatic conflicts and is called on to assume the labor of working through the trauma, a task that the survivor generation was largely unable to perform. In this way, the second generation suffers the effects of a trauma it can never claim as its own. The trauma of the second generation is thus not the trauma of an original event, but rather the cumulative effects of the vicarious experience of ongoing suffering caused by the event.

Of the various features of trauma and PTSD, two symptoms in particular are pertinent to my discussion of *Elijah Visible*. The first is the aspect of repetition, which Freud terms the "compulsion to repeat." Trauma is fundamentally defined by repetition, in which the victim remains within the emotional and linguistic complex of the original event and feels compelled to repeat (and reexperience) certain aspects of that event in an attempt to circumvent the painful awareness of it. According to Caruth, however, it is not just the encounter with death and destruction that is repeatedly reenacted, but the fact that one has eluded death as well: "for those who undergo trauma, it is not only the moment of the event, but of the passing out of it that is traumatic; [. . .] *survival itself,* in other words, can be a crisis" (*Trauma: Explorations in Memory,* 9). Traumatic repetition, whether in the form of repeated acts, or, as in the case of the literary text, in the form of repeated tropological language, is not only the attempt to evade the pain of the traumatic event, but to comprehend the endurance and survival of the event. In this way, it becomes a drama of two acts, the first enacting the crisis, the second, its denouement. Like a play, the trauma is rehearsed again and again, yet the action never moves beyond the last line of the script. The story line may change slightly with traumatic repetition, but in essence it always contains the same dramatic structure.

Repetition is not only a definitive aspect of the trauma of the survivor, but it is also critical for the second generation's assumption of traumatic history. According to Marianne Hirsch, repetition is the hallmark of inherited trauma and thus the primary feature of postmemory; one reason repetition plays such a critical role in postmemorial narratives is because the medium through which the second generation becomes aware of its legacy — namely that of representations — is itself mediated repetitively. For the second generation, the repetitive reproduction of representations of the original traumatic event is the only way to obtain proximity to that event. For this reason, according to Hirsch, postmemorial repetition, though similar to survivor repetition in shape, is different in function, for it is employed in order to conjure up the original traumatic event rather than circumvent it:

> The images that are used to memorialize the Holocaust by the postmemorial generation, in their obsessive repetition, constitute a similar shield of unchanging trauma fragments, congealed in a memory with unchanging content. They can thus approximate the shape of narrative testimonies, *producing* rather than *shielding* the effect of trauma. Rather than desensitizing us to the "cut" of recollection they have the effect of cutting and shocking in the ways that fragmented and congealed traumatic memory reenacts the traumatic encounter. ("Surviving Images," 28–29)

In the second generation, repetition and representation are thus linked together in an attempt to reenact the traumatic event and thus provide a referent for the signifier of traumatic effect.

A second feature of trauma is the element of dissociation, which, in its manifestation, is closely linked to repetition. According to Laurence J. Kirmayer, who compares the trauma narratives of Holocaust survivors with those of adults with a history of childhood abuse, dissociation refers to a response to severe trauma in which the victim survives by psychically separating herself from the experience. As a rupture within consciousness in which the normal integration of memory, identity, and experience is disturbed, dissociation makes itself known in a variety of behaviors, including amnesia, fugue states, and multiple personality. One of the most significant factors of dissociation, according to Kirmayer, is that, despite its depiction in much literature as a state of static rigidity, clinical and experimental evidence show it to be characterized more by fluidity, meaning that victims suffering from dissociation are easily transported from one dissociative state to another. It is this aspect that distinguishes dissociation from outright repression, for repression implies the long-term warding off of painful memories until the moment they are revived in the "return of the repressed." With dissociation, the movement between remembrance and forgetting is constantly active:

> This sensitivity of memory to the metaphoric implications of language is a crucial difference between accounts of repression and dissociation, as the former is portrayed as a rigid barrier overcome at a critical moment of de-repression while the latter involves fluid movements back and forth across an "amnestic barrier" that responds to shifts in metaphor with more or less permeability. (180)

According to Kirmayer, dissociation is frequently operative in the narration of traumatic memories, where it appears in the form of shifts in voice, mental state, or metaphors for the self. However, the telling of a traumatic story may also serve to conceal the dissociation of memory at the same time, giving the dissociative state a protective cover and semblance of normalcy. In this way, narrative unity and dissociation are linked in a dialectical process of covering and uncovering traumatic memories:

> Dissociation is a rupture in narrative, but it is also maintained by narrative because the shape of narrative around the dissociation protects (reveals and conceals) the gap. Dimensions of narrative relevant to the processes of dissociation include coherence, voice, and time: that is, the extent to which the narrative of self is integrated or fragmented, univocal or polyvocal, and whether the flow of narrative time is progressive, regressive, or static. Narrative conventions may give rise to dissociation in several ways: by tolerating gaps in accounts of memory, identity, and experience when they occur; by expecting such gaps and creating a place for them in the story; by hiding gaps from others with diversions; or by hiding gaps from oneself by inventing alternative selves. (181)

Dissociation is one of the most intriguing aspects of trauma narratives, for, unlike repression, which attempts to unequivocally exclude the painful memory from consciousness, dissociation functions in such a way that the hidden secret is partially revealed, yet at the same time any full view of the secret is ultimately deferred, a dialectical problem that Dori Laub and Nanette C. Auerhahn term the "double state of knowing and not knowing" (288). With regard to the members of the second generation, the process of dissociation is one in which the gaps in the parents' integration of identity and traumatic memory are transferred to the children. However, unlike the survivors of trauma, who experience dissociation as a result of the intrusion of painful memories, the second generation is plagued by the absence of memory. Thus, for the second generation, dissociation is largely a metaphorical process. Nadine Fresco's metaphor of the amputated hand that one never had, which I discuss in detail in the introduction, illustrates the second generation's assumption of a trauma that can not be integrated into consciousness. For the second generation, trauma is the phantom pain that finds no referent in experience and is felt as a form of metaphorical dissociation, in which memories of the traumatic event function as a severed limb — an integral part of the body whose existence is perceived most keenly in its radical absence, in its permanent disunion from the body. The gap between traumatic experience and traumatic effect is analogous to traumatic rupture in the integration of identity and experience.

In *Elijah Visible* trauma operates only as a vague residue of suffering, for the original traumatic event occurs in the prehistory of the narrative. The reader never learns the details of the events that occurred before Adam's birth; she is informed only in every story that Adam's parents "had been in the camps." The original traumatic wounds are therefore never fully revealed; they are only perceived by their traces in the characters' lives in a post-Holocaust, apparently normalized world. For Adam, these wounds function rather as Fresco's amputated hand — they are sensed although they are unseen. As the nurse at his school in "The Little Blue Snowman of Washington Heights" remarks, "There are all kinds of beatings that go on in this world. You don't have to leave a bruise to see it" (201). Adam suffers the trauma of the beating without suffering the actual beating itself.

Moreover, the narrative problematic of Adam's polyidentity can be seen as an expression of trauma not only on the level of character but on the level of narrative practice as well, in the ways in which the text negotiates the traumatic Holocaust past. In this way, *Elijah Visible* functions as the traumatized corpus, responding to the trauma of the Holocaust in much the same way that a body responds to physical trauma. As I demonstrate, the features of trauma particular to the second generation, dissociation and the compulsion to repeat, are the symptoms through which this narrative trauma emerges.

Traumatic Dissociation

One of the main forms trauma takes in *Elijah Visible* is dissociation, which occurs both thematically, as a symptom suffered by some of the Adams, and structurally, as a disorder within the narrative itself. In this way, the narrative structure of the stories mirrors the dissociative trauma experienced by the characters. Adam slips into dissociative states in several of the stories. In each case the dissociation arises in response to a "triggering event," an occurrence that symbolizes some aspect of the Holocaust. "Cattle Car Complex," the first story of the collection, offers perhaps the most vivid example of Adam's dissociation. Trapped alone in a malfunctioning Manhattan office-building elevator in the middle of the night, Adam begins to panic, believing that he is actually imprisoned in a deportation train en route to a concentration camp. Elevator car becomes cattle car, triggered by his severe claustrophobia and fear of the dark, and Adam loses all awareness of the true context of the situation:

> Adam's chest tightened. A surge of anxiety possessed him. His mind alternated between control and chaos, trying to mediate the sudden emptiness. His eyes lost focus, as though forced to experience a new way of seeing. He wanted to die, but would that be enough? What had once been a reliably sharp and precise lawyer's mind rapidly became undone, replaced by something from another world, from another time, the imprinting of his legacy. Time lost all sensation; each second now palpable and deafening.
>
> [. . .] Nerves had overtaken his sanity. He was now totally at the mercy of those demons that would deprive him of any rational thought. And he had no one but himself to blame; the psychic pranks of his deepest monstrous self had been summoned, reducing him to a prisoner within the locked walls of the elevator. (6–7)

Adam's confinement in the elevator on the seventeenth floor triggers a transformation: suddenly he is no longer a lawyer on his way home from work, but a prisoner trapped not only by the immobilized elevator but by inner forces as well. Something "from another world, another time" swoops in and dissociates Adam from the context in which he functions as a lawyer, disrupting his ability to distinguish between "control and chaos," "nerves" and "sanity," the actual event of the elevator breakdown and the imagined experience of deportation. The triggering event, which causes the symptoms of physical trauma (tight chest, unfocused eyes) and psychic dissociation is "the imprinting of his legacy," the moment in which his parents' Holocaust experience manifests itself. The physical event of the elevator breakdown summons the unconscious memory of an unknown Holocaust event that had been lying dormant in Adam, causing him to experience it as the return of his own repressed experience. His distress and dissociation from the actual experience of being trapped in an elevator and not in a cattle car becomes so acute that when the security guard begins to speak to him through the intercom, he believes that he hears German. Adam becomes calmer only when his limousine driver, a Russian-Jewish immigrant, arrives and begins to speak to him over the intercom, because he believes that he represents the voice of the liberating Soviet army. In the end, when the elevator finally opens on the ground floor, he emerges, prepared to face the horrors of a death camp:

> Adam was sitting on the floor, dressed in soiled rags. Silvery flecks of stubble dappled his bearded face. Haltingly, he stared at those who greeted him. Were they liberators or tormentors? He did not yet know [. . .] As he lifted himself to his feet, he reached for a suitcase stuffed with a life's worth of possessions, held together by leather straps fastened like a rope [. . .] His eyes were wide open as he awaited the pronouncement: right or left, in which line was he required to stand? (11)

By the time the elevator doors finally open, Adam has become the living embodiment of the unknown memory that has been resting dormant within him. His identity as a lawyer is exposed as the thin and porous superstructure that houses "his deepest monstrous self." Like the leather straps around the suitcase he now carries instead of a briefcase, which can barely contain a jumble of objects that threaten to burst out, Adam's "reliably sharp and precise lawyer's mind" is but a weak dam from behind which a flood of unknown traumatic memory threatens to surge. The triggering event of the broken elevator becomes the violent force that snaps the straps and destroys the dam, allowing unconscious memory of the traumatic past to flood out. The dissociative state experienced by the Adam in the opening story forms a striking image of second-generation trauma, for it demonstrates how the traumatic memory inherited from the parents becomes incorporated in and is suffered intensely by the child.

The dissociation found on the plot level makes itself known as well in the most prominent narrative technique employed in the text, namely, the multiplicity of the character(s) of Adam Posner. The word *dissociate* means, after all, to separate, to disunite, and the psychological definition of dissociation is "the splitting off of certain mental processes from the main body of consciousness, with varying degrees of autonomy resulting" (*Webster's*, 416). Adam is nothing if not split; although all of the Adams share the same name, there is no corresponding union of consciousness. As such, Adam can be seen as a prime example of dissociation, for each of the Adams seems complete in his fragmentation and is unaware of any of the others.

In *Elijah Visible,* the primary dissociation occurs on the level of voice. Although the text's temporality is neither linear nor progressive, the problem of temporality accompanies the issue of voice in that any temporal dissociation is a result of fragmentation of character and not of dislocated chronological memory. The same can be said for coherence: the problem of coherence in the book is a result of Adam's polyidentity, for the respective individual stories retain coherence because of vocal stability within. The dissociation in the book is a matter of voice, although the problem that arises lies less with narrative perspective than with the vocal referent. The element we normally think of as voice, that is, the distinction between first- and third-person narration, is not the aspect of the text over which the reader finds herself stumbling, despite the fact that it is neither unified nor constant throughout the text. The stories alternate between first- and third-person narration, remaining (for the most part) consistent within each story, with the majority told from a third-person point of view (only in one story, "The Pants in the Family," does the voice alternate between first- and third-person within the confines of the narrative). Yet, despite the inconsistencies within the whole of the collection, the element of narrative perspective poses little problem for the reader, for she must only perceive that the situation shifts merely with regard to perspective, and then the changes are easily absorbed and integrated over the course of reading the book. The problem of voice, then, is one of vocal referent. With each new story, the reader asks herself not "Who is telling this story?" but rather "Who is the Adam in this story?" The vocal referent in every story, despite possessing a unifying nomination, is neither unified nor constant. It is characterized, as Kirmayer says of dissociative narratives, by a fluid movement in which the metaphors for the self constantly shift within a complex of amnesia and forgetting. The only stable memory in *Elijah Visible* is that of the reader, who remembers who Adam was and encounters each new shift in identity with unease.[3] Adam, on the other hand, is unable to access a unified memory and so hits the "amnestic barrier" (Kirmayer, 180) over and over again, inventing new and alternate selves after each act of forgetting. The reader eventually comes to question the very possibility of a main body of consciousness, for like the "house of mirrors" (139) to which the text refers, which provides multiple referents for a single signifier and obscures any possibility of a true referent, we are unable to locate any one true Adam.

The narrative stability of *Elijah Visible* is thus split by the dissociative disorder suffered by its structure. But, as Kirmayer reminds us, within and beside the rupture lies the opposite movement of restoration, for the object of narrative is to create a sense of order out of the fragmentation of memory:

> Dissociation is a rupture in narrative, but is also maintained by narrative because the shape of narrative around the dissociation protects (reveals and conceals) the gap [. . .]
>
> Traumatic experience is not a story but a cascade of experiences, eruptions, crevasses, a sliding of tectonic plates that undergird the self. These disruptions then give rise to an effort to interpret and so to smooth, stabilize, and recalibrate. The effect of these processes is to create a specific narrative landscape. (181–82)

---

[3] For Marcie Hershman, Adam's rapidly shifting identity does not present a problem for the reader, for rather than effecting a sort of narrative anxiety, in which the reader can find no referential locus, the narrative changes themselves become a focus of interest and reading pleasure: "The collection's ingenious structure mimics the pull between inheritance and impermanence, as story after story slightly rearranges the reader's assumption of who Adam is [. . .] Rather than create a sense of discontinuity, the shifts become a matter of fascination: Look how different, the author seems to [be] saying, the individual caught in a web of history can be. By the end, the feel is very much like that of a novel" (1). While I agree that the narrative structure is of fascination to the reader, I believe that, rather than causing pleasure, the narrative aberration induces what Roman Ingarden terms "blockage," in which the reader becomes frustrated and anxious, rather than intrigued or surprised. This blockage is caused precisely by the reader's confrontation with the traumatic symptoms of the text.

Kirmayer employs metaphors of geology to investigate the problems of traumatic experience. Like the earth's geological forces, which both mark the earth with tectonic rupture and create new landscapes, trauma narratives attempt to negotiate the rupture of the traumatic experience by conferring to it the coherence of the narrative form. Despite the inevitable splits and dissociations that become an integral part of the telling of the traumatic story, in the space of narration lies the drive toward continuity, the attempt to work through the trauma and heal the self. After all, the stories of *Elijah Visible*, though irreparably divided by the fragmentation of character, are at the same time linked together by the character's name. In this way, although the narrative dissociates into fragments, it tries simultaneously to link these broken bits back together and weave them into coherence.

Traumatic Repetition

The second feature of trauma that emerges in Rosenbaum's text is the compulsion to repeat. As with dissociation, repetition compulsion can be located in the text as both a thematic symptom and a structural disorder. Thematically, Adam is compelled to repeat in two ways. First, he is called upon to repeat the particulars of his parents' experience of the Holocaust. The most striking example of this type of repetition occurs in the opening story, "Cattle Car Complex," in which Adam inherits the psychic wounds of his parents' past, leading him to perceive the stalled elevator as a cattle car on its way to a Polish concentration camp:

> Adam himself knew a little something about tight, confining spaces. It was unavoidable. The legacy that flowed through his veins. Parental reminiscences had become the genetic material that was to be passed on by survivors to their children. Some family histories are forever silent, transmitting no echoes of discord into the future. Others are like seashells, those curved volutes of the mind — the steady drone of memory always present. All one needs to do is press an ear to the right place. Adam had often heard the screams of his parents at night. Their own terrible visions from a haunted past became his.
>
> He carried on their ancient sufferings without protest — feeding on the milk of terror; forever acknowledging — with himself as living proof — the umbilical connection between the unmurdered and the long buried. (5–6)

Adam's parents' memories become his experience and he literally relives the scene of their deportation, repeating the event in the present tense, in their place. As Dina Wardi describes in her therapeutic discussion of the second generation, *Memorial Candles*, this repetition of the original event represents the unconscious role the second-generation survivor plays in the family. He is forced to compulsively "return to the Holocaust," to relive it in order to once again survive it and to attempt to come to terms with and understand his parents' feelings of loss, guilt, and suffering. The operable metaphor of repetition in the above passage is the seashell, the "curved volute," in which sound may remain indefinitely, traveling the spiraling channels over and over again, neither ceasing nor breaking out. In this way, Holocaust memory is a "legacy" that flows through Adam's veins, which, like blood, circulates in the body in incessant repetitive patterns. Adam inherits this self-repetitive legacy through the womb, ensuring the continuity between his parents' memory of suffering and his own suffering of memory. At the end of the story, the reader senses that Adam's episode in the elevator is a scene that, like a theatrical performance, is doomed to be rehearsed again and again:

> The elevator glided to a safe stop. Like a performer on opening night, the car indulged in a brief hesitation — a momentary hiccup, of sorts — before the doors opened.
>
> As the elevator doors separated like a curtain, the four men, in one tiny choreographed step, edged closer to the threshold, eager to glimpse the man inside. Suddenly there was a collective shudder, and then a retreat.
>
> The unveiling of Adam Posner. (11)

Like a choreographed performance, which does not allow for the variation of improvisation and thus can be repeated over and over, this staging of Adam's traumatic memory, a memory of an experience that he can only imagine, points to its own repetition.

The second way the compulsion to repeat appears thematically in the text is the compulsive repetition of certain elements in Adam's own life. With this manifestation of trauma, he is not only forced to repeat the distress and trauma of his parents' Holocaust experiences, but also finds himself caught up in repetitive cycles of his own that are closely linked with to his parents' experience of the Holocaust. However, in this case, the compulsive repetitions are expressions of Adam's own psychic conflicts that revolve around the Holocaust and his link to Jewish tradition. In "Romancing the *Yohrzeit* Light," Adam tries to cast off his Jewishness in an attempt to distance himself from his mother's past, two aspects that are for him intertwined. Yet his rejection of Jewish tradition does not manifest itself in a simple one-time renunciation; it is compulsively repeated in a series of negations:

> His neighborhood on the Upper West Side was filled with synagogues, but Adam acted as though they were virtual leper colonies — cursed concrete structures set in between the familiar brownstones, to be avoided at all cost. He never celebrated Rosh Hashanah (actually, he couldn't tell you exactly what time of the year it even was). During the fall, when fashionably dressed Jewish families all over Manhattan rushed

to services, Adam blankly assumed the coincidence of various nearby, midweek weddings. (17)

Every year, while Jewish tradition renews itself with Rosh Hashanah, the Jewish New Year and the beginning of the High Holy Days, Adam renews his own rejection of Jewish tradition. His renunciation of Judaism thus takes the form of a quasi-religious repetitive ritual in which he alternately avoids Jewish tradition as if it were an agent of biblical infection and ignores it as if either it did not exist or he had no knowledge of its rites. Adam's rejection of Jewishness continues with his choice of a love object, yet here, as well, it is not a simple matter of a one-time renunciation of Jewish women. Rather, it is a scene of rebellion that repeats compulsively: "Recently he had fallen in love with yet another in an unending series of Gentile women [. . .] Misbegotten romances guided by primal, rather than tribal considerations" (17–18). By consciously choosing non-Jewish over Jewish women, Adam posits the erotic as a "primal" or more original power that has a more fundamental and therefore greater hold over him than the "tribal" considerations of Jewish tradition, the community into which he was born. However, rather than making a final break with any identification with Jewish tradition, Adam performs the ritual of renunciation again and again with each sex act, rehearsing endlessly his break with Judaism and his abandonment of his mother's memory.

The most striking aspect of repetition compulsion in *Elijah Visible* can be found in the narrative structure of the text. As we have seen, the textual symptom of dissociation occurs as a problem of character and vocal identity. The compulsion to repeat is active in the text in a similar way, but rather than manifesting itself as a disorder of voice, repetition indicates a violation of narrative practice. Although the collection of short stories appears to function in a conventional narrative manner, the conventional method of making each short story either dependent on the other stories or independent of them is suspended. Thematically and with regard to character, the stories are independent of one another, but semiotically, they are linked by the signifier *Adam Posner*. Even if the reader wants to read each story apart from the others, this desire is thwarted by the persistent nomenclature, and she is forced to link together stories that appear to have no common ground. The reading of each new story emerges as a kind of rereading of the previous one, and thus each story in *Elijah Visible* functions as a revision of the prior stories, but, importantly, *not* their continuation. There is no narrative development between the stories; in each one the narrative elements of exposition, character introduction, moment of crisis and denouement are repeated. Each story appears to be a rewriting of the one before it, with the Adam in each case getting a fresh start. The narrative thus repeats itself — continually and compulsively, by beginning over again and again.

It is this persistent and continual restarting that marks the text's engagement with trauma and its attempt to overcome traumatic paralysis. Each story tries to evade the traumatic past by staging a fresh start outside the shadow of the Holocaust. Adam becomes the protagonist of this recurrent narrative renewal, the main character in a single story that constantly loops back and begins again. Despite the narrative movement within each tale, Adam continually returns to the genesis of his story, where he tries once again to live a life untouched by the trauma of the Holocaust. The scenes of daily life at the beginning of the stories have little or no connection to the Holocaust, and with every new story, the reader is unaware of any legacy of trauma or persecution. In this way, the significance of the name *Adam* is revealed: in each story he is the genesis of the "first man," a fresh, new human manifestation in a world that is not yet fallen. Each story begins on a positive note in anticipation of its own narrative development. It is only later that the Holocaust is introduced, when the reader encounters the one sentence variation that breaks open the text and suddenly reveals its history: "Adam's parents had been in the camps." It is the triggering event that introduces the trauma of the past and mobilizes the traumatic symptoms. At this point, the moment in which the Holocaust past appears in the text, what appears to have been a collection of non-related stories reveals itself to be a single story that repeats itself in different guises. The fresh start untainted by the Holocaust collides into the triggering sentence and begins to unravel into the same tale of the legacy of persecution and suffering. The sentence functions as a signifier for that which the text attempts to evade, disturbing each time the text's carefully constructed normality by revealing the trauma already latent in each story. The narrative drive of the text, which attempts each time to begin anew with the promise of a different story, fails in its project of positive renewal, and its only available option is to spin out of control, self-destruct, and then begin again from the starting position. In this way, the text spirals back on itself in an attempt to continually and compulsively reenact itself. The development of which Burstein speaks reveals itself to be a hollow re-staging of the same story, and Adam comes no closer to understanding his parents' trauma. The texts of *Elijah Visible* become the Holocaust "litany" of which Nadine Fresco speaks, stories and narratives that attempt to fill in the void of Holocaust trauma by their very repetition: "The silence was all the more implacable in that it was often concealed behind a screen of words, again, always the same words, an unchanging story, a tale repeated over and over again, made up of selections from the war" (Fresco, 419).

Elijah Visible is a narrative that neither develops nor is able to work through its own prehistory, but is fractured by dissociation and mired in its own seemingly indefatigable repetition. At the same time, however, as I discuss at the beginning of this chapter, the text attempts to move past its own narrative and historical paralysis by attempting to reinstate on the narrative level the family that was lost historically. In the performance of these two seemingly incompatible aims, *Elijah Visible* thematizes the tension inherent in what I call the double move of recording rupture and restoring continuity in second-generation Holocaust writing, highlighting the relationship between paralyzed despair and restorative imagination. It is not only Adam who is caught up in the machine of Holocaust trauma, but the text as well, which is all but swallowed up by a history that dominates it. By the end of the collection, Rosenbaum's text is exhausted by its attempts to overcome its compulsive repetition and its failure to "escape [. . .] the legacy" (59). The final image in *Elijah Visible* reveals the text's sense of exhaustion and despair at its inability to evade its own compulsive restarting. In this last story, "The Little Blue Snowman of Washington Heights," Adam the kindergartner, who entertains fantasies of escape from his oppressive connection to his parents' traumatic past, eventually returns home to reassume his role as a "memorial candle" in a family paralyzed by trauma:

> The room was cold and damp, as though the storm had followed him inside, or *perhaps this is where it all began*. He entered slowly, afraid of what he would find. A trespasser in his own apartment. The living room was dark. "Momma, Poppa," he repeated, this time in a whisper. All he could hear was a swirling wind, coming from his parents' room. Moving through the corridor, he turned at their room. The door was already open. The room completely dark. By the window, two naked bodies were shuddering in the darkness. Two pairs of terrorized eyes — the withering remains of the master race. (205, emphasis added)

Adam returns home to find his legacy, a story that he can neither own nor evade. He becomes "a trespasser in his own apartment," a witness to an experience he has inherited but cannot call his own. Adam's trauma is the trauma of the unknown, the memory without referent. Unable to access his parents' memory of the Holocaust, but unable as well to escape it, Adam returns to the place "where it all began" to begin again his compulsive engagement with the past.

Rosenbaum's text functions in much the same way as Adam in this passage. Just as Adam is overwhelmed in the face of his parents' trauma and grief and at the same time able neither to find a space for himself within their story nor to evade it altogether, so too the text is paralyzed by the overpowering presence of the Holocaust and its own inability to either integrate that presence and move on or to narrate a space outside it. In the end, the text, exhausted and defeated, interrupts its cyclical attempts to achieve narrative renewal and returns, like Adam, to the scene of a trauma from which there is no escape.

2: "In Auschwitz We Didn't Wear Watches": Marking Time in Art Spiegelman's *Maus*

The horrors of the Holocaust did not last only a day or two. They lasted for six years. I doubt whether there are six years as long as those in all of Jewish history. They were years during which every minute, second, and fraction of a second was filled beyond its capacity.
— Aharon Appelfeld, *Beyond Despair: Three Lectures and a Conversation with Philip Roth*

Turning into the Past

MIDWAY THROUGH THE second volume of Art Spiegelman's comic novel *Maus: A Survivor's Tale*, Vladek, the Holocaust survivor, during a walk through a Catskills resort, explains to his son the procedure for *Selektionen* at Auschwitz, the terrifying periodic physical evaluations in which prisoners were sorted according to those who seemed capable of further performing slave labor and those who were too weak and therefore condemned to be murdered in the gas chambers of Auschwitz-Birkenau:

From Maus II, *page 58.*

A different version of this article was published under the title "No Time Like the Present: Narrative and Time in Art Spiegelman's *Maus*" in *Narrative* 11, no. 2 (May 2003): 177–98. Copyright 2003 by The Ohio State University. Used by permission of The Ohio State University Press.

"In the whole camp was selektions," Vladek begins in the first panel of a four-panel block, "I went two times in front of Dr. Mengele." In the next panel, he continues to narrate his experience in the selections: "We stood without anything, straight like a soldier. He glanced and said: FACE LEFT!" At the same time, Vladek is shown abruptly turning a quarter turn in the image that accompanies this narration; in effect, he is performing his role in the selection for his son, Artie, who stands aside to the left of the panel and watches the recreated spectacle, all the while recording Vladek's narration with a tape recorder that hangs from his shoulder. In the third panel of the sequence, Vladek continues to narrate his experience in the selections, quoting Mengele's order again to "FACE LEFT!" At the same time, he enacts the prisoner's compliance with the order, performing another obedient quarter turn. In the fourth panel, Vladek's explanation continues in a narrative box above the panel ("They looked to see if eating no food made you too skinny"), but here the survivor's reenactment of the selection during a walk through the country is replaced by a depiction of the original scene of the selection. Vladek is now no longer the aged narrator of a past experience, but the naked, emaciated prisoner who is first experiencing the scene of victimization and domination. He performs again a quarter turn, but in this panel it is not Artie who observes and records Vladek's story. Rather, a German camp official (according to Vladek's narration, Josef Mengele), a predatory cat to Vladek's hunted mouse, stands to the left and orders him to "FACE LEFT!" and at the same time records his evaluation of Vladek's physical condition on a clipboard. This last panel effects a visual break in the block of panels, for it suddenly transports the reader from a visual depiction of a present site of verbal narration of the past to a visual depiction of the narrated moment of the past itself. The visual seems to signify the abrupt chasm between past and present (a young, emaciated Vladek versus an aged, well-dressed Vladek), while Vladek's telling of the story appears to hold the two events together, linking the past and present in the process of narration. The comic book format of the scene, with its easily differentiated depictions of two separate temporal levels and two physical manifestations of the same character (young versus old), appears to clarify the disparities between the past and the present and to divide the two temporalities into distinct units in a much more visceral way than narration. For a novel about both the Holocaust past of the survivor and his present-day relationship with his son, *Maus*'s use of visual images as a supplement to narration seems to be an ideal method for demarcating the differences between Holocaust experience and the contemporary lives of the survivor and his son.

 A second look at this sequence of panels, however, belies this easy assumption about the use of visual media to distinguish past and present. The comic images of *Maus*, rather than clearly marking off the past from the present, contribute to a problem in which the present and the past are intimately interconnected and difficult to separate from one another, for the past is revealed as constitutive of the present, and the present makes demands on the ways in which the past is represented. The fourth panel of the block, which at first appears to be cut off from the rest, functions as an extension of the other three panels, as a constituent of a visual and verbal story. This link between the images and the development of the story from the present to the past is above all evident in the *mise-en-scène* of the last panel, which echoes the previous two panels in its structure. Here, as in the panels of Vladek's reenactment, we see a rotating Vladek on the right side of the panel who "performs" in front of an observer standing on the left. The observer in the last panel, Mengele, mirrors Artie's position and posture in the previous panels almost exactly, and, just as Mengele determines and records Vladek's future "fate" (to be sent to the "good side" and not "to the other side," a destiny visually represented by a chimney [58]), Artie watches and records Vladek's story of the selection. It would perhaps be an overstatement to claim that the visual text encourages the reader to conflate the persons of Josef Mengele, a mass murderer, with Artie, the recorder of Vladek's story, but there are clearly echoes of the one in the other, for in a sense, both figures use Vladek, albeit for radically different reasons: Mengele, by controlling Vladek's body; Artie, by controlling his story. By inserting one solitary image of Mengele after a sequence of frames that depict Artie, the text interrupts almost imperceptibly the reader's complacent image of Artie as objective observer and asks her to consider the present recorder of Vladek's story with the past determiner of Vladek's fate in the same context, thus establishing a visual analogue between the representation of an original scene of victimization and trauma and the retelling and representation of the event. When one tracks the movement of the frames in this panel, it appears that Artie, on a purely visual level, transforms into Mengele by virtue of his very capacity as transcribing witness. With this subtle metamorphosis of observer into actor, *Maus* makes an implicit statement about Artie's status as witness to Vladek's story of loss and suffering, marking him visually as a perpetrator, whose drive to learn, record, and represent Vladek's Holocaust experience revives for Vladek an unresolved and painful period of his life and robs him, in a sense, of his own story. Furthermore, the fact that Artie is identified not merely with a Holocaust perpetrator, but with the visual double of Josef Mengele, one of the most notorious agents of the industrial killings at Auschwitz, testifies powerfully to the dynamics of filial exasperation, guilt, and failure that underlie the scene of witnessing and permeate the subtext of *Maus*. In this way, Spiegelman's text depicts not only the father, but the son as well, as indelibly marked by the difficult narration of the Holocaust past.

The continuity between the retelling of the scene and the depiction of it is further underscored by the image of Vladek's rotation, for between the second and the last panels, he progressively rotates a three-quarter circle to the left. Just as in a moving film, which is made up of numerous still pictures that, when projected in rapid succession, contribute to a sense of seamless movement, so too the three panels evoke the idea of continuous, unbroken turning, apart from the abrupt rupture in setting and despite the fact that they are distinct images.[1] Vladek's gesture of turning and the visual representation of its continuation from the present to the past reveal the intricate relationship between the two temporal planes, marking visually the narrative process by which Vladek "returns" to his Holocaust past. As the relationship between the text and image in this instance indicates, however, it is not so much the past that affects the present by means of a story intruding into the present moment of storytelling. Rather, the present, the site of Vladek's verbal narration, is superimposed upon the representation of the past, as embodied in the comic image, and the past story that is narrated bears the visual traces of the act of storytelling. The present, both visually and metaphorically, thus "turns" into the past.

The Temporal Continuum

The representation of Vladek reenacting the *Selektion* in Auschwitz is one of many scenes in both *Maus I* and *Maus II* in which the Holocaust past is an integral element of the present and the present becomes key for representing this past. Even though Spiegelman's comic project appears to contain two separate, seemingly unconnected narrative strands that strictly delineate the *then* of the father's Holocaust story and the *now* of the narration of that story, the text evades attempts on the part of the reader to keep these two chronological levels distinct from one another. This effect of temporal blurring, of the implication of the past in the present and vice versa, has been remarked upon by a number of critics. According to James Young, "In *Maus*, not only are past and present linked, but they constantly intrude and occasionally even collapse into each other" ("The Holocaust as Vicarious Past," 682). Dominick LaCapra holds a similar view: "The past not only interacts with, but erupts into, the present, and at times the present seems to be only a function of, or a diaphanous screen for, the past" (*History and Memory*, 155). For Keith Harrison, by the end of the book, "two places, two times, and two narrative lines movingly converge" (67). A number of critics, however, take issue with the notion of temporal collapse in *Maus* and insist

---

[1] Thomas Doherty remarks on the photographic and filmic qualities of *Maus*, which he claims take advantage of a "grammar of cinema" (78), and Spiegelman himself recognizes the book's parallel with film in the image of Vladek on the exercycle, which he calls "an analogue to the cinematic effect of the whirling wheel where Vladek begins to spin his yarn and you enter into the past for the first time through that wheel" (*The Complete Maus*, 6).

that the then and now in Spiegelman's text, though narratively intertwined and implicated in one another, cannot be normalized into an unbroken continuum in which the past flows evenly and smoothly into a present. Rather, the text, by utilizing certain narrative devices, resists any sort of chronological equilibrium. According to Marianne Hirsch, *Maus* disrupts its own narrative and visual temporal flow by incorporating three actual photographs of the Spiegelman family, severing what she terms the "testimonial chain" ("Family Pictures," 26) that links past and present. For Alan Rosen, the disruption takes place not visually, through photographs, but rather aurally, through Vladek's broken English:

> For episodes in the past, Spiegelman uses fluent, colloquial English to represent the languages of Europe as spoken by their native speakers; for episodes in the present, Vladek's broken, accented English serves as a constant marker [. . .] within the terms *Maus* establishes, Vladek's broken English becomes the means by which Spiegelman articulates the incommensurability between present and past. (258)

For Hirsch and Rosen, the distance between past and present is unbridgeable, despite the easy temporal blurring that appears to take place through the process of reading the comic frames.

Critics have highlighted a further complication in the relationship between temporal levels in *Maus* by pointing out that the text contains not only *two* narrative strands — the narratological categories of story and discourse — but actually *three*. In addition to Vladek's Holocaust experience and his narration of that experience to Artie, the text contains a third layer that consists of Art's reflections on witnessing his father's story and on the problems of shaping it into a visual narrative.[2] According to James Young, this third layer highlights not only Vladek's story itself but also the ways in which the retelling of it becomes an integral component of the narrative process:

> By weaving back into his narrative the constant reflection on his own role in extracting this story from his father, Spiegelman graphically highlights not only the ways that testimony is an event in its own right

---

[2] Following Hamida Bosmajian, I maintain the distinction between Artie, the character who listens to his father's stories, and Art, the character who reflects on his aesthetic project (Bosmajian, 2). (The author of the entire *Maus* project is designated as Spiegelman.) Spiegelman himself maintains the difference between Art and Artie in another way: Artie's statements (like those of Vladek and the other characters in both the Holocaust story and the retelling of it) are designated by uppercase characters. Art's metareflections, on the other hand, are represented by lowercase print (*The Complete Maus*, 178).

but also the central role he plays in this event [. . .] That is, what is generated in the interaction between father and son in this case is not a revelation of a story already existing, waiting to be told, but a new story unique to their experience together. This medium allows the artist to show not only the creation of his father's story but the necessary grounds for its creation, the ways his father's story hinges on his relationship to the listener [. . .] In this way, Spiegelman is both midwife to and eventual representer of his father's story. ("The Holocaust as Vicarious Past," 676–78)

For Young, the third layer reflects on the situation in which Artie, the listening character, finds himself. In this layer, he emerges not as the passive receiver of a story of trauma and loss but as the witness who effectively becomes the coproducer of that story. Stephen Tabachnick, on the other hand, concentrates not on the scene of testimony and the role of witnessing but on Art's struggle to imagine Vladek's story and to find a viable aesthetic form through which he can tell it. Tabachnick orders the three narrative strands according to the generic conventions to which they correspond. The first diegetic (narrative) layer, Vladek's story of his survival in the ghetto, in hiding and in Auschwitz, becomes an epic narrative, "a monstrous *Odyssey*" (156). The middle layer, which focuses on Artie's relationship to his parents and the effects of their Holocaust experience on his own life, corresponds to the *Bildungsroman*. Finally, the third layer, the *Künstlerroman,* narrates the problem of *Maus*'s production, focusing on Spiegelman's concerns about the problems of representation and authenticity, and the difficulty of imagining an event that he never experienced.

My reading of the three layers of temporality combines elements of Young's perspective on the role of witnessing with Tabachnick's ordering of the diegetic levels according to genre and aligns them with Gérard Genette's system of classifying narrative in a tripartite schema of story, discourse, and narrating. The first, innermost level[3] of *Maus* contains the narrative's story: Vladek's life in prewar Poland, his experience of the German invasion as both soldier and civilian, his attempts to elude capture and deportation, his incarceration in Auschwitz, and his liberation. The second, or middle, narrative strand is comprised of the scene of this narration — the times when Artie visits Vladek to listen to and record the first story — which, according to Genette's typology, is the location of the narrative's discourse. In addi-

---

[3] To ensure that my analysis corresponds to previous scholarship on *Maus*, I am reversing Gerard Genette's classification of diegetic levels, which labels the outermost narrative as the first diegetic level, the middle narrative as a narrative of the first degree and the innermost narrative as a narrative of the second degree. In contrast to Genette, critics of *Maus* (with the exception of Tabachnick) have organized *Maus* narratively from the inside out.

tion, the second level is the arena of an additional story — the often difficult relationship between Artie and Vladek. On this narrative level, which locates the scene of testimony and witnessing, Artie, Vladek, Mala, and Françoise are portrayed as mice and are thus depicted according to the same representational logic as the first diegetic level, which casts the characters as various anthropomorphic animal species functioning within the animal kingdom's web of power relations.[4] The visual differences between the first two levels are not distinctions of character representation (the characters are animals in both levels), but ones of the setting in which the characters function (Queens, the Catskills, and Florida of the present versus Poland during the Holocaust). The exception is of course the representation of Vladek, which is perhaps the most striking indicator of the respective narrative levels. On the one level, he is shown as young and physically virile, although the dapper ladies' man at the beginning of the story slowly transforms into the thin, starving slave laborer at the end. But the depiction of a young Vladek clearly differs from that of the middle narrative, which shows him as an old man, wrinkled, stooped, and in poor health, a survivor who visually embodies the cost of survival. By glancing at the Vladek of each frame, the reader can thus immediately orient herself with regard to the narrative level.

Of course, as we saw with the image of Vladek rotating, the visual difference between the inner and middle narrative levels is not always distinct. Vladek's voice penetrates into the visual representations of his Holocaust story, and he quotes his direct speech from the past in panels that refer to the middle narrative, the site of the narration of that story. Furthermore, the text contains dozens of instances in which the two narrative levels exist in close proximity to one another or even within the same panel. As with the scene of Vladek's selection, the text places very similar images from both narrative levels side by side, as in an exemplary scene of Anja's distress in *Maus I*, when in a single panel a depiction of a first-level Vladek wearing a hat is closely followed and echoed by an image of Vladek the narrator, also in a hat, while the verbal text continues unbroken from the past into the present:

---

[4] Since a number of critics have written very good analyses of Spiegelman's use (and potential abuse) of the animal metaphor and the ways in which *Maus* deconstructs its own representational logic, I do not explore the issue in depth here. Particularly insightful interpretations include those by Dominick LaCapra (*History and Memory*), Marianne Hirsch ("Family Pictures"), Keith Harrison, Jeanne C. Ewert, James E. Young ("The Holocaust as Vicarious Past"), Andreas Huyssen, and Michael E. Staub.

From Maus I, *page 122.*

In this example, the blurring of narrative levels takes place not only visually, with the second level's repetition of the first level's *mise-en-scène*, but on the verbal level as well, with the narrator's assumption of the character's dialogue, without quotation or indirect discourse. This instance of the juxtaposition of Vladek the character with Vladek the narrator is but one of many in the two volumes of *Maus*, for the first and second narrative levels (the separate sites of story and discourse), consistently alternate and are interwoven with one another throughout the text. Gérard Genette terms these juxtapositions *narrative metalepses*, which are transgressions that "by the intensity of their effects, demonstrate the importance of the boundary they tax their ingenuity to overstep, in defiance of verisimilitude — a boundary *that is precisely the narrating (or the performance) itself*: a shifting but sacred frontier between two worlds, the world in which one tells, the world of which one tells" (236). The boundary between the two narrative levels, the level of Vladek's Holocaust story and the level of Artie's witnessing, is thus both blurred and highlighted by the abundant visual metalepses that occur throughout the text.

 The third, outer, level of *Maus*, which functions as an instance of the third part of Genette's system, that of narrating, grapples with the connections between the other two layers (the testimonial relationship), Art's problems of imagining, reproducing, and representing Vladek's testimony, and, beginning in the second volume, the role of reception of the first volume of the comic novel. This narrative level operates as a metadialogue on the other two narrative levels, for just as the middle level is a metareflection on Vladek's Holocaust story, so too this third level of narrating examines both the original site of trauma and the traces of this trauma in the witnessing relationship. In addition, this layer investigates Art's struggle with imagining and representing his father's story. Despite the book's apparently easy depictions of Auschwitz and the suffering experienced there, this portrayal is not a self-understood matter of transparent representation. Art must imagine it to be able to draw it, and his fear of not living up to the task points to the text's fragile claim to representational authenticity and even to its potential unauthenticity. This narrative level thus encourages the reader to consider the inability on the part of both Art, and by extension, the text, to decisively or realistically "capture" Vladek's experience and represent it in a narrative.

The third level of narrating is marked off visually from the other levels in two ways. The first is the use of lowercase lettering, which appears briefly in the first volume and more often in the second and marks a stark contrast to the uppercase text that dominates the rest of the book. However, although the third level is limited in its use, it is the narrative mode in which the entire *Maus* project originates. The first panel of *Maus I* begins the narrative with a lowercase introduction to the narrative's impetus: "It was summer, I remember. I was ten or eleven . . . I was roller-skating with Howie and Steve . . ." (5). The use of the lower case, like that of the upper case of the first and second levels, functions here to mark a site of narrating. In this case, however, it is Art who is doing the narrating, not Vladek, who controls the narration in the middle level. Although the dominant story that emerges in the text belongs to Vladek, the first story of the text and the first instance of narrating belongs to Art. Art, like Vladek, has his own story to tell, and, as with Vladek's narration, the narrated event, Art's own story of himself as the second-generation witness, unfolds in uppercase dialogue. In the first volume of *Maus*, however, the use of lowercase lettering is limited and sporadic, appearing as brief introductions to some of the chapters and serving as a prologue to the respective narrative situation. The third level is thus barely discernable in the first volume. In the second volume, the lower case is used more often, especially at the beginning of the second chapter, "Auschwitz (time flies)," where it is sustained for several pages. In this section, the second marker of the level of narrating appears with the depiction of the characters as humans wearing animal masks, rather than embodying anthropomorphic characters.[5] The employment of the mouse mask over the human

---

[5] Several critics compare the use of masks in the "Auschwitz (time flies)" chapter with Vladek's and Anja's employment of them in *Maus I* (Hirsch ["Family Pictures"], Martin, Harrison). While Art's donning of the mouse mask certainly refers to Vladek's and Anja's attempt at "passing" outside the ghetto by wearing pig masks and reminds the reader of the problematic and sometimes arbitrary nature of the construction of racial and ethnic identities, both during the Holocaust and in the present, there are crucial differences between the two uses of the mask. In Art's case, the mask is worn over a human head, reflecting on the strange and "unnatural" gesture of posing as an animal and thus to the aesthetic strategy of depicting a human story in animal form. In the case of Vladek and Anja, they are portrayed as anthropomorphized (but not human) mice wearing the masks of another animal. Although their masking calls attention to the construction of identity, it does not call into question the representational logic that governs both the first and second narrative levels.

head points to the text's self-conscious reflection on its own production, on the representational choices it has made from a spectrum of aesthetic possibilities. Spiegelman's choice of casting his father's narrative as an animal tale, as a fabulous story in which mice are hunted by cats who are in turn hunted by dogs, while pigs selfishly protect their own interests, is thus exposed as an arbitrary (and potentially dangerous) method of framing a story.[6] Rather than allowing the reader to immerse herself comfortably in the mouse-and-cat universe, Art's wearing of the mask, which from the front looks authentic and only from the side and back is revealed as a mask with strings that attach it to a human head,[7] ejects the reader from the complacency of the animal metaphor and points to both its artifice and its effectiveness as a normalized aesthetic device. In addition, Art's role as the author of the Artie and Vladek narratives is made explicit here (he is shown at the drawing table listening to tapes of his father and himself), but the wearing of the mask, which places Art both inside and outside the representational framework that governs the rest of *Maus,* prevents him from assuming a quasi-transcendent, autonomous authorial identity. Art is thus depicted as a character in much the same way as Vladek and Artie, and he too struggles with the same overwhelming forces of history and memory. But his relationship to the past takes on an additional dimension, for he must contend with both his own problems of imagining and shaping his father's story and the reception of the product of his imagination. The third level of *Maus,* which Richard Martin terms "metafictional" (380), Jeanne C. Ewert "metatextual" (93), and Rick Iadonisi a "meta-meta-narrative" (45), thus functions as the outer narrative of the text, the instance of narrating that reflects on the stories of the other two levels. Unlike the first, inner narrative, which is directly

---

[6] Of course, this is not the only device in *Maus* that reflects on the problem of using the animal trope. Other examples that call into question the representational rule include Anja's fear of rats in the cellar in which the couple hides and Vladek's assurances that the rats are only harmless mice (*I*, 147), Artie's discussion with his French wife Françoise about which animal to cast her as (*II*, 11–12), and Art's comments when he goes to see his analyst: "His place is overrun with stray dogs and cats. Can I mention this, or does it completely louse up my metaphor?" (*II*, 43).

[7] Dominick LaCapra does not believe that it can be established with certainty that the faces underneath the masks are indeed human: "When figures wear explicit animal masks (for example, Artie, his TV interviewers, or his analyst), it remains unclear whether there are human faces beneath or whether there are masks all the way down. This *mise en abîme* or bottomless multiplication of the mask may be one of the most radical gestures in problematizing identity" (*History and Memory,* 163). Although I find LaCapra's argument that the mask displaces any notion of essential identity very compelling, I disagree with his assertion that the heads under the mask are not identifiably human, for the backs of Art's, Pavel's and the journalists' human heads are clearly depicted in several of the panels.

concerned with Vladek's story of the Holocaust, the outer narrative struggles with the problems of imagining that experience and transforming it into a visual narrative. The two narrative activities are not directly opposed to one another, but rather function as the diegetic boundaries that delimit the text. The three narrative levels can be viewed as forming a sort of continuum, by which the inner narrative (story) gradually makes its way through the medium of witnessing (discourse) to the outer narrative (narrating). Such a continuum can be imagined as follows, moving from left to right:

1st (inner) narrative	2nd (middle) narrative	3rd (outer) narrative
(story)	(discourse)	(narrating)
Vladek's Holocaust experience	scene of Vladek's testimony	memory and representation
(epic narrative)	(*Bildungsroman*)	(*Künstlerroman*)

In *Maus,* the movement between diegetic levels occurs with the absorption of the father's trauma into the son's memory through the very agency of narrative, the act of storytelling.

The *Super-Present*

If there are indeed three diegetic strands in Maus, then how do they line up with the two temporal levels discussed previously, that is, past and present? According to Gérard Genette, a narrative level is distinguished from other levels not only by the scene and the agent of narration (who tells what story), but, more important, by the time of the narrated story. Each narrative possesses its own temporality, even if the narrative time overlaps with that of other diegetic levels. The temporal dimensions of Vladek's story, the innermost narrative, are relatively easy to identify: the tale that he narrates to Artie is located in the distant past, in the time prior to the German invasion of Poland and in the years that followed, up until shortly after the end of the Second World War. (Easy despite Vladek's own problematic experience of ordering a seemingly fractured and unstable sense of temporality *during* the Holocaust, which then has consequences for his subsequent memory of time. As he says: "In Auschwitz we didn't wear watches" [*II,* 68]). The problem of designating narrative time gets tricky, however, when one looks at the other pole of the past-present temporal continuum. To which narrative strand is the reader to assign the temporal designation of the present? The present of which Young, Hirsch, LaCapra, Rosen, and Harrison speak could refer to the levels of either discourse or narrating. The concept of the present is inadequate for the discussion of the two outermost narrative levels. Of course, one could argue that the level of discourse precedes the level of narrating chronologically, and therefore belongs to a completely different temporality. But the temporal problems to which Young, LaCapra and others refer — namely the conflation of Vladek's Holocaust past with the postwar, more contemporary scenes of which Art/Artie are a part — reduce the text conceptually to a chronological dichotomy of *before/during* and *after*. The text thus refers to the dialectic between an event and its aftermath. The narrative levels in which Art/Artie participate are permanently severed from the Holocaust past and can only access this past through storytelling and imagination. In this way, they necessarily belong to the present, to the time of *after*. As we have seen, however, these outermost narrative levels are separate in terms of their diegetic function: just as the middle narrative reflects on Vladek's telling of the first narrative, so too the outermost narrative contemplates both the middle and the first narratives. Tabachnick separates the two narratives of the present into the genres of *Künstlerroman* and *Bildungsroman*, but how are we to designate their respective temporalities? Spiegelman himself distinguishes between the present of Vladek's storytelling and the present of Art's reflections on the book by employing the terms *present* and *super-present:*

> This section was kind of not one I planned on doing, obviously, when I was planning the book. But it was the only way I could move forward to make the obstacles manifest. So I had to do this thing that now had a different layer of present than anything that happened before. There was a present with Vladek and me talking and then there was the past with his story. All of the sudden we now had a kind of super-present. And the super-present is done with certain devices — for one thing, the upper- and lowercase writing, which is used only a few times earlier in the book. It's used when you very first enter into the story and in a couple of captions, like "I went back to visit my father," or something like that. And that implies that all of that upper and lower case comes from a different present. The other indicator is that we're moving closer to a present where there are people. So that these masks are more obviously masks than ever before. The masks are masks of mice on what's obviously humans wearing them. But I needed some device to allow myself access to this particular anecdote, which was necessary for me to just kind of get it out of the way and get back to business. (*The Complete Maus*, 178)

Spiegelman divides the contemporary temporality of his book into two layers of time that are distinct but at the same time refer to generally the same time period. The present, according to this classification, refers to the time that both narrates and is narrated; it is the time period in which Vladek tells his story to Artie and the time in which their respective lives unfold and move on (Vladek's worsening health and his separation from Mala, Artie's developing book project). Besides containing Vladek's narration of the Holocaust past, this is the temporal space in which the everyday takes place, in which life is lived. The temporality in this level of discourse is fluid and contains movement and development. The super-present, on the other hand, is not a category of everyday life, a fluid, developing temporality that is narrated as a series of events. Rather, it occupies a place outside the movement of life, in a static space that is not the antithesis of life, but a place where life's ebb and flow do not reach. The prefix *super-*, which designates something that is "above, beyond, or over in place or time or conceptually," "to a great or extreme degree" and "of a higher kind" (*Oxford,* 1532), indicates that this super-present is not the present that is usually experienced, but a place apart from the temporal logic of the rest of the book, one that occupies a metaposition with regard to the conventional temporal flow of the present; in short, a sort of timelessness. This is the temporal space that Spiegelman establishes in the level of narrating in order to reflect on his project, a narrative time in which nothing exactly happens,[8] but in which the complexities and contradictions that relate to the other narrative levels are exposed.

Time Flies

As Spiegelman explains, the part of the book in which the super-present of narrating is revealed, apart from a few brief examples in *Maus I,* is the chapter "Auschwitz (time flies)" in *Maus II.* This chapter occurs well into the second volume, after the "Mauschwitz" chapter, which depicts both Vladek's arrival and first months at Auschwitz and Artie's stay with Vladek in the Catskills. The second volume of *Maus* thus begins in much the same way as the first, with chapter 1 continuing the previously established narrative mode, alternating between the first and second narrative levels. Chapter 2, however, marks a break in this narrative continuity, one that can be perceived immediately in its title. To begin with, the title "Auschwitz (time flies)" echoes "Mauschwitz," but at the same time the text corrects and displaces the previous title for the reader, arresting any easy immersion into the text's coy and Disneyesque construction of the animal cartoon. The correct historical German name of the camp following so closely behind the kitschy, revisionist name (perhaps the name of a Holocaust amusement park?)[9] sig-

---

[8] Paradoxically, although there is no real narrative development in the moments of *Maus*'s super-present, Spiegelman employs this temporality in which nothing "happens" in order to induce some narrative movement within the book as a whole, to get things going: "It was the only way I could move forward to make the obstacles manifest" (*The Complete Maus,* 178).

[9] LaCapra writes, "if one were tempted to object that Spiegelman himself does in a sense figure Auschwitz (or Mauschwitz) as Mickey-Mouse land (although he intentionally did not draw the endearing, infantilized types of animals that appear in Disney cartoons), it would be equally important to note that his more challenging move is to bring Auschwitz to Mickey-Mouse land, that is, to bring the Holocaust past to

nals a questioning of the representational logic that has operated heretofore. With the title "Mauschwitz," the text pushes to its breaking point the trope of the cartoon animal and its tendency to erase difference in the pursuit of metaphorical conformity, to the point at which it threatens to displace history and transform it into a commodity of mass culture and cartoon kitsch. The reassertion of and reinsistence on the name Auschwitz both broaches the problem of representation and guides the reader back from the realm of the ever more totalizing tendency of the metaphor to an actual historical space in which the Holocaust took place. At the same time, the second part of the title, "time flies," raises the specter of temporality, alluding both to a time that refuses to stand still and thus transports us ever further and more quickly from the historical event of Auschwitz, and, by ironically referring to the verbal phrase "time flies when you're having fun," to the problem of ordering the experience of time in Auschwitz into a normalized chronology.

It is not only the chapter title, however, that makes a break with the previous narrative mode, but the graphic that accompanies it on the title page as well. This image, as opposed to all of the other title pages in *Maus*, is not contained in the circumscribed frame. Rather, there are little flies (yet another species of animal in Spiegelman's animal fable) scattered around the frame that seem to be climbing out of the image within the frame. The contained image, one of the most violent and disturbing of all of the images in *Maus*, depicts anthropomorphic mice consumed alive by flames, screaming and moaning in agony. As the reader later learns, the image refers to and is repeated with the story Vladek hears from one of the workers in the Auschwitz *Sonderkommando*, who personally witnessed the burning of live people in mass graves (*II*, 72). This image thus viscerally refers to the first part of the title, "Auschwitz." The second part of the title, "(time flies)," the afterthought contained in parentheses, refers to the images not contained in the frame, the flies. The flies emerge from this stark and disquieting image into the non-circumscribed space of the text, from the Auschwitz past contained in the frame into the present in which this past is embedded. They are *time* flies (the substantive phrase rather than the verbal phrase), buzzing reminders of time passed and a past time that carry the trace of the past into the present. Thus, with the trope of the fly, time itself becomes, in a sense, a character in Spiegelman's book.

The chapter opens on the next page with a brief prologue (written in lower case) and a row of two panels depicting Art bent over his drawing desk:

---

the America that must have seemed to survivors like a Disneyworld in its distance from their experience" (*History and Memory*, 160).

80 ◆ MARKING TIME IN ART SPIEGELMAN'S *MAUS*

Time flies...

> Vladek died of congestive heart failure on August 18, 1982... Françoise and I stayed with him in the Catskills back in August 1979.

> Vladek started working as a tinman in Auschwitz in the spring of 1944... I started working on this page at the very end of February 1987.

> In May 1987 Françoise and I are expecting a baby...
> Between May 16, 1944, and May 24, 1944 over 100,000 Hungarian Jews were gassed in Auschwitz...

> In September 1986, after 8 years of work, the first part of MAUS was published. It was a critical and commercial success.

> At least fifteen foreign editions are coming out. I've gotten 4 serious offers to turn my book into a T.V. special or movie. (I don't wanna.)
> In May 1968 my mother killed herself. (She left no note.)
> Lately I've been feeling depressed.

> Alright Mr. Spiegelman... We're ready to shoot!...

From Maus II, *page 41.*

As previously noted, in this section Art wears a mouse mask that is tied around his human head. The flies that appear on the title page surface here as well and buzz annoyingly around him. Art is lit in a stark manner; he is flooded in a bright light that moves around somewhat (in the first panel his chair is in the black shadow; in the second, it is included in the light). This view of Art working while the flies buzz around his head continues in the next row of panels, which, combined with the first row, simulates the movement of a camera zooming out. In the last panel of the page, which in size equals the previous four panels and takes up half the page, the "camera lens" zooms out even further and the reader gets a full view of Art, hunched over his drawing table. The reader suddenly understands why the flies were buzzing around in the previous panels, for Art's table rests upon a mound of naked mouse corpses. The presence of the flies around the anthropomorphic animal corpses takes Spiegelman's animal metaphor a step further; flies are found around both filth and vermin and death and decay. The reader is thus reminded of the short distance from the depiction of Jews as vermin to the specious justification for their destruction, for this metaphorical journey is made through the trope of the fly. Through the window to the right of the panel, one glimpses a watchtower ringed with a barbed-wire fence. A possible source for the stark lighting in the first panels is also suggested in this panel, for it could be the watchtower's searchlight that is producing the moving panes of bright light.[10] Graphically, the different temporal planes of the Holocaust past and the present of Art's life coexist in the same image. On the one hand, Art's artistic production thus shares the same space as the Holocaust victims, and, because his drawing table is mounted directly upon (or perhaps even rises out of) their bodies, his artistic production is thus, to a certain extent, based on their suffering and death. His aesthetic project and its commercial success are predicated on the trauma, loss, and destruction of others and this figures him as a coperpetrator, one who is able to constitute himself by annihilating others. In a sense, by telling his father's story, he reproduces the death of the victims at the same time; he revives them only to have them murdered once more, with him in the director's chair, staging the spectacle.[11] On the other hand, Art is also marked here as a victim, for in this *mise-en-scène* with the barbed wire and watchtower, he becomes the inmate

---

[10] Michael E. Staub sees the black-and-white contrast as part of a larger symbol that can neither be seen nor taken in completely by the reader: "Behind him [Art], shifting right angles of black and white light — like pieces of a giant swastika — frame the action" (42).

[11] I am grateful to my student, Anne Fölting, from the Universität Dortmund, for pointing this out: "With writing *Maus I*, Art has awakened the past — symbolized in the corpses accumulated all around his writing-desk. It seems as if all those people had to die again because Art told the story of their death" (unpublished seminar paper). Ms. Fölting also makes the connection between Art's "perpetration" and the subtitle of the first volume, *My Father Bleeds History*, asserting that Art, through his questioning of Vladek, has opened up his wounds and made them bleed again.

of a concentration camp. The watchtower's searchlight focuses on him, singling him out as a both a potential criminal and a victim. Art thus experiences the scene of the Holocaust past; it becomes the surroundings in which he both lives and works. The first indicators of the presence of this past are the time flies in the first panels, which function as the disturbing residues of a past that, like a pesky insect, will not go away.

Accompanying the graphic elements of the first page of this chapter are several portions of text. Before the visual panels commence, a short two-word prologue, "Time flies . . . ," like Art's introductions to the chapters in *Maus I*, begins the chapter. However, the phrase in this particular context, in the static temporality of Spiegelman's super-present, is employed ironically: time in this narrative mode does *not* fly, does not develop and unfold, but rather stands still. This reference to a temporality that is stuck and unhinged from the conventional movement of life resonates in Art's narration, which he assumes in the first panel. In each panel, he lists different events that have happened in his and his father's lives along with the respective time frames in which they occurred. The events are grouped in a seemingly arbitrary manner, alternating episodes from Vladek's past (in random order) with moments in Art's life (in likewise random order). The chain of time created by the juxtaposition of events appears at first to follow no chronological principle: the text moves from August 1982 to August 1979 to spring 1944 to February 1987 to May 1987 to May 1944 to September 1986 to May 1968 to the present ("lately"). There is an arbitrary logic to this chronology, however, for it seems that Art is comparing a past event that happened during a certain time of year ("May" or "spring") to a present event that happened in the same season. With regard to chronology, the principle of comparison seems to operate here: by situating the events of the Holocaust within a time frame recognizable to both Art and the reader, he pulls his father's experience out of a mythical, achronological, and ahistorical past and places it alongside the more commonplace, "real" events of the present. The reader is thus reminded that the story that she has been reading is not "really" a fictive animal fable but a narrated experience that comes from the same order of reality as the present time of Art's drawing table. At the same time, however, the events, though seemingly arbitrarily arranged, are carefully juxtaposed to evoke the enormous impact of the past on the present and the radical difference between Vladek's Holocaust past and Art's present. In the first panel, Vladek's death in August is paired with Art's and Françoise's visit with him in the Catskills in August, highlighting the chasm between their exasperating experiences with a living Vladek and the finality of his death. This juxtaposition of life and death reveals both Art's sense of loss and his remorse over his troubled relationship with his father. The second panel compares their respective working experiences and at the same time marks the radical difference in the definition of "work" in each case; for Art, work

(work on the present page of text, work on the *present*) means both creative self-expression and the process of mourning (*Trauerarbeit*), while for Vladek, work is slave labor, an exhausting, debilitating form of exploitation that must be performed at all costs if one is to survive. The third panel again juxtaposes life with death; in this case, the upcoming birth of Art's and Françoise's daughter is evoked in the same breath as the murder of over 100,000 Hungarian Jews in the brief period of eight days. The happiness and excitement of a new Jewish life is thus tainted and sobered by the memory of so many Jewish lives annihilated, a number of deaths that can hardly be imagined and that stands in stark contrast to the birth of one child. Once again, the past casts a pall over the present, while the "time flies" buzz around. In the fourth panel, Art raises the issue of his present project, of his commercial and critical achievement with the publishing of *Maus*. He continues to speak of *Maus*'s celebrity in the fifth panel, detailing the markers of authorial success and at the same time his own resistance to his newfound fame and the commercialization of his book ("I don't wanna."). As in the previous panels, death and the past make themselves known here as well with the mention of Art's mother's suicide. Art's success, which, like his drawing table, is based on the suffering and death of countless masses of people, is thus juxtaposed with Anja's lack of success, with her personal failure to "survive" and to make sense of and move beyond the trauma of the Holocaust. Art has outdone his own mother. He has survived her, and his ability to create a written document of himself and his father stands in contrast to Anja's unwritten legacy, pointing to the absence of a suicide note, and by extension, to Vladek's survival of her with his destruction of her diaries.

At the same time, however, Art accuses his mother of not communicating her reasons for killing herself; his parenthetical aside ("(She left no note.)") mirrors the petulant, self-pitying response to his commercial success in parentheses in the previous line ("(I don't wanna.)"). In this large last panel of the page, in which the focus opens up to portray Art hunched in despair on his artist's throne that rests upon a mass of unidentifiable corpses, the seemingly arbitrary listing of events and their respective time frames culminates in his final statement of despair, "Lately I've been feeling depressed." Following as it does his mention of his mother's suicide, this declaration invites comparison between Art's depression and Anja's own desperation, suggesting that the problems that befell the mother also fall upon the child (witness Art's depression as depicted in the "Prisoner on the Hell Planet" narrative in *Maus I*). At the same time, the reader is reminded of Anja's history of trauma as an explanation for her suicide (not to mention her propensity toward suicide[12]), and Art's comparison of his own troubles with those of his mother suggest the problematic conflation of her traumatized past with his inheritance of his parents' legacy, implying a childish and self-centered view on his part ("I don't wanna.").

As a closing statement, however, Art's evocation of his depression is fitting, for the page is inundated with the tragic events experienced by his family — their survival of Auschwitz (along with the mention of the hundreds of thousands who didn't survive), Anja's suicide, Vladek's heart attack. At the same time, Art's own experiences listed on the page function as the radical opposite to his parents' tragedy — his creative work, his new status as father, his success with *Maus*. The depression Art feels arises from the profound incompatibility of his successful contemporary life with the tragic lives of his parents and, by extension, with those of European Jewry. Their experiences can not be assimilated into a well-ordered notion of history and family legacy; as happens frequently in *Maus*, they jut outside the established frame into the surrounding narrative, refusing to stay integrated into a fully comprehended and comprehensible past. Although the events of Art's life give credence to the illusion that he has overcome his parents' trauma and that his life has developed beyond their memory, the fractured chronology he experiences belies the notion of development and moving on. Art becomes a prisoner in this realm of static and dislocated temporality. Like the bodies on which Art's table is propped, the past is left unburied and continues to haunt the present by its very presence.

This feeling of the past's presence, of the presence of death in life, is underscored by the last verbal statement on the page, the only one that does not issue from Art. A voice from the scene says, "Alright Mr. Spiegelman . . . We're ready to shoot! . . ." Although we don't know who utters this state-

---

[12] Anja expresses her despair and suicidal wishes three times during the course of the novel, both before and during the German occupation: "But I don't care. I just don't want to live" (*I*, 31); "Oh God. Let me die too!" (*I*, 122); "Each day I think to run into the electric wires and finish everything" (*I*, 53). Marianne Hirsch ("Family Pictures") and James Young, among others, have discussed the absence, "displacement and violation" (Young, "The Holocaust as Vicarious Past," 686) of Anja's story, alluding to Vladek's destruction of her diaries and Artie's accusation of his father as the "murderer" of her memory. However, critics have ignored Spiegelman's depiction of Anja's own radical tendency toward self-destruction, as well as Vladek's tender words of encouragement to her to stay alive: "No, darling! To die, it's easy . . . but you have to struggle for life!" (*I*, 122); "I beg you, Anja — keep yourself strong. For my sake [. . . .] I . . . I think about you . . . always" (*I*, 56). This reversal of the image of Vladek as Anja's "murderer" is but another example of the ways in which Spiegelman juxtaposes contradictory images and information about both himself and his parents and thus avoids any easy attempt to fit them into generalized characterizations.

ment and are therefore unaware of the context of its utterance, the composition of the *mise-en-scène*, with its corpses, watchtower, and searchlight, encourages an alarming interpretation. For a moment it seems as if Art is about to be called before a firing squad (which might explain another use for his mask) or some other equally frightening and deathly situation and will soon end up as one of the corpses that dominate the bottom of the page. At the same time, the speaker's use of the formal "Mr. Spiegelman" implies that the situation is not really as violent as the statement of shooting and the macabre *mise-en-scène* would lead one to believe. When one turns the page, one immediately sees in the first panel a television film crew ready to film an interview, clambering to turn his father's story into a "human interest" story on the morning talk shows, or perhaps even to "shoot" it as a commercial film or television movie, indicating the commercial momentum Spiegelman's *Maus* project has gained despite his adamant wishes to the contrary ("I don't wanna."). The image of the TV crew thus contextualizes the meaning of "to shoot" as a much less threatening force of the present, despite the image of pushy journalists climbing over dead bodies to obtain interviews[13] and the specter of a possible kitschy *Maus* movie. But for the reader, who for the last two hundred or so pages has been immersed in a world in which people are more likely to be shot by guns than by a camera, the first moment of the utterance is one in which the Holocaust past powerfully marks Art's present.

The first page of the "Auschwitz (time flies)" chapter thus situates the reader within a temporality in which the Holocaust past is felt as a present force, a residue of the *then* that is keenly perceived as existent in the *now*. The next few pages of text continue in the same vein as the first, albeit less powerfully, proceeding according to the narrative logic that Spiegelman designates as the super-present. Accompanied visually by the time flies and the harsh searchlight, Art further explores the problems that he encounters as a result of the *Maus* project. He contends with the media that pressure him

---

[13] This image prefigures one of Vladek's most despairing experiences in the entire book, in which he, as a typhoid prisoner in Dachau, is forced to tread upon corpses. As he explains this horrific experience, the accompanying graphics show his feet stepping on a pile of dead mice, cats, and pigs, echoing literally (with the metaphorical device of the animal fable) the metaphorical trampling of the journalists: "At night I had to go to the toilet down. It was always full, the whole corridor, with the dead people piled there. You couldn't go through . . . You had to go on their heads, and this was terrible, because it was so slippery, the skin, you thought you are falling. And this was every night. So now I had typhus, and I had to go to the toilet down, and I said, 'Now it's **my** time. Now I will be laying like this ones and somebody will step on me!" (*II*, 95). Vladek survives the typhus and does not experience that horror literally, but the image of the journalists who step over the corpses suggests the roughshod trampling of his memory posthumously.

into a producing quick sound bites that encapsulate a quick and easy "Holocaust message" for a public that wants to settle the score with the past, turning him into a kind of poster child for the Holocaust (which causes him to shrink both physically and emotionally into a child). In addition, he is confronted with a publishing and marketing machine that assumes his aesthetic project of testimony and transforms it into a consumer product, turning him into a best-selling author and a darling on the talk-show circuit. Overwhelmed by the media attention and the attendant problems of commercial success, Art visits his psychiatrist, a survivor of the Holocaust himself, with whom he discusses his depression and his feelings of remorse and inadequacy with regard to his father, and the problems he has of imagining his father's experiences, of shaping them narratively and "picturing" them in the visual logic of the *Maus* narrative. At the end of this section of the super-present, he returns home to his desk, still clad in the mask and bathed in the searchlight, and attempts to continue his work. Art's last utterance before the return to the middle level, the scene of Vladek's testimony, is a weary "sigh" (*II*, 47), an overwhelmed and bewildered response to the overpowering presence of Vladek's past.

Polychronic Narration and Timelessness

These pages of the super-present mark a different kind of time structure than exists in the other narrative levels in *Maus,* pointing to a temporal problematic that David Herman investigates in his book on narratology, *Story Logic*. Herman's book calls into question the usefulness of assigning all narrative to the absolute binary of story and discourse, arguing instead for a new way of looking at the broader "ecology of narrative interpretation"(13), a shift in theoretical perspective that would allow more for the ways in which the mode of narrating interacts with what is being narrated. In terms of the temporal relations between the poles of story and discourse, Herman posits the notion of *polychrony,* a temporal designation that takes into account narratives in which the *then* and the *now* are not clearly and unequivocally delineated. He bases his concept of polychrony, or "fuzzy temporality," on recent research on fuzzy logic, which "operates on the basis of multivalence as opposed to bivalence" (212). Herman argues for a multivalent approach to narrative time in response to what he sees as a deficiency in existing narratological frameworks of temporality, particularly those of Gérard Genette. According to Herman, Genette relegates events that the reader is unable to order into the bivalent temporal framework of *then* and *now* to a realm outside the normative temporal logic of narrative, which Genette terms *timelessness* or *achrony*. For Herman, however, the inability to order a narrative event according to the larger, more definite temporal sequence of the narrative does not mean that the event does not possess a connection (however hidden) to the established temporality, or that it hangs suspended outside the temporal plane altogether. Not knowing the exact time designation of an event does not make it timeless. Herman thus proposes reconfiguring the framework of temporality within a system of multivalence, which would include both events that are identifiable according to the binary of *then* and *now* and those that do not adhere to the binary:

> When it involves events being assigned indeterminate temporal positions in a storyworld, fuzzy temporality likewise reconfigures the concepts of "earlier" and "later" as special limiting cases in a multivalent system. What I am calling polychronic narration entails a three-value system spanning Earlier, Later and Indeterminate, where, again, Indeterminate is shorthand for Indeterminately-situated-vis-à-vis-some-temporal-reference-point-X. (212–13)

Herman's notion of a multivalent system that includes events not easily ordered into specific temporal designations as well as textual strategies that resist conventional narrative frameworks is of critical relevance to the complex temporal planes found in Spiegelman's text, for, as we have seen, *Maus* resists the same bivalent temporal logic against which Herman argues. In particular, Herman's linking of polychronic narrative strategies to the textual effects of trauma, memory, and forgetting in narratives by Anna Seghers, Atom Egoyan, and D. M. Thomas demonstrates how texts like *Maus,* which as we have seen, involves "the reconstruction of a traumatic event from the past whose effects live on in and mold a present that in turn gives shape to that past" (Herman, 237), require a more complex temporal framework in order to express traumatic elements that can not be easily evoked within a rigid bivalent system. The openness of Herman's theory of multivalence, which goes beyond the binary of *then* and *now,* thus provides us with a useful vocabulary for examining *Maus*'s intricate temporality.

However, despite our ability to designate *Maus* as polychronic, it is not so easy to align it with the problematic that occupies Herman's analysis, for the temporal difficulty of Spiegelman's text is not one of indeterminacy, the third term in Herman's framework. On the contrary, the temporality of the super-present relates to problems of determinacy, not to the specific designation of indeterminacy. As my close reading of the first page of "Auschwitz (time flies)" indicates, this narrative level of *Maus* grapples with a temporality that is at simultaneously adeterminate, over-determined and clearly determined. Adeterminacy is, as I have argued, a defining quality of the super-present; this temporal plane exists outside the experience of time in the timeless, static space of memory. The image of Art at a drawing table perched upon a pile of corpses is perhaps the best example of this disconnected, disjointed time that is neither part of the developing present nor a part of the calcified past. Despite the super-present's state of suspension above past and present, however, its temporality is not indeterminate; indeed, the opposite is the case: Art conspicuously names the exact time frame during which he sits at the drawing table ("I started working on this page at the very end of February 1987"). Time in this narrative mode does not so much refuse to be ordered into a linear chronology as exempt itself from the notion of a moving and developing temporality altogether, and thus the temporal problematic is not one of determining the *order* of the event, a task that occupies much narratological analysis of time. Furthermore, the temporal aspects of this part of Spiegelman's text are over-determined as well; the litany of dates and traumatic experiences that accompany the image of Art at the drawing table testify to the power that time and its markers have over Art's project. The timeless, adeterminate quality of the time structure of the super-present does not mean that time is somehow unimportant for Art; rather, in these images he is hyper-invested in the issue of temporality, experiencing thus the very painful effects of a fractured chronology of family experience. Moreover, the notion of indeterminacy is not only irrelevant for the pages of the super-present; it is not a factor in the rest of *Maus* either. Throughout the narrative, despite complex shifts back and forth between Vladek's Holocaust past, Art's witnessing present, and the atemporal plane of the super-present, the reader is able to consistently assign the events a temporal designation, for the three temporal levels are, as I have demonstrated, clearly marked, an effect produced by Spiegelman's careful juxtaposition of verbal text and image. The temporal complexity of *Maus* is thus not a problem of indeterminacy, and Herman's three-part framework, which re volves around the question of assigning an event a specific time within a chronological sequence, is inadequate for the discussion of the temporal complexity of the text. However, despite the limitations of Herman's specific temporal structure, his theory of polychronic narrative is an open one, for it is based on the concept of multivalence, which should by definition admit new temporal values. Polychrony, rather than closing itself off from the multiple ways in which time can operate in a narrative (as bivalent temporality does), can admit new positions to its spectrum — temporalities found in *Maus* and in other texts. Alongside Herman's *earlier, later,* and *indeterminate* (temporal positions classified according to order), one can also mark out polychronic sites that concern other types of temporality, such as the subjective quality or experience of time. For this reason, one can argue for the reintegration of Genette's concept of timelessness into a multivalent understanding of temporality on the grounds that it expresses not the disruption of chronological order in the narrative, but the ways in which time is perceived and understood in different ways in the process of narration and the manner by which narrative discourse is figured within the story that it produces.

In the case of the super-present in Spiegelman's text, the past of Vladek's story, the present of Vladek's witnessing, and the timeless plane of Spiegelman's narrating merge, highlighting the ways in which the narrating of *Maus* pervades and is in turn permeated by the story and the discourse it narrates. The temporal structure of *Maus* is closely tied to the ways in which its narration functions; the multivalent temporal character of Spiegelman's text, with its adeterminate, over-determined and clearly determined aspects, exposes the ways in which different levels of narrative, like those of temporality, are experienced simultaneously and are consequently implicated in each other. Rather than remaining fully distinguishable elements of a strictly delineated narrative system, the narrative categories of story, discourse, and narrating in Spiegelman's text commingle with each other, demonstrating that these classifications, while providing useful vocabulary to the critic, are heuristic aids in the study of how narrative functions rather than absolute divisions that are somehow immanent in the nature of narrative itself. Just as his wearing of the mouse mask refers both to the textual world of his narrative fable and to the "real" world in which it is situated and from which the narrating emerges, the Art of the super-present encounters multiple aspects of both time and narrative function — the past of the Holocaust story, the present time of memory and discourse, and the timeless moment of narrating. Vladek's story does not remain a narrative of a concluded past, an experience that is dead and buried; rather, it is perceived as contemporaneous reality, a part of Art's life that cannot be relegated to the past tense. Although the gesture of narrating, of framing Vladek's past in narrative, is a move to solidify his Holocaust experience and turn it into the *then* of history and keep it separate from the *now* of the present, the text acknowledges the impossibility of this move to neatly and decisively distinguish the traumatic past from the present of living and the story and discourse from the narrating instance that produces them. For in this third level of *Maus,* the past is lived as part of the present, as a structure that continues to function and inform the present. The metaphor of the searchlight, which emanates from the watchtower and follows Art visually throughout these pages, is particularly useful for understanding this blurring of temporality and the inability to contain the past outside the present. This searchlight is not Art's concentrated beam upon Vladek's past in order to shed light on it, explain it and condense it into a "message," which is the ostensible goal of a project like *Maus* (at least that is the way the media see Art's book, even if he does not). Rather, the austere gleam of the searchlight issues from the past, from the watchtower of the Holocaust, and this harsh light emits directly onto Art and his present, illuminating the ways in which he continues to "live" the Holocaust even as he narrates it as a past event. The opening panels of "Auschwitz (time flies)," which cast the past as the source that sheds light on the present (while at the same time leaving much of that present in the darkness that surrounds the beam), thus function in an opposite way from the panels that began this discussion of *Maus,* the image of Vladek turning. In that image, as we have seen, Vladek turns "into" the past, and the present scene of storytelling becomes the past scene of experience. Rather than the past informing the present, seeking it out and casting light upon it, the turning Vladek of the present becomes the model for the representation of his past. In both instances, however, in the movement from present to past and in the movement from past to present, the Holocaust story and the present of narrating are figured as constitutive of one another, as inherently linked. Just as Art continues to bear witness to the effects of his father's past ("My father's ghost still hangs over me" [*II*, 43]), his representation of that past is chained as well to the present in which he writes and draws. The temporalities that mark the traumatic experience of the Spiegelman family (the *then* of Vladek's story and the *now* of Art's storytelling) weave in, out, and among one another, each never allowing the other to exist in isolation. Like the time flies that hover around Art, in *Maus* the past buzzes annoyingly around the present and the present swarms persistently around the past, neither leaving the other in peace.

3: "Because We Need Traces": Robert Schindel's *Gebürtig* and the Crisis of the Second-Generation Witness

Memory implies identity, the self caught between its roles as subject and object of memory, the telling and the told.
— Paul Antze and Michael Lambek,
Tense Past: Cultural Essays in Trauma and Memory

Narrative Counterparts

G*EBÜRTIG*,[1] ROBERT SCHINDEL'S NOVEL about the lives of second-generation Austrians in the early 1980s, is marked by a radically heterogeneous narrativity and an almost obsessive concentration on problems of signification and referential representation. The novel's complex, multilayered, decentralized narrative structure, its overabundant significatory synapses, and its dense, often paradoxical poetic language contribute to an exercise in reading that, in its refusal to grant the reader clarity, closure, or narrative certainty, mirrors the confused and impotent struggle of its characters with the presence of the Holocaust past in an Austrian society that, in effect, abdicates responsibility for its perpetration of the Holocaust. The problematic role of the Holocaust in the contemporary relations between Austrian Jews and non-Jews is brought to the fore by the novel's three main narrative strands, two of which occur on the same main narrative level and are linked together by common characters. The first narrative, told largely from the perspective of the second-generation Jewish twin brothers Danny and Alexander (Sascha) Demant, depicts the love affairs and often adversarial relationships between various Jewish and non-Jewish members of the con-

---

[1] Schindel's choice of title for his novel, which Michael Roloff renders as "Born-Where" in his translation of the book, does not possess an exact correlative in English. As an adjective that is related to the noun *Geburt* (birth) it denotes the importance of birthplace for one's identity. One can thus translate the phrase "ein gebürtiger Österreicher" as "an Austrian by birth." Schindel's title evokes the idea of geographical place as a foundational aspect of one's sense of self and the feeling of being at home in one's environment, both of which are critical problems for the novel's Holocaust survivors and children of survivors, who feel both bound to and estranged from their country of origin and residence.

temporary Viennese intellectual scene. The second strand narrates a crisis experienced by a member of "another second generation" (Alan L. Berger and Naomi Berger, 1), Konrad Sachs, the German son of a high-ranking Nazi. The third narrative functions as a novel within a novel, written by Emanuel Katz, an acquaintance of Danny's and the son of a Holocaust survivor. Katz's novel tells the story of Herrmann Gebirtig, a Holocaust survivor residing in New York, who returns to Vienna for the first time since the war in order to testify at the trial of a concentration camp guard. In addition to the three major narrative strands, which weave in and around one another, the novel contains dozens of characters, a complex chronology in which moments of the Holocaust past momentarily intrude into the present, and a number of diverse narrative conventions, including inner monologues, a film within a novel, diary entries, letters, fairy tales, and dream sequences. Moreover, the novel is privy to a multiplicity of voices, for there are a number of partially omniscient, focalized and unfocalized, named and unnamed narrators who, beyond presenting the dialogue, inner monologues, and dreams of various characters, reflect on the role of narration and its ostensible goal of maintaining narrative continuity as well.

The profusion of diverse stories and characters and the decentralization and proliferation of narrative agency in *Gebürtig* evade any fixed, univocal perspective by which the Holocaust is remembered in the second generation. The opposite is the case; rather than narrating a single story of the Holocaust and its aftermath, Schindel's text presents multiple stories of many post-Holocaust experiences that radically supplement each other but resist any single, unified narrative of the legacy of the Holocaust. As Neva Šlibar points out, the novel's characters (both Jewish and non-Jewish) are caught up in a web of relations, whereby they are linked, not always thematically, but structurally, as opposing figures or *Doppelgänger:* "All of the characters in the novel are ordered in mirror-like symmetry into perpetrators and victims or children of perpetrators and children of victims."[2] However, this apparently symmetrical division, once established, is destabilized through the course of the novel, for the characters and stories do not adhere to a one-to-one correlation or clear opposition, but are rather indicative of a radical supplementarity, demonstrating the ways in which not only the Jewish characters, but the non-Jewish ones as well, are caught up in greater or lesser degrees in the problems the Holocaust past poses to the present. As I argue, the linkage between the various otherwise unrelated and even diametrically opposed characters and narrative elements and the ways in which they sup-

---

[2] "In spiegelbildlicher Symmetrie werden alle Figuren des Romans den beiden Tätern-Opfern beziehungsweise Täterkindern-Opferkindern zugeordnet" (Šlibar, 343).

plement each other without contributing to a stable symmetrical closure are the most striking elements in Schindel's depiction of the second generation. These supplemental characters and stories, which relate to one another structurally or with regard to content, are combined by the reader into provisional significatory dualities whereby the one character or experience is compared and contrasted with the other. I say "provisional," for these pairs of counterparts are neither fixed nor absolute, but rather otherwise unrelated characters and narrative elements that combine to create a certain association and then break apart to form other pairs.[3] Each narrative element thus points to another story, another experience, without the two parts becoming either strictly identical or wholly oppositional. In this way, the novel investigates the ways in which the Holocaust past continues to operate in the lives of second-generation Austrians, both Jewish and non-Jewish, and at the same time avoids both conflating their experiences and relegating them to a rigid dichotomy. These pairs of counterparts are evident on a number of levels and with several narrative elements. In addition to the character and story configurations identified by Šlibar, the text posits narrative counterparts with regard to setting (Konzett, 83; Šlibar, 343), chapter titles (Kaiser, 101; Posthofen, 194), the dialectics of reading and writing (Šlibar, 343), fictionality and reality (Posthofen, 194; Šlibar, 245; Kaukoreit, 7–8), and past and present (Šlibar, 344). My analysis of Schindel's novel focuses on the provisional dualities that occur in the processes of signification and narration — among the characters, among their names and stories, and with regard to the function of the narrator — and the ways in which the movement among these counterparts mediates an image of second-generation Holocaust memory.

Counterpart Names

The most obvious counterparts in *Gebürtig* occur with the names of characters, almost all of which have some connection to either the Holocaust past or the present relationship between Jews and non-Jews in Austria. The names either evoke a certain meaning that becomes the counterpart of the character itself or are structurally similar to the names of other characters or narrative elements. In the first case, the reader is called upon to associate the

---

[3] Neva Šlibar terms Schindel's novel "postmodern," in part because of its seemingly never-ending significatory movement and displacement. The postmodern aspect of the novel is reflected as well in its length, extraordinary complexity, and resistance to categorization, all of which frustrate critical attempts to interpret it and to condense its meaning into a palatable argument. My own interpretation in this chapter, which has been significantly edited from a much longer version (!), struggles with the novel's almost infinite chain of signification and its rich abundance of narrative elements as well.

character with certain traits signified by his or her name. One of the most obvious examples is Herrmann Gebirtig, the main character in the novel within the novel, a survivor of the Ebensee concentration camp who immigrates to New York and is persuaded to return to his native Vienna for the first time since the war for the trial of a camp guard. His name instantly reminds us of *Gebürtig,* the title of both the novel and the third chapter, which in German bears connotations of belonging and home.[4] Another major example of the connection between name and meaning occurs with the twin narrators Danny and Alexander Demant, whose last name is reminiscent of their birth in wartime France in the French verb *démanteler,* meaning "to dismantle." The idea of breaking apart is critical, as we shall see, for their joint narrative undertaking. Furthermore, Alexander is also known by his pen name Sascha Graffito, which refers explicitly to his self-appointed mission of narrator and "note-taker." Another example is Christiane Kalteisen, Danny's non-Jewish girlfriend, who sleeps "im eiskalten Zimmer" (107; in an ice-cold room) and whose name, which translates as "Coldiron," reminds the reader of her inflexibility and lack of understanding with regard to Danny's Jewish identity.[5] The characteristics of coldness and metal in turn remind us of two of the chapter titles, "Kälte" (Coldness) and "Egge" (Plow). The image of the *Egge,* or plow, leads to further interdiegetic elements both in the second narrative (the story of Konrad Sachs, the son of a prominent Nazi who was hanged at Nuremburg[6]) and in Katz's novel about Gebirtig, with the character of Egger, a former concentration camp guard who is discovered in Austria, living under the name of Eigler. Just as Sachs's dream depicts the *Egge* plowing under a field full of skulls and smoothing the earth

---

[4] The name Gebirtig also points to the famous Yiddish poet and songwriter Mordechai Gebirtig, who was shot in the Cracow ghetto in 1942.

[5] According to Thomas Freeman, Christiane's name is indicative of how her relationship with Danny will play out: "Another failed relationship is that of Jewish literary editor Danny Demant with the physician Christiane Kalteisen, whose name underscores both her Christian heritage and her attitudes. All along, Christiane has displayed cold indifference to Danny's problems as a Jew in Austrian society" (120). Of course, it is important to point out the moments in which the name is *not* characteristic of the given figure. Christiane is also associated with warmth, above all in the image of her ear burning red as an indicator of her passion for Danny. The names do not completely describe the totality of each character, and contradictions between a name and a character's qualities are frequent.

[6] The character of Konrad Sachs is modeled on the historical experience of Niklas Frank, son of Hans Frank, the Nazi General Governor of occupied Poland. Like the fictional Sachs, Niklas Frank published an autobiography about his experiences as the son of a Nazi luminary, which I investigate at length in chapter 6.

over them, the trial of Egger, "the skull-cracker,"[7] becomes the mechanism that plows up the buried and repressed Nazi past and brings Gebirtig back to Austria. Also in the Gebirtig narrative, we find the character of David Lebensart, modeled on the Austrian survivor and Nazi hunter, Simon Wiesenthal. As his name, which translates as "way of life," suggests, Lebensart is the ultimate survivor: "'I am,' he said to the concern of the woman, 'the one who just won't die.' The idea of living longer than the last Nazi refreshed him."[8] Other examples of nominal meaning include: Käthe Richter (whose last name means "judge"); Mascha Singer, who tells a litany of stories and is described as an "out-of-tune Jewish organ";[9] and Peter Adel (whose last name means "nobility"), the German theater director who attempts to hide his Jewish heritage.

A second practice by which names become elements in the pairing of counterparts occurs on a structural level, with the orthographic or phonetic similarity between the names of characters. The implicit association of two characters with similar names creates a second type of nominal counterpart, and the reader is thus encouraged to look for commonalities between the two characters and to juxtapose their respective experiences, even if they are radically different, as with the legacy of Holocaust survival and that of perpetration. The similarity between names occurs both intradiegetically in the main narrative and interdiegetically between both strands of the main narrative and the Gebirtig novel. At the forefront of the intradiegetic name game are the twin Demant brothers, Danny and Alexander, who share the same last name with each other (this will become more complex when we investigate Alexander's problematic existence) and with other Demants no longer living, who sporadically appear themselves in the main narrative as acting, living characters. Alexander, or as he is frequently referred to in the text, Sascha, locates a further counterpart in Mascha, the Jewish sociologist with whom he falls in love, and who was once Danny's lover. Mascha Singer, in turn, has another counterpart character: Ilse Jacobsohn-Singer, the Holocaust survivor who narrates the story of her experiences in Theresienstadt to Danny. Although there is no evidence that Mascha is related to Ilse, the reader is called upon to wonder about their common bond and to try to discover their possible common link in a familial chain that has been torn apart by the Holocaust. The intradiegetic nominal commonality or similarity thus challenges the reader to compare the characters and to make either implicit

---

[7] "der Schädelknacker" (Schindel, *Gebürtig*, 96).

[8] "'Ich bin,' sagte er zur Sorge der Frau, 'derjenige, der überhaupt nicht sterben wird.' Die Vorstellung, länger zu leben als der letzte Nazi, erquickte ihn" (Schindel, *Gebürtig*, 206).

[9] "verstimmte jüdische Orgel" (Schindel, *Gebürtig*, 106).

links between them (in the case of Sascha and Mascha) or to fill in the many gaps left by the Holocaust in each of their family trees.

In addition to the parallelism between character names on the main narrative level, a nominal semblance occurs between diegetic levels as well. The Gebirtig narrative, as we know, is linked to the main narrative through Emanuel Katz, who writes it, and Danny, who, as Katz's editor, reads it. The similarities between the characters of the two stories are thus for the most part a result of Katz's authorial intervention. One of the most obvious parallelisms occurs between Katz (whose name means "cat") and his character Wendelin Katzenbeißer (whose last name means "cat-biter"). Katzenbeißer is the exceedingly polite Viennese cultural bureaucrat who is determined to exact political profit from Gebirtig's visit by arranging for him to receive the city's highest honor. Despite Gebirtig's adamant refusal to accept the award or to engage in any kind of relationship with Austria, Katzenbeißer ignores the wishes of the survivor and arranges to have him honored anyway. Katzenbeißer does not argue with Gebirtig or aggressively confront him about Gebirtig's justifiable bitterness with regard to Austrians' role in and subsequent denial of the Holocaust; he merely quietly and obstinately manipulates him into an undesired reconciliation. Katzenbeißer is representative of Hannah Arendt's banal bureaucrat who acts not out of immense hatred or sociopathology, but out of his own opportunistic bureaucratic ambition, a willful misunderstanding of history, and a self-centered insensitivity to Austria's Holocaust victims. As such, he echoes many of the people with whom Emanuel Katz himself comes into contact, such as Käthe Richter, who displays both a prurient curiosity with regard to his "exotic" Jewishness and a lack of sensitivity to his experience as a Jew, but who, importantly, cannot be labeled an outright anti-Semite. Katzenbeißer is exactly the type of person Katz is describing when he says "if someone says Jews are people too or but that doesn't matter or one of my best friends is a Jew or even, we're sorry, but what happened has happened, then everything is somehow clear and I can slip away."[10] For Katz, it is this type of person and not the outright anti-Semite who is most dangerous, so it is no wonder that the bureaucrat, whose intentions with regard to Gebirtig appear to be honoring and honorable but actually ignore Gebirtig's wishes, should be called Katzenbeißer. Katzenbeißer is thus the friendly foe who would compliment and flatter Katz and then, the moment Katz turns around, bite his tail.

---

[10] "wenn einer dann sagt, Juden sind auch Menschen oder aber das macht doch nichts oder einer meiner besten Freunde ist Jude oder gar, das tut uns aber leid, aber was geschehn ist, ist geschehn, dann ist irgendwie alles klar, und ich kann mich verdrücken" (Schindel, *Gebürtig*, 115).

A second interdiegetic similarity occurs between the characters of Eggenberger and Egger. Anton Egger is the former concentration camp guard in the Gebirtig novel whose trial impels Gebirtig's return to Austria. As such, he becomes the agent whose capture disrupts Gebirtig's post-survival life in New York and brings about his confrontation with a contemporary Austria that has apparently normalized the memory of its perpetration in the Holocaust. Herrmann Eggenberger, who appears in the Sachs strand of the main narrative, functions in a similar way for Konrad Sachs, for his presence brings about Sachs's crisis with regard to his father's crimes and his own complicity as a child in the Nazi occupation of Poland. When Sachs accidentally meets Eggenberger, a former school friend whose father was also a prominent Nazi, his forgotten childhood and the repressed crimes of his father begin to torment him both in his dreams and during his waking hours and contribute to his nervous breakdown. As I discuss above, the image of the *Egge* (plow) is operational for Egger and for Eggenberger as well: the appearance of both characters plows up the painful past for Gebirtig and Sachs and uncovers a history that refuses to be buried under a layer of normalized forgetting. The two characters thus occupy the same structural and metaphorical position in their respective narratives; the similarities between their names and the associations the names evoke implicitly encourage the reader to compare the situation of Gebirtig, the Holocaust survivor, who travels to the site of both family memory and his persecution during the Holocaust, with Sachs, the son of the notorious perpetrator, who attempts in his own journey to come to terms with his familial legacy of guilt and denial.

The associations between names and the qualities they evoke and the similarities between the names of thematically unconnected characters are thus narrative instruments by which the reader is compelled to compare characters and explore the ways in which each character is caught up in a network of similar but not identical stories. In this way each name becomes the counterpart of another character, another experience, yet because the characters are not mere doubles of one another, the comparisons between any two can only reach so far. They are neither complements nor opposites of each other; rather, the similarities ultimately point to the individuality of each character and his or her experiences. Importantly, as for example in the case of Sachs and Gebirtig, the counterpart relationships cut across the divide between the legacies of perpetration and survival, revealing the tense but often opaque network of relationships between the two experiences and highlighting the ways in which the Holocaust continues to affect both groups.

Counterpart Stories:
Jewish and Non-Jewish Austrians

Gebürtig is a novel not only of multiple narrative strands, but of numerous plots as well. Every character has his or her own story, and just as the name of one character becomes the structural or thematic counterpart of another character, so too the characters' stories form a counterpart to the experiences and stories of other characters in the novel. I have already referred to the similarity in the positions of Konrad Sachs and Herrmann Gebirtig: both receive a call from the past and both must come to terms with the ways in which the Holocaust past is still present in their lives. The one story is the counterpart to the other, but from different perspectives: on the side of the victims on the one hand, and on the side of the perpetrators on the other. However, Schindel's novel is not structured merely as a narrow confrontation between Holocaust perpetration and Holocaust survival; rather, it explores more generally the counterpart experiences between Jews and non-Jews in contemporary Austria, whose relationships to each other, even when not overtly connected to the Holocaust, are never fully able to move out of the shadow of Austria's brutal history of the oppression and murder of its own citizens.

Schindel's novel presents the often unbridgeable gulf between Jewish and non-Jewish Austrians at the outset of the novel, in a scene in the prologue set in a Viennese coffeehouse, when the narrator Alexander (Sascha) remarks:

> Now Mascha sits next to Danny and gives him her report; during which he doesn't look at her, but rather for her is merely an ear. Christiane Kalteisen talks and laughs into her friend, who in a happy way is spun in to this careless mutual game, so that for me, this table breaks into two halves, as though a glass wall were being erected between the two respective pairs, mute, invisible, hermetic.[11]

Thus begins a novel that intermittently juxtaposes the experiences of Jews with those of non-Jews and invites the reader to do the same. Mascha (as I have suggested in my analysis of her last name, Singer) plays here the role of the one who laments; she tells Danny of her anti-Semitic mistreatment by

---

[11] "Mascha sitzt nun neben Danny und berichtet ihm: dabei schaut er sie nicht an, sondern ist für sie bloß Ohr. Christiane Kalteisen redet und lacht in ihre Freundin hinein; diese ist im sorglosen Widerspiel auf fröhliche Weise eingesponnen, so daß dieser Tisch für mich in seine zwei Hälften auseinanderbricht, als baue sich zwischen den jeweils Zweien die gläserne Wand auf, stumm, unsichtbar, hermetisch" (Schindel, *Gebürtig*, 12).

Erich Stiglitz and he listens to this one of her many "melancholy sonatas."[12] Mascha and Danny are thus bound together in this act of Jewish testimony. Christiane and her friend, on the other hand, portray an entirely different image; they are cut off from Danny and Mascha's problems and reside together in a happy, oblivious cocoon of their own making. A transparent but nevertheless impermeable barrier rises between the two groups, with the Jews and their history on the one side and the non-Jewish Austrians on the other, insensible of the presence of this history. This opening scene sets the tone for Schindel's exploration of the relations between Jews and non-Jews in contemporary Austria, and the juxtaposition of Jewish and non-Jewish experience is thematized throughout the novel in a number of narrative contexts.

One particularly striking example of the way in which the text points to the duality of Jewish and non-Jewish experience is located in the chapter "Gebürtig." In this chapter, the reader learns of the respective histories of Christiane's and Danny's families and is thus encouraged to compare the very different origins of the two characters and to reflect on the ways in which these differing legacies contribute to the divide between them. Christiane's father, Leopold Kalteisen, as we learn not from Christiane directly, but from an unnamed narrator (Sascha?), was born in Sankt Ägyd, where he was "so to say, acquainted and intimate with mountain pines, thistles and chamois."[13] Though we learn that he was a local constable and not a Nazi, the text does not reveal Leopold Kalteisen's activities after Austria became a part of the German Reich or during the war years. The text evades the question altogether:

> In May 1938, Augustine and Leopold married in a Catholic ceremony; in spite of *Mein Kampf* as a wedding gift from the *Führer* they both remained Catholic.
> The pine trees bent this way, the pine trees bent that way, and the war was over.[14]

The seven years between the *Anschluss* and the end of the war are thus marked with a single sentence that vaguely associates historical events with the ordinary cycles of nature and avoids any discussion of what Austrians, and specifically Kalteisen the policeman, did during this time. The absence of

---

[12] "melancholische Sonaten" (Schindel, *Gebürtig*, 39).

[13] "sozusagen mit Latschen, Disteln und Gemsen bekannt und intim" (Schindel, *Gebürtig*, 107).

[14] "Neunzehnhundertachtunddreißig heirateten Augustine und Leopold katholisch und im Mai; trotz 'Mein Kampf' als Hochzeitsgeschenk des Führers sind sie beide katholisch geblieben. Die Föhren bogen sich so, und die Föhren bogen sich anders, und der Krieg war aus" (Schindel, *Gebürtig*, 108).

information regarding his wartime experience is made all the more astonishing because the next two pages of text are devoted to the time of the Russian occupation immediately following the war. This irregularity is perhaps understandable if one reads the narrative as a summary of what Christiane herself has told Danny, for the narrative focuses on family experiences at the expense of macrocosmic historical events. Yet this postwar section of the narrative is not without its ties to the larger events of the time; Christiane's birth on the seventeenth of June 1953 is associated by Kalteisen with an important political incident that takes place at the same time and thus it becomes part of the family mythology: "Later the elder Kalteisen did take notice of the events in distant Berlin, and thus Christiane knew early that she was born on the day of German unity."[15] Christiane thus knows and reports the details of her family's history except events that took place during the critical war years. The gap in information about the Kalteisens' wartime experience marks a break in the narrative's continuity and indicates Christiane's own ignorance of what exactly happened. The narrative's silence about this period of history mirrors the silence of so many German and Austrian parents after the war who neglected to integrate their experiences and actions during the Nazi years into an oral legacy that could be passed down to their children.

Danny's account of his origins, also reported to us by an unnamed narrator and combined with bits of dialogue about the past, begins, like Christiane's, with a discussion of place: "Demant was also born in a village. It's called Moussac, lies on the Vienne and in 1940 found itself in France's unoccupied zone. His parents had fled there and were active in the resistance against Hitler."[16] In contrast to Leopold Kalteisen's ties to Sankt Ägyd, however, which express the notions of home and belonging to a place (hence the title of the chapter, "Gebürtig"), Danny's account of his birth begins with displacement and exile. His story, in direct opposition to that of Christiane, emerges from and is fixated to the war years. Unlike Christiane, who either does not know what her parents did during the war or knows but chooses not to tell, Danny knows the exact details of what his parents did during the occupation of France, at least until his father was arrested by the Gestapo. The family's experiences during the war and in the Holocaust become central to its chronicle, just as the Kalteisens' trials and tribulations

---

[15] "Später nahm der alte Kalteisen aber doch Notiz von den Ereignissen im fernen Berlin, und so wußte Christiane schon früh, daß sie am Tag der deutschen Einheit geboren worden war" (Schindel, *Gebürtig*, 110).

[16] "Auch Demant war in einem Dorf zur Welt gekommen. Es heißt Moussac, liegt an der Vienne und befand sich neunzehneinundvierzig in der unbesetzten Zone Frankreichs. Seine Eltern waren dorthin geflohen und im Widerstand gegen Hitler tätig" (Schindel, *Gebürtig*, 156).

during the Russian occupation make up their story. It is only after this concentration on the displacement of the war years that Danny's tale moves on to a chronicle of his extended family, to the place in which they were *gebürtig,* or at home:

> "Simon Demant, my grandfather," Danny told Christiane, "was an innkeeper in Leopoldstadt. The inn was founded by my great-grandfather, I think his name was Jakob. It existed even until 1938. On my father's side there has always been a line of innkeepers; they were the first born."
> [. . .]
> "My mother Ida, previously Landau, comes from Brünn, as is fitting for a Viennese. In general my parents are true Viennese; my mother is in love with Vienna to this day, despite everything."[17]

Danny, like Christiane, is able to access his lineage and connect his life to both a family history and a location in which that history unfolded. The difference between the two lies in what remains of the family connection to a specific place. Although Christiane's parents leave Sankt Ägyd and relocate to Lilienfeld during the Russian occupation, they have not lost their tie to location of their family's history ("The parents are long since back in Sankt Ägyd"[18]). Danny's family, on the other hand, is not able to retrieve this familial continuity and link to a location, even though his mother moved back to Vienna after the war, "despite everything." The same year in which Christiane's parents were married, 1938, is the year in Danny's account of his father's family that announces the loss of the family business (which, the reader assumes, was expropriated by the Nazis) and marks the rupture in the continuity between family and home. For Danny, it is precisely the Kalteisens' unbroken connection between prewar and postwar existence that separates his experience and familial legacy from that of Christiane: "That's the way it is. The people of this region come from here and the surrounding area. They're all simply always there. People, like trees. They bend back and

---

[17] "'Simon Demant, mein Großvater,' erzählte Danny der Christiane, 'war Gastwirt in der Leopoldstadt gewesen. Gegründet hatte das Gasthaus mein Urgroßvater, ich glaube der hat Jakob geheißen. Es hat noch bis neunzehnhundertachtunddreißig existiert. Väterlicherseits hat's immer eine Gastwirtslinie gegeben, das waren die Erstgeborenen.' [. . .] 'Meine Mutter Ida, vormals Landau, stammt aus Brünn, wie sich's für eine Wienerin gehört. Überhaupt sind die Eltern echte Wiener, meine Mutter ist bis heute in Wien verliebt, trotz alledem'" (Schindel, *Gebürtig,* 157–58).

[18] "Die Eltern sind längst wieder in Sankt Ägyd" (Schindel, *Gebürtig,* 138).

forth and a century has already passed."[19] Danny's thought echoes the one-sentence description of the Kalteisens' experiences during the war. For him, Christiane's family is essentially rooted in a familial location, and the winds of war may blow it back and forth a bit, but it is never uprooted. Danny's family, on the other hand, has been torn from its roots and forcefully displaced by these same winds. Danny is not *gebürtig* in the same way as Christiane, for he has neither clan nor home. The text, by situating these two familial accounts within the "Gebürtig" chapter, locates part of the division between Christiane and Danny in their radically different experiences of home and family.

"Double Otherness"

As we have seen, the opening scene in the Viennese coffeehouse, with the construction of the "glass wall," posits the experiences of Jews and non-Jews as supplemental stories. In this case, however, it is not only the categories "Jews" and "Gentiles" that are set up as counterparts, but also more specifically the figures of Mascha and Christiane, whom the novel frequently compares and associates with each other. As we learn, Danny was Mascha's lover and later he becomes Christiane's, and Sascha (whose problematic status with regard to Danny will be discussed later) falls in love with Mascha. Mascha, as Hildegard Kernmeyer points out, is described as "the black one,"[20] while Christiane is the "snow queen."[21] The two women are established as near opposites; Mascha as a beautiful Jewess who likes to taunt Danny with her exploits with stereotypically non-Jewish Austrian men, and Christiane as the provincial Catholic who struggles with her relationship with a Jew. At one point, as Danny visits Christiane's birthplace in Lilienfeld on the Traisen, Alexander ruminates,

> Mascha Singer's discordant Jewish organ is very nice for my future stories, but how will the woman born Kalteisen from the quiet Traisen valley resound? Will she show herself to be a triangle amid thundering marches and Sunday country folk, or am I harboring my favorite prejudice?[22]

---

[19] "Das ist eben so. Die Leute dieser Gegend kommen eben von da und aus der Umgebung. Die sind alle eben immer da. Leute wie Bäume. Sie biegen sich hin und her, und schon ist ein Jahrhundert um" (Schindel, *Gebürtig*, 119).

[20] "[die] Schwarze" (Schindel, *Gebürtig*, 10).

[21] "Schneekönigin" (Schindel, *Gebürtig*, 160).

[22] "Mascha Singers verstimmte jüdische Orgel ist ja ganz hübsch für meine künftigen Geschichten, aber was wird erst die gebürtige Kalteisen aus dem stillen Traisental er-

In this passage, Mascha and Christiane are thus juxtaposed against one another according to the "sound" they make; Mascha is described as a Jewish organ, heavy with sonorous memory and melancholic, who constantly and compulsively plays "her discordant song."[23] Christiane, on the other hand, "die gebürtige," plays a light, fanciful tune on the triangle that is almost drowned out by Austrian patriotic folk music. Jewish music versus Austrian music, two different musical traditions. The stories Mascha sings become "melancholy solo concertos"[24] of the past, while Christiane's voice becomes subsumed into the larger Austrian retelling of history.

Although Mascha and Christiane occupy opposite positions on either side of the glass wall that separates second-generation Jews and non-Jews, their apparent polarity is neither absolute nor stable, for at times they share similar experiences. As women, the two sometimes occupy a similar status vis-à-vis other characters in the novel, for both are often portrayed as objects of sexual desire by the male-focalized narrators and characters. Sascha's preoccupation with the kinds of music the two women make carries traces of this sexual desire, for he fantasizes about "playing" them sexually to discover their own personal song. Throughout the novel, both women are often subtly objectified as they are gazed at and reduced to their sexual body parts. In the beginning sequences of the novel, for example, the narrator Sascha remarks that "Mascha waits for friends and acquaintances and allows herself to be looked at."[25] She becomes the beautiful object of the male gaze of both the narrator and the characters, above all, Erich Stiglitz, who tries to provoke her by combining jokes about the Mauthausen concentration camp and her Jewishness with sexual innuendo ("He says simply, says Mascha to Demant, that I have to screw him, because Austria thrives on foreign tourism"[26]). For Stiglitz, Mascha becomes "breasts and legs."[27] Christiane is also characterized by a certain sexual objectivity, although perhaps less openly so than Mascha. During his estrangement with Christiane, Danny fantasizes about specific parts of her body (266) and, because of these fantasies, finds it impossible to concentrate on work: "[Danny] tried to get back into the stuff.

---

klingen lassen? Wird sie sich als Triangel erweisen inmitten Marschgebraus und Sonntagsländlern oder hege ich da mein liebstes Vorurteil?" (Schindel, *Gebürtig*, 106–7).

[23] "ihren verstimmten Song" (Schindel, *Gebürtig*, 337).

[24] "melancholische Solokonzerten" (Schindel, *Gebürtig*, 40).

[25] "Mascha wartet auf Freunde und Bekannte und läßt sich anschauen" (Schindel, *Gebürtig*, 10).

[26] "Er sagt schlicht, sagt Mascha zu Demant, daß ich vögeln muß mit ihm, denn Österreich lebt vom Fremdenverkehr" (Schindel, *Gebürtig*, 15).

[27] "Brüste und Beine" (Schindel, *Gebürtig*, 14).

But Christiane's breasts, legs, and eyes locked him out of it."[28] Despite their differences and the glass wall that separates them, the two women are often seen as mere breasts and legs, and in these moments of the narrative gaze, their sexualized body parts[29] become metonymies for their entire persons. The women are not only seen as sexual objects through the agency of narration, they are also marked by the male characters according to their sexuality; for Danny, Christiane is a "sex heart"[30] that threatens to overwhelm him, and Stiglitz is attracted to Mascha because of her "coincidentally Jewish pussy."[31] Both women find this objectification problematic, for it automatically reduces them to pieces and parts and precludes an identity that embodies more than sexuality. As Mascha says of non-Jewish men like Stiglitz, "And they pick me apart. And I exist in pieces. And what I am is foreign to me."[32] Mascha's self-alienation is echoed by Christiane as well. When she and Danny play the game "What would you most like to be?," she avoids responding to the question at first, but then she answers him, betraying the identity crisis from which she suffers: "'A man,' she burst out and stood up quickly. The conciliation had already failed. She noticed it and added quickly: 'Or a woman. Or I want somehow to be me.'"[33] Both women feel determined by the sexual desire the men feel for them, a desire that fetishizes parts of their bodies. Both attempt to circumvent their object status; Mascha through telling stories to Sascha[34] and through the radical self-assertion (or

---

[28] "[Danny] versuchte, wieder in das Zeug hineinzukommen. Doch Brüste, Beine, und Augen der Kalteisen verriegelten es gut" (Schindel, *Gebürtig*, 236).

[29] Once again, it is critical to point out that the novel allows no absolute interpretive claims. Importantly, it is not only the women who are reduced to body parts in the novel, but the men as well. In the quote cited above, Danny is for Mascha "merely an ear"("bloß Ohr" [Schindel, *Gebürtig*, 12]). His ear becomes a metonymy for both himself and his function as listening witness to Mascha's stories. Of course, this metonymy is not one of sexual objectification, but it does appear that Mascha is guilty of a transgression similar to that of Stiglitz: she does not perceive Danny as a person but values him only for his function as listener.

[30] "Geschlechtsherz" (Schindel, *Gebürtig*, 36).

[31] "zufällige Judenscheide" (Schindel, *Gebürtig*, 14).

[32] "Und mich zertrennen sie. Und ich existiere in Stücken. Und was ich bin, ist mir fremd" (Schindel, *Gebürtig*, 15).

[33] "'Ein Mann,' platzte sie heraus und stand rasch auf. Die Beschwichtigung war bereits gescheitert. Sie bemerkte es und fügte rasch hinzu: 'Oder eine Frau. Oder ich will sein irgendwie Ich'" (Schindel, *Gebürtig*, 48).

[34] Sascha functions as the transcribing witness who validates Mascha's sense of self by listening to her stories. Although Sascha is the subject of the male gaze in some of the episodes, in this case, he is not the agent of Mascha's fragmentation but a force that helps her feel more integrated. As with so much in Schindel's novel, Sascha's po-

self-denial) of an eating disorder,[35] and Christiane, first by leaving her husband and children, and then by suddenly fleeing to Italy and France to escape the social expectations that crush her: "The main thing is that I'm a good girl and I let myself be fucked."[36]

Hildegard Kernmeyer devotes a good deal of her article on the dialectics of identity and Jewishness in *Gebürtig* to the problem of sexual alterity. For Kernmeyer, women function as the objectified other in society and language: "Women are by definition foreign in masculine discourse [. . .] Defined as the *other sex*, they stand outside masculine discourse. Their existence itself signifies the crossing of boundaries."[37] As Kernmeyer asserts, Christiane and Mascha both function as sexualized objects that, according to Hegelian principles, become the foundations of masculine subjectivity. However, as Kernmeyer points out, Mascha's status in the book is even more precarious than that of other women, for her Jewishness adds another layer of alterity to her marginalization, which Kernmeyer terms her "double otherness."[38] Mascha is doubly marginalized in the society of Schindel's novel; even though her Jewishness links her to Danny and Sascha, the brothers are unable to understand her rage at Stiglitz's sexual objectification of her. However, although her observations are certainly astute with regard to Mascha's status as object for Stiglitz and, to a lesser extent, Danny, Kernmeyer ignores the romance between Sascha and Mascha (the novel suggests that Sascha loves Mascha and perceives her as more than a mere sexual object) and regards the objectification of her as constant and absolute. Moreover, Kern-

---

sition vis-à-vis Mascha is not fixed, and there is no quick and easy way to characterize his relations with her.

[35] None of the critics, even the ones who have analyzed Mascha in detail (Kernmeyer, Freeman, and Nabbe), have mentioned her eating disorder, which becomes progressively worse throughout the novel. Her illness is partly tied to her propensity for telling stories about the past: "Thus the stories remain in her and literally hang out of her mouth; she can neither swallow them nor spit them out" ("So bleiben die Geschichten in ihr über, hängen ihr buchstäblich aus dem Mund heraus; sie kann sie weder schlucken noch ausspeien" [Schindel, *Gebürtig*, 40]). Mascha's role as witness, as the one who narrates the past, precludes any kind of normalization or digestion of history. The past remains undigested and unassimilated and she in turn begins to starve. Alexander makes the connection between her anorexia and Holocaust memory in particular when he compares her to a concentration camp victim (201).

[36] "Hauptsache, ich bin ein braves Mädchen und laß mich ficken" (Schindel, *Gebürtig*, 313).

[37] "Frauen sind per definitionem Fremde im männlichen Diskurs [. . .] Als das *andere Geschlecht* definiert, stehen sie außerhalb des männlichen Diskurses. Ihre Existenz selbst bedeutet Grenzüberschreitung" (Kernmeyer, 183).

[38] "doppelte Andersheit" (Kernmeyer, 184).

meyer herself effectively endorses Mascha's objectification by casting her only in the role of object and by denying Mascha's own agency in her storytelling, in her radical assertion of will with an eating disorder, and in her choice of "blonde mothers' boys"[39] as love objects. Finally, by eliminating Christiane from her discussion of sexual alterity, Kernmeyer misses the one character in the book who recognizes Mascha's double marginality. Although Mascha and Christiane at times occupy opposing positions on either side of the glass wall, there are moments in which the two women are able to defy the strict oppositions of "the black one" and "the snow queen." Christiane is the only person besides Sascha who really perceives Mascha at all. Despite the fact that the reader is unaware of any contact at all between the two women, Sascha reports that it is Christiane who first recognizes Mascha's eating disorder and intervenes by bringing her to the hospital (234). And at the end of the novel, in Danny's retelling of Sascha's opening scene (the scene in which the glass wall is erected), Christiane comes to recognize Mascha's "double otherness":

> On the way home Christiane tells me that she's completely on Mascha's side and she proposes the theory that, as a woman and a Jewess, one has a doubly tough time of things with such shitty men. I look at her amazed, pull lightly on her ear and inquire how all the sudden she has developed a Jewish soul, even if it's only a feminine one. At the word "only," one of the usual fights flares up, and out of a desire for peace I admit to her that this was a macho comment. But with that I lose the point, and the question that I posed goes unanswered.[40]

In the first telling of this scene, as we have seen, Mascha and Christiane are set up in opposition to one another; their relationship is almost adversarial, for Mascha sees Danny (her ex-lover) as abandoning solidarity with her in favor of his new, non-Jewish girlfriend: "Oh, you [Danny] want to be like him. Once again. Or like her. And Mascha looks with an expressionless face

---

[39] "blonde Muttersöhne" (Schindel, *Gebürtig*, 14).

[40] "Auf dem Heimweg teilt mir Christiane mit, daß sie völlig auf seiten Maschas sei und stellt die Theorie auf, daß man es als Frau und Jüdin doppelt schwer hat mit so beschissenen Männern. Ich schaue sie erstaunt an, ziehe sie leicht am Ohr und erkundige mich, woher sich ihr auf einmal eine jüdische Seele erschließe, und sei es auch bloß eine weibliche. Am Wort 'bloß' entzündet sich dann eine der üblichen Streitereien, und ich gebe ihr um des lieben Friedens willen zu, daß dies eine machistische Bermerkung war. Dabei verlier ich aber den Faden, und die Frage, die ich gestellt habe, bleibt unbeantwortet" (Schindel, *Gebürtig*, 337).

over at Christiane Kalteisen."[41] In the second and final retelling of the same scene, the antagonism between the two women is gone and Christiane empathizes with Mascha's problem. Importantly, this is not an instance of narrative evolution gained by temporal development (as if Christiane had learned something or changed her perspective between the two episodes), for the second telling of the scene is merely a structural analogue to the first, told from the point of view of a different narrator (Danny instead of Sascha). Mascha and Christine are counterparts in both narrative retellings of the scene, yet their position vis-à-vis one another is not constant, nor is the second telling evidence of character development or a move toward narrative closure. What changes is not the content, but the narrative perspective, which casts the episode in a different light and encourages the reader to reflect on two tellings of the same story. Moreover, Christiane's empathy with Mascha does not signal the novel's reconciliation of Mascha's "double otherness." Both the question of Jewishness (Danny's question to Christiane about her sudden recognition of Jewishness) and that of gender (Christiane's objection to Danny's "only") remain unanswered and unassimilated.

The Split Narrator

Arguably the most complicated of all counterpart relationships in Schindel's novel is to be found in the narrative function. In addition to the division of narrative labor between two diegetic levels, logically requiring the reader to respond to at least two narrative identities, the narrative agency on the main diegetic level is dispersed among several narrators, both named and unnamed. Although the novel's vocal perspective is decentralized among a number of narrators in all three of the main narratives, the most critical narrative agency resides with the character-narrators Danny and Alexander (Sascha) Demant, the twin sons of Holocaust survivors. In spite of the fact that their combined narrative activity occupies roughly only half of the novel, the brothers are the only named narrators in the entire novel, and they are therefore often seen as narrating the novel as a whole.[42] The two characters alternate their narrating responsibilities, with Alexander taking over most of the duties during the first half of the book and Danny appear-

---

[41] "Ach, du [Danny] willst sein wie er. Schon wieder einmal. Oder wie sie. Und Mascha schaut mit versperrtem Gesicht zu Christiane Kalteisen hinüber" (Schindel, *Gebürtig*, 16).

[42] Several critics (Kernmeyer, Kaiser, Posthofen) concentrate on Danny and Alexander as "the" narrators of the novel and do not distinguish their narrative passages from the sections of the text in which either the narrator is unidentified or the twins can not logically tell the given story (as with the beginning of Sachs's story).

ing as narrator more often toward the end. The most striking example of this gradual transfer of narrative power is the discrepancy between the opening and closing scenes of the book, both of which report on the same coffeehouse scene, albeit from two different narrative perspectives. Although the general narrative responsibility passes from Alexander to Danny during the course of the novel, the division of narrative agency does not fall into even, clearly demarcated territories of their own respective experiences. There are moments when it is not clear to the reader which brother is acting as narrator, and there is one instance in which the narration switches abruptly and confusingly from Danny to Alexander within a single, continuous passage (23–26).

The narrative relationship between the two brothers becomes even more complicated when the reader begins to suspect that Alexander does not function according to the established reality of the novel. As Thomas Freeman and Volker Kaukoreit both point out, certain passages in the text, most notably the narration of Danny's family history discussed earlier, strongly suggest that Alexander does not actually exist: "Father Heinrich Demant worked under a false name at a firm that collaborated with the Nazis [. . .] His wife Ida and Daniel, the son, stayed hidden in the small village."[43] In this passage, the narrator (who is unnamed) excludes the possibility of Danny's having a brother. By using the definite article "the" and not the possessive adjective "his" (as with "his wife Ida"), which would admit the small possibility of another son, the narrator makes an unequivocal declaration that Danny is the sole offspring of his parents. This admittedly obscure reference is the only moment in the novel that directly contradicts Alexander's many assertions that he is Danny's twin brother, although there are certainly instances in which Alexander's presence in the novel appears to have minimal or no effect on the characters or the action. It is tempting to use this passage as indisputable evidence of Alexander's non-existence (Volker Kaukoreit writes that Danny's family history, "on the level of pure fact, excludes the existence of a twin brother"[44]), but there are no textual indicators that would lead the reader to believe that this unidentifiable narrator is more authentic, reliable, or veritable than Alexander himself. The reader is caught in a dilemma; on the one hand, she must admit that Alexander's "existence is never established with certainty" (Freeman, 121), yet on the other hand, the many passages in which he functions as the narrator and claims his existence belie for the reader the apparent "fact" that he doesn't exist. Alexander thus pre-

---

[43] "Vater Heinrich Demant arbeitete unter falschem Namen bei einer Handelsfirma, die mit den Nazis kollaborierte [. . .] Seine Frau Ida und Daniel, der Sohn, blieben in dem kleinen Ort verborgen" (Schindel, *Gebürtig*, 156–57).

[44] "rein faktisch die Existenz eines Zwillingsbruders ausschließt" (Kaukoreit, 6).

sents a problem of narrative verifiability for the reader: he cannot be perceived as a fully present, active, real character, and yet his presence and his investment in the text cannot be ignored either.

Critics have attempted to explain Alexander's problematic narrative authority over the actual character of Danny by attributing it to what Konstantin Kaiser calls "the division of the narrating subject into a double figure."[45] For Renate Posthofen and Volker Kaukoreit, the two brothers represent the fragmentation of the role of the narrator. According to Posthofen, Danny and Alexander function differently in the narrative; Danny acts and Alexander shadows him as his double and then reports on this action. The relationship between the two brothers and their narrative functions exposes the dialectic of the narrator — the difference between acting (the narrator as character) and reporting (the narrator as witness). The integrated narrator is thus divided into entities that either act or report, and each brother performs one part of the duty of a focalized narrator who is both within the story and reports on it from without. According to Volker Kaukoreit, this split not only is indicative of the narrative problematic but also becomes a metareflection on the role of the writer. Alexander, as the one who observes and notates (as Danny says to him, "you're the one who has to note it down"[46]), becomes a figure for the writer, who in his authorial program is cut off from life: "This division, which sustainably destroys the illusion of an omniscient narrator and at the same time evokes the existential inner conflict of the author, is, simply stated, the discrepancy between living and writing."[47] The counterpart character-narrators Danny and Alexander, according to Kaukoreit, point to the dialectic between literature and life: either one can live or one can write about living, but one can not act and write at the same time. For Kaukoreit, the identity and integration of the traditional, omniscient, I-protagonist narrator is thus exposed as a construct that serves to disguise the fragmentation inherent in narration.

Matthias Konzett and Hildegard Kernmeyer, on the other hand, view the two brothers as doubles of one another, as mutually entwined character-narrators who are intricately bound to one another both structurally and thematically. Although the twin brothers are fragmented and relegated to one side of the action-narration dialectic on their own, according to Matthias Konzett, their collaboration in the living and telling of their story allows for a sort of narrative unity. The twin brothers "are symbiotically connected to

---

[45] "die Aufspaltung des erzählenden Ich in eine Doppelfigur" (Kaiser, 100).

[46] "dann bist du der, welcher aufnotiert" (Schindel, *Gebürtig*, 18).

[47] "eine Aufspaltung, die nachhaltig die Illusion eines allwissenden Erzählers zerstört und gleichsam einen existentiellen Zwiespalt des Autors beschwört, schlicht gesagt, die Diskrepanz zwischen Leben und Schreiben" (Kaukoreit, 6).

one another as passive observer-narrator and acting characters respectively, thus producing together a narratively enframed life or story" (82). Rather than emphasizing the inherent split of narration and the crisis of narrative identity, Danny and Alexander, though fragmented and cut off from one another, together are able to produce a coherent, unified story. Hildegard Kernmeyer takes this analysis one step further; in her opinion, the fact that the responsibilities of acting and narrating are divided gives Alexander a stability that is absent in the other characters: "Sascha Graffito preserves 'the peace and the overview,' he guarantees the unity of the narrative strands. He alone offers certainty; his writing creates the illusion of identity."[48] In Kernmeyer's view, Alexander, though not a character in his own right, is paradoxically the most stable figure in the entire novel. He achieves this certainty and equilibrium not by participating as a character in the action, but by exempting himself from it and watching and reporting Danny's activities and interactions with other characters. Precisely because Alexander is not caught up in the problems of identity and memory afflicting the characters, he is able to maintain a reliable and veritable narrative perspective.

What all of these analyses neglect to consider are the ways in which Alexander and Danny do not conform to a strict living-writing dialectic. While the text certainly supports the idea that Alexander functions as Danny's alter ego and that he takes on the role of the passive narrator as counterpart to Danny's activity, this paradigm does not operate consistently throughout the novel. I maintain that there is a strong move on the part of Alexander to break out of his position on the narrative dialectic. What results is not a structure of stable narration, in which Alexander is able to guarantee "unity" and "certainty," but a narrative crisis that resounds throughout the rest of the novel.

Narrative Parturition

In the beginning of the first chapter, "Enge" (Narrowness), Alexander's role as the writing observer vis-à-vis Danny's acting character is established. At the same time, his existence is made problematic, although the text only hints subtly at this through Danny and Alexander's witty, ironic conversation, which I quote here at length:

> When there's no room to the left or the right. It's dripping from above, spraying from below. So just take a path. From the back comes crying,

---

[48] "Sascha Graffito bewahrt 'Ruhe und Übersicht,' er garantiert die Geschlossenheit der Erzählstränge. Er allein hat Gewißheiten zu bieten, sein Schreiben stiftet die Illusion von Identität" (Kernmeyer, 187).

in the front you have only thoughts that you yourself have exuded. But write, Alexander Graffito. Always keep writing after the people:

"Nothing is genuine about you, Sascha," Danny Demant says to me shortly after the beginning of this complicated story, through which I would like to develop him. We both are sitting in the Zeppelin, shortly after it opens, eye to eye, between us the table. No Stiglitz, no Singer, Christiane Kalteisen in counter-rhythm to his fearful heart, and so on.

"Nothing's genuine about me? Hopefully," I say elegantly to him across the table. "The genuine — you can keep it."

[. . .]

Demant nods to me. "That's okay," he says. "The main thing is that you write it down afterwards, quickly and precisely, because we need traces. It's dreary to think that everything is the way it is, or different and the same."

"I know," I calm him, "you'd rather have it too cramped than go up in the sky in a puff of smoke."

[. . .]

"If one of us has *zores* [misfortune], then you're the one who has to note it down. Although," he pauses and takes his hands out of his shirt, "it's a shame that what I do doesn't speak for itself, doesn't bring itself into the story."

"Where there's no room, there's no room," I say again over the table. "But I find it completely in order that I'm so tenacious when I'm taking notes. As a twin brother I don't like to move in windy words, smoky words, and other edifying words. Let that be my concern, brotherheart, and finally do something."

[. . .]

Later we part, as if each of us had a life of his own.[49]

---

[49] "Wenn links und rechts kein Platz ist. Von oben tropft's, von unten sprudelt's. Geh halt einen Weg. Aus den Rücken kommt Geplärr, vor dir lauern bloß die Gedanken, die du selbst abgesondert hast. Aber schreiben, Alexander Graffito. Immer den Leuten hintennach schreiben: 'An dir ist nichts echt, Sascha,' sagt mir Danny Demant kurz nach Beginn dieser verwickelten Geschichte, mit deren Hilfe ich ihn entwickeln möchte. Wir sitzen beide beim Zeppelin, kurz nach dem Aufsperren, wir beide, Aug in Aug, zwischen uns der Tisch. Kein Stiglitz, keine Singer, die Christiane Kalteisen im Gegentakt seines bangen Herzens und so weiter. 'An mir ist nichts echt? Hoffentlich.' Elegant sag ich ihm das über den Tisch hin. 'Das Echte kann mir gestohlen bleiben.' [. . .] Demant nickt mir zu. 'Schon gut,' sagt er. 'Hauptsache, du schreibst hintennach auf, hurzig und präzise, denn Spuren müssen her. Mir wird öd bei dem Gedanken, daß alles so ist oder anders und egal.' 'Ich weiß,' beruhige ich ihn, 'dir ist es lieber zu eng als daß du in den Himmel qualmst.' [. . .] 'Wenn einer *Zores* hat von uns beiden, dann bist du der, welcher aufnotiert. Obwohl,' er hält inne und zieht

Although it is not clear at the beginning, the narrator of the passage is eventually revealed to be Alexander, who then establishes himself as the primary narrator of the "complicated story." The first paragraph, which contains a second-person address to Alexander, thus appears to be a case of Alexander commanding himself to take up the pen. On the other hand, this imperative to write is very similar to Danny's instructions later on in the passage ("The main thing is that you write it down afterwards, quickly and precisely"). The narrator of this first paragraph could therefore just as well be Danny. If this were the case, then it would be Danny who complains, "When there's no room to the left or the right," and Alexander's response, "Where there's no room, there's no room" would then be an admonition to Danny to accept reality. But then again: the command, "So just take a path," is very similar to Alexander's later command to Danny: "finally do something." The text thus cleverly conceals the identity of the narrator of this passage. This ambiguity is further enhanced by the colon that separates this paragraph from the rest of the (Alexander-narrated) passage, which suggests that the two texts are very different in their composition and should be considered apart from one another. My reading is that the colon marks the transition from an apparently integrated narrator to "the division of the narrating subject into a double figure," for, as we learn both in this passage and in later sections of the novel, this scene takes place at the beginning of the story — shortly before Danny meets Christiane and well before the scene in the coffeehouse described in the prologue. The event that precipitates this story is not Danny's affair with Christiane, but the creation of a new narrative consciousness. In this first paragraph, the narration is not yet doubled and organized into two distinct parts, but rather contains inner contradictions. A split in the narrative consciousness then takes place with the introduction of the address to Alexander and the reference to writing, and the colon marks this moment of partition/parturition, the birth of a twin narrative consciousness.

The post-colon text begins with a dialogue between the two brothers. Danny's first words, "Nothing is genuine about you, Sascha," can be read as both a quasi-hidden, ironic reference to Alexander's non-existence as an acting character and a paradoxical intimation to a situation in which Danny converses with an apparently real figure about his inauthentic existence. Fur-

---

sich die Hände aus dem Hemd, '. . . schade, daß, was ich tu, nicht von selbst redet, sich nicht selbst in die Geschichte bringt.' 'Wo kein Platz ist, da ist kein Platz,' sag ich wieder über den Tisch. 'Aber ich find's ganz ordentlich, daß ich so zäh bin beim Notieren. Als Zwillingsbruder mag ich mich nicht in Windwörtern, Qualmwörtern und sonstigen Erbauungsworten bewegen. Laß das meine Sorge sein, Bruderherz, und tu endlich was.' [. . .] Später gehen wir auseinander, als habe jeder sein Leben" (Schindel, *Gebürtig*, 17–18).

thermore, the dialogue introduces the first narrative intrusion, in which Alexander lays out his plans for the story and ruminates on his ability, as a narrator, to "develop" Danny as a figure. In addition, the paragraph establishes Danny and Alexander as counterparts and even stages this connection spatially for the reader, for the scene has them sitting at a table across from one another, "eye to eye." One can read this scenario as a site of negotiation between the two, a meeting in which the terms of this new arrangement are discussed and agreed upon.

The following paragraphs establish the division of responsibility. On the one hand, Alexander is charged with keeping track of the activity and then reporting on it. He is designated not only as a writer in the creative sense of the term — he intends on becoming famous with his writings (40) — but as one whose role is above all to observe and note everything down, and, importantly, to leave behind a written document of what happened ("because we need traces"). Alexander is to become the writing witness who testifies to Danny's activity and his relationships with the other characters in the novel. Moreover, the text suggests that this job of bearing witness is somehow connected to Holocaust memory, for Alexander's statement "you'd rather have it too cramped then to go up in the sky in a puff of smoke" (which he repeats later in the novel [201]) is a reference to both the title of this first chapter and to imagery in Paul Celan's "Todesfuge" ("Death Fugue"), arguably the most well-known poem in German about the Holocaust: "He shouts play death more sweetly this Death is a master from Deutschland / he shouts scrape your strings darker you'll rise then as smoke to the sky you'll then have a grave in the clouds where you won't lie too cramped" (*Selected Poems*, 33).[50] Alexander alludes to Celan's imagery in an effort to assure Danny that he indeed understands what is at stake here — that his job is to bear witness to the effects of Holocaust memory on Danny and to the legacy of the Holocaust in the everyday life of contemporary Austria. For Danny, this act of witnessing and the production of testimony are absolutely critical, for, unlike the smoke that curls into the air, leaving no trace of the existence of the burnt victim behind, Alexander's writing and note-taking must rescue Danny's life from oblivion and permanently record exactly what happens, "that everything is the way it is." In short, Alexander functions as what Alan Berger and others have called the "second-generation witness," one who is witness not to the actual events of the Holocaust, but rather to the traces of these events in familial and social memory. His task is to provide a corpus of testimony that both attests to the ways in which Holocaust

---

[50] "Er ruft spielt süßer den Tod der Tod ist ein Meister aus Deutschland / er ruft streicht dunkler die Geigen dann steigt ihr als Rauch in die Luft / dann habt ihr ein Grab in den Wolken da liegt man nicht eng" (Celan, *Die Hand voller Stunden*, 32).

memory functions in the present and, to some extent, stands in for the absent testimony of those who perished without leaving so much as a trace behind.

Danny, on the other hand, assumes the other side of the living/writing dialectic. Just as Alexander is called to testify, Danny is called to act. "Finally do something," says Alexander, a phrase he repeats often throughout the course of the novel, and Danny himself complains of his own inactivity on the very next page. As a protagonist of a novel, Danny is noticeably inactive and, at the same time, worried about this chronic passivity. It appears that he needs the admonishments of the story's narrator to behave like a character and actually do something. Moreover, in order for his action to be meaningful, it requires the counterpart of the observing witness who perceives that something has happened and orders this event into a narrative: "it's a shame that what I do doesn't speak for itself, doesn't bring itself into the story."

The end of this scene signals the beginning of the new narrative arrangement, in which each of the brothers steps into his prescribed role and begins performing his duties. Alexander's language points out the ambiguity of this new structure: "Later we part, as if each of us had a life of his own." The use of the conditional in this sentence calls into question the apparently separate lives the brothers are to lead in the novel from this point forward. Although the brothers settle the matter in this opening section, the evidence of this negotiation is not allowed to recede into the background, and therefore the reader is prevented from accepting the new terms of narration as natural. The text's insistence on keeping this arrangement in the foreground is underscored at the beginning of the next section, which is narrated by Danny in his first appearance as a narrator. Although Alexander takes on responsibility for narrating by the sixth section of the first chapter and remains the sole identifiable narrator through the next four chapters, Danny does not give up the narrating function as easily as the first section suggests.

The event that marks the transformation of Danny from a self-narrating figure to an acting character is his affair with Christiane Kalteisen. He gives up his participation in narrating the novel (at least until the last third) in the moment immediately preceding her initial entrance (25). Significantly, this occurs in the section in which the narration abruptly transfers from Danny to Alexander within a single, continuous passage. Danny is thrust onto the center stage of the story, in which he is called on to act, and Alexander must suddenly assume the narrative responsibility. Danny thus makes the transition from passive narrator to active character in his own story of his relationship with Christiane. The narrative significance of the meeting between Danny and Christiane, an encounter that the novel stages as an attempt to revive the old dream of a "symbiosis" between Germans/Austrians and Jews, is then revealed to us by Alexander, who states, "And so a story begins again, as if it could never end."[51]

"Because Here I Know Everything"

What follows this abrupt transition is a period of relative stability, in which both brothers settle into their respective roles. Danny pursues his relationship with Christiane, and Alexander plays the part of the observing witness whose job is to report from a distance:

> While I observe my twin, how he is torn between Christiane and "beautiful Venice," between being a lazy bones and a top editor, a contentment spreads out in me. It's a fine thing to sit on your ass and merely turn your ear to your surroundings, note down what happens, and occasionally, how should I say it, intervene wordlessly [. . .]
>
> It makes me very happy when I have an overview of everything; the outcomes are humming along [. . .]
>
> I still know way too little about the life that I presume to live. I'm a mere stone in the debris of the present, but what of it? It may be like that for most people, but for me it's different, because here I know everything.[52]

For Alexander, the role of the notating narrator is one in which he feels comfortable, for it allows him a measure of certainty and security he does not possess in life. As the agent of storytelling, he wields the power to govern the actions of all the characters, for as he says, nothing happens without his shaping the actions in language. Alexander holds the narrative overview, the ultimate control over the story, which contrasts sharply with his feelings of powerlessness as an actor in life. As a character, Alexander is insignificant and without control, but as the narrator, he appears to be all-knowing. It is because of these statements by Alexander that critics have commented on Alexander's apparent omniscience as a narrator, yet in contrast to Hildegard Kernmeyer's assertion that this omniscience makes him the most stable and

---

[51] "Und wieder beginnt eine Geschichte so, als ob sie nimmer aufhören könnte" (Schindel, *Gebürtig*, 26).

[52] "Während ich meinen Zwilling beobachte, wie es ihn hin und her reißt zwischen Christiane und 'schönes Venedig,' zwischen Faulian und Spitzenlektor, breitet sich die Behaglichkeit in mir weiter aus. Ist schon eine feine Sache, auf dem Hintern zu sitzen, bloß der Umgebung die Ohren zuzuwenden, aufzunotieren, was passiert und gelegentlich, wie soll ich sagen, wortlos einzugreifen [. . .] Mich freut auch sehr, wie ich alles im Überblick habe; schon schnurren die Verläufe ab [. . .] Ich weiß ja noch viel zu wenig vom Leben, in dem ich selbst zu leben mir anmaße, ein Steinchen bin ich bloß in Geröll der Gegenwart, aber was tut's? Möge es den meisten so gehen, mir geht's anders, denn hier weiß ich alles" (Schindel, *Gebürtig*, 97–98).

certain character in the novel, it appears here that this knowledge derives not from an inherent stability or superior perspective, but from his voluntary withdrawal from the action of the story. Behind the all-knowing, all-powerful perspective crouches a figure who avoids the uncertainty and insignificance of his own life by exerting narrative control over the stories of other characters' lives. Alexander thus embraces one extreme of the living/writing dialectic by becoming a memory scribe, whose textual function is to bear witness to the events around him. He is the immobile witness whose constant observation and narration bars him from being present in the narrative as a character. Because the position he occupies on the dialectic is directly opposed to living, Alexander effectively exempts himself from life. His writing becomes a sort of deathly paralysis that assumes and determines his existence ("my papery existence"[53]), and he likens himself to a dead written document, a corpus of testimony, a "paper body."[54] Alexander embodies the textual functions of narrating and notating, and in doing so, renounces his status as a body in the text and instead becomes the body of the text.

Although Alexander assumes the role of the witness who is immobilized by becoming his own written text, his paralysis does not guarantee that he is the most stable and unified character in the text. He must constantly battle a sense of crisis and chaos that threatens his apparently immutable perspective:

> Now and then I can barely suppress the desire to throw myself into the action. My contact with Mascha Singer threatens to draw me in, and that will probably bring the great overviews to an end. I have resolved to note instead of act, because only so will I grow into the role that an unknown talent has allocated to me. If Danny weren't my twin brother, I would never have succeeded in leaving life to him and remaining seated on my ass, omniscient and all-feeling.[55]

The narratorial arrangement requires from Alexander some amount of self-restraint and suppression of desire, for he admits that he often wishes to take up his own action in the novel. In particular, his burgeoning relationship with Mascha mobilizes Alexander's desire to become the hero of his own

---

[53] "mein papierenes Dasein" (Schindel, *Gebürtig*, 234).

[54] "Papierkörper" (Schindel, *Gebürtig*, 245).

[55] "Bisweilen kann ich die Lust, mich selbst hineinzuwerfen ins Geschehen, kaum unterdrücken. Mein Kontakt mit Mascha Singer droht mich hineinzuziehen, und dann ist's wohl vorbei mit den großen Übersichtlichkeiten. Ich hab mir nun mal vorgenommen zu notieren statt zu handeln, denn nur so werde ich in die Rolle hineinwachsen, die mir ein unbekanntes Talent zugewiesen hat. Wäre Danny nicht mein Zwillingsbruder, nie hätte ich es geschafft, das Leben ihm zu überlassen und allwissend und allfühlend auf dem Hintern sitzen zu bleiben" (Schindel, *Gebürtig*, 99).

story. As we learn in the first chapter, Alexander meets secretly with Mascha in his capacity as listening witness (39). For Mascha, Alexander provides a forum for her to tell her stories; although at first she sees him only as a version of Danny, after he begins to listen to her (which, as it is hinted at in the prologue, Danny did not do), he becomes Danny's antithesis. Alexander becomes unique to Mascha precisely for his function as a witness who provides her with a confirmation of identity (40).

As the novel progresses, however, Alexander finds it more and more difficult to maintain his narrative distance. He feels increasingly threatened in his role as the overseer of the narrative:

> But it could happen that I have to lean far forward from the seat of my entangled soul in order to look down at what is developing down there. Under no circumstance may I fall down, rather I must stay up here [. . .]
>
> For I am convinced. Everyone may lack an overview, someone must see the whole picture, that's me, otherwise the notetaking doesn't make sense.
>
> [. . .] As such I watch over his [Danny's] sleep and sit in his life, prepared for the possibility that he will get the idea to drive me away.[56]

Alexander feels threatened in his narrative position for two reasons: on the one hand, he fears that if he is not able to maintain his distanced perspective above and over the events, he must relinquish his privileged narrative stance and no longer function as the witness. On the other hand, he also worries that Danny will disrupt the established division of responsibilities and prevent Alexander from withdrawing into "Demant's inner geography."[57]

The event that finally precipitates Alexander's full-blown crisis is the deterioration of Mascha's health and her hospitalization for anorexia:

> After Mascha Singer's weight had sunk to 39 kilos, Christiane intervened and took Mascha to the hospital [. . .]
>
> In general I can't get her out of my senses and she muddles up my papery existence [. . .] It seems to me as if I were already sitting like my twin brother between the furniture and doing as little as he [. . .]

---

[56] "Doch es könnte mir nun passieren, daß ich mich vom Sitz des Seelengeflechts weit vorbeugen muß, um hinunterzuschauen, was sich da unten anbahnt. Keinesfalls darf ich hinunterfallen, sondern heroben muß ich bleiben [. . .] Denn ich bin überzeugt. Allen mag es an Übersicht mangeln, einer muß drüberschauen, das bin ich, sonst macht das Aufnotieren keinen Sinn [. . .] Als solcher wache ich über seinen Schlaf und sitze in seinem Leben, gefaßt darauf, daß er auf die Idee kommen wird, mich von dort zu vertreiben" (Schindel, *Gebürtig*, 106).

[57] "Demants innere Geographie" (Schindel, *Gebürtig*, 57).

> I would so like to see Mascha, to do something myself, to live myself and to no longer write afterward. This danger is growing. It still suffices for me, I hope, to emulsify my annoyance in the notes [. . .] Most of all I would like to rip the text from my body and run naked into my own life.
>
> I hear though, that with notetaking comes a half insipid composure. I probably have to wring myself out a bit, in order that this troublesome lust for life drips out of me; above all the desirous fantasies of Mascha must flake into sentences and paragraphs, otherwise I would have to get up and disappear from the written action.[58]

In this passage, Alexander undergoes a severe struggle with himself. His desire for Mascha comes to preoccupy him to such extent that he is unable to concentrate on witnessing and writing, which threatens his function and identity as narrator and thus his "papery existence." Alexander is attracted to the idea of living; he longs to cast off his role as memory scribe and "run naked into his own life." Although he is able to continue writing, it is only with the utmost concentration; and still his sentences suffer from a lack of fluidity. He admonishes himself to shut out the distractions, to expel his desire, to suppress "this tiresome lust for life" so that he can retain his narrative perspective, exert control over the text, and continue as the immobile witness. Yet despite his efforts he finds it increasingly difficult to remain motionless inside his textual corpus; his greatest desire, as he states, is to shed the text from his body and to escape the realm of the non-living witness, to become an actor in life instead of its narrator.

Alexander's much-feared, much-desired exit from the post of witness occurs at the beginning of the sixth chapter, "Weite":

> I can't hold myself back. I regret nothing. Scarcely had I heard of Mascha's recuperative stay when I began to cower, stick my ears into the wind and move my nostrils. My crotch itched, my heart palpitated,

---

[58] "Nachdem Mascha Singer auf neununddreißig Kilo heruntergekommen war, intervenierte Christiane Kalteisen und brachte Mascha ins Spital [. . .] Überhaupt geht sie mir nicht aus den Sinnen heraus und bringt mein papierenes Dasein durcheinander [. . .] Mir kommt's vor, als säße ich bereits wie mein Zwillingsbruder zwischen den Möbeln und täte so wenig wie er [. . .] Ich möchte so gerne Mascha sehen, selber etwas tun, mich leben und nix mehr nachschreiben. Diese Gefahr ist im Wachsen. Noch genügt es mir, ich hoffe es, meinen Ärger in die Notizen zu emulgieren [. . .] Am liebsten würde ich mir den Text vom Leibe reißen und nackt in mein eigenes Leben rennen. Ich höre aber, zum Notieren gehört eine halbfade Gelassenheit. Ich muß mich wohl wieder etwas auswringen, damit diese lästige Lebenslust aus mir heraustropft, vor allem die begierlichen Phantasien zu Mascha müssen sich zu Sätzen und Absätzen flocken, sonst müßte ich wohl aufstehen und aus dem aufgeschriebenen Geschehen verschwinden" (Schindel, *Gebürtig,* 234–35).

in the mirror I actually caught sight of the brilliance of my eyes in my face, the rustling of the paper body was over [. . .]

What does Danny matter to me, this silly brother? He constantly half-lifts himself out of his chair and then lets himself fall back in it again; for months it's been the same. When there's nothing to register the notekeeper can only pick his nose until it becomes an obsession.[59]

In this passage, Alexander makes the transition from the recording narrator to a full-blown character. He appears to come to life here, or at least his body does; all of his organs and body parts suddenly announce their existence, and only at this point does the reader realize that Alexander has been almost without a concrete body in the previous sections of the narrative. One thinks back to the prologue, in which he writes: "By the way, I'm spread out somewhat in the bar, because I write down whatever comes to me so that the various silences take on a trace."[60] Until this sudden assumption of a body, Alexander has been diffuse and lacking any sense of corporeality; unlike Danny, who possesses ears (12), eyes (12), mouth (18), hands (23), face (24), hips (32), arms (40), and sex organs (46), Alexander has not been identified with any body part at all. His text enjoys the carnality that he himself lacks; in the above quote from the prologue, he is dispersed all over the room, as if he were a gaseous substance, while his writings assume a concrete corporeality. Alexander thus sheds his paper body and assumes the body of a living, breathing character. In this later quote, he also spreads himself out, but in this case he has picked up a body and a sense of physicality; just one paragraph later he is endowed with shoulders, back, cheek, forehead, and chin (246). Alexander marvels over his new physical presence ("I felt my existence in the strongest possible way"[61]), and his obvious pleasure in doing something corresponds to his frustration over Danny's own lack of activity. This frustration, combined with his desire to act with regard to Mascha, effects Alexander's transformation from textual body to bodily character. Danny is not performing his duty, leaving Alexander nothing to wit-

---

[59] "Ich kann mich nicht zurückhalten. Ich bereue nichts. Kaum hörte ich vom Kuraufenthalt Maschas in Aflenz, schon kauerte ich mich zusammen, steckte die Ohren in den Wind und bewegte die Nüstern. Mir juckte der Damm, es pochte das Herz, vorm Spiegel erblickte ich tatsächlich im Gesicht die Leuchkraft der Augen, das Rascheln des Papierkörpers war dahin [. . .] Was ficht mich Demant an, dieser verblasene Bruder. Ständig erhebt er sich halb aus dem Sessel und läßt sich wieder nieder, seit Monaten immer dasselbe. Wo nichts zu registrieren ist, hat ein Notierer bloß das Nasenbohren, bis es zum Zwang wird" (Schindel, *Gebürtig*, 245–46).

[60] "Ich bin übrigens einigermaßen im Lokal verteilt, denn ich schreibe auf, was mir entgegenfällt, damit die diversen Wortlosigkeiten eine Spur bekommen" (Schindel, *Gebürtig*, 8).

[61] "Ich spürte mich aufs Stärkste vorhanden" (Schindel, *Gebürtig*, 247).

ness or report, so Alexander throws off the limitations of watching, waiting, and witnessing and steps into the action himself.

Thus begin both Alexander's love affair with Mascha, whom he visits in Aflenz, and his debut as a character. At the end of the section, after he and Mascha have promised themselves to each other and he returns to Vienna, he tells Danny what has happened:

> "Stalin was our matchmaker," I say to Danny [. . .] He stands up, takes from the desk drawer the notebook I gave him and throws it in my lap.
> "*Mazel tov*," he says and goes to the window so that I can see only his back.
> "Okay, then," I say after I had stared for a while, getting up. "Do your own reporting, twin heart." Since he doesn't answer I exit the apartment and enter my life, but that's my own business.[62]

At this point, Alexander's transformation from witnessing narrator to acting character is made complete. He hands over his narrative duties to Danny and exempts himself from the role of witness in order to enter into his own life. This transfer of narrative responsibility is represented by the notebook that Alexander gave Danny before his trip to Venice (57), which Danny takes out and throws at Alexander. Although Alexander feared previously that Danny would assume narrative power, at this point this no longer is a concern. Alexander overcomes his anxiety and walks away from both Danny and the role of narrator.

"Things Have Happened That Hollow Me Out"

Alexander's defection from the narrative order and his renunciation of witnessing initiate an immediate narrative vacuum, signaling a crisis that resounds throughout the rest of the novel and forcing Danny to take up his own narration and to integrate the functions of acting and witnessing. Danny assumes the role of the narrator two sections later at the first possible opportunity. He then goes on to report on every other section of the text in which he is involved (a total of twelve sections, as opposed to the two sections he partially narrates at the beginning of the novel), with the exception of one episode, which will be discussed later. Despite Danny's immediate assump-

---

[62] "'Stalin war unser Kuppler,' sage ich zu Danny [. . .] Er steht auf, nimmt das Notizbuch, das ich ihm seinerzeit geschenkt habe, aus der Schreibtischlade und wirft es mir in den Schoß. '*Mazel tow*,' sagt er und stellt sich zum Fenster, so daß ich bloß in seinen Rücken schauen kann. 'Also dann,' sage ich, nachdem ich das eine Zeitlang tat, und erhebe mich. 'Berichte du nun selber, Zwillingsherz.' Weil er nicht antwortet, gehe ich aus der Wohnung heraus und hinein in mein Leben, doch das ist nun meine Angelegenheit" (Schindel, *Gebürtig*, 248–49).

tion of narration, however, the transition from Alexander to Danny is not an easy one. Danny has trouble assuming the voice of the writing witness, for he feels alienated by his writing; he is nauseated by his own words and states "I noticed that someone besides me was talking out of me."[63] Moreover, he doubts his ability to actually own the language he uses and employ it to create a meaningful text, something more than mere intellectual ornamentation: "When I speak I'm a word-polishing head-man."[64] Despite Danny's misgivings about his own project, however, he continues to narrate and even finds that he is able to replace some of Alexander's narrative importance.

However, Alexander still exists as a possible counterpart to Danny; as the reader learns a few sections later, Alexander has not disappeared at all, but has just given up narration for his love affair with Mascha. The pleasure he once took in being the distanced narrator he now finds in his role as lover: "My change from notetaker to lover gradually acquired one and the same aura; in the meantime I had more and more the feeling that I was doing one and the same."[65] In this last section in which he appears as a narrator, however, Alexander describes the demise of the relationship. Mascha has returned to her old boyfriend Fritz Untner, and now Alexander is left with neither identity, which leaves him feeling empty and without direction: "Things have happened that hollow me out."[66] He then seeks to take back the role of the witness-narrator from Danny and to continue as before, as if nothing had happened:

> Now I sit once again in my folding-chair. I just phoned Danny. I told him that Christiane had called me. Told him that Mascha had simply turned the thing with me off [. . .]
> "I'll resume the notetaking again, brother heart."
> "If you want. But not about me, Alexander."
> "What?"
> "Don't get excited! Now you just have to deal with yourself. And I with myself. It should stay that way."
> "I don't have anything to do. Absolutely nothing."
> "Then finally do something."[67]

---

[63] "Ich merkte, daß wer anderer als ich aus mir redete" (Schindel, *Gebürtig*, 264).

[64] "Wenn ich also rede, bin ich ein wortwichsender Kopfmann" (Schindel, *Gebürtig*, 263).

[65] "Mein Wechsel vom Notierer zum Liebhaber bekam langsam für mich ein und die gleiche Aura; in den Zwischenzeiten hatte ich mehr und mehr das Gefühl, ein und dasselbe zu tun" (Schindel, *Gebürtig*, 321).

[66] "Dinge sind vorgefallen, die mich aushöhlen" (Schindel, *Gebürtig*, 321).

[67] "Jetzt sitze ich wieder in meinem Klappsessel. Habe eben mit Danny telefoniert. Habe ihm erzählt, daß mich Christiane angerufen hat. Habe ihm erzählt, daß Mascha

Alexander has lost both his roles, as lover and as narrator, and now he is without any responsibilities; as he says, he has absolutely nothing to do. He tries to reassume the job of the narrator of Danny's story, to reestablish a sense of purpose or identity for himself, but Danny rejects his offer. Although Danny was annoyed with Alexander for leaving his post as the witness-narrator, in the meantime he has learned to narrate his own story. In short, the symbiotic relationship between the two brothers has been severed. In an inversion of the brothers' relationship at the beginning of the novel, in which Alexander became the observer who encouraged Danny to act, it is now Danny who turns the tables on Alexander and encourages him to do something. Although Danny does not let Alexander resume telling Danny's story, he advises him not to give up on notetaking, but to combine the witnessing with the action and thus to renounce the rigid writing-living dialectic.

Shortly after this passage, Alexander closes this section and thus ends his narration in the novel: "'All right,' I tell him, hang up and stand there. I sit down and write a long letter to Mascha Singer. She will never receive it."[68] Importantly, Alexander does not give up writing. But just as Mascha does not receive his letter, we as readers are not privy to it either. For the text we are reading has become Danny's novel, a chronicle of Danny's life. Alexander's letter no longer belongs in Danny's text, but rather to Alexander's own story, to another text. Not only is Alexander no longer Danny's narrator-witness, but he has also ceased to be his alter ego, the double of the protagonist in this novel. The struggle between the two brothers over the narration is over and the narrative crisis has been resolved. Alexander has been ousted as the witness and continues in the novel only as a figure described by Danny's narration. Although he is mentioned twice more in the novel (331, 337), as a double, he is effectively dead. Danny becomes a witness to his own memory, to his own inner split, to his struggle with his twin counterpart, to the death of that double, and finally, to the assumption of his own story, which is predicated on that death.

---

das Ding zu mir einfach ausgeknipst hat [. . .] 'Ich nehme das Notieren wieder auf, Bruderherz.' 'Von mir aus. Aber nicht bei mir, Alexander.' 'Was?' 'Reg dich nicht auf! Du hast doch nun mit dir zu tun. Und ich mit mir. Dabei soll's bleiben.' 'Ich hab gar nichts zu tun. Überhaupt nichts.' 'Dann tu endlich was!'" (Schindel, *Gebürtig*, 323).

[68] "'Ist recht,' sage ich ihm, lege auf und stehe nun da. Ich setze mich hin und schreibe einen langen Brief an Mascha Singer. Sie wird ihn nie erhalten" (Schindel, *Gebürtig*, 323).

"I Am Perfect Because I Was Born After"

The end of *Gebürtig* sees the resolution of all of the novel's major narrative strands. Konrad Sachs battles his demons and overcomes them by exposing them to the light (with the help of Danny and Emanuel Katz), Anton Egger is acquitted, Gebirtig comes to the realization that Austria will never again be his home, and Danny, despite having recovered from a car accident, ends up exactly where he started, with the repetition of the prologue. For Volker Kaukoreit and Hildegard Kernmeyer, there is a discrepancy between Sachs's success in freeing himself from the past and the Jewish characters' own failure to do the same: "No one (except for Sachs) is truly redeemed";[69] "The Jewish protagonists cannot free themselves from the image, that is to say, from the past. Their otherness is codified [. . .] whereas Konrad Sachs, the son of the master race, becomes *identical with himself*."[70] Although the character of Konrad Sachs does represent the most dramatic development among all of the major plots, Kernmeyer and Kaukoreit ignore the real changes that occur on the novel's structural level. Although nothing *happens* to Danny besides his off-again-on-again relationship with Christiane, he does undergo a real transformation. As we have seen, Danny becomes the witness to his own life, the narrator of his own story, and as such, has acquired a voice with which he can testify to his legacy. His narration of the second version of the prologue can be seen as the result of a long process of integrating acting and witnessing, by which he is able recognize and give voice to his own experience and memory. Danny's transformation is certainly not as overtly dramatic as that of Konrad Sachs, who appears able to "master" his past; however, if one accepts the notion that Danny and Alexander are the splitting off of a single character, then the narrative death of Alexander and Danny's quiet assumption of testimony can be interpreted as a more profound example of what Kernmeyer terms becoming "identical with himself." Moreover, Danny, unlike Sachs, does not wish to escape his legacy of the Holocaust. Instead, he seeks a way to bear witness to the Holocaust and to integrate his connection to his murdered family with his own life and thus to bridge the gap between past and present, original experience and inherited legacy. In the novel's epilogue, in which Danny participates as an extra in the filming of a movie about Theresienstadt, he approaches this goal, for he narrates his experiences in revisiting a site of Holocaust memory, "in which the

---

[69] "Wirklich erlöst wird (bis auf Sachs) niemand" (Kaukoreit, 7).

[70] "Die jüdischen Protagonisten können sich aus dem Bild (sprich: aus der Vergangenheit) nicht befreien. Ihre Andersheit ist festgeschrieben [. . .] Konrad Sachs hingegen, der Sohn des Herren-Menschen, wird *sichselbstgleich*" (Kernmeyer, 188).

present is forced behind the mask of the past."[71] This is not to say that Danny has become secure and self-sufficient in his role as integrated narrator and has resolved the tensions inherent in bearing witness to the past. Rather, he is at times overwhelmingly aware of the sheer presumption involved in attempting to write about the Holocaust, an event that he has not experienced: "How should I note it down, I can't note it down. To write about the forty as the forty-first, that's writing from the hip, from the throat, oh well."[72] Danny understands the problem of writing about a legacy that for him is not lived experience; it is at times both impossibly outrageous and outrageously impossible. At the same time, however, he recognizes the privilege inherent in his position as both distanced observer and active participant, in short, as the second-generation witness, who can bridge the gap between experience and legacy by narrating his own experience.

---

[71] "in denen die Gegenwart hinter der Vergangenheitsmaske eingezwängt ist" (Schindel, *Gebürtig*, 342).

[72] "Wie soll ich's notieren, ich kann nicht notieren. Als einundvierzigster über die vierzig notieren, das ist ein Schreiben aus der Hüfte, aus der Gurgel, ach was" (Schindel, *Gebürtig*, 342).

4: Documenting Absence in Patrick Modiano's *Dora Bruder* and Katja Behrens's "Arthur Mayer, or The Silence"

I have also suggested that there is such a thing as memory-envy. It shows itself in writers who seek to recover an image of their community's past — a past deliberately destroyed by others or which was not allowed to form itself into a heritage. Memory-envy also touches a generation that feels belated: the "generation after" which did not participate directly in a great event that determined their parents' and perhaps grandparents' lives.

— Geoffrey H. Hartman,
The Longest Shadow: In the Aftermath of the Holocaust

Detective Stories

IN KATJA BEHRENS'S 1993 short story, "Arthur Mayer oder das Schweigen" ("Arthur Mayer, or The Silence," 2002), the autobiographical narrator becomes aware of a neglected stone monument that commemorates Arthur Mayer, a Jewish doctor whose family, prior to the Holocaust, had lived in her small German town for over 200 years. The text of the monument reads: "In memory of Dr. Arthur Mayer. Born 20 January 1888, died at Auschwitz. We remember him in place of all those who lost their lives for political, racial, or religious reasons. The Citizens of Town S" (Behrens, "The Silence," 34).[1] The narrator is intrigued by the monument, which she had never before noticed, and its memorialization of the town's former doctor, which, although it lists his death as occurring in Auschwitz, characterizes him as the sole representative of a mass of people who died (or, as the German original phrases it, "had to leave their lives") for unclear reasons in vague circumstances in an unnamed event.

Frustrated and intrigued by the cryptic memorial, Behrens begins to query her fellow townspeople in an attempt to reconstruct the story of Arthur Mayer's life and death, a project that Leslie Morris and Karen Remmler

---

[1] "Dr. Arthur Mayer — Ruhe. Geboren 20.1.88, gestorben in Auschwitz. Wir gedenken seiner stellvertretend für alle Menschen, die aus politischen, rassischen oder religiösen Gründen ihr Leben lassen mussten. Die Bürger der Gemeinde S" (Behrens, "Das Schweigen," 68–69).

term a "detective story" (11). In particular, she endeavors to fill in the discursive gaps in the text of the memorial by trying to engage in dialogue with the townspeople who still remember him in order to create a biographical document of his existence. As she optimistically says at the beginning of her text, "I think there are still people who knew him. I could try to bring him back to life with words" (35).[2] Behrens's text chronicles the narrator's twofold quest: to locate the missing or forgotten details of one man's existence, and to transform these facts and anecdotes into a biographical narrative that will rescue his memory from the arcane opacity of the monument by restoring the individuality of both his life and his death.

In a similar fashion, the beginning of Patrick Modiano's 1997 novella *Dora Bruder* (English translation 1999) describes the autobiographical narrator's discovery of an advertisement in a December 1941 issue of the newspaper *Paris-Soir* that reads: "Missing, a young girl, Dora Bruder, age 15, height 1 meter 55, oval-shaped face, gray-brown eyes, gray sports jacket, maroon pullover, navy blue skirt and hat, brown gym shoes. Address all information to M. and Mme Bruder, 41 Boulevard Ornano, Paris" (3). The narrator becomes fascinated by this report of a girl with what appears to be a Jewish name reported as missing from a convent during one of the most brutal winters of the Occupation, during which the notorious roundups of French Jews were taking place. After investigating further, he learns that Dora Bruder was interned at the French transit camp Drancy in August 1942 and then in September was deported to Auschwitz, where she perished. Modiano becomes increasingly preoccupied with documenting the story behind the brief announcement, and over the course of the next eight years he attempts to reconstruct in particular the months between the time she went missing (he later learns that she ran away from the Catholic boarding school to which her parents had sent her less than a year before) and the time of her arrest. Like Behrens, he endeavors to fill in the gaps left by the sparse text; however, unlike in the case of Arthur Mayer, who is well remembered in the small town of S almost half a century after his death, there is almost no one remaining in Paris who can testify to the memory of Dora Bruder. Modiano thus redirects his inquiry into the past away from personal memory and instead focuses on the documents that organize Dora's legal and bureaucratic existence and on the Paris streets that function as the setting of her last months, an endeavor that Geoffrey Hartman, in echoes of Morris and Remmler's assessment of "Arthur Mayer," likens to a "detective story" (Meyers, Martin, and O'Brien, 115). As in Behrens's text, the narrator here is optimistic about his biographical detective work:

---

[2] "ich denke, es gibt ja noch Leute, die ihn kannten. Ich könnte versuchen, ihn mit Worten lebendig zu machen" (Behrens, "Das Schweigen," 70).

It takes time for what has been erased to resurface. Traces survive in registers, and nobody knows where these registers are hidden, and who has custody of them, and whether or not these custodians are willing to let you see them. Or perhaps they have quite simply forgotten that these registers exist.

All it takes is a little patience. (9)

Just as Behrens sets out to reconstruct the missing story behind the monument, the narrator in Modiano's text attempts to work back from the newspaper announcement in order retrace Dora's movements during her last months in Paris. However, whereas Behrens attempts to document Arthur's life by asking her neighbors to recount their memories of Arthur, Modiano must rely on the archives to speak in the place of those who once knew Dora.

Unknown Missing Persons

Like Art Spiegelman's *Maus,* which is not only the story of a Holocaust survivor but also an account of the artist's attempt to recover and shape that story, Katja Behrens's and Patrick Modiano's narratives both recount the difficulties of piecing together individual stories of the Holocaust, one generation removed. Their texts are particularly compelling because, although both authors are members of what we generally refer to as the second generation, neither author has any personal connection to Arthur Mayer or Dora Bruder. Despite their own biographical connection to the Holocaust, the main focus of their respective documentary projects, unlike that of many second-generation writers, is not the wartime and Holocaust experience of their own parents (although Modiano does briefly refer to the parallels between his father's experience and that of Dora Bruder). Rather, both writers choose to reconstruct the histories of unknown missing persons who perished in the Holocaust. For this reason, their texts veer slightly from a strict definition of second-generation Holocaust literature and are perhaps more appropriately classified under the rubric of postmemory, which Marianne Hirsch has characterized as "an identification with the victim or witness of trauma, modulated by the unbridgeable distance that separates the participant from the one born after" ("Surviving Images," 10), a description that goes beyond the second generation's biographical relationship to the Holocaust to include the identification with and adoption of Holocaust trauma by parties who have may no personal connection to the Holocaust at all. As I discuss in the introduction and chapter 1, postmemory is fundamentally defined by displacement, vicariousness, and belatedness, in which the original experience of trauma cannot be accessed by personal memory, but is always mediated through representation and imagination. In this way, because of their struggle with displaced trauma, all of the texts discussed in this book can be described as postmemorial; Behrens's and Modiano's texts represent a further form of displacement in which the stories of the unknown title characters exist in tension with and become signifiers for the unevoked stories of the authors' parents.

In addition to a driving desire to reconstruct the lives of unknown victims of the Holocaust (figures who, in both books, function as metonymies for the erasure of whole communities), Modiano's and Behrens's narratives have a number of further aspects in common. Chief among these is both the deployment of imagination, whereby the narrators highlight the speculative nature of their projects by repeating, almost as a litany, phrases such as "I imagine," "I wonder," and "I have a feeling," and at the same time emphasize the inability of the imagination to restore the lost information. Furthermore, because the genre of detective story requires the collection and analysis of different types of evidence, the two narratives contain a number of intertexts, including bureaucratic documents produced by the German and French police that are both reprinted and, in the case of Arthur's Auschwitz file, visually reproduced; reproductions of photographs; passages from other literary texts and from personal letters; citations from contemporary anti-Semitic flyers; and, in the case of *Dora Bruder,* reproduced maps of Paris.[3] Moreover, both texts alternate between focusing on the past lives of the objects of their investigation and on the contemporary lives of their narrators, revealing the extent to which the narrators themselves are slowly changed by both the process of writing about the traumatic experiences of another and the considerable setbacks they encounter as they attempt to document the existence of two people whose lives have been effectively effaced from postwar memory.

From "Perfect Memory" to "Poor Memory"

For her part, Behrens must contend with the stubborn and often threatening refusal of the townspeople to talk with her about the town's Nazi past, a hostility in which their "perfect memory" (35)[4] for remembering their prewar lives and their own suffering during the war suddenly becomes "a poor memory" (36)[5] when it comes to the disappearance of the town's Jewish citizens. The silence to which the title of the story refers is selective; while the townspeople are happy to discuss Arthur Mayer's abilities as a doctor and

---

[3] The two maps and four photographs in the 1999 English translation are not found in Modiano's original 1997 text in French. I thus refer only to the English edition when discussing these elements of the text.

[4] "Tadelloses Gedächtnis" (Behrens, "Das Schweigen," 71).

[5] "ein schlechtes Gedächtnis" (Behrens, "Das Schweigen," 72).

his generosity as one of the town's leading citizens, they quickly become reticent when her questions turn to the years after the Nazi ascendance to political power. The citizens of S thus discursively cordon off the years under the Nazi regime with a wall of mute obstinacy; as the non-Jewish wife of Willi Goldschmidt, a Jewish survivor of Auschwitz, demonstrates when she refuses to allow him to speak to the narrator, "That was fifty years ago. It's all forgotten and over" (56).[6]

As the narrator comes to learn, this careful discursive containment is controlled by a certain "Herr C," a retired teacher who, as the self-proclaimed "expert on Jews" (43),[7] has organized an exhibit and is writing a book about the town's former Jewish population. However, at the opening of the exhibit, which is held on the fiftieth anniversary of *Kristallnacht*, the narrator is disturbed by both the role Herr C expects her to play at the event and the way in which the exhibit characterizes the sudden disappearance of the Jews:

> When I entered the hall, I was met by a tall, good-looking elderly gentleman, who extended his hand.
> I'm particularly glad to greet *you*.
> Since we didn't know each other, I presumed what he meant was that a Jewish woman was an adornment for his exhibit. Still chatting, he led me around. I was somewhat confused. The photos, the letters from survivors to Mr. C, all gave the impression that sometime, *somehow*, a natural catastrophe had befallen the Jews. (36)[8]

The narrator confides to Herr C her intention to document the life of Arthur Mayer, but rather than giving her help, he considers her project dangerous competition, especially because her questions attempt to puncture his carefully constructed image of the "natural catastrophe," a terrible disaster in which there were no human perpetrators and therefore no uncomfortable questions as to who, specifically, was culpable (a characterization that, in its vagueness, echoes the text of the monument). Moreover, because of Herr C's refusal to identify or even admit the existence of the responsible actors in

---

[6] "Das ist fünfzig Jahre her. Das ist doch vergessen und vorbei" (Behrens, "Das Schweigen," 113).

[7] "Judenfachmann" (Behrens, "Das Schweigen," 86).

[8] "Als ich den Raum betrat, kam ein großer, gutaussehender älterer Mann auf mich zu, streckte mir die Hand entgegen. *Sie* begrüße ich hier besonders gern. Da wir uns nicht kannten, nahm ich an, er meinte, eine Jüdin schmücke seine Ausstellung. Plaudernd führte er mich umher. Ich war etwas verwirrt. Die Fotos, die Briefe von Überlebenden an Herrn C, alles erweckte den Eindruck, als sei irgendwann *irgendwie* eine Naturkatastrophe über die Juden hereingebrochen" (Behrens, "Das Schweigen," 72–73).

the town's persecution of the Jews and his discretion with "intimate things" (44),[9] namely their incriminating secrets, the citizens of the town (including the town council) invest their full trust in him, granting him "a monopoly on Jews" (43).[10] For this reason, not only does Herr C enjoy exclusive access to the town archives, including records pertaining to the current owners of confiscated Jewish property, but he is also the person to whom almost all of the townspeople refer the narrator once she begins to ask delicate questions. Her quest thus continually loops back to Herr C, who in turn continually refuses to help her discover anything beyond "mere facts, [. . .] what is known anyway" (44).[11] According to Petra S. Fiero, Herr C functions in the town of S, on the one hand, to allow public acknowledgement of the obvious disappearance of the town's Jewish citizens during the Nazi years (and thus to evade the potential accusation that the town has completely forgotten this era), and on the other, to minimize opportunity for both general self-recrimination and accusations against specific individuals:

> With the word "trust" [. . .], Herr C means rather the "conspiracy" of the people of Schönberg to prevent the *whole* truth from coming to light. Herr C symbolizes the type of philo-Semite who curries favor with Jews; who acts as if he's interested in their history, when in reality he wants, through his "monopoly in the matter of Jews," to guarantee that the history of the Jews is written by non-Jews. In this way, he is able to stamp *his* interpretation, *his* mark on the facts, and moreover can proceed so selectively with the examination of materials that he is thus able to protect his fellow citizens.[12]

As the vigilant gatekeeper to the town's Jewish history (or, as the townspeople call him, the "Jew king" [52][13]), Herr C is able to retain careful control over the official narrative of both the onetime existence and the violent eradication of the Jewish population. The narrator threatens the coherence of that narrative with the very questions she poses. Despite the

---

[9] "intime Dinge" (Behrens, "Das Schweigen," 88).

[10] "das Judenmonopol" (Behrens, "Das Schweigen," 87).

[11] "die reine Information [. . .], was man sowieso weiß" (Behrens, "Das Schweigen," 88).

[12] "Mit dem Wort 'Vertrauen' [. . .], meint Herr C. wohl eher 'Verschwörung' der Schönberger, die *ganze* Wahrheit nicht ans Licht kommen zu lassen. Herr C. symbolisiert den Typus des Philosemiten, der sich an Juden anbiedert, so tut, als interessiere er sich für deren Geschichte, in Wahrheit aber durch sein 'Monopol in Sachen Juden' sicherstellen will, daß die Geschichte der Juden von Nichtjuden geschrieben wird, da er so *seine* Interpretation, *seinen* Stempel den Tatsachen aufdrücken kann und außerdem so selektiv bei der Sichtung des Materials vorgehen kann, daß er damit seine Mitbürger schützen kann" (Fiero, 148).

[13] "Juddekönig" (Behrens, "Das Schweigen," 105).

considerable resistance on the part of Herr C and his cohort (and despite the suddenly frequent appearance of threatening right-wing, anti-Semitic literature in her mailbox), however, she continues to insist on breaking through the town's selective silence, and her documentary project becomes an obsessive quest from whose grip she is unable to loosen herself; she soon finds herself aggressively confronting her neighbors in the stores and on the streets. As she states midway through her inquiry, "I am no longer the same person I was at the beginning of my investigation. Now I take the bull by the horns with questions I wouldn't have dared ask a few weeks before" (57).[14]

"This Mute Block of the Unknown"

Whereas the narrator in Behrens's story struggles against the town's carefully controlled discourse about its former Jewish citizens, which, as she discovers, contains an oppressive silence about the violence inflicted on them, the narrator in *Dora Bruder* must contend with a different sort of memorial effacement. Just as Behrens begins her quest for the memory of Dr. Mayer by questioning the people who knew him, Modiano commences his investigation by searching for clues of her existence, both legally, as a citizen, and physically, as a body who occupied the Paris cityscape. He starts by making the rounds of the Paris municipal registries in order that he might reconstruct her life before the war as well as retrace her bureaucratic transit through the French and Nazi police network. But, as he tells us, his progress is painfully slow and the results meager: "It took me four years to discover her exact date of birth: 25 February 1926. And a further two years to find out her place of birth: Paris, 12th arrondissement" (10). He also finds that, although he is able to discover the most rudimentary facts about Dora's family — such as the fact that her father, born in Vienna, came to France after a stint with the Foreign Legion — their marginalized existence as working class immigrants, especially in the period before the Occupation, went largely unrecorded: "They are the sort of people who leave few traces. Virtually anonymous [. . .] Often, what I know about them amounts to no more than a simple address. And such topographical precision contrasts with what we shall never know about their life — this blank, this mute block of the unknown" (20). With regard to the war years, however, the narrator comes to realize that the absence of documents is not merely a matter of the Bruders' relative anonymity in Parisian social life. On the contrary, he discovers that, during this time, the French bureaucracy suddenly began to take notice of its

---

[14] "Ich bin nicht mehr dieselbe wie zu Beginn meiner Nachforschungen. Jetzt trete ich mit Fragen, die ich vor ein paar Wochen nicht zu fragen gewagt hätte, die Flucht nach vorn an" (Behrens, "Das Schweigen," 115).

marginalized Jewish residents, requiring them to register their families at police stations (indeed, it is from these registry documents that Modiano learns of Ernst Bruder's service as a Legionnaire). However, Modiano finds that most of the documents that recorded the registration, arrest, and deportation of the Jews have been destroyed, either as a matter of routine ("No doubt local police stations destroy documents of that kind as they become obsolete" [62–63]), or, as he implies, more likely, to erase the complicity of the French police: "Also dead [. . .] are the street police, known to us as the 'press-gang,' who signed the transcript of every interview with those whom they arrested during the roundups. Every one of those tens of thousands of transcripts was destroyed, and we shall never know the identity of the 'press-gang'" (69).

Unable to reconstruct Dora's life solely from the archives, the narrator looks to the physical environment in which Dora lived. He studies old maps of Paris in order to determine where Dora resided and the precise streets in which she walked to travel from school to home to the cinema. In an attempt to make "the link between Paris then and Paris now" (41), he puts on the shoes of the *flâneur* and walks through the city, identifying the buildings in which she was housed and, in particular, the sites of her arrest and deportation. He hopes to thus create an intuitive connection to Dora's existence, to glean a sort of spatial knowledge of her life by literally walking in her footsteps (39). However, in this endeavor as well, he confronts an environment that is all but purged of traces of the Holocaust, for like the documents he seeks, which have largely been destroyed in a postwar attempt to conceal French collaboration in the deportation of the Jews, the physical landscape has been altered in such a way that the memory of the violence has been effectively paved over. As the narrator comments in response to his visit to the old Jewish quarter,

> Once again, I had a sense of emptiness. And I understood why. After the war, most buildings in the area had been pulled down, methodically, in accordance with a government plan [. . .] And here, on this wasteland, they have put up row upon row of houses, altering the course of an old street in the process.
>
> The facades are rectangular, the windows square, the concrete the color of amnesia [. . .] They have obliterated everything in order to build a sort of Swiss village in order that nobody, ever again, would question its neutrality. (112–13)

The narrator thus interprets what otherwise might be considered the fairly organic (if bureaucratically planned) process of urban decay and renewal as a sinister design to obliterate the sites of Jewish prewar existence and thus to cover up French participation in the genocide of the Jews. Rather than achieving a greater comprehension of Dora's story by obtaining a sense of her spatial presence in Paris, he can only experience a certain "sense of emptiness that comes with the knowledge of what has been destroyed, razed to the ground" (29). Despite his years of careful detective work, Modiano is only able to produce a few random, disconnected details of the life and death of Dora and her family, for the very environment in which Dora lived resists his attempts to reconstruct her last months there.

Buried Secrets

In the cases of both Dora Bruder and Arthur Mayer, the narrators simply do not learn enough about the lives of their subjects to produce coherent narratives. Rather than rescuing their memory from oblivion by documenting the story of their deaths, the narrators can only write of their own failure to produce this story. In this way, the dominant narrative that emerges in both texts is one not of biographical presence but of overwhelming absence. At the heart of both texts is the resistance the narrators encounter while attempting to uncover secrets, but whereas for Behrens the "life-threatening secret" (38)[15] is concealed in the townspeople's discourse and their obstinate silence on the subjects of their former Jewish neighbors and their own wartime activities, for Modiano, Dora's "poor and precious secret" (119) is buried not only in the bureaucratic archives of Paris but also in the very urban environment in which she once lived. Because of these impediments, the promise of documentary evidence that at first encouraged both narrators is borne out in neither case, and Modiano's and Behrens's books thus become more a response to the post-Holocaust erasure of memory and the ultimate impossibility of recovering the personal details of an individual life, and less reconstructed biographies of the lives of Arthur Mayer and Dora Bruder.

Because they fail in their attempt to bring their subjects "back to life with words," Behrens and Modiano must either abandon their proposed biographical projects or find another viable narrative form through which they tell both the absent stories of their missing protagonists and their own stories of documentary failure. In order to highlight the disconnect between their intended endeavors and the discursive and documentary resistance they encounter, both texts utilize postmemorial narrative strategies of textual documentation that resemble what are best described as encyclopedic genres, such as the lexicon and the atlas. By employing reference forms that explicitly endorse the idea that knowledge can be collected and synthesized into an accurate representation of empirical reality, the two writers mark the gap between the ideal biographical project, which attempts to create a virtually seamless depiction of an individual's life, and the meager collection of un-

---

[15] "ein lebensbedrohendes Geheimnis" (Behrens, "Das Schweigen," 76).

connected and often irrelevant facts they manage to assemble. Modiano and Behrens press their flawed and fragmented narratives into generic molds that connote certainty and veracity, yet rather than endowing the stories of their subjects with a sense of biographical integrity and authority, the resulting forms ironically underscore the absence of reliable knowledge about them and reveal skepticism about the quest of reconstructing the lives of forgotten Holocaust victims in a world that insists on forgetting them. At the same time, however, because of their refusal to leave these stories of memorial effacement unwritten, choosing instead to secure them in the unlikely form of reference texts, the narrators are able to paradoxically rescue Arthur Mayer and Dora Bruder from collective oblivion and write them back into history.

Lexicon of Silence

In "Arthur Mayer, or The Silence," Behrens creates a lexicon of German resistance to the uncovering of the Holocaust past by taking the disordered, episodic, and, above all, failed encounters with her fellow townspeople and organizing them alphabetically in numbered sections. The characters in her narrative are denied individual names; rather, each person she encounters is represented by a different letter of the alphabet and an option of names. The first entry of the story thus describes the narrator's conversation with a certain "Mr. A, as in Anders or Anhalt" (33),[16] who tells her of the monument to Arthur Mayer, and the narrative proceeds alphabetically through the characters she encounters, ending with the newspaper editor "Mr. Z, as in Ziegler or Zeiler" (76),[17] who lectures the narrator that the town's hostile silence about the Holocaust must be respected. The alphabetic figures in the story possess no fixed name, for in most cases, as in the examples above, the respective letter is followed by "as in" along with two example last names. The text thus displaces the idea of a fixed identity, suggesting that the narrator is not dealing with the idiosyncratic attitudes of a few individuals but rather with a pattern of silence and evasion indicative of the town in general. As the "as in" reminds us, the people with whom the narrator speaks could be any ordinary Germans. Moreover, the names the narrator employs suggest a number of meanings relevant to her struggle to uncover the town's past. Many are common German words and names — Fischer (fisher), Gärtner (gardener), Stein (stone) — or possess German literary meaning — Faust, Grimm, Hoffmann — underscoring the notion that the town is a microcosm of both ordinary and higher German culture. However, the text employs not just names that represent the benign side of German culture, an

---

[16] "Herr A wie Anders oder Anhalt" (Behrens, "Das Schweigen," 67).
[17] "Herrn Z wie Ziegler oder Zeiler" (Behrens, "Das Schweigen," 151).

image that the town carefully cultivates; several of the names evoke the period about which the townspeople are silent, either through reference to Nazi history — Brauner (suggesting the SA, known as the Browns) and Sturm (reminiscent of the anti-Semitic Nazi organ, *Der Stürmer*) — or by their often violent discursive associations — Anders (other/different), Jäger (hunter). Moreover, a number of the names also connote Jewishness, either directly, as with "Mr. D, as in Daniel or David, my fellow Jew in Schönberg" (41),[18] or indirectly, with names that are Germanic (and in the text refer to non-Jews) but are also often Ashkenazic family names (Stein, Veit).[19] The text reminds us with its employment of such ambiguous names that, even if the notion of a one-time German-Jewish symbiosis is largely a myth, the history of Jews in Germany was not only one of separation and otherness. Furthermore, in contrast to the figures to whom she gives two names along with the "as in," the narrator designates the few people who attempt to help her with her inquiry by their first names and an alphabetic letter (Hilde T), a gesture that designates a certain intimacy that is juxtaposed with the distance and hostility she experiences with the other characters. However, the people with whom she is on a first-name basis are few, and here, too, the names are both truncated and integrated within the alphabetical logic of the narrative, suggesting that these characters, despite their willingness to help, are implicated as well in the town's general silence about its sinister past. Finally, in a moment of frustration at the town's refusal to discuss or identify the people responsible for the deportation and murder of the town's Jews (or, just as important, those who took possession of their property after they were gone), the narrator invents a new figure in the story — "N, as in nobody" (61)[20] — to designate the unidentified perpetrators. "Nobody" thus functions as an additional character in the text, one upon whom the responsibility and culpability the townspeople refuse to assume is displaced.

Because of the text's narrative strategy of providing the townspeople with either provisional or truncated names, the presence of the actual full name of Arthur Mayer is all the more noticeable. Indeed, the only people whom the text designates with full names are the Jewish citizens who were deported from the town, including Arthur Mayer, Willi Goldschmitt, and a list of citizens who perished in camps and ghettos (59),[21] suggesting that

[18] "Herr D wie Daniel oder David, mein Schönberger Mitjude" (Behrens, "Das Schweigen," 83).

[19] When I taught this text in English to my students in Jewish Studies, several assumed that many of the names in the text were Jewish and were thus confused by the characters' reactions to the narrator's inquiries.

[20] "N wie Niemand" (Behrens, "Das Schweigen," 123).

[21] Behrens, "Das Schweigen," 118.

while the non-Jewish townspeople were able to evade their identities as perpetrators and collaborators, the Jewish victims of the Nazis could not escape the fated planned for them. The text insists on them as real, historical persons, refusing on the one hand to fictionalize them (and thus to run the risk of falling into the hands of the anonymous authors of the anti-Semitic leaflets who accuse the narrator of "lies and untruths" [68][22]), or on the other hand to universalize their existence with imaginary or vague "everyman" names that would rob them of their individuality. The stark contrast between the two narrative systems of naming — on the one side, the insistence on the names of the historical victims of the Holocaust, and, on the other, the slippery displacement and elision of the names of the perpetrators and bystanders — thus highlights the disparity between Jewish memory of that period of the town's history and its German counterpart.

The narrator extends her system of identifying the town's citizens to the town itself, designating it simply as "S, as in Schönberg or Schwarzdorf" (34).[23] In this way, the text suggests that, just as the townspeople could be any ordinary Germans, the town itself is but one of a multitude of similar towns throughout Germany, functioning as a microcosm of daily life during the Third Reich and a metonymy for an entire country that endeavored to rid itself of its Jewish population (and, of course, that of its neighbors as well). However, in the case of the town's name, the careful reader of the text will notice that Behrens violates her own strategy of anonymous alphabetization with her reproduction of Arthur Mayer's Auschwitz file, which, in its neatly typewritten bureaucratic text, clearly names Seeheim, the actual town in which Behrens lives, as his birthplace. This moment of textual disclosure authenticates Behrens's narrative as an actual encounter in contemporary German discourse on the Holocaust and challenges the contention of her local anti-Semitic detractors that she writes lies and fictions. Moreover, her latent revelation of the town's real name functions as a counterpart to her lexical strategy of eliding the names of the individual townspeople, highlighting the fact that, while she is unable to assign culpability to specific people and must thus resort to encyclopedic types to depict them, she is unambiguously able to identify the role of the town itself not only in the story of Arthur Mayer's death, but also in the collective effacement of that story. In this way, though her narrative documents mainly her failure to puncture the town's silence about Arthur Mayer and to write a biography of his life, it also partially resists that silence and manages nevertheless to produce a text about him, however fragmented.

---

[22] "Lügen und Unwahrheiten" (Behrens, "Das Schweigen," 136).

[23] "S wie Schönberg or Schwarzdorf" (Behrens, "Das Schweigen," 69).

Atlas of Absence

Modiano, as we have seen, recounts a similar tale of failed biography. However, in contrast to Behrens, who creates a lexicon of silence in which the story of Arthur Mayer is eclipsed by a town's denial of the Holocaust that runs the gamut from A to Z, Modiano adopts a different reference genre to tell of the obscure fate of Dora Bruder. Just as Behrens finds that Arthur's story is concealed in the discourse of the townspeople, from which she hopes to extract a few clues about his life, Modiano believes that Dora's destiny is "inseparable from those Paris streets, those suburban landscapes" (20), and thus he develops a sort of narrative atlas in which he attempts to reconstruct her final months in the streets of wartime Paris by obsessively tracing her movements in present-day Paris. In a gesture of postmemorial cartography, he superimposes the cityscape of the present onto that of the past, exposing the ways in which the past is covered over and forgotten. Modiano's literary atlas includes a number of narrative strategies, chief of which are the two reproduced maps of the 12th and 18th arrondissements in Paris that he inserts at the beginning of the narrative. By looking at these maps, the reader is able to locate the numerous buildings that housed Dora's existence, track her movements as a runaway through the streets of Paris, and most of all imagine a concrete geographical existence for a person whose traces in the bureaucratic register are close to nonexistent. These maps are supported by Modiano's own narrative cartography, in which he takes the reader on a journey through Paris with his obsessive descriptions of house and street, district and neighborhood. Modiano's narrative travels are not only intended to supplement the faint trace of Dora's bureaucratic existence; he uses them as well to highlight the tenuous nature of the memory of her life, for while it is undeniable that she was there, this is something that cannot be verified by the documentary record: "It is said that premises retain some stamp, however faint, of their previous inhabitants. Stamp: an imprint, hollow or in relief. Hollow, I should say, in the case of Ernest and Cécile Bruder, of Dora. I have a sense of absence, of emptiness, whenever I find myself in a place where they have lived" (21). Modiano attempts not only to locate in space the people who in the past were undeniably present but who left few physical traces, but also to mediate that radical sense of absence in the present day. Thus, while his atlas concentrates primarily on the space in which Dora moved and lived, the element of temporality is also critical for the form he creates, for the essential difference between the Paris streets in which he presently walks and those in which Dora fled in fear or in excitement is one of time. Modiano continually reminds himself of the interval between Dora's actions and his attempt to reconstruct those actions:

> I'm writing these pages in November 1996 [...] Tomorrow we shall be in December, and fifty-five years will have passed since Dora ran away [...] I feel as though I am alone in making the link between Paris then and Paris now, alone in remembering all these details. There are moments when the link is strained and in danger of snapping, and other evenings when the city of yesterday appears to me in fleeting gleams behind that of today. (40–41)

For Modiano, the difference "between Paris then and Paris now" is not merely the objective temporal distance between the biographer and his subject; rather, he feels that the space of Paris connects him profoundly and intimately to Dora, and he attempts to make this link manifest in different layers of time. He repeatedly highlights the connections between Dora's life and his own experiences (such as his own endeavor to run away as a teenager), as well as between Dora's wartime actions and those of his father, who, as an alien Jewish black-marketeer, lived the same sort of underground existence as Dora before her arrest and deportation. These multiple autobiographical and biographical experiences exist for Modiano on a temporal continuum in a fixed point in space; therefore, as he tracks Dora Bruder's journeys through the Paris streets, he not only registers her movements intellectually but also senses her presence palpably and personally. He even retroactively assigns his own meandering walks in certain neighborhoods long ago, before he knew of Dora, to an unconscious but profound compulsion to literally walk in her footsteps:

> In 1965, I knew nothing of Dora Bruder. But now, thirty years on, it seems to me that those long waits in the cafés at the Ornano crossroads, those unvarying itineraries [...] all that was not simply due to chance. Perhaps, though not yet fully aware of it, I was following the traces of Dora Bruder and her parents. Already, below the surface, they were there. (6)

In reconstructing Dora's story, the narrator simultaneously relates the story of his own feeling of connection to her existence, not only intuitively, through a second-generation sense of solidarity, but physically, as an unmistakable bond between bodies in space and through time. His method of narrative cartography thus encompasses much more than an attempt to simply map out where she spent her last months; in good postmemorial fashion it emphasizes the ways in which the landscape of the present still suffers from the scars of the past. By locating himself in Dora's environment, Modiano writes himself into her story and tries to narrow the conceptual gap between the living and the dead, insisting that, although evidence of Dora's struggle in Paris is all but non-existent, it can be made manifest for the reader by the joint exercise of memory and imagination. In this way, despite the nearly total resistance to the reconstruction of her life he encounters in the archives,

Modiano is nevertheless able to recover Dora's memory by writing her into his text as a real body on the street. Moreover, this act of cartographic imagination of the past transforms Modiano's present, just as Dora's retroactive reinscription in the Parisian landscape of the past alters its contemporary manifestation. By the end of narrative, he remarks that, despite the fact that he will "never know how she spent her days" (119), his awareness of her existence, along with his unanswered questions, will forever mark the environment in which he lives:

> Ever since, the Paris wherein I have tried to retrace her steps has remained as silent and deserted as it was on that day [the day after Dora's transport left for Auschwitz]. I walk through empty streets. For me, they are always empty, even at dusk, during the rush hour, when the crowds are hurrying toward the mouths of the métro. I think of her in spite of myself, sensing an echo of her presence in this neighborhood or that. (119)

Postmemorial Lexica and Atlases

Katja Behrens and Patrick Modiano have thus created two texts that, because of a postwar silencing of memory of those who were murdered in the Holocaust and a contemporary refusal on the part of their former neighbors to revive their memory, are unable to narrate the biographies of their title characters. The narrators' investigation and attempt to record the lives of Dora Bruder and Arthur Mayer document rather the profound indifference and even resistance to their memory in the places in which they lived. Modiano's narrative mapping of Dora's Parisian environment is analogous to Behrens's lexicon of the townspeople's denial about and hostility to her questions about Arthur; both encyclopedic forms chronicle the narrators' endeavors to collect information about real people who once existed in time and space. However, in contrast to conventional reference genres, which attempt to organize and authoritatively communicate knowledge, the atlas and the lexicon in this case convey a radical absence of knowledge. The precise, organized structure of these texts contrasts with the loose uncertainty of what is known about their protagonists and emphasizes the authors' inability to fully recover their memory and create conventional biographies of them. Modiano's and Behrens's narrative strategies of lexicalization and cartography thus produce postmemorial genres that not only highlight the problematics of documentary projects but also, at the same time, embody a narrative that memorializes, however inadequately, their protagonists.

Part II. The Legacy of Perpetration

5: "Under a False Name": Peter Schneider's *Vati* and the Misnomer of Genre

Without his desire and knowledge, in a weaker form, he imitated the nature of his father.
— Christoph Meckel, *Suchbild: Über meinen Vater*
("Picture Puzzle: About My Father")[1]

Born Guilty

PETER SCHNEIDER'S 1987 NARRATIVE *Vati* ("Daddy") tells the story of the relationship between a notorious Nazi, in hiding to escape prosecution for atrocities he committed as a concentration camp doctor, and his adult son, who in the late 1970s secretly travels to Brazil to meet his father for the first time since his infancy. Written as a sort of letter from the son (who, like his father, remains unnamed in the story) to a childhood friend, the narrative documents the son's attempt to get to know his father and his struggle to come to terms with his father's culpability in the perpetration of the Holocaust. As the narrator-son endeavors to make clear to his friend, his father's legacy is not simply a matter of involvement in an event that lies in the past and is therefore no longer of relevance to the son's life. Rather, the son perceives his relationship to his father's crimes as an inheritance of both biblical proportion and genetic character that is fundamental to his own identity. Despite the fact that, as a child, he was unaware of both the existence of his father and the crimes of which he was accused, and thus was innocent in that he neither could be implicated in nor had any knowledge of his father's violation, he nevertheless felt a vague sense of culpability for an unknown transgression. As he explains to his friend, even as an innocent schoolboy, he felt somehow tainted by his father's past, a secret that he was unable to interpret:

> Later on, in high school, I noticed that I carried the secret around with me like an inscription on my forehead that everyone but me could decipher. As if I were stricken by a deadly illness that one would rather conceal from the patient. Some stain — invisible to me — seemed to cling to me — but how did you all recognize it? Was it an

---

[1] "Ohne sein Wollen und Wissen, in schwächerer Form, imitierte er die Wesensart seines Vaters" (Meckel, 18).

odor, my way of speaking, my clothing, a facial twitch? Over and over I observed myself in the mirror, I turned around and around, I sought the stigma and didn't find it. For years I felt like the class fool who goes to the chalkboard and doesn't notice that someone has fastened a condom to his back.[2]

The child perceives that he carries a physical mark of difference that distinguishes him from the rest of his classmates, something that is almost congenital in its origin, for it has always been with him, an essence that, like an odor, emanates from his body. However, though he is keenly aware of the fact that he is singled out by his secret branding, despite obsessive scrutiny he is unable to locate the actual signifier of his distinction either within his body or without. Furthermore, not only is he ignorant as to the location and form of his identifying mark, but he is also at a loss for its significance, for the mark is not his own scar of experience, but rather one that indicates an experience that he cannot access — indeed, that he is unable to even name. He is thus conscious of being caught in a powerful web of signification, one that points to his inherent difference, despite the fact that he can determine neither signifier nor referent. He likens his condition to being marked by a sort of writing on the forehead, a script that is legible to everyone but himself, a story that determines his identity but that he himself cannot read. Colin Riordan has identified the script on the forehead as an allusion to the mark of Cain (81), which, as discussed in the introduction, is a biblical signifier for the perpetual, irresolvable guilt of the murderer. With the image of Cain's mark, the narrator thus alludes to a discourse of guilt in which he is already inscribed, a story of perpetration and continually deferred punishment that is written on his body for everyone to read and understand but that remains indecipherable to him. However, unlike Cain, who not only knows the significance of his marking but is also forever bound to his crime by his stigma, the narrator is marked for a crime of which he is not only innocent but ignorant as well. Like an inherited genetic trait, the ever-present but incomprehensible stigma of the father's crime is bequeathed to the son, who is thus born into a state of guilt that is powerfully sensed but whose

---

[2] "Später dann, im Gymnasium, merkte ich, daß ich das Geheimnis mit mir herumtrug wie eine Schrift auf der Stirn, die jeder außer mir selber entziffern konnte. Als wäre ich von einer jener tödlichen Krankheiten befallen, die man dem Patienten lieber verschweigt. Irgendein mir selber nicht sichtbarer Makel schien an mir zu haften — aber woran habt ihr ihn erkannt? War es ein Geruch, meine Art zu sprechen, die Kleidung, ein Zucken in meinem Gesicht? Immer wieder habe ich mich im Spiegel betrachtet, ich drehte mich um und um, ich suchte den Fehler und fand ihn nicht. Über Jahre habe ich mich gefühlt wie der Klassendepp, der zur Tafel geht und nicht merkt, daß jemand ein Präservativ auf seinem Rücken befestigt hat" (P. Schneider, *Vati*, 12).

meaning eludes him. As the narrator confesses to his friend, "long before I knew it, I sensed that I was born guilty."[3]

"The Belated Attempt to Fill in the Gap"

As indicated by its title, *Vati* is a narrative that focuses on the figure of the father, examining the ways in which the legacy of the Third Reich lives on in the relationship between the Nazi parent and the child who feels stigmatized by his father's crimes. Because of this focus on the parent-child relationship as the locus of inherited guilt, Peter Schneider's text has much in common with the "wave" (Peitsch, 71) of writing that emerged in West German literature during the 1970s and 1980s, marked by a preoccupation with Germany's fascist past.[4] The autobiographical texts associated with this trend explore thematically the legacy of the Nazi past on the most intimate level of transmission — that of the postwar family. An entire generic category, known as *Väterliteratur* (father literature) has been created to describe these texts.[5] In 1981, Michael Schneider (Peter Schneider's brother) became the first critic to identify the phenomenon of father literature as part of a massive postwar generational conflict that began as a political rebellion with the student movement of the late 1960s and only emerged as a literary topos in the late 1970s. Despite problems associated with its limited scope,[6]

---

[3] "Ich spürte lange, bevor ich es wußte, daß ich schuldig geboren war" (P. Schneider, *Vati*, 14).

[4] The metaphors critics use to describe the multitude of texts that explore the fascist past in the family reveal their perception of the books' sudden, violent appearance in German public discourse. In addition to Peitsch's "wave," critics employ a vocabulary of natural disaster such as "flood" ("Sturzflut"; Grimm, 168), "avalanche" (Schlant, 96), and "boom" (Brandstetter, 35).

[5] *Väterliteratur* (father literature) is the term I have chosen from among several to serve as my nominal designation for the genre (as do Bagley, Frühwald, Segebrecht, Moffit, Schlant, Vormweg, Riordan, Klages, and Figge). Other critics have used the terms *Väterbücher* or *Vaterbücher* (father(s) books; Brandstetter, Fröhlich, Peitsch, Segebrecht, Gehrke, Figge, Vormweg, Weigel [*Die Stimme der Medusa*], Snyder Hook, and Moffit), *Väterromane* (father novels; Bagley, Bullivant, and Kenkel), *Vaterbilder* (father portraits; Frühwald, Kenkel, Segebrecht, Vormweg, and Bagley), *Vatergestalten* (father figures; Grimm and Frühwald), *Vaterdarstellungen* (father representations; Gehrke), *Erinnerungsbücher* (memory books; Mayer), *Lebensdarstellungen* (life representations; Grimm), *Elternbücher* (parent books; Grimm and Gehrke).

[6] Reinhold Grimm points out a number of deficiencies in Schneider's essay, including Schneider's limited investigation, his tendency toward "gross simplification" ("grobe Vereinfachung"; 172) and his problematic framing of the conflict in *Väterliteratur* as almost exclusively one between father and son. This third criticism is addressed at length in chapters 6 and 7.

Michael Schneider's essay, "Väter und Söhne, posthum: Das beschädigte Verhältnis zweier Generationen" ("Fathers and Sons, Retrospectively: The Damaged Relationship between Two Generations," 1984), has become the most frequently cited analysis of this genre, providing both a useful vocabulary for reading the works and a basic framework with which later critics have debated the texts, and thus its author can be considered the "father" of the genre *Väterliteratur*.[7]

In his article, Schneider identifies a sudden flood of literary father biographies by authors attempting to excavate the fascist past of their fathers, impelled in part by the West German broadcast of the American television miniseries *Holocaust*.[8] Shown over the course of four evenings in January 1979 to an combined audience of over twenty million viewers (nearly half of the adult population of West Germany), *Holocaust* sparked intense public debate about Germany's past and introduced the term "Holocaust" into everyday German usage, making it a watershed event in German postwar discourse about the genocide of the Jews (Magnus, 223). Despite the indisputable impact of the film on German consciousness, however, Michael Schneider views the timing of this sudden flood of books about the fathers' Nazi past as suspect, not least because most of the books were written after the fathers had died. He considers most of books "obituaries" ("Father and Sons," 4)[9] and asks why the authors did not choose to investigate their fathers' actions during the Nazi period while their fathers were still living, when they might have conducted an interactive conversation with them about the past. In his opinion, the belated character of this attempt to come to terms with the fascist past of the fathers has two critical consequences that doom the sons' project to failure. First, because the fathers themselves left no record of their experiences during the Third Reich, the sons lack both literary models to emulate[10] and detailed accounts that would provide possible explanations for the fathers' activities:

---

[7] In the critical literature on *Väterliteratur*, M. Schneider has been characterized as the "founder" of the genre. Several critics, including Frühwald, Figge, Grimm, Haubl, Kenkel, Segebrecht, Moffit, Riordan, Gehrke, and Schlant, discuss his essay in their work.

[8] M. Schneider's claim that the broadcast of *Holocaust* was the critical impetus for the father texts is misleading. In fact, as Sandra Frieden's list of autobiographical works of the 1960s and 1970s shows, many of the works Schneider mentions (and many he does not) were published before the telecast in 1979.

[9] "Nachrufe" (M. Schneider, "Väter und Söhne," 9).

[10] In this regard, the difference between the situation of the children of perpetrators and that of the children of survivors is striking. Since the perpetrators of the Holocaust, almost without exception, kept silent about their actions during the Holocaust, they bequeathed no texts that might have served as literary models for the second

With few exceptions, the fathers and mothers in question left behind no biographies in which they could have explained to their offspring how it was that they happened to "go along" with or even become actual supporters of National Socialism. Thus, each author had to assume responsibility for the still unsettled questions in the political past of their parents' time and, at the same time, had to make the belated attempt to fill in the gaps in the life histories of their parents. ("Father and Sons," 4)[11]

Second, Michael Schneider views this mass attempt to uncover the fathers' fascist involvement in and subsequent silence about the Nazi period, which he terms a "collective blackout used by the older generation to obliterate its monstrous past" ("Father and Sons," 5),[12] as evidence of a deep-seated conflict between the war generation and their offspring that eventually erupted into the student revolution. In Michael Schneider's opinion, the parents' silence about their role in the Holocaust and the absence of an intergenerational dialogue about the past are not something that can be righted by the sons' literary efforts to excavate the fathers' fascist background and to question their complicity in Nazi crimes. Rather, he implicates the sons for engaging in the dialogue too late and thus precluding any real understanding or reconciliation between the generations: "It takes two to maintain a silence; the one who remains silent, and the one who either doesn't ask questions or who is satisfied with unsatisfactory answers" ("Father and Sons," 5).[13]

Although Michael Schneider himself does not use the term *Väterliteratur* to designate the objects of his study, he does term the project of the father texts "the literary coming-to-terms with the past of the fathers" ("Father and

---

generation. The children of survivors, on the other hand, grew up with an increasingly abundant literature by Holocaust survivors and thus had access to a kind of literary tradition. In this respect, at least, there is a sort of paradoxical continuity on the side of the legacy of survival that is entirely absent on the side of perpetration.

[11] "Von wenigen Ausnahmen abgesehen, haben die Väter und Mütter keine Biographien hinterlassen, in denen sie ihren Nachkommen hätten begreiflich machen können, wie sie zu Mitläufern oder aktiven Vertretern des Nationalsozialismus werden konnten. So mußten jene die noch immer unbeglichenen Wechsel aus der politischen Vergangenheit ihrer Eltern gleichsam übernehmen und versuchen, die eklatanten Lücken in den Lebensläufen ihrer Erzeuger nachträglich auszufüllen" (M. Schneider, "Väter und Söhne," 8–9).

[12] "kollektive[s] Black-Out [. . .], durch das die Väter-Generation ihre monströse Vergangenheit wie ausgelöscht hat" (M. Schneider, "Väter und Söhne," 10).

[13] "denn auch zum Verschweigen gehören zwei: Der eine, der schweigt, und der andere, der nicht gefragt oder sich mit unzureichenden Antworten begnügt hat" (M. Schneider, "Väter und Söhne," 10).

Sons," 4),[14] an attempt on the part of the sons to examine the fascist past of their fathers and to question their involvement in Nazi crimes in order to understand the relationship between history, authoritarian structure, and their own identity. However, although he recognizes the literary character of the biographies of the fathers (and despite his reference to the figure of Hamlet as a model for the second generation and his comparison of the student revolution of 1968 with the *Sturm und Drang* literary movement of the eighteenth century), Michael Schneider does not focus on them as literature *per se* (that is, texts that employ figurative language and various narrative strategies in traversing a particular problem). Rather, he prefers to concentrate on their sociological and psychological content at the expense of their aesthetic and formal aspects. In short, he reads the novels as transparent, self-evident historical documents whose value lies in what they can tell us objectively about the postwar generation's inability to come to terms with the Holocaust past, the relations between that generation and their children, and the current state of German society. While Michael Schneider's method of examining the father texts is certainly a legitimate sociological enterprise, yielding a number of striking observations about the psychopathology of the postwar West German family, as an exercise in literary criticism his reading is inadequate, for his view of autobiographical literature as primarily a window into the social and psychological makeup of both its author and the greater culture thus obscures its literary aspects, such as the dialectical struggle between fiction and historical reality and the ways in which the I is self-consciously staged as a literary figure. This tendency to read *Väterliteratur* as a mere case study of social conditions, a practice found not only in Michael Schneider but in other critics of the genre as well, results in a one-sided interpretation and a reduced understanding of how the texts function as literature. Because of Michael Schneider's prominent influence as the first critic to investigate the phenomenon of *Väterliteratur*, his referential mode of reading the father texts as transparent representations of reality has consequences for subsequent analyses of the texts. Schneider bequeaths his limited perspective to the critical analysis of the genre, which for the most part takes its cue from him, accepting only self-evidently autobiographical prose narratives and excluding other literary forms such as poetry and drama (Grimm, 167). Thus Gisela Moffit defines *Väterliteratur* narrowly as "father memoirs written by sons and daughters of the post-war era who have professional credentials (or have established them through their father book) and who undertook the painful journey to their past" (2). In this way, autobiography is given exclusive rights to the realm of *Väterliteratur*, a critical limitation that has conse-

---

[14] "die literarische Auseinandersetzung mit der Vergangenheit der Väter" (M. Schneider, "Väter und Söhne," 9).

quences for the ways in which father texts that are not straightforwardly autobiographical are received. As we shall see in the case of *Vati*, the equation of *Väterliteratur* with ostensibly referential representations of West German attempts to come to terms with the Holocaust is so entrenched in the critical community that texts that do not meet this criterion, such as fictional depictions of fathers and sons, have often been met with vehement criticism and outright hostility.

Vati — Fiction or *Väterliteratur?*

Peter Schneider's *Vati*, a text that focuses on the attempts by the son of a notorious Nazi to work through and understand his relationship to his father's criminal past, quite consciously aligns itself with the problematics of *Väterliteratur* as outlined by Michael Schneider. However, despite its obvious thematic alignment with the latter's concerns, *Vati* differs from the texts grouped together by him in two critical ways: it is neither the product of Peter Schneider's own autobiographical expression nor a biographical depiction of his father. Rather, Schneider's narrator, a fictional character based on Rolf Mengele, son of the infamous Auschwitz doctor, Josef Mengele, performs the role of the typical autobiographical author of a biography of his father: he writes of his relationship with his father only after the father has died. According to Colin Riordan, the publication of the book was accompanied by a critical firestorm that focused precisely on this fictional aspect of Schneider's narrative.[15] Schneider's assumption of the Mengele story in order to produce a father text outraged critics, who were agitated by his pretense of utilizing the conventions of a genre that so clearly belonged to the category of non-fiction:

> It is possible to read *Vati* as an attempt to represent the issues which Michael Schneider outlined, and to restore some of the deficits which he identified in his essay [. . .] But there is more to it than that: *Vati* differs from other examples of *Väterliteratur* in various crucial respects. Firstly, it is not autobiographical; Peter Schneider is tackling a literary and historical problem, rather than an explicitly personal one [. . .] and secondly, [there is] an implication that fiction is not an appropriate means to deal with a topic such as this [the relationship between the son and the Nazi father] [. . .]
>
> Finally, Schneider has chosen to fictionalise a real case whose facts were known, and it is this which led to widespread misinterpretation. Other books which began for the first time in the late 1980s to exam-

---

[15] More detailed analyses of the controversial critical response to *Vati* can be found in the work of Riordan, Burgess, Morgan, Jensen, Brasch, and Snyder Hook.

ine the fates of the children of Nazis came in for no such condemnation; both Peter Sichrovsky's *Schuldig geboren* (1987) and Dörte von Westernhagen's *Die Kinder der Täter* (1987) are historical, psychological and sociological case studies which make no claim to literary status (although Sichrovsky's book does seem to have recourse to rhetorical devices, if nothing more). It seems, then, that a story which fictionalised real events, written by an author with no autobiographical axe to grind, yet tackling the sensitive issue of the legacy of Auschwitz, aroused inordinate, sometimes emotional reactions in the German press. (Riordan, 26–27)

Riordan documents the strong resistance by the German press to designating *Vati* as *Väterliteratur,* including the accusation by Gerda-Marie Schönfeld in the *Spiegel* that Schneider commits plagiarism by appropriating passages without acknowledgement from a series of interviews with Rolf Mengele published in the German magazine *Bunte*. The virulent denunciation of Schneider's narrative revolves around particular critical assumptions about literary referentiality, namely that literature and history, especially a history as fraught as that of the Holocaust, are incompatible — even mutually exclusive. According to this line of reasoning, texts that make an attempt in good faith to come to terms with the legacy of the Holocaust must approach their topic from a perspective that is as empirically reliable as possible in order to avoid charges of mystification or even fabrication. The more imaginative a text is, the more it may threaten to distort (and thus potentially deny) the history it attempts to depict. Furthermore, critics argue that Schneider does not provide a politically and ethically exemplary method for coming to terms with the Holocaust. Instead, in their opinion, his use of conventional fictional and literary devices to approach the Mengele story, in particular his adoption of an ambivalent first-person perspective akin to that of Rolf Mengele (a voice that, critically, Schneider refuses to identify as belonging to Rolf Mengele), represents nothing less than a depiction in bad faith of an established historical record. However, *Vati*'s alleged distortion of history is for many critics not its only failure, nor even its principal failure. Rather, the more serious shortcoming of Schneider's imaginative rendering of Mengele is that its ambitious, even brazen assumption of its subject matter causes it to fail aesthetically as well. According to Gordon Burgess, Schneider's transgression is not one of plagiarism (a charge that several critics, including Uwe Wittstock, Gabriele Kreis, Peter Morgan, and Birgit A. Jensen have dismissed as over-exaggerated or beside the point), but one, simply put, of writing "bad literature" (116):

> In all his substantial literary works, Schneider has employed fundamentally the same compositional technique: using authentic material in the creation of an imaginative work of art [...] Why, then,

should it have failed him in this case? Why should *Vati* be as aesthetically wanting as the works of pop art with which Schneider took issue in 1966? There are two main reasons, I would suggest, both of which are to be sought outside the text itself. The first lies in the very nature of literature, which is essentially a product of the imagination and claims to be a fictional retelling of reality. *Vati* endeavors to deal imaginatively with the unimaginable, and fictionalizes dreadful fact. In so doing, it is not equal to the subject-matter and as a result trivializes it [...] The second, allied to the first, concerns Schneider himself. *Lenz, ... schon bist du ein Verfassungsfeind,* and *Der Mauerspringer* all deal with themes which Schneider had himself experienced: indeed, they all represent to a greater or lesser degree his coming to terms with problems of his own life: the failure of the student movement, the consequences of the *Radikalenerlaß,* and the problem of being a writer in a divided Berlin, a divided Germany. It is, perhaps, after all in this unfashionable approach of interpreting literature through the biography of the author that the key to Schneider's success and failure as a writer in the 1980s is to be found. (120)[16]

According to Burgess, who approaches *Vati* from the perspective of a "literary critic" (115), not a historian, Schneider, with his earlier works, is able to successfully synthesize the competing claims of history and aesthetics. It is only with *Vati* that he fails to transform history into a work of literature, a failure that Burgess attributes to Schneider's lack of autobiographical authority over the events he depicts. Aside from implicitly positing in this statement a definition of literature that factors the literary value of texts according to the degree of their biographical veracity (a definition that is not only "unfashionable" but also logically excludes a great portion of the traditional Western canon), Burgess claims that the story of the relationship between a Nazi father and his son exists outside the realm of the imaginable and can not be accessed by any "fictional retelling." Burgess therefore suggests that the larger project of *Väterliteratur,* with its focus on the "dreadful fact" of the father's fascist past, must fundamentally and exclusively remain an autobiographical one. Fictional texts like *Vati,* for which, despite its title, any referential relationship to reality is missing, can only mimic the more earnest autobiographical exploration of fascism and the family and thus trespass onto illegal territory. In this view, *Vati* not only violates the memory of the Holocaust with its arrogant aesthetics but also mocks the attempts of the "real"

---

[16] Peter Schneider has responded to Burgess and other critics who claim that the Holocaust does not lend itself to fictional, aesthetic literature: "The aesthetic criticism betrays elitist biases. In West Germany at least, reference to the 'unspeakable' has too often served the purpose of not speaking at all" ("German Postwar Strategies of Coming to Terms with the Past," 285).

(autobiographical) father texts to come to terms with the fathers' participation in Nazi crimes. Schneider's text may be a story about a Nazi father, but according to this line of reasoning the signifier suggested in the title is misleading, for *Vati* is definitely not *Väterliteratur*.

"The Final Solution of Your Little Father Problem"

As if anticipating the critical firestorm to come, *Vati* itself struggles with its own possible inclusion in the genre of *Väterliteratur* because of the way it relates to the bitter battle between the second generation and its Nazi parents. On the one hand, by virtue of its very title, Peter Schneider's narrative links itself self-consciously to the tradition identified by Michael Schneider. Moreover, the narrator in *Vati* echoes many of the themes found in Michael Schneider, including a criticism of the West German government's record of persecuting left-wing terrorists while allowing Nazi criminals to remain at large, an assertion that generational conflict fueled the student movement, and a demonstration of the schizoid situation in which the accusing/protecting son finds himself. On the other hand, the narrative is explicitly critical of the project of *Väterliteratur*, distinguishing itself from father texts in its relationship to the past and arguing against its own systematic inclusion into what it characterizes as a problematic genre. At one point the narrator addresses the intended reader of the narrative, his school friend, as one of the students who rebelled against their fathers in the late sixties and who then went on to write accusatory books about them in the seventies and eighties. Describing this rejection of the fathers as patricide, the narrator criticizes the sons for their hard-hearted treatment of their fathers and for their ridiculous "revolution," which he sarcastically names "the final solution of your little father problem,"[17] making an explicit connection between the National Socialist term *Endlösung* (final solution) and the sons' attempts to effect an ultimate, violent solution to the problem of the Holocaust past in their condemnation of their fathers.[18] According to the narrator, many of the

---

[17] "[die] endgültige Lösung deines Vaterproblemchens" (P. Schneider, *Vati*, 24).

[18] At several points in the text, *Vati* makes the explicit connection between the notion of a "Final Solution," the Nazi euphemism for the Nazis' plan to decisively solve what they saw as Germany's (and Europe's) persistent problem of the other, namely European Jewry, and postwar German attempts to put behind it the otherness of its historical crimes in the Holocaust. The text thus abounds with different forms and cognates of *lösen* (to solve), including *erlösen* (to save or redeem) and *auflösen* (to dissolve). There is a crucial distinction, however, in the ways in which the narrator employs these cognates. In his description of the student revolutionaries' attempt to

texts of *Väterliteratur* reproduce fascist discourse under the guise of revolutionary anti-fascism and a radical coming to terms with the past:

> You say I shouldn't have listened to him, that I should have — how was it called back then — "emancipated" myself from him. Back in the late sixties, there were classmates like you who would accept nothing but money from their parents and who seemed to follow only one goal in life: not to become like their fathers! I can remember exactly how you talked of your "patricide" with a victorious smile, how you showed me the photocopied piece of evidence that you used to carry with you instead of an identity card: an article of your father's from 1943 that you came across, after years of research, in an East German documentary account. The wording of the article has slipped my mind. But the way you deduced the "fascist disposition" of your father from mere echoes of the vocabulary of National Socialism seems nothing more to me than brazen and unfeeling. In my eyes, you didn't expose your father back then, but rather yourself. And then, as you explained further that your "old man" was "dead" to you now and that you had severed every tie to him, I only thought: yeah, except for the monthly check, he'll still take that![19]

---

solve their relationship to their parents' past, the narrator chooses the term "Final Solution" quite consciously and ironically. In his own description of his quest to come to terms with his father's legacy, however, he reproduces the terminology largely unconsciously.

[19] "Du sagst, ich hätte nicht auf ihn hören müssen, hätte mich — wie hieß es damals — von ihm 'emanzipieren' sollen! Es gab ja, Ende der sechziger Jahre, Kommilitonen wie dich, die von ihren Erzeugern nichts weiter annahmen als Geld und nur ein Lebensziel zu verfolgen schienen: nicht so zu werden wie ihre Väter! Und ich erinnere mich genau, wie du mit Siegerlächeln von deinem 'Vatermord' erzählt, wie du mir das fotokopierte Beweisstück vorgelegt hast, das du damals statt eines Identitätspapiers bei dir trugst: einen Artikel deines Vaters aus dem Jahr 43, auf den du nach jahrelangem Forschen in einer DDR-Dokumentation gestoßen warst. Der Wortlaut dieses Artikels ist mir entfallen. Aber die Art, wie du aus bloßen Anklängen an den Wortschatz des Nationalsozialismus die 'faschistische Gesinnung' deines Vaters erschlossen hast, ist mir nichts weiter als vorlaut und lieblos erschienen. In meinen Augen hast du damals nicht deinen Vater, sondern dich selbst entlarvt. Als du mir dann noch erklärt hast, dein 'Alter' sei nun für dich 'gestorben' und jede Verbindung zu ihm abgebrochen, habe ich nur gedacht: bis auf den Monatsscheck, den nimmt er!" (P. Schneider, *Vati*, 23). The narrator's recollection of his friend's discovery of his father's article recalls a similar situation described by Michael Schneider, in which a fellow student comes across his father's 1935 law thesis, which analyzes the moral and legal concept of race in Hitler's *Mein Kampf* ("Väter und Söhne," 16; "Fathers and Sons," 10).

The narrator argues that the sons, who rejected their fathers as fascists simply on account of their overtly fascist vocabulary, were far from ideologically free from their fathers' influence,[20] for despite their criticisms of the fathers' bourgeois economics, they were willing to remain economically dependent on them. Moreover, the narrator sarcastically derides the sons, and by extension, their biographies of their fathers, for their purported goal of overcoming their fathers' legacies. According to the narrator, the father texts are unable to gain ultimate clarification and mastery over Germany's Holocaust past; rather, through their attempts to demonize and distance themselves from their fathers, the sons reveal their own implication in fascist modes of thought. Rather than displaying sympathy with the struggles of German youth against their parents, the narrator delineates his own experience from the situation of the sons who had denounced their fathers in the 1960s and then went on to write bitter biographies of them once they had died. Characterizing his position within history as unique and distinguishing his project of approaching the past from that of the texts of *Väterliteratur*, he argues that condemning his father as a mere Nazi sympathizer was never an option for him, given the circumstances of the notorious atrocities his father committed during the Holocaust and his father's status as the "most hunted man in the world":[21]

> It became clear to me then that there was an important difference between us [. . .]
> It seemed to me as if I alone was forced to carry a burden the rest of you had only talked about. I sympathized with the attempted escape of '68 that named itself a "movement" in involuntary self-denunciation. But I was never allowed the hope that I could free myself from my father through a pair of hastily learned quotes from Mao or Che Guevara.[22]

---

[20] There is some indication that the narrator believes that it is precisely the ideology of the student movement that links the students to the fathers' fascist past, for although the student movement's leftist political goals contrasted sharply with those of fascism, its hegemonic ideology resembled the Nazi world view in its quest for totality. In this way, according to the narrator, it is not only fascism that is criminal, but any strongly ideological system: "The greatest crimes are committed in the name of an idea" ("Die größten Verbrechen werden im Namen einer Idee verübt" [P. Schneider, *Vati*, 52]).

[21] "der meistgesuchte Mann der Welt" (P. Schneider, *Vati*, 24).

[22] "Damals wurde mir klar, daß es einen wichtigen Unterschied zwischen uns gibt [. . .] Es war mir, als hätte ich allein und als einziger eine Last zu tragen, von der ihr alle nur geredet habt. Mit dem Ausbruchsversuch von 68, der sich in unfreiwilliger Selbstanzeige 'Bewegung' nannte, habe ich sympathisiert. Die Hoffnung

In the narrator's view, the authors of *Väterliteratur* are self-deceptive in that they cast their fathers in the role of authoritarian perpetrators and brand themselves as victims, without taking into account the ways in which their own discourse resembles that of their fathers. They thus displace the status of the historical victims of the Third Reich's genocidal policy in order to proclaim for themselves an original innocence that contrasts sharply with the stain of guilt associated with their fathers.[23] On the other hand, the narrator, son of a hunted Nazi criminal, must actually experience the drama that the other sons only pretend to rehearse. For him, a solution to his father's past would require more than a mere performance of rebellion or a recitation of leftist political ideology in a bid to erase the stigma of Germany's past and free his own conscience. He reminds his school friend that, in spite of their often cold and authoritarian upbringing and regardless of their attempts to cast off the history of their fathers, the children of perpetrators must abandon their own narrow conception of the victim-perpetrator dichotomy and realize that they cannot in good faith be included among the historical victims of the Nazis: "But in that second I was forced to comprehend: we are, no matter how we deal with it, the sons and daughters of the perpetrators; we are not the children of the victims."[24] To overcome their fathers' past by equating themselves with actual victims of the Holocaust (however much the sons feel they are able to sympathize with them and however much they have "suffered" under the authoritarian hands of their fathers) would be a distor-

---

aber, ich könnte mich durch ein paar hastig erlernte Zitate von Mao und Che Guevara von meinem Vater befreien, war mir nie erlaubt" (P. Schneider, *Vati*, 24).

[23] Ernestine Schlant investigates the tendency on the part of the narrators of *Väterliteratur* to self-style themselves as victims and effectively ignore the historical factors that defined the status of victim during the Holocaust. One the one hand, this strategy involves equating themselves with the Jewish victims of the Nazis: "Since the fathers remain inaccessible, some members of the younger generation try a different approach. They establish an identity with the realization, even fantasy, that they are partly of Jewish descent. But this fantasy has nothing to do with an attempt to understand what it means to be (or to have been) a Jew in Germany; rather it instrumentalizes and idealizes being Jewish, for altogether personal purposes" (94). On the other hand, the actual Jewish victims themselves are often absent in the texts or relegated to the status of secondary victimhood, taking a back seat to the victimization of the authors themselves: "In almost all the situations depicted in these novels Jews are peripheral" (92). *Vati*, with its criticism of the former tendency (the instrumentalization of the status of victim), reproduces the latter, for the word *Jew* and the mention of Jewish victims are strikingly absent in the entire narrative.

[24] "Aber ich mußte in jener Sekunde begreifen: wir sind, wie immer wir uns dazu verhalten, die Söhne und Töchter der Täter, wir sind nicht die Kinder der Opfer" (P. Schneider, *Vati*, 34).

tion of history and would only serve to prohibit a meaningful attempt to work through the past.

In addition to a thematic criticism of *Väterliteratur,* in which the narrator exposes the ideological blind spots of the generation of '68's depiction of its relationship with its parents, Peter Schneider's text addresses the problematic aspects of the genre on an aesthetic level as well. In this case, the narrative, rather than merely making explicit the ways in which its project of coming to terms with the past is markedly different from that of the student revolutionaries and of *Väterliteratur,* performs its critique of the genre and its conventions poetically through its enactment of certain tropes. In particular, Peter Schneider's narrative exposes the inherent problems of the project of the father texts, in which the sons, through the process of autobiographical writing, attempt to come to terms with their father's crimes, solving once and for all their problematic family histories, an activity known in German as *Vergangenheitsbewältigung,* or "mastery over the past." As *Vati* suggests, the narrator's impetus for telling his father's story is not the drive to uncover the objective truth of what his father actually did in the Holocaust, but rather an overwhelming anxiety about his own connection to his father's guilt, impelling him to undertake violent measures to distance himself from and rewrite the oppressive legacy he has inherited from his father. As I demonstrate through a careful reading of certain tropes within *Vati,* namely those of *reading, writing,* and *naming,* the son, caught up in a crisis of signification in which he feels controlled by the narrative of his father's crimes, attempts to solve his dilemma by renouncing the story and the name imposed on him by his father and by wrenching narrative control from his father. However, as I shall argue, this attempt fails because the narrator comes to recognize that, by attempting to rewrite his father's past so that it is forced to conform to his own desired story of self, he implicates himself in the violent discourse of his father's ideology. Thus the goal of finally solving the father's past begins to resemble its semantic relative, the "Final Solution." The son, rather than achieving distance from his father's crimes in the Holocaust, finds himself repeating the very behavior that he finds so objectionable in his father. In this way, *Vati,* by attempting "to deal imaginatively with the unimaginable" and to make fiction out of "dreadful fact" (Burgess, 120), turns the tables on the very project of *Väterliteratur* and, rather than attempting to conform to its conventions, exposes the problematic nature of its autobiographical quest to master the fathers' criminal past.

Naming the Unknown Transgression

As the reader learns at the beginning of *Vati,* the narrator develops an anxiety about signification when he is still a small child, particularly with regard to nomenclature. His anxiety manifests itself as a feeling of distinct but unidentifiable difference that separates him from his classmates: "Some stain — invisible to me — seemed to cling to me — but how did you all recognize it? Was it an odor, my way of speaking, my clothing, a facial twitch? Over and over I observed myself in the mirror, I turned around and around, I sought the stigma and didn't find it."[25] At first, he believes that the mark of difference he carries is due to some obvious bodily affliction, a sign of critical meaning that is decipherable to everyone else but that he, despite obsessive searching, is unable to locate. Slowly the narrator's ignorance of his difference transforms into a vague understanding of what it is that distinguishes him, as he becomes aware that his mark is not a physical flaw or affliction, but rather another sort of signifier whose meaning is comprehended by the world around him: "For years I felt like the class fool who goes to the chalkboard and doesn't notice that someone has fastened a condom to his back. Until I hit upon the absurdly simple solution: the name. Hardly anything and yet everything: the name!"[26] The narrator thus solves his dilemma, discovering that the mark he bears — his own surname — is a signifier with portent. The discovery of the name as the source of the narrator's difference, however, does not at first provide illumination, for he is unable to decipher its significance. In its form, it appears to resemble the less mysterious names of his classmates, yet the manner in which others speak his name signifies that there is something extraordinary about it:

> At first the tone with which the teachers called on me irritated me, a hesitation, a lowering of the voice before the three syllables, almost as if the solid Swabian surname were completely unpronounceable. It seemed to recall something terrible, perhaps something great, in any case something unspeakable.[27]

---

[25] "Irgendein mir selber nicht sichtbarer Makel schien an mir zu haften — aber woran habt ihr ihn erkannt? War es ein Geruch, meine Art zu sprechen, die Kleidung, ein Zucken in meinem Gesicht? Immer wieder habe ich mich im Spiegel betrachtet, ich drehte mich um und um, ich suchte den Fehler und fand ihn nicht" (P. Schneider, *Vati*, 12).

[26] "Über Jahre habe ich mich gefühlt wie der Klassendepp, der zur Tafel geht und nicht merkt, daß jemand ein Präservativ auf seinem Rücken befestigt hat. Bis ich auf die lächerlich einfache Lösung stieß: der Name. Nichts weiter als und doch alles: der Name!" (P. Schneider, *Vati*, 12).

[27] "Zuerst irritierte mich der Ton, mit dem die Lehrer mich aufriefen, dieses Zögern, dieses Senken der Stimme vor den drei Silben, ganz so, als sei der gut schwäbische Familienname ganz unaussprechbar. Er schien an etwas Schreckliches, vielleicht etwas Großes, jedenfalls an etwas Unaussprechliches zu erinnern" (P. Schneider, *Vati*, 13). According to Riordan, the narrator's description of his name "is the broadest possible hint to the reader that the name alluded to is 'Mengele,' with its three syllables and typical Swabian diminutive ending" (81).

From his teachers' obvious reluctance to say his name, the narrator becomes aware that it must be a signifier for some horrific transgression about which the teachers would prefer to remain silent. As the narrator suggests, the teachers' disinclination is not so much a problem of the articulation of the name itself; rather, its unpronounceability is an indicator for the greater unspeakability of its unknown significance. His name thus functions as a hypercharged signifier for an enigmatic signified content that resists linguistic attempts to capture and interpret it.

At last aware that his name is the signifier for an unknown and uncannily significant meaning of which everyone else is aware but about which no one dares to speak, the narrator seeks to relieve himself of the burden of his name's unspeakable meaning. Thus he is quick to acknowledge an alternative name given him by his classmates, a name that is assigned to him pejoratively: "Until my high school graduation I was halfway protected from my name since only grown-ups addressed me with it. For you and most of my classmates I was known as 'the Pig,' and no one considered any longer that this nickname was in reality an insult."[28]

As the narrator then explains, he is given this new nickname "Pig" by Heitzmann, a classmate who uses it for the first time when he blames the narrator for stealing the teacher's pen (a crime of which Heitzmann himself is actually guilty):

> When asked about how he had come to possess the pen, Heitzmann pointed with his finger at me and uttered the strange sound three times: Pig, Pig, the Pig did it!
>
> Even today I don't know if the Hanseatic Heitzmann knew this word or just invented it out of necessity. I stood up, red from head to toe, and proclaimed myself guilty. I understood the harmless insult as a sign of recognition, almost a word of redemption. In any case, I quickly got used to the nickname, even if I never completely forgot that it stood for a crime I hadn't committed.[29]

---

[28] "Bis zum Abitur blieb ich vor meinem Namen halbwegs geschützt, denn nur die Erwachsensen redeten mich damit an. Für dich und die meisten Mitschüler war ich 'der Wutz,' und niemand dachte mehr daran, daß dieser Spitzname in Wahrheit ein Schimpfwort war" (P. Schneider, *Vati*, 14).

[29] "Zur Rede gestellt wie er in den Besitz des Kulis gelangt sei, hatte Heitzmann mit dem Finger auf mich gezeigt und dreimal den seltsamen Laut ausgestoßen: Wutz, Wutz, der Wutz hat es getan! Bis heute weiß ich nicht, ob der Hanseat Heitzmann dieses Wort kannte oder in seiner Not erfand. Ich bin damals, rot bis unter den Scheitel, aufgestanden und habe mich damit schuldig bekannt. Ich verstand das harmlose Schimpfwort als ein Zeichen der Anerkennung, fast als ein Erlösungswort. Jedenfalls habe ich mich rasch an den Spitznamen gewöhnt, wenn auch nie ganz vergessen, daß es für ein Vergehen stand, das ich gar nicht begangen hatte" (P. Schnei-

In this childhood scene, the narrator both accepts the disparaging nickname and admits guilt for stealing the pen, a crime he did not commit, even going so far as to accept responsibility for it publicly. The new name, Wutz, like the narrator's family name, is thus associated with a particular transgression and becomes a signifier for it. In this case, however, the narrator is fully aware of the content to which the signifier refers. Rather than representing a terrible violation for which there are no words, the name Pig possesses banal meaning that, though negative and unflattering in its reference to a farm animal, is easily identifiable, for it refers to a specific violation, the theft of a pen. In this way, the name functions as a signifier for guilt, much like the mark of Cain. However, in contrast to Cain's mark, which represents a transgression that is perpetually present and irresolvable, the narrator's nickname, because of the certainty of its meaning, becomes a mark of "recognition" that promises him something like redemption, absolving him of the unspeakable and unidentifiable crime to which his last name is connected.

The moment of redemption provided by the alternative name, however, is short-lived, and the narrator's crisis intensifies when he finally learns the meaning of his last name. When he is deemed an appropriate age, his mother and his aunt (his father's new wife) take it upon themselves to "enlighten" him[30] and to include him in the "circle of 'initiates'"[31] by explaining who his father (the man he thought was his uncle) is and what crimes he is accused of. The narrator's immediate reaction to the sudden revelation of the meaning of his name and the transgression that it represents is to deny his connection to his father and to insist on his nickname, a name he previously preferred to his real name without knowing why:

> None of it's true, I thought. The person sitting here isn't me, this woman is not my mother, it must be a mix-up, a mistake like back then, when the German Air Force bombed the city because the pilots confused the Freiburg Cathedral with the one in Strasbourg. Leave me alone, take somebody else, my name is Pig![32]

---

der, *Vati*, 14). Because "Wutz" is a word that originates in the local Alemannian dialect (Jensen, 88), Heitzmann, who comes from the Hanseatic realm of northern Germany, could be expected not to be familiar with it.

[30] "heute klären wir ihn auf" (P. Schneider, *Vati*, 17); In her description of the act of informing the narrator of his legacy, the aunt employs the word *aufklären*, which in German connotes both enlightenment and the process of explaining sex to children, thus revealing the ways in which the adults regard the father's identity as a "dirty little secret" that is for the most part repressed.

[31] "Kreis der 'Eingeweihten'" (P. Schneider, *Vati*, 20).

[32] "Es is alles nicht wahr, dachte ich. Der hier sitzt, bin ja nicht ich, diese Frau ist nicht meine Mutter, es muß eine Verwechselung sein, ein Irrtum wie damals, als die

The narrator's comparison of his suddenly revealed paternal legacy with the German bombing of the German city of Freiburg is significant, for it reveals his belief that this legacy is a violation foisted upon him in error, as if he, like the cathedral in Freiburg, were the victim of mistaken identity. In any case, the enigmatic content of his name is finally revealed, exposing the transgression that it represents, in all of its unspeakability (significantly, this revelation is only experienced by the narrator, not the reader, who, never informed as to the father's specific identity or crimes, is still left to wonder what the content, which thus remains unspeakable in the narrative, is). Unlike his nickname, which provides "Erlösung" (redemption) for the guilt of the petty crime of theft, the narrator's surname becomes "die lächerlich einfache Lösung" (the absurdly simple solution) that represents his father's perpetration and culpability, a mark of identity that is literally branded upon the son, because despite the fact that the son is innocent of any crime (even the crime of theft), he bears the name of a mass murderer and thus his own name becomes a signifier for the crimes of the past.

The narrator tries thereafter to distance himself from the names that signify both petty and unspeakable transgression by detaching himself from his father's past and by convincing himself that he, in fact, possesses another name, one that is not tainted with his father's history. Wandering through the forest, he is certain that nature knows him under a different name, and he is overcome by emotion at this recognition of an identity apart from his father's:

> Sometimes, when I lay under a cliff and looked up at the trunk of a spruce tree, up to the treetop [...], I believed that I was being called. Someone called me by a name that I had never heard, and without warning tears streamed from my eyes.[33]

Longing to escape the certain identification with unspeakable atrocity that accompanies his surname, the narrator imagines himself the possessor of another name, one that, if not recognized by the human world, is at least sensed by nature, a neutral force that, in the narrator's mind, attaches no ominous significance to the nominal signifier. The narrator thus indulges in a Romantic idealization of nature, which promises him a notion of a self that is untainted by human transgression.

---

deutsche Luftwaffe die Stadt bombardierte, weil die Piloten das Freiburger Münster mit dem von Straßburg verwechselten. Laßt mich, nehmt einen anderen, ich heiße Wutz!" (P. Schneider, *Vati*, 17).

[33] "Manchmal, wenn ich unter einem Felsen lag und am Stamm einer Fichte hinaufschaute, hinauf zu den Wipfeln [...], glaubte ich, ich würde gerufen. Jemand rief mich bei einem Namen, den ich noch nie gehört hatte, und ohne Vorbereitung schossen mir Tränen in die Augen" (P. Schneider, *Vati*, 15).

The possibility of a name free of the guilt associated with his surname, hinted at in nature, is finally realized when the narrator listens to music:

> I was calm only when I heard music, always the same music, the String Quintet by Brahms, G-Major, I think. When I heard the cello in the slow movement, it was as if I were called at last by my true name, a name known only to me. The edges of objects dissolve, the room and the house fill with water, my body loses its weight, it swims and rolls, is thrown from side to side — not by the waves, but rather by invisible currents deep underneath the sea — in unconscious alertness it hears the melody, the message written in tones, but it doesn't understand this message, because the melody doesn't come from the outside at all, it fills the body like the water fills the drowned man.[34]

The narrator's experience of listening to the Brahms quintet, much like his relationship to nature, is characterized by a markedly Romantic sensibility that evokes a sense of complete emotional fulfillment that threatens to culminate in self-annihilation and death. However, in this instance, the promise of another identity, merely hinted at in nature, is finally realized in music, which provides the narrator with another name, one that does not automatically signify either his own difference or his father's crimes. In contrast to his father's surname, whose function as a mark of difference and whose corresponding significance were once known to all but the narrator, this "true" name is known only to him. Moreover, not only is the narrator the sole "initiate" to his new signifier, he is also the only one who is aware of what it signifies. The content of his true designation, the "message written in tones," is not a mark branded upon the narrator by the outside world, a cryptic text that he must first discover and then decipher, but a fluid energy that emanates from within his own body, a force that need not be decoded because it is identical to him. In the discovery of his true name, the narrator seems finally to solve the crisis of signification that has plagued him, for in the experience of music he is able to seamlessly join a chosen signifier to a desired signified, achieving a moment of unproblematic identity. Significantly, the ultimate moment of the achievement of this identity, as revealed in the im-

---

[34] "Ruhig wurde ich, wenn ich Musik hörte, immer dieselbe Musik, das Streichquintett von Brahms, G-Dur, glaube ich. Wenn ich das Cello hörte im langsamen Satz, war es, als würde ich endlich bei meinem wahren, nur mir bekannten Namen gerufen. Die Ränder der Gegenstände lösen sich auf, das Zimmer, das Haus füllt sich mit Wasser, der Körper verliert sein Gewicht, er schwimmt und schlingert, wird hin und her geworfen, aber nicht von den Wellen, sondern von unsichtbaren Strömen tief unten im Meer, in bewußtloser Wachheit hört er die Melodie, die in Klang geschriebene Botschaft, aber er versteht sie nicht, denn die Melodie kommt ja gar nicht von außen, sie erfüllt ihn wie das Wasser den Ertrunkenen" (P. Schneider, *Vati*, 15).

age of drowning, is one of death, when the anxiety over signification is imagined to be resolved once and for all.

The narrator's solution to his crisis is, however, only fleeting, for even the "true" name he is able to locate in music links him to his father. Later, as an adult, he finally travels to Brazil to get to know his father and to confront him about his genocidal past. On the third day of his visit, his father arranges an outing to a nearby rainforest, bringing along a tape recorder; according to the father, who also displays a Romantic attitude toward both nature and music, "there's nothing more beautiful than listening to German music in the middle of a primeval forest."[35] Once in the forest, in preparation for a lecture he gives to the son on the importance of National Socialist racial theory, the father begins to play the Brahms quintet. The son's reaction is one of immediate trepidation:

> He took the tape recorder out of the backpack and without a word of explanation pushed the play button. There is no word for the horror that seized me as I heard the first bars of music coming from the stereo speakers. In a frantic rewinding of my memory through all the letters that I had written to my father, I searched for the sentence, the inadvertent hint, with which I could have initiated him. I was sure that there was never such an indication. But the tones that filled the wild dome above us were the introductory chords of the String Quintet in G major by Brahms, and from these notes I now heard, like a sixth instrument, my father's voice break forth.[36]

The music that earlier had filled him, providing a moment of relief in which the signifier and signified were joined together, is now the element that reinstates the narrator's crisis of signification. Along with the "message written in tones," the meaning that belongs only to the son, his father's voice is revealed to be an integral part of the music. Thus the father's history is once again thrust back onto the narrator. The son comes to realize with horror that, even when he chooses to identify himself with another name, the signi-

---

[35] "Es gebe nichts Schöneres, als mitten im Urwald deutsche Musik zu hören" (P. Schneider, *Vati*, 44).

[36] "Er holte den Kassettenrecorder aus dem Rucksack und setzte ihn, ohne ein Wort der Erklärung, in Gang. Es gibt kein Wort für das Entsetzen, das mich ergriff, als ich aus den Stereoboxen die ersten Musiktakte vernahm. In einem rasenden Rücklauf meines Gedächtnisses durch sämtliche Briefe, die ich meinem Vater geschrieben hatte, suchte ich nach dem Satz, dem versehentlichen Hinweis, mit dem ich ihn eingeweiht haben könnte. Ich war sicher, einen solchen Hinweis hatte es nie gegeben. Aber die Klänge, die den wilden Dom über uns füllten, waren die Einleitungsakkorde des G-Dur-Streichquintetts von Brahms, und aus diesen Klängen hörte ich nun, wie ein sechstes Instrument, die Stimme meines Vaters" (P. Schneider, *Vati*, 47).

fied content remains the same. He can neither discard the name that he bears nor create his own identity apart from his father with a new referent that contains no transgression.

Moreover, in the course of the narrative, the notion of the father's name as a signifier for an unspeakable past to which the narrator is mistakenly linked is undermined and exposed as a construction, a misnomer. Midway through the book, the son, still trying to escape the father's name, signs in at a hotel "under a false name."[37] At the end of the narrative he learns that on the father's gravestone "a false name"[38] has been inscribed as well. Both father and son try to escape the past by discarding their names, hoping that, by changing the signifier, they might erase the referent. The son, in his assumed anonymity, is once again linked to the father, yet this time, rather than severing himself from his father's crimes, he ends up reproducing his father's strategy for evading responsibility for them and thus he becomes a nominal participant in the willful concealment of the past.

Decoding the Father's Story

Closely linked to the issue of the father's *name* in the narrative is the matter of the father's *story*. The narrator (as a figure in a *father story*) displays a desire to appropriate and rewrite his father's story (the signified content) within the text. The narrator's letter to his childhood friend chronicles this endeavor, and his journey to visit his father to confront him and force him to reckon with his criminal past becomes a metaphor for his attempt to solve his crisis of signification by controlling his father's story. In this way, the present narrative becomes obsessed with determining the narrative of the past, and the son hopes that mastery of his father's story will simultaneously guarantee mastery over the processes of signification that oppress him.

From the very beginning of the narrative, we learn that reading and writing are characteristic of the son's relationship to the father. In fact, the son's engagement with the unknown father begins when he learns to read: "As I began to learn to read, letters from overseas arrived, from an uncle, they said, letters with beautiful stamps that depicted a blond, angelic woman."[39] The son first begins to read the letters from his "uncle" (whom he later learns is actually his father), which he believes contain a crucial narrative that, although written only for him, resists his comprehension: "I

---

[37] "unter falschem Namen" (P. Schneider, *Vati*, 44).

[38] "ein falscher Name" (P. Schneider, *Vati*, 62).

[39] "Als ich anfing, lesen zu lernen, kamen Briefe aus Übersee, von einem Onkel, hieß es, Briefe mit wunderschönen Briefmarken, auf denen eine blonde, engelsgleiche Frau abgebildet war" (P. Schneider, *Vati*, 11).

thought that if I only read them often enough, they would reveal a secret to me, something forbidden and fantastic that I would need only to decipher."[40] He associates these letters with his own story, which is just as puzzling to him, for it too is encoded, a narrative of self that is incomprehensible to him. He characterizes himself as "the allegedly blank page,"[41] an apparent tabula rasa positioned prior to any narrative of history, but that is actually already inscribed with a story. As a textual body he carries this unknown story "like an inscription on my forehead that everyone but me could decipher."[42] As with his anxiety over his name, the son is aware that he embodies a story unknown to himself, a narrative with grave import and critical meaning, and his goal is to decode this story. At this point the project of reading transforms into that of writing, for he believes that he can decipher the story by manipulating it. He first tries to gain control over his father's story by rewriting it, in the hope of discovering some hidden meaning: "After that I began to transcribe my uncle's letters [. . .] But however much I studied them in bed at night by the light of a flashlight and tried to rearrange them according to the initial letters and the beginnings of the lines, they told me nothing."[43]

Despite his best efforts, the son is able neither to decode nor to rewrite the puzzling letters into a narrative that he is able to comprehend. He does not give up his project of writing, however, for after he finally is enlightened as to his father's identity, he begins to write his own letters to his father in order to understand and control the narrative that marks him. He professes himself ready to accept his father's name, as long as his father will help him understand his own prehistory:

> At this time I began to write letters to him. I informed him that I now belonged to the circle of "initiates" and that I was ready to accept my father's name. At the same time I asked him to abandon all allowances he had previously made for my youth; I offered myself as a friend and someone to converse with. I didn't expect confessions, but rather

---

[40] "Ich dachte, wenn ich sie nur oft genug läse, würden sie mir ein Geheimnis verraten, etwas Verbotenes, Unerhörtes, das ich nur enträtseln müßte" (P. Schneider, *Vati*, 12).

[41] "das angeblich unbeschriebene Blatt" (P. Schneider, *Vati*, 12).

[42] "wie eine Schrift auf der Stirn, die jeder außer mir selber entziffern konnte" (P. Schneider, *Vati*, 12).

[43] "Danach begann ich, die Briefe des Onkels abzuschreiben [. . .] Aber sooft ich sie nachts im Bett, im Licht einer Taschenlampe, studierte, sie nach Anfangsbuchstaben und Zeilenanfängen neu zusammensetzte, sie erzählten mir nichts" (P. Schneider, *Vati*, 12).

clues that would allow me to understand him, and if possible to defend him.[44]

The son identifies himself to his father as one of the "initiates," a person who is familiar with his father's story, and in this way requests that his father impart the secrets that he in turn can decode and rewrite into a new story that would exculpate his father, thus providing a new identity for himself. His father, however, is ready neither to confess his secrets to his son nor to give him control of the narrative: "I was taken aback by his answers. Although at first I avoided every accusatory word, he wrote me letters that seemed to be directed more to a prosecutor than to a son. An official, even hostile tone emerged."[45] Despite the son's inclusion in the "circle of 'initiates,'" however, it is clear that the father regards his son not as a sympathetic correspondent with whom he wishes to share the "clues" of his past in a mutual project of defense and exculpation, but rather as a prosecutor who seeks to use his father's narrative against him. In this way the relationship between father and son, despite the son's stated intention to help defend his father, develops into an adversarial one, in which the father resists the son's attempts to comprehend the narrative that precedes his birth.

Thereafter the narrative becomes a bitter struggle between father and son for control of the father's story. The adult son, realizing that he has heretofore been unable to come to terms with his father's legacy, a failure that he likens to a "decades-long conversation with himself in the park of an insane asylum,"[46] decides finally to travel to South America to seek out his father and engage him in a dialogue. As he later explains to his friend, his intention was to somehow loosen the grip his father has over his life:

> I've explained to you what I wanted in Belem. I wanted to compel him to speak, to convince him to justify his deeds before a German court. Today I know that this explanation merely serves to obscure my plan. I wanted to confront him, to bring about his downfall with the justice of my innocently guilt-laden life. No, I want to say it with

---

[44] "In dieser Zeit fing ich an, ihm Briefe zu schreiben. Ich teilte ihm mit, daß ich nun zum Kreis der 'Eingeweihten' gehörte und bereit sei, meinen Vatersnamen anzunehmen. Gleichzeitig bat ich ihn, alle Rücksichten, die er bisher auf meine Jugend genommen hatte, fallenzulassen, ich bot mich als Freund und Gesprächspartner an. Nicht Geständnisse erwartete ich, sondern Hinweise, die mir erlaubten, ihn zu verstehen, ihn womöglich zu verteidigen" (P. Schneider, *Vati*, 20).

[45] "Seine Antworten befremdeten mich. Obwohl ich zunächst jedes anklagende Wort vermied, schrieb er mir Briefe, die eher an einen Staatsanwalt als an einen Sohn gerichtet schienen. Ein offizieller, ja feindlicher Ton entstand" (P. Schneider, *Vati*, 20).

[46] "aus einem jahrzehntelangen Selbstgespräch im Park eines Irrenhauses" (P. Schneider, *Vati*, 10).

simpler words that are just as false: I wanted to be saved through him — or to save myself and the world from him.[47]

Armed with the intention to challenge his father, the son arrives at his father's house. Almost immediately, however, it is his father who takes control of the visit, confronting the son with his own challenge: "'Why are you hiding?' said my father suddenly. 'You wanted a conversation: the notorious game of questions and answers! Begin!'"[48] With these words of provocation, the two begin their conversation, which the son, using the language of military maneuvers ("tactics," "encircle," "attack"[49]), describes as an epic battle between mortal enemies, a characterization that, despite his overt intentions to force his father to renounce his racist ideology, implicates the son in the fascist, militaristic, social-Darwinistic discourse of the father. As the son states, he has arrived prepared for this violent struggle, having devised a "conversational strategy [. . . in order] to learn the truth"[50] and armed himself rhetorically: "During that night, I finally asked him the question that over and over I had polished, expanded, dismissed, and then sharpened anew. Yes, I worked on this question like an outcast who tries to form an axe from a boulder with his bare hands."[51] Despite his best efforts to force his father to submit to his questioning, however, the son comes up against a powerful narrator in the figure of his father, whom he characterizes as the "word leader and language giver."[52] Suddenly realizing that his father is winning this battle, and afraid of being "intellectually overrun,"[53] he relinquishes the hope that his father will answer his questions and finally desires merely to

---

[47] "Was ich in Belem wollte, habe ich dir erklärt. Ich wollte ihn zur Rede stellen, ihn dazu bewegen, sich vor einem deutschen Gericht zu verantworten. Heute weiß ich, daß diese Erklärung eher dazu taugt, mein Vorhaben zu verschleiern. Ich wollte ihn stellen, ihn mit dem Recht meines schuldlos schuldbeladenen Lebens zu Fall bringen. Nein, ich will es mit einfacheren, ebenso falschen Worten sagen: ich wollte durch ihn erlöst werden — oder mich und die Welt von ihm erlösen" (P. Schneider, *Vati*, 25).

[48] "'Warum versteckst du dich?' sagte mein Vater plötzlich. 'Du wolltest doch ein Gespräch: das berühmte Frage- und Antwortspiel! Fang an!'" (P. Schneider, *Vati*, 26).

[49] "Taktik," "einkreisen," "Angriff" (P. Schneider, *Vati*, 27).

[50] "Gesprächsstrategie [. . . um] die Wahrheit zu erfahren" (P. Schneider, *Vati*, 26–27).

[51] "In jener Nacht [. . .] habe ich ihm schließlich die Frage gestellt, die ich für mich immer wieder zugespitzt, erweitert, verworfen und neu zugeschliffen hatte. Ja, ich habe an dieser Frage gearbeitet wie ein Verbannter, der mit bloßen Händen aus einem Felsblock eine Axt zu bilden versucht" (P. Schneider, *Vati*, 27).

[52] "Wortführer und Sprachgeber" (P. Schneider, *Vati*, 30).

[53] "intellektuell überrannt zu werden" (P. Schneider, *Vati*, 27).

bring an end to his father's verbal superiority: "I just wanted to silence him."[54]

Shortly after his defeat in the verbal battle with his father, the son displaces his violent desire for domination over the father by aggressively stalking a young Brazilian woman, encouraged by the possibility of narrative control that she represents. Unable to reason with his father and overwhelmed by his father's linguistic mastery, the son leaves his father's house and begins to roam the city. For reasons unclear to him, he begins to follow this young woman, whom he describes in language that echoes the racist and sexist attitudes of his father:

> In the teeming mass I noticed a girl who, a head taller than everyone around her, overtook the other passersby with a long stride. Since she was walking in front of me I couldn't see her face, just her dark neck and her damp legs that were naked up to the thigh. The astonished and sometimes shamelessly leering faces of the men coming the opposite way led me to guess that she was beautiful, or at least striking [. . .]
>
> Yes, she was beautiful, sullen and beautiful, but her beauty seemed to have a negative effect on me, it reminded me of nothing.[55]

The son, unable to determine the woman's beauty on his own, reads the narrative of her beauty as it is written on the faces of the men who look at her. The woman herself remains "a blank page" on which a story is yet to be written, a body without story or meaning ("she reminded me of nothing"). He eventually becomes sexually aroused by his act of stalking: "The fact that in a totally unknown city, I was following someone, anticipating someone, excited me. I was filled with a lust that made my body heavy."[56] His arousal is triggered by the idea of the unknown woman, a blank text onto which he might project his own story. However, he is not only attracted to the

---

[54] "ich wollte ihn nur zum Schweigen bringen" (P. Schneider, *Vati*, 33).

[55] "In dem Gewimmel fiel mir ein Mädchen auf, das alle vor und neben ihr Gehenden um Haupteslänge überragte und mit ausgreifendem Schritt überholte. Da sie vor mir herlief, konnte ich ihr Gesicht nicht sehen, nur ihren dunklen Nacken und ihre nassen, bis zum Oberschenkel nackten Beine. Daß sie schön, jedenfalls auffallend war, ließ sich aus den erstaunten, manchmal schamlos grimassierenden Mienen entgegenkommender Männer erraten [. . .] Ja, sie war schön, trotzig und schön, aber ihre Schönheit wirkte eher abweisend auf mich, sie erinnerte mich an nichts" (P. Schneider, *Vati*, 36–37).

[56] "Die Tatsache, daß ich in einer wildfremden Stadt jemandem folgte, jemanden erwartete, erregte mich. Eine Gier, die den Körper schwer macht, erfüllte mich" (P. Schneider, *Vati*, 37).

unwritten text of her body, but also becomes interested in an object that accompanies her:

> The naked female leg, splashed with mud, next to it the bulky writing instrument, improbable in this place, which at times knocked against her knee when a passerby came too close — both affected me like a sign, and so I hurried aimlessly after her.[57]

The woman's leg, a metonymy for the sexual allure of her textual body, combined with the typewriter that, like its own keys that strike the blank page, enticingly strikes up against this leg, represents to him the possibility of writing and thus he is encouraged and aroused. Importantly, the prospect of writing is linked in his mind with the woman he objectifies; together the woman and the typewriter affect him in an almost prophetic manner ("like a sign"). The possibility of dominating her thus functions as a signifier for the possibility of narrative control and mastery of his father's past.

In the end, the woman, aware of the son's presence, turns around to confront him: "The moment I was close enough to either grab her by the arm or at least to greet her, my chest tightened. Drag her into the hall of the building, tear the clothes from her body or throw myself on my knee before her — I wasn't capable of a middle gesture."[58] Suddenly he loses his nerve and quickly withdraws, unable to conclude his pursuit and take control of the woman through either outright violence or ostensible chivalry.

Despite his failed attempt at dominating the woman, however, he returns to his father's house rejuvenated by a desire to aggressively take control of his father's narrative: "The entire time he was talking I waited for a pause, for a chance to interrupt him."[59] However, the struggle between the two continues as before, culminating in the confrontation in the rainforest, in which the father successfully deflects his son's questions and tries further to indoctrinate him into Nazi ideology. At this point, the son begins to acknowledge the ultimate impossibility of his project. He realizes that trying to master the father's story is futile, and instead hopes to suppress his father's narrative agency: "Only one thought stood like flaming script before my

---

[57] "Das nackte, vom Schlammspritzern bedeckten Frauenbein, daneben das sperrige, hier unwahrscheinliche Schreibgerät, das manchmal, wenn ein Passant zu nahe kam, gegen ihre Knie schlug — beides wirkte auf mich wie ein Zeichen, und so hastete ich, ohne Ziel, hinter ihr her" (P. Schneider, *Vati*, 36).

[58] "In dem Augenblick, da ich nahe genug war, um sie an diesem Arm zu ergreifen oder sie wenigstens zu begrüßen, krampfte sich meine Brust zusammen. Sie in einen Hausflur zerren, ihr die Kleider vom Leib reißen oder mich vor ihr auf die Knie werfen — zu einer mittleren Geste war ich nicht fähig" (P. Schneider, *Vati*, 39).

[59] "Die ganze Zeit, während er sprach, wartete ich auf eine Pause, auf eine Gelegenheit, ihm das Wort abzuschneiden" (P. Schneider, *Vati*, 48).

eyes: Prohibit! Eradicate! He should be forbidden to think and to speak."[60] The son's quest for the story becomes a "flaming script" that depends upon the violent suppression of the father's narrative agency in order to survive. The son thus reproduces his father's fascist language in an attempt to isolate himself from his father's discourse.

At the end of the narrative the son becomes aware of the impossibility of controlling his father's story, for he finds himself implicated in the very language he employs to perform the task. He senses the problem during the discussion in the rainforest, when his father plays the music that had earlier revealed his son's "true name." The son is horrified to find, not only that the music he considers his private language is also a favorite piece of his father's, but also that his father's speech becomes a part of that music: "and from these notes I now heard, like a sixth instrument, my father's voice break forth."[61] Earlier, the son had attempted to become initiated into his father's narrative, looking for "hints" to his father's past. Here, the reverse has occurred: the father is initiated into his son's story and assumes his son's identity as his own voice. Thus the son's "true" name and his father's voice are intertwined together. At this point the son finally learns what "the message written in tones" that the Brahms piece represented for him is, namely, his intimate connection to his father's past. Unable either to control his father's story or to keep it separate from his own identity, the son flees the rainforest and returns to the hotel, hoping to simply escape his father's narrative control and go home.

However, although the son breaks off the conversation with his father and flees, he is unable to throw off his father's legacy. Upon arrival at the hotel, he immediately becomes further implicated in his father's narrative of guilt when, adopting his father's racist language, he accuses the hotelier of stealing money from his room. At the beginning of this incident, he transfers the unspoken accusation that he had formulated against his father ("He's guilty! A trial must be held!"[62]) to the hotelier ("He's lying, he's guilty, a trial must be held"[63]). The accusation, however, remains internalized as a silent reproach with regard to the father, and it becomes vocalized in the case of the latter only when the son releases his pent-up fury: "'How you lie,' I

---

[60] "Nur ein Gedanke stand, wie eine Flammenschrift, vor meinen Augen: Verbieten, ausrotten! Man muß ihm das Denken und Sprechen verbieten" (P. Schneider, *Vati*, 52).

[61] "aus diesen Klängen hörte ich nun, wie ein sechstes Instrument, die Stimme meines Vaters heraus" (P. Schneider, *Vati*, 47).

[62] "Er ist schuldig! Es muß ein Gericht gehalten werden!" (P. Schneider, *Vati*, 53).

[63] "Er lügt, er ist schuldig, es muß ein Gericht gehalten werden" (P. Schneider, *Vati*, 56).

scream. 'Nothing is sacred to you people, not even your children!'"[64] In his outburst of anger, the son not only shows himself willing to openly accuse the hotelier without any proof but also goes on to displace the hotelier's ostensible crime onto "you people," meaning the native Brazilians, relocating an individual act to an entire national group and thus replicating his father's fascist discourse.

While making a formal complaint at the police station shortly thereafter, the son, confused by the proceedings that are incomprehensible to him, begins to conflate the hotel owner's crime (a petty theft of five hundred dollars) with that of the father, a suspected mass murderer, and fears he has somehow betrayed his father while reporting the theft. The father's legacy, which the son had carefully attempted to rewrite, suppress, and keep apart from himself, breaks down and becomes indistinguishable from his own: "Suddenly the text that I had prepared for myself disappeared without a trace from my memory. Only letters remained before my eyes, letters that didn't want to assemble themselves into the right syllables."[65] The son comes to connect his own story with that of his father when he realizes that the boundaries separating his own culpability (the sexual stalking of the woman and the accusation against the hotel staff) and the crimes of his father blur: "The official seemed to be completely indifferent as to whether he was filing a theft, a sexual assault, or a mass murder."[66] The son's ability to distinguish and thus control the different narratives of guilt so deteriorates that, in contrast to his admonition to his friend about the necessity of remembering that one is the child of perpetrators, he himself suddenly loses the capacity to decisively distinguish between perpetrators and victims: "About twenty figures — men, women, children — sat on a shabby bench at the rear of the room, immersed in timeless waiting. It could not be determined whether they came here as accused or accusers. And in the heat the difference seemed absolutely trivial."[67] The son recognizes here that he has failed in his attempt to clearly demarcate his father's story from his own, for his use of language, rather

---

[64] "'Wie du lügst,' schrie ich. 'Nichts ist euch heilig, nicht einmal eure Kinder!'" (P. Schneider, *Vati*, 55).

[65] "Plötzlich war der Text, den ich mir zurechtgelegt hatte, spurlos aus meinem Gedächtnis verschwunden. Es blieben nur Buchstaben vor meinen Augen, die sich nicht zu den richtigen Silben zusammensetzen wollten" (P. Schneider, *Vati*, 57).

[66] "Dem Beamten schien es völlig gleichgültig zu sein, ob er einen Diebstahl, ein Sexualverbrechen oder einen Massenmord zu den Akten nahm" (P. Schneider, *Vati*, 57).

[67] "An der Rückseite des Raumes saßen etwa zwanzig Gestalten, Männer, Frauen und Kinder, auf einer schäbigen Bank, in ein zeitloses Warten versunken. Es war nicht zu erkennen, ob sie als Angeklagte oder als Beschwerdeführer hierhergekommen waren. Dieser Unterschied schien bei der Hitze auch völlig belanglos" (P. Schneider, *Vati*, 56).

than aiding him in this division, persists in linking him to his father's legacy. Earlier in the narrative, the son queries, "What does one inherit from a father whom one doesn't know? His eyebrows, a bald head, the hands, what else?"[68] At this point, the son finds an answer to this question: he has inherited his father's language, the language of National Socialist discourse. As the son leaves the hotel, his thoughts echo the violent language to which he earlier objected in the case of the student rebels: "A knife! If I had a knife I would hold it to the old liar's neck until he confessed. And if the five hundred dollars were worth more to him than his life, I would let him pay this price!"[69]

At the end of his journey, the narrator acknowledges the futility of his quest for control of his father's legacy when he meets the chambermaid held responsible for the crime and becomes aware that he is guilty of accusing an innocent woman:

> I saw her become terribly frightened as she noticed the policemen; she broke into tears with the first questions. I placed myself between her and her inquisitors, swore that I had never seen her, never met her, that she was innocent. The two men grinned at me with repulsive chumminess. They liked the woman too, but on account of my accusation they would have to go home with her for a moment. The woman looked at me with complete contempt. Her gaze told me that my protestations came too late, that a house search in this country was tantamount to extermination.[70]

The son realizes at this moment that, rather than making an unequivocal accusation against his father and forcing him to admit to his crimes, he has pointed the finger at someone else, an innocent person. In reaction to his inept and unsuccessful attempt to gain mastery over his father's past, he has

---

[68] "Was erbt man von einem Vater, den man nicht kennt? Seine Augenbrauen, die Glatze, die Hände, was noch?" (P. Schneider, *Vati*, 18).

[69] "Ein Messer! Wenn ich ein Messer hätte, ich würde es dem lügnerischen Alten an die Kehle setzen, bis er gestand. Und falls ihm die fünfhundert Dollar mehr wert waren als das Leben, würde ich ihn diesen Preis zahlen lassen!" (P. Schneider, *Vati*, 61).

[70] "Ich sah sie furchtbar erschrecken, als sie die Polizisten bemerkte; schon bei den ersten Fragen brach sie in Tränen aus. Ich stellte mich zwischen sie und ihre Vernehmer, schwor, daß ich sie niemals gesehen habe, ihr niemals begegnet, daß sie unschuldig sei. Die beiden grinsten mir in widerwärtiger Kumpanei zu. Auch ihnen gefalle diese Frau, nur müßten sie aufgrund meiner Anzeige für einen Augenblick mit ihr nach Hause gehen. Die Frau sah mich voller Verachtung an. Ihr Blick sagte mir, daß meine Beteuerungen zu spät kamen, daß eine Hausdurchsuchung in diesem Land einer Vernichtung gleichkam" (P. Schneider, *Vati*, 60).

displaced his aggression and desire to master onto someone less powerful, thus reproducing his father's ideologies of domination. Looking at the frightened chambermaid, he suddenly comprehends that there will be no "final" solution to his relationship to his father's crimes, for the narrative control he desires is beyond his reach: "But when I looked her in the eyes, full of fear of a sign, I suddenly realized: I would never again recognize the woman I had followed without the typewriter."[71] The sign that, in the case of the woman with the typewriter, represented the possibilities of both sexual domination and narrative mastery, now becomes a threatening reminder, not only of the impossibility of gaining control over his crisis of signification, but also of his own inability to separate himself from his father's language. The blank page onto which he had wished to violently inscribe a new story is elusive. The son is left with his own story, the one that links him to his father's language and criminal past.

Vati and the Failure of *Väterliteratur*

In *Vati*, the narrator's quest to rewrite his oppressive legacy is an example of what Miriam Hansen terms the "double bind" of the project of working through the Holocaust past in the German second generation, where the attempt to come to terms with the parents' crimes slips into a "discourse of denial" (quoted in Santner, 100). In this way, the ostensible narrative goal of *Vati* — the narrator's attempt to solve and thus free himself from his father's criminal past — fails. However, the failure of the narrator does not equal the failure of the narrative itself. For *Vati*, through its careful deployment of tropes of signification, orchestrates the narrator's failed attempt by linking his quest to rewrite his father's story to the problematic motivations of the autobiographical texts of *Väterliteratur*. In this way, the fictional text, rather than trivializing its subject through the attempt "to deal imaginatively with the unimaginable" (Burgess, 120), highlights the problematic assumption that the autobiographical text is more successful in coming to terms with and thus solving the historical past because it is ostensibly better equipped to determine objective truth.[72] The narrator-son in *Vati* functions in the text as a metaphor for the problematic relationship between the past

---

[71] "Aber als ich ihr in die Augen sah, voller Furcht vor einem Zeichen, wußte ich plötzlich: ich würde die Frau, der ich gefolgt war, ohne die Schreibmaschine niemals wiedererkennen" (P. Schneider, *Vati* 60).

[72] Colin Riordan also takes issue with the position represented by Burgess: "This seems to betray [. . .] an implication that fiction is not an appropriate means to deal with a topic such as this. Yet it is precisely the fictional medium which allows *Vati* to confront issues which are more delicate, controversial and painful than those dealt with in other novels of 'Väterliteratur'" (26–27).

and the present as well as the impossibility of a full *Vergangenheitsbewälti- gung*. In the attempt to rewrite his father's story, the son becomes aware of the impossibility of writing the "father story" as a means of coming to terms with the past. The authority of *Väterliteratur*, a genre of autobiographical texts that attempt to write objectively about the parents' past in order to free their authors of it, is thus aesthetically resisted by *Vati*, a text that at the same time demands inclusion into the genre. In writing itself into the tradition of *Väterliteratur*, Peter Schneider's text deconstructs its project of coming to terms with the past. The genre *Väterliteratur* therefore becomes a misnomer for that which it attempts to nominate, that is, the individual text (*Vati*). A gap between text and genre is thus exposed, and the relationship between the two is radically called into question. This gap, the space between memory and language, is alluded to in Peter Schneider's text by the metaphor of *Vati*, or "Daddy." As the signifier for a relationship the narrator never experienced with his father (indeed, as a signifier for the child's ideal of the loving, good father) the designation *Vati* becomes not only a metaphor for the unattainable but a trope for the position of the writer as well, straddling the space between the personal and the political, between memory and language, between desire and mastery. Furthermore, *Vati* represents the gap between genre and text in that it underscores the problem of naming: the illusion that the name (*Väterliteratur*) is identical with that which it names (text). Peter Schneider's text *Vati* reveals that *Väterliteratur*, like the metaphor "Daddy," in trying to recoup that which cannot be attained and solve that which cannot be solved, is actually a misnomer, "a false name."

6: My Mother Wears a Hitler Mustache: Marking the Mother in Niklas Frank and Joshua Sobol's *Der Vater*

A fascinating, pure ideological regime like that of the Nazis, covering up undiscussable crimes of ordinary men (Browning, 1992), could elicit fantasies in almost any mind, especially when born long after its collapse into a regime which went on silencing and covering up these issues [. . .] As almost every adult was emotionally involved in one way or another in something (fascination, bystanding or evil making) during the Nazi era, it was much more difficult to create a fresh and distinct comprehensive authority which the children could lean on. With the help of such an authority they could perhaps have developed a clear demarcation between those Nazi crimes and other, more ordinary, family life events and secrets.

— Dan Bar-On, *The Indescribable and the Undiscussable: Reconstructing Human Discourse after Trauma*

Seeking the Mother in *Väterliteratur*

IN THE PREVIOUS CHAPTER I explored the discourse that defines *Väterliteratur*, citing in particular Michael Schneider, whom I term the "father" of *Väterliteratur*. Michael Schneider claims that the father texts represent a particular historical problem of the "generation damaged by its fathers" ("Fathers and Sons," 4),[1] a group of rebellious adult children (mostly sons) who question their fathers' participation in Germany's fascist past. Although this rebellion and challenge on the part of the sons fall under the general concept of generational conflict, Schneider stresses the unique historical position of this particular nexus of texts. According to Schneider, the conflict around which *Väterliteratur* is centered "far exceeds the classical Oedipal complex which stamps every generational relationship to a greater or lesser degree at any given time" ("Fathers and Sons," 5),[2] for in this case, the sons

---

[1] "vätergeschädigte Generation" (Schneider, "Väter und Söhne," 9).

[2] "weit über jenen klassischen (ödipalen) Konflikt hinausgeht, der jedes Generationen-Verhältnis zu bestimmten Zeiten mehr oder weniger prägt" (Schneider, "Väter und Söhne," 9).

attempt not only to battle the authority of the fathers but also to achieve *Vergangenheitsbewältigung,* or mastery over Germany's past. Despite Schneider's claim that the texts are not conventional reenactments of the classical Oedipal drama, however, he continues to make use of the Freudian father-son generational paradigm in his discussion of the texts. He characterizes the genre as a whole as a "literary coming-to-terms with the past of the fathers" ("Fathers and Sons," 4)[3] in order to "overcome" the fathers in an aggressive struggle for dominance. Although he does mention father texts written by two women, Ruth Rehmann's *Der Mann auf der Kanzel* (1979; *The Man in the Pulpit,* 1997) and Brigitte Schwaiger's *Lange Abwesenheit* (Long Absence, 1980), Schneider subsumes their writings under the label "father-son conflict" (as the title of his essay indicates) without questioning the ways in which aspects of gender affect the writer's investigation into the father's history and without examining how female writers themselves fit into his model of literary Oedipal patricide.

Susan Figge, in her essay, "Fathers, Daughters, and the Nazi Past: Father Literature and Its (Resisting) Readers," takes Schneider and subsequent studies on *Väterliteratur* to task for concentrating primarily on the texts written by sons at the expense of those written by daughters. She revises Schneider's father-son paradigm by showing that a large number of the texts of *Väterliteratur* are written by women who, like the sons, attempt to discover their fathers' involvement in the Nazi era, but who furthermore are interested in exploring the fathers' role as representatives of patriarchy. Figge stresses that, however much Schneider and other critics argue that postwar father biographies transcend the notion of a "classical generational struggle," critical studies of *Väterliteratur* situate themselves within a broader tradition in German literature of father-son conflict, a tradition that necessarily precludes gender-conscious discussion of narratives written by daughters. According to Figge,

> It is helpful to look first at some early 1980s general assessments of the father literature [. . .] In this interpretive tradition, by no means limited to the twentieth century, the literary overthrow, defeat, or death of the father is understood to signify both the individual son's liberation from the bonds of particular authoritarian psychological and familial constraints and the potential creation of wider social and political freedoms [. . .] Clearly, however, the use of this literary paradigm of father and son conflict must either subsume or exclude consideration of fathers and daughters. (275–76)

---

[3] "die literarische Auseinandersetzung mit der Vergangenheit der Väter" (M. Schneider, "Väter und Söhne," 9).

Figge objects not only to the exclusion of daughter texts from traditional generational categories but also to the historically specific ways in which critics of *Väterliteratur* read these texts, arguing that they ignore gender as a site of struggle in the postwar family. By attempting to open up the genre of *Väterliteratur* to include narratives authored by daughters, Figge's essay effectively posits gender as a crucial factor in evaluating postwar autobiographical texts and thus rewrites the critical notion of *Väterliteratur*. Like Schneider and other critics of *Väterliteratur*, however, Figge accepts without question the primacy of the father in the text, and in this way aligns herself with the critical reception of the genre, which attributes the authoritarian nature of postwar child-rearing and the oppressive family environment of the authors' childhood primarily to the father. By concentrating solely on the father-daughter paradigm as the critical gendered relationship in the fascist family and ignoring any configurations in which the mother operates, Figge undermines her own efforts to bring the issue of gender fully into critical discussions.

So what about the missing member in this familial drama, the figure of the mother? Has she no relation to the postwar presence of fascist discourse in the home? What is the role of the mother in these autobiographies that focus so obsessively on the father's past? Is she completely absent from these texts? Does the term *Väterliteratur* adequately describe the texts under discussion, or does it in fact posit a mode of reading that, in privileging the figure of the father in the narrative, precludes discussion of the mother? For the most part, critics have ignored these questions. According to Eveline Kanes, the figure of the mother is absent from discussions of *Väterliteratur* and of family in the Third Reich in general: "one might ask about the commitment of the mothers, aunts, or grandmothers involved in these histories. By and large, there is little discussion of the women's views on the Nazi regime and its policies" (11). Those few critics who do mention the problem of the mother in *Väterliteratur*, such as Konrad Kenkel, either dismiss texts written about mothers or attribute the paucity of mother narratives to women's supposedly non-political role in society:

> As one might expect, in the father novels, the respective relationship to the father occupies the center of such a figuration of the past. The fact that it is thus a matter of fathers (that is to say, men), excluding to a large extent mothers, reflects the society of the late 1960s and its political history, which was dominated by men both publicly and in the family. Even when a woman — the example here is Elisabeth Plessen — examines the relationship with her father, the non-treatment of mothers is obvious.[4]

---

[4] "In den Väterromanen steht, wie nicht anders zu erwarten, die jeweilige Beziehung

Konrad Kenkel does not investigate texts written about mothers because, as he says, he does not expect to find any. He argues that, because women had no prominent role in political life in either the Nazi era or in postwar West Germany, they bore little culpability for Nazi crimes or the subsequent repression of them and therefore cannot expect to be objects of an attempt to come to terms with the past. Michael Hulse agrees:

> Perhaps because the element of historical confrontation is absent, or at all events not present in the same degree, German writing about mothers has not had the same intensity as writing about fathers. Writers come *after* their mothers just as they come *after* their fathers, it is true; but it was the fathers who created the Nazi Reich and who fought its war, and so it is rightly the father who must answer to the generation that is left its legacy of doubt and barbarity. Mothers are often approached in a more intimate mood, not without recrimination but nonetheless without that extra dimension of historical hatred or despair. (138–39)

Hulse and Kenkel privilege readings that concentrate on the father because, in their opinion, only in the writer's engagement with the father does the historical moment make itself known. Because of their supposedly intimate subject matter, narratives written about mothers cannot be classified as historical texts that address the continuing influence of Nazi discourse in the family. Hulse opposes the "historical," which he sees as having the most merit and application for the study of *Väterliteratur,* to the "intimate," a loaded concept that frequently functions as a signifier for a lesser-valued, less intellectually rigorous private sphere associated with women.[5] His dichotomy

---

zum Vater im Zentrum solcher Vergangenheitsgestaltung. Daß es sich dabei unter weitgehendem Ausschluß der Mütter um die Väter, d.h., um Männer handelt, reflektiert die Gesellschaft der späten sechziger Jahre und ihre politische Geschichte, die sowohl in der Öffentlichkeit als auch in der Familie von Männern beherrscht wurde. Auch da, wo eine Frau — das Beispiel hier ist Elisabeth Plessen — sich mit ihrem Verhältnis zum Vater auseinandersetzt, bleibt die Nichtbehandlung der Mutter offensichtlich" (Kenkel, 168).

[5] Hulse applies his logic of the supposed "intimacy" associated with women to explain why women have written about mothers in greater numbers: "If the study of fathers is equally the province of male and female writers, it is immediately striking that the majority of works about mothers are by women, partly no doubt out of a doctrinaire sense of shared sisterliness" (139). Writing on fathers and the father-son relationship thus merits further inquiry, according to Hulse. Writing on mothers, on the other hand, is only "doctrinaire" and therefore not of value to the supposedly ideologically neutral project of literary analysis. Furthermore, rather than investigating the motives behind the daughters' texts about their mothers, he reflexively assumes that they are the result of a feminist solidarity with the mothers, and thus of

of gender and history thus provides him with justification for his singular concentration on the role of the father, which then allows him to exclude mothers from the discussion altogether.

The grounds Hulse states for ignoring or minimizing the role of the mothers in literary accounts of the postwar family are questionable enough, but perhaps more problematic is his assertion that women of the Nazi era carry no responsibility for "its legacy of doubt and barbarity" and therefore can freely be excluded from any study of *Väterliteratur*. It is admittedly very difficult to determine the actual roles women played in the Third Reich, since much of the historical data available concern the political and military arenas. Certainly women did not number among the high-ranking Nazis who developed German fascism, nor were they, for the most part, among the agents to whom we usually assign responsibility for the Holocaust. However, it cannot be denied that many non-Jewish German women were at some level complicit in the Nazi regime. Women belonged to the electorate that voted the Nazis to power and they did live and function in a fascist state. In many cases, they benefited as much as their male counterparts from the racist and militaristic policies of the Third Reich. While it is true that women were oppressed by Nazi gender policy and the biological role it assigned to women, it is historically inaccurate to describe them only as victims of fascism. According to Ulla Roberts, the role of women in Nazi society is much more complex:

> But women were not merely and predominately passive recipients or victims of National Socialist women's politics [. . .] Rather, in view of the current state of critical women's studies, we can assume that many women welcomed the early changes in the quality of life in Germany after the assumption of power by Hitler and the National Socialist Party. Furthermore, the majority of women were silent during the horrifying persecution of Communists, Socialists, Jews, and resistance fighters, which began as early as 1933; and more than a few "just" did their duty by reporting to the Gestapo neighbors who were Jewish or political dissidents. From this we can conclude that there was an affirmation, at the very least, of authoritarian measures and, in many cases, even of violent solutions to social conflicts.[6]

---

no interest to a non-female audience, in contrast to the more compelling historical struggle between fathers and sons.

[6] "Frauen waren aber nicht nur und überwiegend passive Empfängerinnen oder Opfer der NS-Frauenpolitik [. . .] Vielmehr können wir nach dem Stand heutiger kritischer Frauenforschung annehmen, daß viele Frauen die anfänglichen Veränderungen der Lebensumstände in Deutschland seit der Machtübernahme durch Hitler und die NSDAP begrüßten. Auch bei der schon ab 1933 einsetzenden Verfolgung

As Roberts explains, women's roles in the Nazi era were multiple and diverse and demonstrate a more active participation in the structures of National Socialism than Hulse would lead us to believe. To be sure, one can describe German women of the Third Reich as "passive victims" in certain contexts, but to characterize them wholly as such is misleading and historically deceptive, for it effectively relegates millions of women to one narrow category. To deny German women's various activities in support of the Nazi regime and its criminal policies is to exhibit historical bad faith and to court an essentialized view of women that promotes a notion of their inherent "goodness." Unfortunately, this essentialist view of women as morally superior pervaded much of the research on women in the Nazi era until the late 1970s. Not only does the critical literature on *Väterliteratur* tend to view mothers as innocent (and therefore unimportant to the author's engagement with the Nazi past), but a great deal of feminist scholarship has held the same view. According to Karin Windaus-Walser, there is a tendency on the part of many feminist scholars to characterize non-Jewish German women under Nazi rule as unwitting and powerless victims who stood outside Nazi society and were therefore unable to persecute others, a relativistic assertion that not only fails to distinguish between the various power and victim groups under Nazi rule but also maintains rigid and mutually exclusive definitions of perpetration and victimization.[7]

Since the eighties, scholars have interrogated the roles and activities of women in the Third Reich, demonstrating the ways in which they partici-

---

von Kommunisten, Sozialisten, Juden und Widerstandskämpfern hat die Mehrheit der Frauen geschwiegen, und nicht wenige haben 'nur' ihre Pflicht getan, indem sie jüdische und politisch andersdenkende Nachbarn bei der Gestapo meldeten. Daraus können wir auf eine Bejahung von mindestens autoritären, in vielen Fällen sogar gewalttätigen Lösungen gesellschaftlicher Konflikte schließen" (Roberts, 36–37).

[7] According to Karin Windaus-Walser, "When some feminist historians, linguists, and theologians draw a parallel between the oppression of women and the persecution and annihilation of the Jews, these images take on irrational features. Such a refusal of empathy with regard to the real female and male victims of National Socialism is related to the denial of one's own guilt as a member of the female sex for National Socialism and anti-Semitism. Conversely, in this denial there lies the most recent justification for the idea of woman as victim (which by the way is also perpetuated by men)" ("Wenn von manchen feministischen Historikerinnen, Linguistinnen und Theologinnen in der Unterdrückung von Frauen eine Parallele zur Judenverfolgung und Judenvernichtung gezogen wird, nehmen diese Vorstellungen irrationale Züge an. Eine solche Verweigerung von Einfühlung den wirklichen, weiblichen und männlichen Opfern des Nationalsozialismus gegenüber hängt mit der Verleugnung jeglicher eigener Schuld des weiblichen Geschlechts an Nationalsozialismus und Antisemitismus zusammen. Umgekehrt liegt darin der jüngste Grund für die (im übrigen auch bei Männern verbreitete) Denkfigur der Frau als Opfer" [60]).

pated in Nazi crimes both actively and in the more domestic roles in which they supported Nazi men's activities. As Claudia Koonz concludes, "Far from remaining untouched by Nazi evil, women operated at its very center" (6). Most recently, Gudrun Schwarz has documented the large-scale involvement of hundreds of thousands, perhaps even millions, of German women, especially single women, in the Nazi military occupation of Eastern Europe:

> These women [white-collar, blue-collar, and medical workers employed by the Wehrmacht, SS-Women's Corps, and the German Red Cross] were involved in the crimes committed by the Wehrmacht and the SS in various ways. They lived and worked in an atmosphere of murder and crime, were bystanders and, as such, witnesses. Many were profiteers, some became accomplices, and still others became perpetrators themselves. (131)

Schwarz argues that, despite evidence of the massive participation of German women in activities associated with war crimes and the Holocaust, the memory of their involvement was quickly effaced from the historical record after the war, a repression made possible by a "masculine myth" (123) that denied the pervasive influence of Nazi ideology and the war in all aspects of society, including the spheres in which women operated. Postwar narratives of women's involvement in the Nazi period reinscribed German women back into the supposedly non-political, transhistorical sphere of the family, thus ignoring the ways in which the "intimate" arenas of women's lives (not to mention their very public presence as employees of the German military) were in their own way permeated by Nazi society and its crimes.

However critical it is to determine women's exact participation in Germany's fascist history, with regard to the presence of mothers in *Väterliteratur,* the historical reality of women's roles in the Third Reich and the Holocaust is perhaps of less interest to our inquiry than the revisionist narrative of which Schwarz speaks, for it cannot be forgotten that the father books are not the results of historical research but rather the autobiographical expression of the authors' attempt to come to terms with the legacy of the Nazi period within the family. Although it is true, as Hulse and Kenkel assert and Figge implies, that the majority of autobiographical narratives written about the postwar family focus on the father and the legacy of his participation in the Nazi period, the figure of the mother is by no means absent from these texts. On the contrary, it occupies a meaningful albeit small presence in many of the books that purport to come to terms with the father. Rather than viewing the mothers as apart from fascist discourse or as victims of Nazi policy, narrators often identify them as representatives of Nazi society to the child, especially in the absence of the father, who was often away serving in the German military. According to Ulla Roberts, the absence of the father meant that the mother became for the child the mediator of the outside world, including Nazi society: "Certainly *the other division of roles in the family* was of considerable importance. *The mothers* henceforth had to be for the children *the leading mediator of both worlds of socialization: that of the intimate inner space in the family and that of the position in the world outside,* which up to then had belonged to the duties passed down to the fathers."[8] Furthermore, not only was the mother the sole parent present during the war, but in many accounts, such as the short narrative by Irene Anhalt discussed in the introduction, the father either was killed during or immediately after the war or spent as long as a decade after the war in Soviet captivity. In these cases, the mother and her representation of the years under Hitler are the only link the narrators have to the father and to memory of the Nazi past. For this reason, much of what Hulse terms the "historical hatred or despair" the author feels for the father is simultaneously (although often unconsciously) directed at the mother, belying her supposedly ahistorical image for the child. According to Wolfgang Frühwald, "The intensification of literary conflicts today reveals itself among other things in the fact that the texts of the modern *Väterliteratur* give shape to a leave-taking from the parents, not only from the father. The destruction of the mother world and even hatred toward the mother in such texts are almost more grave than the decomposition of the father."[9] Frühwald does not pursue the particular forms the hatred for the mother takes in relation to the aggression toward the father, allowing it to remain a project for further scholarship; but his point is well taken. Any study of the phenomenon of *Väterliteratur* (a genre that revolves around familial generational conflict) must take into account the role of the mother, the family's structural analogue to the figure of the father, in order to excavate the role of the family in Nazi society. In many cases, as Frühwald intimates, it is not the "historical" father who bears the greater brunt of textual aggression, but the "intimate" mother, who signifies the Nazi past as it was represented in the familial sphere in which the children grew up.

---

[8] "Ganz wesentlich war sicher *die andere Rollenverteilung in der Familie. Die Mütter* mußten fortan für die Kinder *die tragende Vermittlerin der beiden Sozialisationswelten sein: des intimen inneren Raumes in der Familie und der Position in der Welt draußen,* die bis dahin zu den tradierten Aufgaben der Väter gehörte" (Roberts, 31).

[9] "Die Verschärfung der literarischen Konflikte heute zeigt sich unter anderem darin, daß die Texte der modernen Väterliteratur Abschiede von den Eltern, und nicht allein vom Vater gestalten. Die Destruierung der Mutterwelt, ja der Mutterhaß ist in solchen Texten fast gravierender als die Dekomposition des Vaters" (Frühwald, 350).

Writing the Mother in the Father Text

One text of *Väterliteratur* in which the author's project of coming to terms with the past of the father becomes an exploration of the mother and her role in fascism is the autobiography written by Niklas Frank, whose father, Hans Frank, the General Governor of the occupied territories in Poland during the war, was tried and executed in Nuremburg in 1946. Entitled *Der Vater: Eine Abrechnung* (the English translation is entitled *In the Shadow of the Reich;* translated literally, the title reads "The Father: A Reckoning"), Frank's book is composed as a dialogue between the narrator and his father's diaries and speeches. Because of its aggressive, violent confrontation with the father's legacy, the narrative is generally considered one of the most extreme of all texts associated with *Väterliteratur*.[10] The book is an extended chain of insults and invectives hurled at his father by a bitter and unforgiving narrator who, according to Peter Schneider, "verbally annihilates his criminal father" in an "attempt to execute his father a second time" ("German Postwar Strategies," 287).[11] The son's position toward the father is unambivalent: he fashions himself as his father's judge and proceeds to try and execute the father with little filial affection, a stance that elicited vehement criticism on the part of the *Stern* readership when the book was first serialized in the

---

[10] Heinrich Vormweg terms Frank's book a "ruthless reckoning with the father" ("rabiate Abrechnung mit dem Vater" [220]), while Ralph Giordano, in his foreword to the 1993 paperback edition of the book, writes: "Niklas Frank spews his entire disgust on paper; no, he pukes directly at the reader's feet the betrayal of the desires of early childhood, the indissoluble binding of the son to the horrific biography of this father, and the horror about it" ("Niklas Frank speit seinen ganzen Ekel auf Papier, nein, er kotzt den Verrat der frühkindlichen Sehnsüchte, die unlösbare Sohnesbindung an die Horrorbiographie dieses Vaters und das Entsetzen darüber dem Leser direkt vor die Füße" [9]).

[11] Peter Schneider is highly critical toward Niklas Frank's project, which he sees as Frank's attempt to push all responsibility for the past onto his father and in so doing to clear his own name: "In his unquestionable solidarity with the victims of his father, he seems to suggest a hidden personal motive: to depict himself as a pure victim. He certainly is a victim, but there is a difference between being the victim of bad conscience and being the victim of physical extermination" ("German Postwar Strategies," 287). Moreover, Schneider claims that Frank's goal with his book "is to set a model for his generation" (287), meaning, in effect, that he posits himself as an exemplary text of *Vergangenheitsbewältigung* and *Väterliteratur*. Although Frank's text first appeared as a series of articles in the *Stern* about the same time that *Vati* was released, one could read Schneider's critique of the goals of *Väterliteratur* in *Vati* in part as a reaction to precisely the sort of model Frank provides (see chapter 5).

magazine in 1986.[12] On the other hand, the role of the mother, who criminally exploited her position as the "first lady" in Hans Frank's General Government, occupies a proportionally much smaller place in the text, but the narrator's often lurid imagination of his mother gives her prominence, constructing her as an overpowering representative of the Nazi era and keeper of the father's memory.[13] The figure of the mother becomes even more powerful when we turn from Frank's narrative to the dramatic adaptation of it, written by Niklas Frank and the Israeli playwright Joshua Sobol. In the play, which bears the same title as the German edition of the book, the mother is figured as both a primary mouthpiece of fascist discourse and a threatening maternal character who comes to represent for the son the most pathological aspects of the Third Reich.

While the book's German title leads one to believe that it is the father who is under principal investigation, the narrator also imagines his mother and her influential role in Nazi society. It is in fact his mother whom the narrator first mentions when he describes the moment of his conception: "She had no orgasm when you came — when I came" (*In the Shadow of the Reich*, 3).[14] With this first sentence, the narrator establishes the configuration that will dominate the book, that of the familial ménage à trois, an incestuous variation of the psychoanalytic primal scene in which the mother occupies a primary place. Through the ambiguous use of "to come" — intimating that it is not only the father (the "you") that orgasms, but the son as well — the narrator emphasizes the importance of his relationship to his mother, Oedipal-sexual and otherwise. The mother-son relationship is made problematic from the outset, for here the narrator claims partial responsibility for his mother's lack of orgasm, thus admitting his filial failure to please her. Despite the fact that the narrator leaves his mother unnamed in the novel, rarely

---

[12] According to Henryk Broder and Ralph Giordano, many readers felt that the book made Niklas Frank guilty of a greater crime than those for which his father was convicted — the crime of filial disregard and hatred. According to one reader, the son's literary betrayal was "much worse than what the father did" ("noch viel schlimmer als das, was der Vater gemacht hat" [quoted in Giordano, Foreword, 6]), while another wrote: "Whatever Hans Frank may have done, his most abominable deed is without a doubt the fathering of this perverse monster of a son" ("Was auch immer Hans Frank getan haben mag, seine größte 'Schandtat' besteht zweifellos in der Zeugung dieses perversen Monstrums von Sohn" [quoted in Broder, 167]).

[13] In 2005, Niklas Frank published a book that concentrates exclusively on his mother. Entitled *Meine Deutsche Mutter* (My German Mother), this recent work is structured more novelistically than *Der Vater*, which is more of an autobiographical family portrait. In any case, the more recent text is more than twice the length of the earlier work.

[14] "Sie hatte keinen Orgasmus, als Du kamst, als ich kam" (Frank, *Der Vater*, 11).

addressing her in the second person, as he does his father, his ambivalent image of her, which is marked by his own overwhelming aggression, self-pity, and self-stylization as a victim, occupies a good portion of the book. He alternates between feelings of admiration and desire for his mother and intense fear of her and contempt for her activities as the self-proclaimed "Queen of Poland" (*In the Shadow of the Reich*, 109).[15] At one point in the narrative he professes his love for her and at another the same passionate hatred he feels for his father: "There are letters of hers [. . .] that make me hate Mother the way I hate you" (*In the Shadow of the Reich*, 106).[16]

In contrast to the figure of the mother in Michael Hulse's definition of *Väterliteratur*, Frank's book constructs the mother as the narrative's looming authority figure. Moreover, the narrator often characterizes her as more "masculine" and politically competent than the father, a reversal of official Nazi gender discourse, which diametrically opposes a passive and nurturing mother to a strong, mythically heroic warrior. In this case, it is the mother whom the narrator imagines in terms of the mythic and heroic. Throughout the book, the son remains in awe of what he sees as her almost supernatural stature and abilities. Referring to her influence with Hitler and other high-ranking Nazis, he writes, "But then, the Lord God (who had played along without showing any mercy, right up to the gas chambers), did not reckon with Mother" (*In the Shadow of the Reich*, 209).[17] The mother is thus figured as a force that challenges the authority of God (here figured as a coperpetrator of the Holocaust) and whose power exceeds the banal functionalism of National Socialist genocidal discourse. The narrator portrays his father, on the other hand, as weak and ineffective, emasculated by the mother: "But Mother was better than you — she wasn't as effeminate" (*In the Shadow of the Reich*, 106).[18] By reversing Nazi gender ideology and characterizing one of the highest-ranking Nazis as effeminate in comparison with his wife, the narrator tears at the fabric of Nazi constructions of masculinity, characterizes his powerful father as a laughable figure, and imagines his mother as the super-powerful, hyper-masculine center of fascist dominance.

Haunted throughout the novel by the crimes both parents commit while plundering Poland, the narrator also figures himself as one of their victims. Here again, although the book's title announces itself as a settling of accounts with the father, the powerful mother figure looms largest. The narra-

---

[15] "Königin von Polen" (Frank, *Der Vater*, 94).

[16] "Es gibt Briefe, wo ich sie hasse, so wie ich Dich hasse" (Frank, *Der Vater*, 92).

[17] "Der Herrgott, der hat ja bis zu den Gaskammern gnadenlos alles mitgemacht, aber er hat einfach nicht mit Mutter gerechnet" (Frank, *Der Vater*, 179).

[18] "Aber Mutter war besser als Du, sie war einmal nicht so weibisch wie Du" (Frank, *Der Vater*, 92).

tor perceives the mother and her criminal past as a real and immediate threat of mythic origin and proportion, imagining her as a fury out to avenge crimes of kinship, most notably the filial betrayal of his writing (*In the Shadow of the Reich*, 157).[19] Furthermore, he feels that he is unable to escape her threatening influence and sees himself as indelibly marked by her participation in Nazi history. He represents himself as the present injured party of her past crimes against others (ostensibly Poles and Jews, who largely remain nameless others within the text) and appropriates the status of the persecuted victim to represent the wrongs that she has allegedly committed against him. The son feels the mother's oppressive omnipresence and persistent influence at the present moment of writing, when he is trying to free himself from her criminal past and the dominance she continues to wield over him from the grave. Even the typewriter with which he writes his reckoning with his father is inextricably linked to the mother and her role as a fascist *grande dame*; as he notes, she employed it to correspond with Nazi luminaries, and after the war she used it to promote his father's autobiography to those same people, now exculpated and restored to powerful positions in postwar Germany. Although his stated project is to free himself from his father's influence through the medium of writing, the typewriter remains a visceral reminder of his inability to sever his connection to his parents and his mother's continuing influence over him. His writing is thus tainted by its association with his mother's Nazi activities, and the language that emerges from it carries the stigma of fascist discourse.

In an effort to rid himself of what he sees as his mother's pervasive influence and authority, the narrator confronts her directly: "Wherever you may now be orbiting in the universe, no matter how hard you try to put spiral nebulae between yourself and me [. . .] Mother, don't try to hide from me in one of those black holes — you won't be able to avoid hearing this" (*In the Shadow of the Reich*, 148; the literal German translation of the last clause is "you will hear it").[20] The narrator insists that his mother, here imagined as an all-powerful cosmic force, acknowledge both her complicity in the barbarity that occurred in Poland and her transgressions against him. "You will hear it" thus becomes a call of reckoning of almost biblical proportion, a demand for judgment and confession from a universal maternal force guilty of an enormous but unspecified violation.

---

[19] Frank, *Der Vater*, 136.

[20] "Wo immer Du jetzt durch die All-Systeme fliehst, Spiralnebel zwischen Dich und mich zu schieben suchst [. . .] Mutter, verschwind mir nicht in einem dieser Schwarzen Löcher, Du kriegst Deine Ohren nicht zu, Du wirst es hören" (Frank, *Der Vater*, 127).

In addition to being a powerful participant in the Nazi era in her own right, the figure of the mother functions for the narrator as the keeper of his father's memory and a vital link to the Nazi past. Through her mediation the son comes to learn about his father, who was hanged when he was a small boy, although the image relayed by the mother is anything but the negative one the son carefully cultivates: "I grew up in an atmosphere of almost total admiration for your life. Mother no longer felt in the slightest burdened by your crimes" (*In the Shadow of the Reich*, 350).[21] His mother becomes the official curator of Hans Frank's memory; after the war she publishes his memoirs and aggressively markets them to an enthusiastic postwar readership, much of which includes well-known Nazis who were reinstated to positions of power in the Federal Republic and with whom she regularly corresponds. The narrator thus represents his mother as an apologist for the Nazi regime, someone who refuses to acknowledge Germany's culpability in the war and the Holocaust and wallows in nostalgic hero worship. As an avowed advocate for National Socialism, she endeavors to reinstate its former glory by invoking God to avenge the Nazis (4).[22] For the son, she becomes the living embodiment of fascism and the father's Nazi crimes; her body and voice transmit this past to him. Although the father, the Nazi hanged for his crimes against humanity, is the functional fascist according to the text's title and overt content, the text's living memory of the past is channeled through the mother; through her mouth both the Nazi past and its reigning ideology of fascism speak into the present.

Staging the Mythology of the Fascist Mother

In 1995, *Der Vater: Eine blutige Komödie* ("Der Vater: A Bloody Comedy"), the dramatic adaptation of Niklas Frank's autobiographical novel, written by Joshua Sobol and Frank, premiered in Vienna. In this version of the Frank family story, the son, Niklas, becomes one character among a diverse cast that includes his parents, Adolf Hitler, Heinrich Himmler, Martin Bormann, the American hangman at Nuremburg, God, postwar Germans, and even the audience. As in the novel, the play depicts the son's attempts to exhume his father's memory and come to terms with the legacy he has inherited. However, his reckoning with his father becomes here the domain of theater, a problem to be staged and performed. At the beginning of the play, the son acknowledges the self-consciously theatrical character of his project. He refuses to grant his relationship with his father the quality of a classical

---

[21] "ich wuchs in einer Atmosphäre der totalen Anerkennung Deines Wirkens auf. Mutter fühlte sich gar nicht mehr verbrecherisch belastet" (Frank, *Der Vater*, 294).

[22] Frank, *Der Vater*, 12.

drama of father-son conflict, however, by associating his performance of reckoning instead with seedy burlesque entertainment: "I'll make a peep show out of your heroic life! The stinkiest coming-to-terms with the past that you can imagine — I'll drag you through it!"[23] The play depicts a messy excavation of a dead and buried history that waltzes and wallows in images of filth and decay, as demonstrated viscerally by the stage directions to the first scene: "Niklas rolls in Hans, who is lifeless like a figure from a wax museum, in a wheelbarrow. Hans is covered with a dirty sheet. Niklas rips the cloth off. Hans is covered with dust, dirt, and spider webs."[24] As this image indicates, the son refuses to let his father "rest in peace"; he exhumes his filthy corpse and revivifies him in order to compel him to answer for his crimes. In the process Niklas becomes a *Nestbeschmutzer*, a term that designates someone who fouls his own nest, defiling himself and his own life in his attempt to expose the filth of his parents' crimes.

This dirty engagement with the Nazi past is not limited to the son. The confrontation that in the book is played out exclusively between the narrator, the father, and the mother (albeit under the eyes of the reader) becomes in the theater a vicious vortex into which the audience can not help but be drawn, for this postwar familial drama forces the audience to examine its own personal connections to the Nazi era.[25] The play thus reflects on its own provocation of contemporary society. In the same scene, as Niklas tidies up Hans, he suddenly turns to the audience and implicates its members in his battle with the past, accusing the viewers of voyeuristically invading his privacy rather than investigating their own families' activities in the Nazi era: "What are you gawking at? This isn't a show, it only concerns me and my father. Go worry about your own damn fathers!"[26] The address to the audience is particularly interesting as a theatrical device in that it functions as a Brechtian alienation effect that denies itself as such; at the same time that he claims "This isn't a show," implying that what is happening on the stage is somehow supposed to represent reality, Niklas acknowledges the theatrical construction of his statement by addressing it to the audience. The specta-

---

[23] "Eine Peepshow mach ich aus deinem Heldenleben! Die stinkigste Vergangenheitsbewältigung, die du dir nur vorstellen kannst, zieh ich mit dir durch!" (Sobol and Frank, 125).

[24] "Niklas fährt auf einer Schubkarre Hans herein, leblos wie aus dem Wachsfigurenkabinett. Hans ist mit einem schmutzigen Leintuch bedeckt. Niklas reißt das Tuch herunter. Hans ist voller Staub, Dreck und Spinnweben" (Sobol and Frank, 124).

[25] The play premiered in Austria and has been performed in Germany. Sobol and Frank's intended audience is thus a group of adults whose parents and grandparents were living and active in the Nazi era.

[26] "Was glotzt ihr so blöd? Das ist keine Show, das geht nur mich und meinen Vater was an. Kümmert ihr euch doch um eure Väter!" (Sobol and Frank, 124).

tors of *Der Vater* are regarded not as passive and ahistorical consumers of entertainment, but as an interested and integral party to this particular attempt to work through the past. Sobol and Frank thus fashion theater as an alternative space of *Väterliteratur* in which the reader of the *father text* (now the viewer) is invited, even compelled, to participate in the son's engagement with the past.

As in the novel, the figure of the mother in the play operates in a critical way, despite the title's insistence that its focus lies elsewhere. Here too, the mother is imagined as an intensely powerful force, while the father is portrayed as weak and pitiful, a "loser."[27] The son constructs his mother's authority in the opening scene, using her as a weapon in his confrontation with his father. After Hans, still lying motionless in the pushcart, stretches out his leg and trips his son, Niklas threatens, "You and your mean tricks! You backstabbing dog! I'll tear your chest open and shit into your heart! Worse than that! I'll do something that you really hate. I'll bring Mama."[28] The play, much like Frank's book, stages his mother's fearsome dominance over his father, opposing her strength to his weakness and cowardice and belying her supposedly passive status as a non-actor in the Nazi era.

Later on in the same scene, the audience experiences the mother's dominance and authority in an elaborate slapstick routine involving eggs. Eggs, according to Frank's book, figure prominently and somewhat bizarrely in the historical Hans Frank's story. According to the narrator, his father allegedly confiscated for personal consumption 200,000 eggs that were slated for delivery to German troops at the eastern front, an action that led to an investigation by Heinrich Himmler. The play also addresses the subject of the stolen eggs, but here it picks up an extra layer of meaning, for in German, the word *Eier* has a double connotation anatomically and sexually. Not only does it refer to the female reproductive ova, it can be used colloquially to signify testicles, much like the English word "balls." In its reference to both male and female sexual anatomy, the German word thus cuts across the rigid divide between conventional physical signifiers of gender and sex and renders sexual difference an ambiguous construct. Eggs become a major leitmotif in the play and Sobol and Frank constantly tinker with its double meaning. In this first scene, Hans receives a pair of eggs from the girlfriend of his youth, Lilly, who tries to thereby induce Hans's sexuality so that she may seduce him. She fails in her attempt, for although she performs a striptease and speaks enticingly to him, he can only think about the future glory of Germany:

---

[27] "Versager" (Sobol and Frank, 124).

[28] "Du und deine miesen Tricks! Du hinterhältiger Hund! Ich reiß dir die Brust auf und scheiß dir ins Herz! Schlimmer als das! Ich werd dir etwas antun, was du wirklich haßt. Ich werd Mama bringen" (Sobol and Frank, 124).

HANS: Oh Lilly, there is so much energy hidden in me, I feel a will that is full of restlessness, I glow with the urge to be the pilot of this ship. A great new Germany will arise from this rubble, a Reich that will represent the world of culture and whose founder will be adorned with the diadem of redemptive humanity. Mankind, awake!

[...]

LILLY: Germany, Germany, always your Germany! We've loved each other since we were children. But now, Hans, it's time to grow up. Shall we try the classical Greek way? Or the way the French do it? Just us two?

HANS: Don't remind me of the French! After Versailles![29]

For Lilly, the nation is a signifier for sex. Hans, on the other hand, misreads her references to France, Greece, and (later) Hungary, interpreting them according to his own view of nationalist and fascist ideology, for which he sublimates his own sexual desire. He reserves his passion for his view of the greatness of Germany, and he seems ignorant about sex, an inexperience that is depicted theatrically as weakness and emasculation. As we learn from the stage directions, "he doesn't know what he should do with the eggs,"[30] although he is "fascinated by the eggs."[31] Lilly finally abandons the seduction and exits, yelling, "If you ever show up at my place again, then you'd better put hard-boiled eggs on my table, you wimp."[32] Brigitte, Niklas's mother, then enters (in a simulation of the couple's first meeting) and immediately takes possession of the eggs, demonstrating her sexual dominance by assum-

---

[29] HANS Oh Lilly, welche Energie steckt in mir, ich fühle diesen unruherfüllten Willen, ich glühe vor Drang, Lotse zu sein auf diesem Schiff! Ein neues, großes Deutschland wird aus diesen Trümmern erstehen, ein Reich, das die Welt der Kultur bedeutet und dem Gründer dieses Reiches das Diadem erlösender Menschlichkeit gewährt! Menschheit, erwache! [...]

LILLY Deutschland, Deutschland, immer nur dein Deutschland! Wir lieben uns, seit wir Kinder waren. Doch jetzt, Hans, ist es Zeit, erwachsen zu werden. Wollen wir nicht mal den klassischen griechischen Weg probieren? Oder wie es die Franzosen machen? Nur wir zwei?

HANS Erinnere mich nicht an die Franzosen! Nach Versailles!" (Sobol and Frank, 130)

[30] "der weiß [nicht], was er mit den Eiern anfangen soll" (Sobol and Frank, 130).

[31] "von den Eiern fasziniert" (Sobol and Frank, 130).

[32] "Wenn du je wieder bei mir auftauchst, dann leg mir gefälligst harte Eier auf den Tisch, du Weich-Ei!" (Sobol and Frank, 131).

ing the signifiers for both feminine and masculine sexuality: "She takes the eggs from him and begins to juggle with them."[33] She then breaks the eggs and "lets the yolks flow into Hans's hands,"[34] effectively emasculating him. As she declares her interest in him and her desire to possess him — "You're the one I want, Hans. You're mine,"[35] the stage directions indicate that "she holds his shaking yolk-hands,"[36] emphasizing her control of the frightened and sexually inept Hans. Finally, in a moment of climactic passion, Hans confesses his desire to climb the ranks of the Nazi party. As he fervently exclaims, "Oh, Brigitte, for once to earn 1,000 Marks a month. And to offer it all to you. That's all that I want,"[37] he suddenly, passionately and unconsciously squeezes the egg yolks, which drip to the floor. "Oh, crap!"[38] he cries, upset by his premature ejaculation, but Brigitte overlooks the "accident" and says comfortingly, "That can happen, my little piglet. Come, they're waiting for us at the church."[39] She then leads him "like a good little boy"[40] to the wedding. Hans performs the role of obedient son and "holds her hand and follows her docilely."[41] At the same time, however, he attempts to characterize the nuptials as his own subjugation of Brigitte, parroting the Nazi line on masculine superiority: "The sign of man is unconditional mastery. Weak men are much worse than women, because then they are cripples."[42] After the ceremony, in which the couple is blessed with the Nazi salute, the priest carefully cleans up the spilt egg and offers it to Niklas, thus blessing Niklas's symbolic conception. As this scene amusingly demonstrates, the play, like the book, constructs the mother in active terms. As her confident possession of the eggs demonstrates, she, with her double anatomy that renders her both masculine and feminine, wears the pants in the family. She is depicted as clearly dominating Hans, one of the highest-ranking officials of the Third Reich. Moreover, the play implies in this scene

---

[33] "Sie nimmt ihm die Eier ab und fängt an, damit zu jonglieren" (Sobol and Frank, 131).

[34] "läßt das Eidotter in Hans' Hände fließen" (Sobol and Frank, 131).

[35] "Du bist es Hans, den ich will. Du bist mein" (Sobol and Frank, 131).

[36] "Sie hält seine zitternden Eidotterhände" (Sobol and Frank, 131).

[37] "Ach, Brigitte, einmal 1000 Mark monatlich verdienen. Und sie dir darbieten. Das ist doch alles, was ich will" (Sobol and Frank, 131).

[38] "Oh Mist!" (Sobol and Frank, 132).

[39] "Das kann doch passieren, mein kleines Schweinchen. Komm, sie warten in der Kirche auf uns" (Sobol and Frank, 132).

[40] "wie einen braven kleinen Buben" (Sobol and Frank, 132).

[41] "folgt ihr brav an der Hand" (Sobol and Frank, 132).

[42] "Zeichen des Mannes ist unbedingtes Herrsein. Schwache Männer sind weit schlimmer als Weiber, denn jene sind dann Krüppel" (Sobol and Frank, 132).

that her ambition is the decisive factor that leads Hans to Nazi politics and installs him there as a leader.

The play's imagination of the mother's dominance over the father and her stature as an authority figure is further exemplified in a humorous scene in which Hans is appointed the General Governor of occupied Poland. He receives a phone call from Hitler while in the bathtub, and thus he takes his orders from Hitler while Brigitte dries him off:

BRIGITTE: Hans! Hans! The *Führer!*

HANS: My God! *He suddenly springs up in the bathtub, completely covered with suds, and stands at attention. To Brigitte:* Give him . . . to me! *Then into the telephone:* Heil Hitlerjawoll!

BRIGITTE: Get out of the water!

HANS: Jawoll. *Brigitte dries Hans with a giant red swastika towel.* Jawoll, my *Führer. He kneels.*

BRIGITTE: Stand up!

HANS: Jawoll.[43]

The comedic quality of this scene, which much like Sobol's widely-acclaimed play *Ghetto,* violates an unwritten taboo on humor about the Holocaust, functions theatrically as a Brechtian *Verfremdungseffekt,* in that it exposes the latent power relations between the characters while at the same time entertaining the audience. Hans, who comically bobs up and down, alternately sitting, standing, and kneeling, is portrayed as little more than a puppet in both his public and his private personae. Brigitte continues her role as the powerful, masculine mother figure, drying the naked but emasculated Hans as she would a young boy (effectively reducing Hans to the same status as Niklas). Furthermore, Hans takes orders from his wife in the same manner as he does from the dictator. Brigitte commands perhaps as much respect and fear from Hans as Hitler himself, for she receives as many "Jawoll"s as the

---

[43] BRIGITTE Hans! Hans! Der Führer!

HANS Mein Gott! *Er steht — über und über mit Schaum bedeckt — blitzschnell in der Badewanne auf und nimmt Haltung an. Zu Brigitte* Reich . . . mich ihm dar! *Dann ins Telefon* Heil Hitlerjawoll!

BRIGITTE Steig doch aus dem Wasser!

HANS Jawoll. *Brigitte trocknet Hans mit einem riesigen roten Hakenkreuz-Badetuch ab.* Jawoll, mein Führer. *Er kniet nieder.*

BRIGITTE Steh auf!

HANS Jawoll." (Sobol and Frank, 133).

Führer. Despite Hans's appearance as "a Roman emperor,"[44] wrapped in his bath towel, there is no question as to who is in charge. From her position as mother and caretaker, Brigitte is depicted as dominating Hans, establishing herself as the effective authority in the family, despite Hans's standing with Hitler and his new position.

Hitler, the Phallic Mother

The mother as a dominating fascist figure, which is operative in Frank's autobiographical representation, is radically reimagined in the theatrical space, for not only does Brigitte's authority over Hans equal that of Hitler, she actually *becomes* Hitler. According to the list of characters at the beginning of the play, "Hitler and Brigitte should be played by one person,"[45] the only instance of a double role in the play. Brigitte transforms into Hitler several times in the course of the play, and in one particular production I observed, this metamorphosis occurs onstage when the actress puts on a "Hitler mustache," an action that in its significatory potential is analogous to Brigitte's assumption of the eggs. By donning the mustache, she presents for the audience a figure who, on the one hand, is clearly a woman, but who, on the other hand, through a seemingly minor physical trait, becomes masculine. The mustache, an unmistakable physical marker of masculine virility, thus functions as a powerful phallic symbol, providing Brigitte with the penis to accompany the testicles she already possesses so confidently. In this way, Brigitte becomes the literal embodiment of the phallic mother, the fantasy of the all-powerful maternal figure who assumes attributes of masculine sexuality and refuses to be confined to socially-determined gender roles. She represents a certain sexual ambivalence, in that she possesses signifiers of both masculinity and femininity but does not fuse them into a resolved image of identity or a third gender that supersedes the male-female binary, remaining instead both phallic and maternal. At the same time, as Marcia Ian argues, the phallic mother is the result of a psychic drive toward identity and meaning, for she functions as "the symptom of a compulsion to resolve ambivalence by dissolving it into a specious equivalence" (6). Her very existence is formulated as a psychic solution to anxiety about contradiction, multiplicity, and ambiguity. In other words, she is the product of a crisis of signification, and her presence represents the son's attempt to resolve his epistemological anxiety and his ambivalence toward his project of excavating the past.

---

[44] "ein römischer Kaiser" (Sobol and Frank, 133).

[45] "Hitler und Brigitte sollten von einer Person gespielt werden" (Sobol and Frank, 123).

Moreover, with this particular choice of a phallic signifier, the mother becomes both ominously threatening and uncannily familiar. The mustache, arguably Hitler's most identifiable physical mark, functions in the contemporary cultural imagination as a metonymy for him, as well as an absolute sign for fascism, Nazism, and genocide (obscuring the origins of that particular style of mustache, which was made famous by Charlie Chaplin, after which Hitler's is rumored to have been based). As a visual mark the mustache effects a sort of codified shortcut to the identification of its bearer; without resorting to verbal discourse, it calls forth the specter of Hitler and the Nazi period in a visceral way, thus accessing immediately a cache of cultural associations without referring to particular historical events or constructions. According to Alvin H. Rosenfeld, the cultural sign *Hitler* conveys an almost unlimited number of meanings that not only are functional in contemporary cultural mythology but also continue to multiply as time carries us ever further from the historical figure:

> Hitler, one comes to understand, simultaneously haunts and defies the contemporary imagination, which, with respect to the whole Nazi past, seems drawn between a willed forgetfulness and a kind of mythologizing memory. As a consequence, the ghost of Hitler has been set free from the strictures of historical consciousness and enjoys a second life through art. (xx)

Rosenfeld elaborates further:

> Far from fading back into the past, they [Hitler and his henchmen] have emerged as a primary code of our cultural mythology, a code that has its own distinctive vocabulary, recognizable symbol system, ordered hierarchy, significant place names, familiar songs and slogans, established manner of dress. We are, in other words, in possession of, and in no small manner possessed by, a whole world of resonant meaning, replete with its own sources of pathos and signification and evocative of a life that has far from run its course. (19)

As Rosenfeld points out, although the image of Hitler evokes a multitude of associations, the most prominent reading for the sign *Hitler* is the notion of evil; in both popular culture and intellectual debate his name is synonymous with pathology, horror, and death. By comparing a person to Hitler, the agent making the comparison can convey the idea of absolute evil without having to elaborate the ways in which that person's activities resemble Hitler's crimes. In his book *Imagining Hitler* (1985), Rosenfeld investigates the appropriation of Hitler as a character in popular fiction, especially when he appears in the guise of a different character:

> As our writers have tended to dream him up, he is likely to be found almost anywhere, almost any time, and in the shape of almost any-

body. So long, that is, as the body has been heavily brushed at some time or other by evil, tainted by sorcery or one of the other black arts, participated in or perpetrated exceptional pain [...] The brand of the beast must be evident at least as background coloration for Hitler to be our Hitler though; otherwise, all our efforts to mine him for metaphor would fail. (5)

According to Rosenfeld, as long as he or she can display a history of evil or sociopathic criminality, almost any figure can function as a blank canvas onto which Hitler may be painted. Although Rosenfeld is primarily interested in what happens to the sign *Hitler* when it is associated with disparate characters, rather than what happens to a character when he or she is associated with Hitler, the inverse of his claim can be true as well. To stage a particular character as Hitler thus provides him with a rich background of absolute evil, and he immediately becomes representative of fascist sadism and Nazi power. Importantly, the character does not have to display the actions or behaviors generally associated with Hitler in the cultural imagination (racism, fanaticism, genocide, warmongering, and so on); by mere association with Hitler, the figure is automatically imbued with the idea of many of these qualities. By physically constructing Brigitte as Hitler, the play thus displaces both the mythical quality of evil associated with him as well as the historical crimes committed by him onto the private domain of the family and, in particular, the intimate figure of the mother. In direct opposition to Hulse's assertion that the postwar mother is "rightly" absent from representations of German historical confrontation with the past, Sobol and Frank's play thus constructs the threatening, phallic mother as the primary agent responsible for Germany's crimes, thereby effectively acquitting the father of his participation in them.

In her book *Feminism, Film, Fascism* (1998), Susan E. Linville makes an explicit connection between the sign *Hitler*, the concept of the phallic mother, and postwar German attempts to come to terms with the past. In her discussion of postwar German psychoanalytic research on *Vergangenheitsbewältigung*, she takes issue with the influential work of Alexander and Margarete Mitscherlich, who in their 1967 book *Die Unfähigkeit zu trauern* (*The Inability to Mourn*, 1975) attribute the failure on the part of West Germans to take responsibility for the Holocaust and empathize with the victims of the Nazi regime to their refusal to acknowledge their own psychic losses in the Second World War, chief of which was the loss of Hitler as their *Führer* and collective ego-ideal. Linville exposes some of the blind spots in the gender discourse in both the Mitscherlichs' book and a related work by Alexander Mitscherlich, *Auf dem Weg zur vaterlosen Gesellschaft* (1965; *Society without the Father*, 1969). In particular, she objects to their obsessive concentration on patriarchal authority and father-son Oedipal conflict, their privileging of the "masculine mythos of melancholia" (5) as opposed to the "traditionally feminine ritual function" of mourning "that has been privatized and repressed" (4), and their "theorizing of Hitler as an internalized maternal imago" (5). For Linville, these aspects of the Mitscherlichs' analysis fit into a larger pattern of postwar discourse that displaces the father's culpability onto the role of the mother:

> Far from innocent, their work was made to order for the official needs of a postwar society that, into the 1960s and beyond, was still struggling to rigidify the social gender hierarchy and to exonerate patriarchy in its role in the fascist past. Their exculpation of the paternal function, moreover, occurs at the expense of that familiar postwar scapegoat, the "mother" — whatever "her" guise. (5)

Linville examines in particular the Mitscherlichs' characterization of Hitler as a "variant on the so-called pre-oedipal, phallic mother" (6), "an evil primitive mother figure, a Clytemnestra in drag" (8) that "depends upon a retrospective view that Hitler was not *really* an introjected father figure, despite innumerable testimonies about the idealism Germans felt he represented" (6). According to Linville, this "revisionist view of Hitler as maternal" (6), which transforms the male figurehead of the Fatherland into a pathological mother who led her country to both defeat and culpability for genocide, underlies not only the Mitscherlichs' view of *Vergangenheitsbewältigung,* but also other postwar "cultural product[s]" (4) that thematize the struggle over the Nazi past within the family, including the texts of *Väterliteratur*. In this view, behind the mythic struggle between father and son lies a "bad mother fantasy [. . .] that [. . .] in turn helps sustain the fiction of the sufficiency and integrity of the classical male subject" (6). Linville's reading of the ways in which postwar German culture charges the mother with responsibility for Germany's crimes while absolving the father thus exposes the hidden discourse of gender operative in German attempts at *Vergangenheitsbewältigung* and directly contradicts the prevalent critical notions of *Väterliteratur,* which hold that the mother, as an ahistorical figure, is absent from German historical confrontation with the past.

This hidden discourse of gender is the operative mechanism at stake in Sobol and Frank's staging of Hitler in the figure of Brigitte Frank. By employing her body as the canvas onto which the sign *Hitler* is painted, the play endows the mother with Hitlerian qualities and at the same time accesses the mythology of evil with which Hitler is associated. In addition to assuming the shape of Hitler, she becomes quite literally a mouthpiece for his words and his ideology (and conversely, Hitler becomes a mouthpiece for her speech: at one point in the seventh scene, a film of the historical Hitler appears on a screen, mouthing a speech and lip-synching to the spoken words of Brigitte/Hitler [149]). Importantly, however, she does not transform into Hitler, or even into a man, for her body and voice do not change. For the audience, she remains partially recognizable as the female figure of Brigitte Frank, wife to Hans and mother to Niklas. By performing the sign *Hitler* as a woman, she becomes simultaneously the phallic mother and a staging of Hitler mythology. The process of signification operates in both directions: on the one hand, by assuming the phallic signifier, the mother is imbued with the threatening power of the patriarchal figure, thus negating Hans's statement that "the sign of man is unconditional mastery" and displacing him from his seat of power. On the other hand, she herself is displaced in the act of becoming Hitler, for her body and her voice are literally appropriated in this performance in the service of fascist ideology and the Hitler myth. Thus, according to the code of the play, the sign *mother* is to be read by the audience as a signifier for fascism, while at the same time the sign *Hitler* becomes a referent for pathological female power. The mother is imagined in the theatrical space as critically bound to fascism, power, and evil, for she signifies the Nazi past merely through her body, while the father is evacuated from his position as primary representative of the Third Reich and absolved of responsibility for his crimes.

During the course of the play, Brigitte performs Hitler several times, usually in situations where it serves her interest to evoke the authority of the dictator, such as in Hans's conflict with Himmler. If fact, there is no moment in which the audience is privy to the mother as an "intimate" individual untainted by Nazi discourse, for the first time we are introduced to her, she appears in the form of Hitler:

> *Niklas rolls in a second character in the wheelbarrow, which is covered with a second dirty sheet* [. . .] So then, here is the figure you love most on God's big round earth: Papa, Mama — be pleased to meet each other! *Niklas rips the sheet off. In the wheelbarrow stands Hitler, played by Brigitte.* Shit! What's that?[46]

Niklas is as surprised as the audience to see his mother as Hitler, although the transformation has no effect on Hans, who, interestingly, reacts to her as Hitler in the same way as he does otherwise, displaying utter submission to both *Führer* and *Frau,* a reaction that Niklas characterizes as sexual. Niklas blames his father for Brigitte's appearance as Hitler, for he believes the admiration Hans feels for Hitler is merely a thinly veiled expression of homosexual desire for the *Führer* combined with a masochistic submission to his

---

[46] "*Niklas fährt eine zweite, mit schmutzigem Leintuch verdeckte Figur auf einem Schubkarre herein* [. . .] Sodala, hier ist die von dir am meisten geliebte Figur auf Gottes weitem Erdenrund: Papa, Mama — freut euch aneinander! *Niklas reißt das Leintuch herunter. Auf der Schubkarre steht Hitler, dargestellt von Brigitte.* Scheißdreck! Was ist das?" (Sobol and Frank, 125).

wife. After Hitler/Brigitte appears, Hans speaks for the first time, exclaiming, "This is the first time in the history of German law that love for you, my *Führer*, has become a component of our constitution,"[47] to which Niklas replies,

> "Love for you, my *Führer*"? Wait a minute. Is this an outing? Are you blathering to the *Führer* as a man or a woman? Oh, who cares! Do I really care if you had a homosexual penchant for your fucking *Führer*?[48]

For Niklas, the desire Hans shows for the Hitler-mother poses an epistemological dilemma — is Hans responding to him/her as a woman or as a man? If he professes his desire for Brigitte, the woman, then Hans embodies the masochistic, emasculated weakling who allows his phallic wife to assume authority. If his admiration is for Hitler, he becomes for Niklas the decadent Nazi, whose homosocial preoccupation with Nazi ideology disguises a repressed homosexuality. Because, at this moment, Brigitte and Hitler are one, however, the distinction in desire cannot be determined. Masochistic obedience to a patriarchally constructed authority thus conflates with homoerotic desire for this authority. As Andrew Hewitt convincingly argues in his book *Political Inversions: Homosexuality, Fascism and the Modernist Imagination*, the mythology of Nazism (and with it the mythology of Hitler) is intricately bound to a reading of fascism as homosexual, a significatory conflation that is operative at the levels of both critical theory and the popular imagination. For Hewitt, the parallel unrepresentability of both fascism and homosexuality propels the association between the two:

> [Ernst] Bloch's essay points out that there always was something *unsäglich* — unspeakable — about fascism, something that confounded conventional political terminology [...]
>
> The second thing that Bloch's essay alerts us to [...] is the very structure of *das Unsägliche*, for has not homosexuality too — that "love that dare not speak its name" — been historically unspeakable? [...] If homosexuality dare not speak its own name, it will nevertheless serve as the "name" of something else that cannot be spoken — fascism. In other words, I am suggesting that the conflation of homosexuality and fascism — while not grounded in historical fact — is by no means accidental. (8–9)

---

[47] "Es ist das erste Mal in der Geschichte des deutschen Rechts, daß die Liebe zu Ihnen, mein Führer, ein Bestandteil unserer Verfassung geworden ist" (Sobol and Frank, 125).

[48] "'Die Liebe zu Ihnen, mein Führer'? Moment mal. Ist das ein Outing? Quatschst du den Führer als Mann oder Frau an? Ach, was soll's! Kümmert's mich wirklich, ob du eine homosexuelle Neigung zu deinem verfickten Führer hattest?" (Sobol and Frank, 125).

Because both homosexuality and fascism are, as Hewitt quotes Bloch, unspeakable, unable to be contained in discourse, they each become signifiers for the other. Thus to evoke fascism, in this case in the guise of Brigitte, the Hitler-mother, the woman with the phallic mustache, is necessarily to raise the specter of homosexuality, to point to the associated other of fascist discourse. Niklas's Hitler-mother functions as the site of multiple discourses on gender and sexuality represented in the theatrical space as signifiers for each other. On the one hand, she is figured as the phallic mother, the reverse image of the nurturing mother found in Nazi ideology, the evil monster that usurps and emasculates masculine authority and is responsible for perpetrating Nazi crimes. On the other hand, with her female body she paradoxically embodies the masculine ideology of fascism, a discourse conflated with homosexuality and predicated, as Klaus Theweleit argues, on the disavowal of women's bodies. The play's theatrical fusing of the mother with Hitler thus makes possible the performance of images and ideologies that, like the eggs that represent both masculine and feminine sexuality, would otherwise contradict each other or cancel each other out. Brigitte/Hitler thus functions as a site of impossibility in the play, a metaphor for the impossibility of solving the dilemmas of the past in a way that (like Ian's phallic mother) would erase contradictory images and ideologies and allow the past to finally be laid to rest.

In Niklas Frank's autobiography, the mother functions as a mediator for the fascist past of the father and for the *Nazizeit*. In the play, she not only bequeaths fascism to the son, she quite literally embodies it. For the son, National Socialist discourse is not relegated to the public sphere; it takes root in his very home at one of the most intimate points of connection the child has to the outer world — the mother. The mother, rather than providing a shelter from fascism for the child, is constructed as the literal mouthpiece of its discourse, reproducing it in the home and foisting it upon her son. In this way, she becomes as critical as, or more critical than, the father, the "real" Nazi criminal, for the son's experience of National Socialism and his engagement with the Nazi past.

7: The Future of *Väterliteratur:* Bernhard Schlink's *Der Vorleser* and Uwe Timm's *Am Beispiel meines Bruders*

For the inheritors of the Nazi legacy, a moral life seemed to require a condemnation of their parents — an excruciating, an almost impossible, conflict. How do you feel about someone you love whom you have a duty to hate?

— Eva Hoffman, "The Uses of Illiteracy"

I come to speak of these father books because inherent in them is a structural problem that concerns me once again in connection with your, as I have said, far more important text: How can one speak about perpetrators who at the same time were one's own fathers (or brothers)?

— Robert Cohen, "Letter to Uwe Timm about His Book *In My Brother's Shadow*"[1]

The Future of *Väterliteratur*

ACCORDING TO MOST histories of postwar West German literature, *Väterliteratur* is a phenomenon that erupted onto the literary scene in the late seventies and dominated German literary representation of the Nazi past through the mid-1980s. This conception of the genre certainly aligns with the notion of the *Tendenzwende* (change in trend), which holds that the very public political activism that marked the art and literature of the late 1960s and early 1970s gave way to a withdrawal into the private sphere, which in turn manifested itself as a concentration, often in autobiographical form, on the subjective individual experience of social structures and on the ways in which power is enacted and negotiated in personal relationships. This introspective turn toward the self and questions of identity, termed by literary critics variously as *Neue Subjektivität* (New Subjectivity), *Neue Sensibilität* (New Sensibility), and *Neue Innerlichkeit* (New Inwardness), thus trans-

---

[1] "Brief an Uwe Timm über sein Buch *Am Beispiel meines Bruders.*" "Ich komme auf diese Väterbücher zu sprechen, weil ihnen ein strukturelles Problem inhärent ist, das mich im Zusammenhang mit deinem, wie schon gesagt, weit bedeutenderen Text erneut beschäftigt: Wie kann man über Täter sprechen, die zugleich die eigenen Väter (oder Brüder) waren?" (Cohen, 8).

formed the literary agenda of the second generation. Whereas the student revolutionaries of 1968 had previously publicly denounced the entire parent generation for its activities in the Nazi period and had combined these incriminations with often violent protests against what they saw as the "fascist," authoritarian character of the West German state, the authors of New Subjectivity now grappled with their parents' past in a much more intimate form: the father novel. With their intensive focus on the parents' role in the crimes of the Nazi regime, the authoritarian structures that dominated postwar childrearing, and, most important, the ways in which both of these factors affected the authors' sense of themselves,[2] the father texts were seen as a "new sub-genre" (Bullivant, 222) of the new subjective trend of investigating one's own emotional and social roots. Perhaps for this reason, critics invariably view the flood of *Väterliteratur* as trickling out not long after the demise of New Subjectivity. However, this conflation of the two literary trends ignores the fact that, while *Väterliteratur* is certainly linked to the increase in autobiographical writing and the focus on self-exploration, it is not entirely subsumed under this trend. Moreover, New Subjectivity is generally considered to have ebbed by the end of the seventies, whereas, according to Wulf Segebrecht, the bulk of the father biographies appeared "around the year 1980."[3]

Although critics prefer to terminate *Väterliteratur* with New Subjectivity, however, the second generation's engagement with the past did not end in the mid-1980s. Rather, throughout the decade, German society turned toward the Nazi and Holocaust past as never before, as controversies such as the Historians' Debate, Ronald Reagan's visit to the SS cemetery at Bitburg, and the fiftieth anniversary of *Kristallnacht* dominated public discourse. The end of the decade, with the sudden unification of East and West Germany, saw a brief lull in German dialogue about the Holocaust, when the anniversary of the fall of the Berlin Wall threatened to eclipse the anniversary of *Kristallnacht* and both German and Jewish intellectuals feared that Germany would now proclaim its past as fully mastered. However, the Holocaust reemerged more strongly as a prominent topic in the early nineties, a fact that Bill Niven sees as a direct outcome, not a contradiction, of unification and the end of the postwar rift between the two German states:

> Yet while the political impact of National Socialism and its aftermath had come to an end, there was a veritable explosion of discussion

---

[2] According to Ernestine Schlant, the authors of the father texts often fused these two separate problems into a single complex: "In many cases, the parents' breathtakingly barbarous child-rearing methods were coupled in the minds of the authors with the Nazi past" (85).

[3] "um das Jahr 1980 herum" (Segebrecht, 80).

about the National Socialist past in the public realm. The media, intellectuals, politicians of all parties and the general public were involved in this discussion. Indeed the Germans set about debating the Nazi past as never before. (1)

A number of events and issues centering specifically on German crimes during the Holocaust dominated public discussion for most of the decade: the release of Steven Spielberg's film *Schindler's List,* which was immensely popular in Germany; the controversy over Daniel Goldhagen's book *Hitler's Willing Executioners;* the considerable attention given to the shocking photographs of the *Wehrmachtsaustellung* (*Wehrmacht* exhibit); the ongoing debates about the planned Memorial to the Murdered Jews of Europe (which finally opened in Berlin in 2005 over a decade-and-a-half after it had originally been conceived); and the conflict between Martin Walser and Ignatz Bubis, head of the Central Council of the Jews in Germany, about the speech Walser gave in 1998 upon receipt of the Peace Prize of the German Book Trade. The various debates and events, according to Niven, reflected a willingness on the part of the German public both to confront more directly German crimes during the Holocaust and at the same time to move beyond an obsession with the perpetrators to consider their victims as well: "Increased interest since 1990 in the true extent both of crime, and of involvement in it, has been matched by increased interest in learning about the range of victims" (3). At the same time, the increased readiness to acknowledge the scope of Germany's role meant that Germans needed to focus less on admitting the crimes of the Nazi period and instead could concentrate more on *how* the Holocaust should be remembered, producing a number of highly sophisticated discussions on memory, representation, and the extent to which a "normalized" Germany must include an ongoing discussion about National Socialism and the Holocaust.

Since the late nineties, German discourse on the Nazi past has expanded its focus to look at the German victims of the period, particularly the victims of the Allied firebombing of German cities, the mass rape of German women by the Soviet army, and the plight of the millions of German refugees who fled westward in advance of the Soviets. During the postwar period and, in particular, after 1968, discussion of German suffering was all but absent from intellectual and literary discourse, even as it continued to dominate German private memory and conservative public narratives of the war years, a phenomenon W. G. Sebald documents in his 1999 collection of essays *Luftkrieg und Literatur* (*On the Natural History of Destruction,* 2003). The challenge of introducing the question of German victims into public conversation about the Nazi period has been to acknowledge and investigate the history of German suffering without removing it from the greater context of German crimes in the Holocaust or sliding into what the historian Hans-

Ulrich Wehler terms "a cult of victimhood that represents the German people as stigmatized."[4] As demonstrated by debates that have accompanied literary attempts to represent German suffering so far, such as that chronicled in the 2002 *Spiegel* article "Unter Generalverdacht" ("Under General Suspicion"), which discusses the depiction of German victims in such recent literary works as Günter Grass's 2002 novel *Im Krebsgang* (*Crabwalk*, 2002), contemporary discourse in Germany is concerned with balancing the representation of German victimhood with the ethical necessities of acknowledging German guilt and the suffering of Jews and other non-Germans in the Holocaust.

Given the changing nature of German discourse on the Holocaust and the Nazi period over the last two decades, it is no wonder that critics prefer to view the mid-1980s as marking the end of *Väterliteratur* and are reluctant to recognize more recent literary works as belonging to that tradition. Not only did the intimate autobiographical impulse of the 1970s' New Subjectivity abate in the more political atmosphere of the 1980s, but the public debate about the Nazi past changed as well and to a certain extent moved beyond the generational polarization and sense of victimization by the parents that dominated the father texts. However, as Ernestine Schlant points out, though literary works that thematized the legacy of Nazism in the German family did not appear nearly as frequently as they had around 1980, works by the German second generation continued to be published throughout the eighties and nineties:

> While autobiographical fiction covered a wide territory, the so-called *Väterliteratur* (novels about fathers — or, more correctly, novels about fathers and mothers) was particularly prominent in the years surrounding the 30th anniversary of the Federal Republic, from the middle of the 1970s into the 1980s. The specific characteristics of these novels became blurred in subsequent years, but variations on the main themes continue to be published into the present. (85)

Schlant is one of the few critics to extend the purview of *Väterliteratur* past the era of New Subjectivity and thus to allow the genre to account for texts that approach the legacy of perpetration in the German family in ways that follow some of the more recent developments in German discourse on the Holocaust.

In this chapter, I explore two second-generation works that both align themselves with the tradition of *Väterliteratur* and emerge from German discourse on the Holocaust in the post-unification period: Bernhard Schlink's *Der Vorleser* (*The Reader*) and Uwe Timm's *Am Beispiel meines Bruders* (*In My Brother's Shadow*). In the case of Schlink's novel, the focus shifts from the son's engagement with the father's past to an intergenera-

---

[4] "Ein Opferkult, der das deutsche Volk als stigmatisiert darstellt" (Wehler, 52).

tional love relationship between a Holocaust perpetrator and a member of the German second generation. Significantly, however, the second-generation protagonist's understanding of his connection to the Holocaust past does not undergo a similar shift; rather, he reads his relationship to the guilt of his lover through the lens of the student movement, the conflict between the German war generation and their children, and the genre of *Väterliteratur*. Timm's text, on the other hand, concentrates on the past of Timm's brother, who died on the eastern front as a member of the Waffen SS. Despite the title's stated focus on the memory of his brother, however, Timm's father remains a central figure in his attempt to understand the past. Yet Timm's text is not simply another example of conventional *Väterliteratur*; rather than directing its investigation exclusively against his father in an attempt to expose him as fascist and authoritarian, *Am Beispiel meines Bruders* examines the subtle ways that language circulated within Timm's family to uphold his brother as a model hero, contribute to the family's sense of loss and victimhood, defer acknowledgement of German culpability for the war and the Holocaust, and preserve a rigid, authoritarian view of both the family and the individual.

The Fate of a Generation

Since its publication in German in 1995, Bernhard Schlink's *Der Vorleser* has achieved enormous international success, making it the most well-known of second-generation novels that address the German legacy of perpetration and prompting Steven Erlanger of *The New York Times* to proclaim Schlink "the bard of his generation." In contrast to the texts one usually associates with *Väterliteratur*, however, *Der Vorleser* locates the conflict between the generations over the crimes of the Nazi period with neither the father nor the mother but rather outside the family altogether. The novel, organized in three parts, is narrated from the point of view of Michael Berg, a German man who recounts his lifelong struggle to come to grips with a passionate love affair he had as a teenager in the late 1950s with a thirty-six-year-old woman, Hanna Schmitz. However, although the entire first part — almost half the novel — concentrates specifically on the brief duration of their sexual relationship, Berg's narrative is no mere love story told with nostalgic longing or retrospective regret. In part 2, Michael, now a law student in the mid-1960s, attends a trial of former concentration camp guards as part of a seminar and finds that Hanna, whom he has not seen since the affair, is on trial for her activities as an SS guard. The relationship he had long considered simply an instance of first love is thus suddenly imbued with the added dimension of historical significance when Michael is presented with the question of Hanna's culpability as a Holocaust perpetrator. While the facts of Hanna's criminal actions are indisputable — she was a guard at

Auschwitz and a subcamp, she participated in the forced march of Jewish prisoners, and she was involved in an incident in which prisoners on the march were left to burn to death inside a locked church — Michael finds it difficult to believe in her guilt, for he is unable to reconcile his knowledge of Hanna the perpetrator with his experience of Hanna the lover. His ambivalence is further complicated when, midway through the trial, he realizes that Hanna has long harbored a secret that Michael feels mitigates, at least partially, her agency for the crimes for which she is being tried: she is illiterate. Michael decides that Hanna's efforts to hide her illiteracy propelled her into her role as a camp guard and he considers informing the court of Hanna's handicap, since it bears directly on the degree of her culpability in the church fire.[5] Ultimately, however, he decides to protect her secret, and Hanna is pronounced guilty. Part 3 chronicles Hanna's subsequent imprisonment and Michael's attempts to deal with the debilitating effects of these events on his life. Almost a decade after the trial, he begins to record himself reading his favorite books aloud and then sends the tapes to Hanna in prison. With the help of the tapes, she learns to read. After eighteen years of prison, Hanna is paroled, but the night before she is released, and shortly after her first meeting with Michael since the end of their affair, Hanna commits suicide.

In the mid-1990s, roughly a decade after Hanna's death, Michael decides to write his chronicle of their love affair in order to consolidate it with all the events that followed: the trial, Hanna's imprisonment, her death, and his own troubled relationships with women. In short, he attempts to connect his experience with Hanna as a lover with his knowledge of Hanna as a perpetrator. However, his task of integrating these two narratives proves difficult, for he has been unable to find the language to describe his relationship with Hanna, an experience that he feels has set him apart from his peers. During the affair, Michael is unable to confide in his friends about what at the time is simply his first love with an older woman, and later, he neglects to tell his wife Gertrud, whom he meets shortly after the trial, about his former liaison with a convicted Holocaust perpetrator. In order to write of his relationship with Hanna, Michael requires a narrative form with which he can integrate his private experience of pain and loss into a larger historical

---

[5] Michael claims that Hanna's illiteracy caused her to join the SS and commit crimes, but this is speculation on his part; over the course of the novel, it is, however, accepted as self-evident truth. Except for exonerating her of the responsibility for writing the report of the church fire, the text offers no proof that Hanna's illiteracy was a contributing factor in the crimes she committed. For a detailed analysis of the ways in which Michael's interpretation of Hanna's behavior is presented as truth, see my article "Theorizing the Perpetrator in Bernhard Schlink's *The Reader* and Martin Amis's *Time's Arrow*," forthcoming in *After Representation?* edited by R. Clifton Spargo and Robert Ehrenreich.

framework that links him to his contemporaries. Because the character of his situation resembles that of his fellow students who struggle with their parents, where love for the parent collides with horror upon learning of the parent's criminal past (which, with the so-called student revolution, is historicized as generational conflict), Michael aligns his experience with Hanna with his peers' struggle with their parents. He assumes the trope of generational discord over the Nazi past and reinterprets his intimate relationship with Hanna as a second-generation encounter with the legacy of perpetration. In this way, rather than remaining "a sad story" (*The Reader*, 217)[6] of a secret so shameful that it appears to have led Hanna to commit criminal acts, of an intergenerational love affair that ended painfully without explanation, of Michael's lifelong inability to conduct lasting, intimate relationships, and of Hanna's suicide, Michael rewrites their private, idiosyncratic experience into a public narrative emblematic of an entire generation. At the beginning of part 3, he writes that, whereas during the trial he was shamed and paralyzed by his situation, he has come to the conclusion that his story was not as anomalous as he had assumed:

> How could it be a comfort that the pain I went through because of my love for Hanna was, in a way, the fate of my generation, a German fate, and that it was only more difficult for me to evade, more difficult for me to manage than for others. All the same, it would have been good for me back then to be able to feel I was part of my generation. (*The Reader*, 171)[7]

Michael thus deliberately connects his experience to that of the students of the second generation, "who had dissociated themselves from their parents and thus from the entire generation of perpetrators, voyeurs and the willfully blind, accommodators and accepters, thereby overcoming perhaps not their shame, but at least their suffering because of the shame" (*The Reader*, 171).[8] He equates his love relationship with a perpetrator with the students' familial ties to the Nazi generation and compares his complex feelings of guilt, shame, and betrayal to their conflicted love for their parents. At the same time, however, as the above quote demonstrates, he not only appropriates

---

[6] "eine traurige Geschichte" (Schlink, *Der Vorleser*, 206).

[7] "Wie sollte es ein Trost sein, daß mein Leiden an meiner Liebe zu Hanna in gewisser Weise das Schicksal meiner Generation, das deutsche Schicksal war, dem ich mich nur schlechter entziehen, das ich nur schlechter überspielen konnte als die anderen. Gleichwohl hätte es mir damals gutgetan, wenn ich mich meiner Generation hätte zugehörig fühlen können" (Schlink, *Der Vorleser*, 163).

[8] "die sich von ihren Eltern und damit von der ganzen Generation der Täter, Zu- und Wegseher, Tolerierer und Akzeptierer absetzten und dadurch wenn nicht ihre Scham, dann doch ihr Leiden an der Scham überwanden" (Schlink, *Der Vorleser*, 162).

the narrative of generational struggle to explain his story with Hanna but also fashions himself and his experience into an emblem for the students' struggle with their parents' past. By positing Michael's experience with Hanna as representative of an entire generation's encounter with the past, Schlink's novel transforms the relationship between the generations from one of fractured filial connection to one of ambivalent erotic attachment and in the process redefines the German second-generation quest to assume and comprehend the legacy it has inherited.

Critics of *Der Vorleser,* including Schlant, Helmut Schmitz, Daniel Reynolds, and Ursula R. Mahlendorf, generally tend to follow the narrator's lead and read Michael's story in the context of the German second generation's relationship to the parent generation in general and of *Väterliteratur* in particular. According to Schmitz, "*Der Vorleser* is thus a narrative institutionalisation of the central conflict between perpetrator and second generation which inherits the 'unbewältigte Vergangenheit' from the parents who have been silent about their Nazi past" (58), while Froma Zeitlin writes that "*The Reader* is and is not a parable of the haunted relationships between German children and their parents in the aftermath of the war" ("New Soundings," 192). In this view, *Der Vorleser* transcends its own erotic narrative; because of the intergenerational focus and Hanna's past as a perpetrator, it resembles in crucial ways the problematic relationships between perpetrator parents and their children born after the war, thus evoking the father narratives even as it remains differentiated from them. For this reason, Schlant argues that *Der Vorleser* is an example of how *Väterliteratur* has diversified since its heyday in 1980:

> Born in 1944, Schlink belongs to the generation of the 1968ers, who published their autobiographical novels during the late 1970s and the 1980s. *The Reader* might be seen as a latter-day example of this trend. It shows a thorough acquaintance with all the issues addressed in the "literature about fathers and mothers" and recapitulates and simultaneously criticizes them [. . .]
>
> Schlink uses the generational discrepancy that was at the core of the "literature about fathers and mothers" to new purpose when he makes the bond of love between the generations sexual rather than biological. (210)

According to Schlant, *Der Vorleser* consciously aligns itself within a continuing tradition of *Väterliteratur*. However, as the quote by Zeitlin implies, the novel deviates significantly from the formula of the father texts in that the site of conflict no longer resides in the family, but rather in the sexual relationship between the generations, a development that critics have viewed as both positive and negative.

For Ursula R. Mahlendorf, such a displacement "sexualizes the conflict as well as the coming to terms" and also "highlights the issues of power at stake in all human social relations whether familial or personal and intimate" (459). By locating the transmission of Nazi history outside the narrow confines of the family, Schlink's novel demonstrates how the postwar German struggle over the past transcends conventional intergenerational or Oedipal struggle and points to the extent to which not only familial bonds but also all interpersonal relations in postwar Germany are affected by its legacy of fascism and genocide. In this view, the novel exposes some of the discourses that are immanent but just below the surface in many of the father texts, such as general questions of gender, sex, and class; and problems of guilt, shame, self-victimization, and displacement that are more specific to the engagement with Germany's Holocaust past. For Mahlendorf, by "sexualizing the generational divide" (459), *Der Vorleser* succeeds like no other text in illuminating "the *private* sphere" of "the Holocaust and its heritage" (460), and therein lies "the genius of the novel" (459).[9]

William Collins Donahue holds the opposite opinion of Schlink's work and its use of the sexual relationship between Michael and Hanna to represent Germany's generational struggle over the Holocaust. Rather than increasing our understanding of intergenerational conflict over the past, Donahue argues that *Der Vorleser* distorts it by appointing Michael the "virtual spokesman for an entire generation" (64) and by positing Michael's singular experience with Hanna (as well as Hanna's anomalous illiteracy) as paradigmatic of relations between the second generation and the perpetrators. For this reason, Donahue considers the novel's employment of the erotic plotline a narrative trick that serves to make Michael the "object of

---

[9] Several critics, Heidi Schlipphacke and Joseph Metz among them, have written excellent gender analyses of *Der Vorleser,* but only Mahlendorf has questioned Schlink's decision to cast the novel's perpetrator as a woman: "Why use a woman as *the* perpetrator when the overwhelming number of guards and SS were men?" (459–60). Although Mahlendorf does not pursue answers to this question in her article, she makes a critical point. According to Patricia Heberer of the Center for Advanced Holocaust Studies at the United States Holocaust Memorial Museum, "women could not be members of the SS proper [; . . . they] were technically termed 'weibliche SS-Gefolge' [female SS attendants] and were [. . .] an auxiliary group of SS. They were a minority in the concentration camp world (circa 3,500 women guards compared to nearly 51,000 male SS guards involved in concentration camp activity)." Schlink's novel thus to a certain extent misrepresents the historical role of women in SS posts when it characterizes Hanna simply as a member of the SS. Moreover, the actual relative participation of women compared to men in SS activities suggests that the specific character of Hanna's and Michael's situation precludes it from being representative of the fate of a generation. More likely in this regard would have been a love relationship between a former male SS guard and a younger German woman.

sympathetic identification" by encouraging the reader to ignore the "not insignificant errors of [Michael's] own thought and (in)action" (61):

> Under pressure to "explain" an entire generation's vexed relationship to its parents, it is not difficult to see how Hanna must perforce appear both likeable and, in a sense, reproducible. If we are to understand, rather than condemn the second generation's attachment — and recall that Berg insists that we cannot have it both ways — then we, as readers, must have some sympathetic experience of this inter-generational bond. Schlink achieves this through a sleight of hand that has been lauded by numerous critics: he introduces a weighty issues book with an unlikely erotic preamble that readers simply love. (64)

According to Donahue, with its manipulation of conventional romantic emplotment, *Der Vorleser* thus elicits sympathy for Michael's position and disarms any critical objection the reader might have to Michael's view of Hanna's handicap as a mitigating factor in her culpability for her crimes, his statements of guilt for having loved her, his assessment of the second generation, and his "right to speak for this broad demographic group" (64). Donahue believes that critics (in particular, German critics) readily accept Michael's claim that he is emblematic of the second generation because, even though the love affair between a fifteen-year-old boy and a thirty-six-year-old woman is hardly a typical connection between the perpetrator generation and the second generation, it substitutes a more palatable narrative for the more common relationship between perpetrator parents and second-generation children:

> To second-generation German readers eager to understand (and, perhaps, justify) their own attachment to the generation of perpetrators and bystanders, this underprivileged figure [Hanna] seems to have provided a seductively simple answer both to the question of how they could have loved a morally compromised parent, and how a basically good person might end up as an SS guard. (63)

As Donahue implies, *Der Vorleser* is readily viewed by readers not only as a paradigmatic second-generation text, but, indeed, as a better, more accurate version of *Väterliteratur*. Such a reading reveals a false understanding of the inner workings of the text, yet it is the text (or more precisely, Michael's overt claims to generational representation) that promotes this misreading.

"What Was Truly Surprising"

A careful reading of the text shows that, despite Michael's claim that his love for Hanna is prototypical for his generation, his reaction to Hanna's past in no way resembles the way in which he describes the response of his peers. According to Michael, the student generation's project of confronting the crimes of the Nazi period in general and the participation of their parents in particular was meant to shake up the stolid paralysis of postwar German society:

> Exploration! Exploring the past! We students in the seminar considered ourselves radical explorers. We tore open the windows and let in the air, the wind that finally whirled away the dust that society had permitted to settle over the horrors of the past. (*The Reader*, 91)[10]

The second generation, as Michael describes it, threw themselves passionately into their interrogation of the past, and approached their task with "energy, activity, aggression" (*The Reader*, 170),[11] expressing their outrage against their parents with "rhetoric: sounds and noise" (*The Reader*, 171).[12] Initially, before he encounters Hanna at the trial, he identifies with the other students' energetic passion: "At first, I pretended to myself that I only wanted to participate in the scholarly debate, or its political and moral fervor. But I wanted more; I wanted to share in the general passion" (*The Reader*, 93).[13] However, Michael's sense of excitement and "the good feeling [. . .] that I belonged" (*The Reader*, 93)[14] transforms radically once he attends the trial:

> Some of the defendants and their lawyers were sitting with their backs to us. One of them was Hanna. I did not recognize her until she was called, and she stood up and stepped forward. Of course I recognized the name as soon as I heard it: Hanna Schmitz. Then I also recognized the body, the head with the hair gathered in an unfamiliar knot, the neck, the broad back, and the strong arms [. . .] I recognized her, but I felt nothing. Nothing at all. (*The Reader*, 95)[15]

---

[10] "Aufarbeitung! Aufarbeitung der Vergangenheit! Wir Studenten des Seminars sahen uns als Avantgarde der Aufarbeitung. Wir rissen die Fenster auf, ließen die Luft herein, den Wind, der endlich den Staub aufwirbelte, den die Gesellschaft über die Furchtbarkeiten der Vergangenheit hatte sinken lassen" (Schlink, *Der Vorleser*, 87).

[11] "Energie, Aktivität, Aggression" (Schlink, *Der Vorleser*, 162).

[12] "Rhetorik, Geräusch, Lärm" (Schlink, *Der Vorleser*, 163).

[13] "Zunächst machte ich mir vor, ich wolle nur den wissenschaftlichen oder auch den politischen und den moralischen Eifer teilen. Aber ich wollte mehr, ich wollte das gemeinsame Eifern teilen" (Schlink, *Der Vorleser*, 89).

[14] "das gute Gefühl, dazuzugehören" (Schlink, *Der Vorleser*, 89).

[15] "Einige Angeklagte und Verteidiger saßen mit dem Rücken zu uns. Hanna saß mit dem Rücken zu uns. Ich erkannte sie erst, als sie aufgerufen wurde, aufstand, und nach vorne trat. Natürlich erkannte ich sofort den Namen: Hanna Schmitz. Dann erkannte ich auch die Gestalt, den Kopf fremd mit zum Knoten geschlungenen

In contrast to his fellow students, who retain their outrage with the older generation in general and with the horror revealed in the trial in particular, Michael suddenly shuts down the moment he encounters Hanna as a defendant. He registers no surprise at all that the woman whom he had so passionately loved is suddenly accused of brutal crimes: no anger, no astonishment, no sorrow. (Incredibly, to my mind, critics have accepted Michael's lack of surprise and have themselves displayed remarkably little surprise about how coolly and insensibly he accepts this shocking new information about Hanna.) His feelings — or more precisely, utter lack of feeling — contrast sharply with both his previous vows to expose and condemn the perpetrator generation and the reactions of his fellow students, whose protests against their parents grow louder and more violent over the course of the next several years.

Michael goes on to explain to the reader that, throughout the trial and for a good while afterward as well, he was unable to register feeling of any kind — neither love for Hanna nor shock about her crimes. He compares his feelings of numbness to an arm that has been anaesthetized, a metaphor that presents an interesting parallel to Nadine Fresco's image of the phantom pains of a hand that never existed. In this case, however, the relationship between cause and effect (or, if you will, between signified and signifier) is reversed; here you have an extant limb without feeling, whereas with Fresco's hand, the sensation of the hand exists despite its absence. Michael is presented with the evidence of Hanna's participation in the Holocaust, but its impact on him remains unacknowledged and thus unrepresented. However, rather than downplaying his lack of feeling, he discusses it at length and attempts to justify it as natural and appropriate in two ways. First, he maintains that his numbness is not unique to the situation and believes he perceives it in others: "After a time I thought I could detect a similar numbness in other people" (*The Reader*, 101).[16] Second, he implies that such a response has less to do with the person who is numb and more to do with the horror of the subject matter by maintaining that the same sort of insensibility had plagued both prisoners and guards in the camps. He thus links himself and the post-war spectators at the trial with the victims and the perpetrators in a "general numbness" (*The Reader*, 103),[17] an outrageous relativization that, according to Schlant, betrays Michael's "lack of a moral compass" (214) and, as Mahlendorf reminds us, may have applied to the perpetrators and bystand-

---

Haaren, den Nacken, den breiten Rücken und die kräftigen Arme [...] Ich erkannte sie, aber ich fühlte nichts. Ich fühlte nichts" (Schlink, *Der Vorleser*, 91).

[16] "Nach einer Weile meinte ich, ein ähnliches Betäubtsein auch bei anderen beobachten zu können" (Schlink, *Der Vorleser*, 97).

[17] "Gemeinsamkeit des Betäubtseins" (Schlink, *Der Vorleser*, 99).

ers, but certainly not to the prisoners themselves (471). By way of what Donahue terms Michael's "dubious 'numbness' doctrine" (61), in which he projects his own inability to react to Hanna's crimes onto anyone else who encounters them, Michael thus justifies his own lack of compassion and outrage and at the same time attempts to bypass any possible criticism by fully acknowledging his insensibility.

Michael's inability or unwillingness to register surprise or emotion upon learning of Hanna's crimes is made all the more evident by his almost diametrically opposite reaction to his discovery of her secret:

> In thinking about Hanna, going round and round in the same tracks week after week, one thought had split off, taken another direction, and finally produced its own conclusion. When it did so, it was done — it could have been anywhere, or at least anywhere the familiarity of the surroundings and the scenery allowed what was truly surprising, what didn't come like a bolt from the blue, but had been growing inside myself, to be recognized and accepted [. . .]
> Hanna could neither read nor write. (*The Reader*, 131–32)[18]

Whereas Michael registered almost no surprise or astonishment upon learning of Hanna's indictment for crimes as a concentration camp guard (on the contrary, he tells us he found her imprisonment "natural and right" [*The Reader*, 97][19]), he reacts intensely to the realization that she is illiterate, claiming that this one factor, among the many of her trial, is "truly surprising." Immediately upon realizing her secret, he spends several pages ruminating on the implications of her handicap for unresolved incidents in their relationship and for her crimes. The questions he neglected to ask when he discovered her past as a camp guard now come pouring out; whereas before he did not dare to pose them, now he allows himself to ponder her past because he can immediately respond with answers:

> No, Hanna had not decided in favor of crime. She had decided against a promotion at Siemens, and fell into a job as a guard [. . .] And no, at the trial Hanna did not weigh exposure as an illiterate against exposure

---

[18] "Beim Nachdenken über Hanna, Woche um Woche in denselben Bahnen kreisend, hatte sich ein Gedanke abgespalten, hatte seinen eigenen Weg verfolgt und schließlich sein eigenes Ergebnis hervorgebracht. Als er damit fertig war, war er damit fertig — es hätte überall sein können oder jedenfalls überall da, wo die Vertrautheit der Umgebung und Umstände zuläßt, das Überraschende, das einen nicht von außen anfällt, sondern innen wächst, wahrzunehmen und anzunehmen [. . .] Hanna konnte nicht lesen und schreiben" (Schlink, *Der Vorleser*, 126).

[19] "natürlich und richtig" (Schlink, *Der Vorleser*, 93).

as a criminal. She did not calculate and she did not maneuver. (*The Reader*, 133)[20]

In this way, Michael wakes from his numbness and begins to react to Hanna's criminal past, devising an elaborate theory for both Hanna's actions as a guard and her behavior during the trial. However, this sudden engagement with Hanna's crime occurs only because it is mediated through the element of her illiteracy; as he immediately perceives, it can be interpreted as a mitigating factor in her crimes, and thus reduces greatly the horror of them. Hanna's inability to read, in Michael's view (importantly, the reader never gets Hanna's perspective on this theory or, for that matter, any outside evidence to support it), thus transforms her from an agent whose motivation for perpetrating crimes he does not dare to fathom to a passive object caught in the unpredictable current of history. This new view of Hanna brings about a sudden thaw in Michael's frozen feelings, and, at the end of his ruminations on her secret, he is finally able to express emotion. Again, however, his feelings do not concern Hanna the perpetrator, but rather Hanna the lover: "I was oddly moved by the discrepancy between what must have been Hanna's actual concerns when she left my hometown and what I had imagined and theorized at the time" (*The Reader*, 134).[21] With regard to Hanna's crimes, and in particular, the victims of those crimes, Michael continues to feel nothing.

Acting Out, Working Through, and Denial

Michael's claim that his story mirrors that of his generation is, at best, misleading, for his reaction to Hanna's past as a perpetrator little resembles his contemporaries' aggressive attack on their parents. Whereas the students angrily reprove their parents for crimes for which they often have little evidence, Michael observes the detailed testimony of Hanna's participation with quiet dispassion. At worst, his assumption of representation is an attempt to link his own failure — that is, his disturbing detachment in the face of Hanna's crimes — to his contemporaries' inadequate confrontation with their parents. Yet, importantly, his failure does not equal their failure. The student generation's attempt to confront their parents was certainly, in large

---

[20] "Nein, habe ich mir gesagt, Hanna hatte sich nicht für das Verbrechen entschieden. Sie hatte sich gegen die Beförderung bei Siemens entschieden und war in die Tätigkeit als Aufseherin hineingeraten [...] Und nein, im Prozeß wog Hanna nicht zwischen der Bloßstellung als Analphabetin und der Bloßstellung als Verbrecherin ab. Sie kalkulierte und taktierte nicht" (Schlink, *Der Vorleser*, 128).

[21] "Seltsam berührte mich die Diskrepanz zwischen dem, was Hanna beim Verlassen meiner Heimatstadt beschäftigt haben mußte, und dem, was ich mir damals vorgestellt und ausgemalt hatte" (Schlink, *Der Vorleser*, 129).

part, misguided; in their zeal to expose the parents as criminals and postwar German society as a disguised version of the Nazi state, the students appointed themselves their parents' judges, a role Michael Schneider terms "truly arrogant and monstrous" ("Fathers and Sons," 12).[22] This self-assumed perspective of superiority with regard to the parents, according to Schlant, allowed the students to neatly and decisively distinguish themselves from both their parents and the unwanted legacy of the Holocaust: "Furious attacks on the parent generation were meant to demonstrate that one was not like the parent and was therefore released from a heinous past" (82). From there, they needed only to travel a short journey to self-pity and the assumption of victimhood, in which memory of the actual victims of the Nazi regime was eclipsed by the students' insistence on their own grievances. For Schlant, therein lay the failure of the student generation: "This shortcut avoided any true confronting of the past and its legacy and any concern for the victims; it was motivated not by sorrow and shame but by rage and despair" (82).

In this way, the student generation engaged in what Dominick LaCapra terms "acting-out," a psychic response to traumatic loss that can be experienced by both survivors and perpetrators (although in different ways) and the descendants of both groups. According to LaCapra, "In acting-out, the past is performatively regenerated or relived as if it were fully present rather than represented in memory and inscription, and it hauntingly returns as the repressed" ("Trauma, Absence, Loss," 716). LaCapra distinguishes acting out from "working-through," a psychic process that enables the person attempting to overcome traumatic loss "to distinguish between past and present and to recognize something as having happened to one (or one's people) back then that is related to, but not identical with, here and now" ("Trauma, Absence, Loss," 713). Although acting-out and working-through utilize different methods and may appear to have opposite aims, LaCapra insists that they are not binary opposites but two closely connected positions on the spectrum of response to trauma. Indeed, as he suggests, acting-out does not always preclude the process of working-through; rather, its manifestation may signal that the person, while still enacting a repetitive struggle with the past, is oriented toward a more critical perspective that could eventually result in working-through: "with respect to traumatic losses, acting-out may well be a necessary condition of working-through" ("Trauma, Absence, Loss," 716–17).

Without question, the students' actions tended more toward the acting-out side of LaCapra's spectrum. Their inability to distinguish between the Federal Republic of the late 1960s and the Third Reich, their at times hys-

---

[22] "wahrhaft anmaßend und monströs" ("Väter und Söhne," 18).

terical accusations against their parents, and their own self-image as the victims of the war generation certainly indicate that they rarely possessed the critical distance LaCapra deems necessary for working-through. However, despite their ineptitude, in acting out, the students *did* act; they refused to accept the status quo and threw themselves against a German society that had calcified into denial of its Holocaust past. Michael, on the other hand, remains passive and observes both the students' theatrical confrontation with their parents' opaque past and Hanna's courtroom drama with detachment. In contrast to his peers, who histrionically exaggerated their parents' involvement in atrocity, Michael, as we have seen, staunchly disavows the evidence that implicates Hanna as a criminal and constructs an elaborate narrative that, in his mind, exonerates her. In short, he engages in neither acting-out nor working-through, but in the psychic complex of denial, a disengagement with the traumatic past that, according to LaCapra, "may involve intricate and subtle modes of evasion, often through relatively complex (if at times paranoid and circular) modes of argumentation" ("Representing the Holocaust," 358 n 6). Michael's methods of evasion are multiple; not only does he concoct a complex theory for Hanna's actions based on scant evidence, but he also develops a convoluted explanation for his own numb lack of response to the discovery of Hanna's past and even goes so far as to extend it to the victims of the Holocaust. Moreover, by positing himself as the yardstick of his generation and claiming his experience with Hanna as representative of their encounter with the past, he co-opts their struggle with the parent generation, thereby camouflaging his passive failure to act. At the same time, by asserting that his numb torpidity with regard to the trial and the crimes it exposed is shared by his fellow students, Michael makes them complicit in his disturbing lack of emotion and thus mitigates his own singular failure to acknowledge the extent of Hanna's involvement in murder.

Michael's claim that his narrative represents the fate of his generation is thus spurious at best, for though his situation of being suddenly confronted with the crimes of Hanna's generation is certainly one that is shared by his peers, his distinct method of trying to reconcile his relationship to the Holocaust past differs from their confrontation with their parents. His narrative, along with *Der Vorleser* as a whole, is thus not a chronicle of an entire generation's attempt to come to terms with their parents' past, but an idiosyncratic account of an anomalous sexual relationship that may at times resemble the greater conflict between the generations but, importantly, cannot be called upon to stand in for this conflict. At the same time, however, Schlink's text, by explicitly connecting itself to the German generational struggle and literary attempts to represent it, demands to be read in the tradition of *Väterliteratur*. In this way, it contributes, like Frank's *Der Vater*, to an expanded understanding of the genre, one that acknowledges that the legacy of the Holocaust past is transmitted through various configurations of personal relationships and not exclusively from father to son. It is through such variations on the father-son paradigm, and not rigid reproductions of it, that *Väterliteratur* proceeds into the future.

"The Danger of Smoothing It All Out in the Telling"

One of the most recent German texts to explore the legacy of the Nazi period in the postwar German family is Uwe Timm's 2003 memoir *Am Beispiel meines Bruders*. The brother to whom Timm's title refers is Karl-Heinz, who, as a soldier in the Waffen SS in Ukraine, died in 1943 after being wounded and having both legs amputated. Timm, who was only three when Karl-Heinz died and can recall only one memory of him, decides after the deaths of his remaining family members (his father, mother, and older sister) to reconstruct his brother's life from a variety of sources: the mediated memories of his parents, his brother's letters from the front, and his brother's brief and at times cryptic wartime diary. Not only does Timm endeavor to discover and document what his brother actually did in the war — he hopes for some evidence that his brother avoided or even resisted brutal orders, yet he fears that Karl-Heinz might have participated in atrocities against civilians — but he also desires to understand how Karl-Heinz viewed himself and his voluntary service with the Waffen SS.

While Timm is empathetic in his attempts to give shape to the life of the brother he barely knew, he also insists on critically reviewing his brother's adherence to authority, enthusiasm for the military, and blithe indifference to the sufferings of the Soviet population (as opposed to Karl-Heinz's outrage at the Allied bombing of German cities). In order to avoid creating a pathetic narrative that valorizes his brother's tragic death and the traumatic loss of the family's apartment in the Hamburg firestorm of 1943 (an account that his parents maintained after the war), Timm supplements the stories of his family with other narratives that situate their loss in the greater context of the Holocaust and German military aggression. He quotes passages from the writings of Holocaust survivors Primo Levi and Jean Améry and of several German generals and discusses Christopher Browning's book *Ordinary Men: Police Battalion 101 and the Final Solution in Poland* (1992), which documents the participation of average Germans in the murder of tens of thousands of Jews. According to Brigitte Rossbacher, Timm's "highly constructed montage" (238) represents a conscious attempt to make connections between the intimate stories of German suffering that Timm heard at home while he was growing up and more comprehensive historical research that documents the widespread participation of Germans in the Holocaust:

> By utilizing a genre that contextualizes personal experiences within public historical discourse, Timm engages in a dialogic process in which he both investigates the wartime experiences of his parents and brother as encoded in long-standing family narratives of suffering, loss, and guiltlessness and rereads these narratives in light of more recent public debates on German perpetration and culpability. (238–39)

For Timm, the juxtaposition of his family's narrative of the war with historical research is critical, for it allows him to move past his parents' narrow understanding of what happened, which calcified into a simple spoken formula: "*Bombed out, and the boy fell soon afterward.* That was the blow Fate had dealt our family, that was war. *Everything destroyed*" (*In My Brother's Shadow*, 29).[23] Timm's project is to break through such rigid codifications to show how his family not only suffered under the Nazi regime and in the war but also may have tacitly supported Nazi efforts and activities as well. By questioning the ways in which his parents characterized their experiences and by allowing other voices with radically different perspectives into the dialogue, Timm hopes to avoid the simple reproduction of the family mythos that comes with retelling their stories: "The danger of smoothing it all out in the telling. *Speak, Memory.* Only from today's perspective do we see the chains of cause and effect ordering things, enabling us to understand them" (*In My Brother's Shadow*, 31).[24]

Skeletons in the Closet

Early on in the book, Timm writes of his anxiety about learning more about his brother's past. In particular, he fears what he might find in Karl-Heinz's diaries and letters and compares his aversion to reading them to his childhood sense of foreboding upon hearing his mother read aloud the famous Grimm story of Bluebeard:

> The moment when Bluebeard's wife tries to enter the locked room after he has gone away, in spite of his prohibition, was so sinister. When my mother came to that point I would ask her to stop reading. Only years later, when I was grown up, did I reach the end of the fairy tale.
> *Then she turned the key in the lock. As the door opened, a torrent of blood flowed out to meet her, and she saw dead women hanging from the*

---

[23] "*Ausgebombt und kurz darauf der Junge gefallen.* Das war der Schicksalsschlag der Familie, und das war der Krieg. *Alles vernichtet*" (Timm, *Am Beispiel meines Bruders*, 37).

[24] "Die Gefahr, glättend zu erzählen. *Erinnerung, sprich.* Nur von heute aus gesehen sind es Kausalketten, die alles einordnen und faßlich machen" (Timm, *Am Beispiel meines Bruders*, 38).

> walls. Some of them were only skeletons. She was so frightened that she closed the door at once, but the key jumped out of the lock and fell in the blood. She quickly picked it up and tried to wash the blood away, but in vain, for when she had wiped it off one side of the key it appeared again on the other side. (*In My Brother's Shadow*, 5)[25]

Timm makes the connection between his childhood fear of finding out what lies behind Bluebeard's door and his current apprehension about opening the door to his brother's past. Just as Bluebeard's wife is prohibited from unlocking the door, so too is Timm subject to a family injunction against investigating the skeletons in their closet, a prohibition that is no less powerful for being undeclared.

Later, as he is reading Karl-Heinz's diary, he comes across the passage that, like the point in the Bluebeard story when he could listen no longer, is so disturbing to him that it previously kept him from reading further: "*21 March. Donez. Bridgehead on the Donez. 75 m away Ivan smoking cigarettes, fodder for my MG*" (*In My Brother's Shadow*, 12).[26] Timm reacts vehemently to his brother's blithe, almost humorous reference to shooting a Russian soldier: "This was the place where, when I came upon it earlier — and it positively leaped out at me from the top left-hand side of the page — I read no more but closed the notebook" (*In My Brother's Shadow*, 12).[27] This passage functions as an analogue to the passage from the Bluebeard tale Timm quoted for us earlier. Indeed, he uses much the same language as the Grimm brothers to describe his horror upon encountering evidence of his brother's nonchalance about violence and his casual dehumanization ("Ivan") of the Soviet soldier. Just as the key in Bluebeard's story jumps out of the lock and falls into the blood, the passage from the diary jumps into Timm's eye (the literal translation of the German reads "it positively jumped from the top

---

[25] "So unheimlich war es, wenn Blaubarts Frau nach dessen Abreise, trotz des Verbots, in das verschlossene Zimmer eindringen will. An der Stelle bat ich die Mutter, nicht weiterzulesen. Erst Jahre später, ich war schon erwachsen, habe ich das Märchen zu Ende gelesen. *Da schloß sie auf, und wie die Türe aufging, schwomm ihr ein Strom Blut entgegen, und an den Wänden herum sah sie tote Weiber hängen, und von einigen waren nur die Gerippe noch übrig. Sie erschrak so heftig, daß sie die Türe gleich wieder zuschlug, aber der Schlüssel sprang dabei heraus und fiel das Blut. Geschwind hob sie ihn auf und wollte das Blut abwaschen, aber es war umsonst, wenn sie es auf der einen Seite abgewischt, kam es auf der anderen Seite wieder zum Vorschein*" (Timm, *Am Beispiel meines Bruders*, 11).

[26] "*März 21. Donez. Brückenkopf über den Donez. 75 m raucht Iwan Zigaretten, ein Fressen für mein MG*" (Timm, *Am Beispiel meines Bruders*, 19).

[27] "Das war die Stelle, bei der ich, stieß ich früher darauf — sie sprang mir oben links auf der Seite regelrecht ins Auge —, nicht weiterlas, sondern das Heft wegschloß" (Timm, *Am Beispiel meines Bruders*, 19).

left-hand side of the page into my eye"). Bluebeard's wife picks up the bloody key and tries to clean it, but she is unable to erase the evidence of her transgression against Bluebeard's dictum and her discovery of his violent secret. Timm is likewise marked by his violation of the unspoken family prohibition; later we learn that he begins to develop an ailment in precisely the spot where the story leaped out at him:

> Since I have been working on this book, reading my brother's letters and diary over and over again, as well as many files, reports, and books, rereading Primo Levi, Jorge Semprun, Jean Améry, Imre Kertész, Browning's *Ordinary Men*, since I have spent day after day reading of these incomprehensible horrors I have had pain in my eyes, first in the right eye, a torn cornea, then for a few weeks later in the left eye, now recurring for the fifth time, a burning, unbearable pain [. . .] It is a pain that makes not only the injured eye weep but the other eye too, and I, one of a generation to whom tears were forbidden — boys don't cry — I weep as if I had to shed all my mother's, my father's, my brother's suppressed tears, the tears of those who didn't know, who didn't want to know what they could have known, should have known. *Wissen*, to know, derives from an Old High German root, *wizzan*, to see, to look. They did not know because they would not see, they looked away. (*In My Brother's Shadow*, 135–36)[28]

The violent impact of what Timm learns when he begins to really look at his family's implication in a nation's collective crimes manifests itself physically as a wound that both registers and expresses intense pain. Like Bluebeard's wife, whose key betrays what she has seen, Timm's eyes become the psychosomatic record of the terrible truths that his family would not regard, and he is forced to weep all of their unshed tears. In the case of Bluebeard's wife, the blood is the ever-present reminder of both the horror she has seen and the infraction she committed in order to learn of her husband's crimes; in

---

[28] "Seit ich an diesem Buch arbeite, seit ich lese, wieder und wieder, die Briefe, das Tagebuch, aber auch die Akten, die Berichte, die Bücher, abermals Primo Levi, Jorge Semprun, Jean Améry, Imre Kertész und Brownings *Ganz normale Männer*, seit ich Tag für Tag das Grauen lese, das Unfaßliche, habe ich Augenschmerzen, erst am rechten Auge, ein Abriß der *Hornhaut*, einige Wochen später am linken, was sich wiederholte, jetzt zum fünften Mal, ein brennender, unerträglicher Schmerz [. . .] ein Schmerz, der nicht nur das verletzte Auge tränen läßt, sondern auch das andere, ich, der einer Generation angehört, der man das Weinen verboten hatte — ein Junge weint nicht — weine, als müßte ich all die unterdrückten Tränen nachweinen auch über das Nichtwissen, das Nichtwissenwollen, der Mutter, des Vaters, des Bruders, was sie hätten wissen können, wissen müssen, in der Bedeutung von wissen, nach der althochdeutschen Wurzel, wizzan: erblicken, sehen. Sie haben nicht gewußt, weil sie nicht sehen wollten, weil sie wegsahen" (Timm, *Am Beispiel meines Bruders,* 147).

Timm's case, the tears function as the traumatic mark of his unwavering look at their unacknowledged secrets and his transgression against the family code in order to learn of these secrets.

In the Shadow of the Father

Although his brother's service in the Waffen SS is one of the family skeletons Timm attempts to uncover, it is by no means the only one, or even the most important, the book's title to the contrary. As Timm states, the memory of his brother is enmeshed with and compounded by what other family members did during the war and the way they remembered these events. He therefore writes intermittently of his mother, his father, and his sister, and how their different memories contributed to the family narrative of the war, his brother's death, the family's suffering, and Germany's defeat, and their inability to admit to German guilt. In particular, his father plays an integral role in the maintenance of the family's collective memory of Karl-Heinz. For that reason, Timm writes, "Writing about my brother means writing about my father too. My likeness to him can be seen in my likeness to my brother" (*In My Brother's Shadow*, 14).[29] As Timm states, his only access to his brother is through his father, and any attempt to reconstruct his brother's life must necessarily investigate that of his father as well, for Timm's memory of one is inseparable from that of the other. According to Jürgen Wutschke, this complex and uneasy conflation of brother with father obscures Timm's original goal of concentrating on his brother's life and becomes the driving force behind not only *Am Beispiel meines Bruders* but all of Timm's work: "Uwe Timm has published the meta-narrative of his literary work in book form. It concerns the triangular relationship between himself, his father, and his brother."[30] For Wutschke, Timm's brother, despite his prominence in the book's title as its professed subject, operates only as the ostensible concern of the narrative. The real object of Timm's memoir is his father, the family skeleton who looms largest in the narrative. Timm's focus on Karl-Heinz thus exists to serve the more pressing problematic of his memory of his father: "Timm works actually in retrospect to understand his father. The fact that this functions only in a roundabout way via the brother makes this little

---

[29] "Über den Bruder schreiben, heißt auch über ihn schreiben, den Vater. Die Ähnlichkeit zu ihm, meine, ist zu erkennen über die Ähnlichkeit, meine, zum Bruder" (Timm, *Am Beispiel meines Bruders*, 21).

[30] "Uwe Timm hat die Metaerzählung seines schriftstellerischen Schaffens in Buchform veröffentlicht. Es handelt sich dabei um die Dreieckbeziehung zwischen ihm, seinem Vater und seinem Bruder" (Wutschke).

book so unique."[31] Other reviewers agree with Wutschke and believe that, despite Timm's stated focus on the brother, the book eventually metamorphizes into an investigation of the father. According to Simone Dattenberg, Timm's conflict with his father is "the actual crux of the discussion,"[32] while according to Roger K. Miller, "it is not Karl-Heinz's shadow that Mr. Timm seems to have been in most of his life, but that of his father."

Timm's more intensive focus on his father would seem to push this "brother book" more in the direction of *Väterliteratur,* and indeed, some critics tend to read it in the tradition of the genre. Stuart Taberner terms Timm's novel "a throwback to the *Vaterroman*" (109) on account of its evaluation of the postwar German family in general and the role of the father and his "pedagogical and political failure" (109) in particular. However, as Taberner suggests, on account of its historicized image of the family, which situates their private loss within the greater context of German perpetration, *Am Beispiel meines Bruders* provides a much more differentiated perspective than the typical father novel. Robert Cohen agrees and argues that Timm expands the parameters of *Väterliteratur.* He believes that Timm's narrative achieves what most of the father books could not by virtue of a delicate balance that attempts to explain the father's and brother's behavior without thereby letting them off the hook. In an open letter to Timm, Cohen writes,

> You don't give (explanatory and therefore reassuring) answers, but rather you burden your readership and above all yourself with this agonizing inability to understand — but without thereby fetishizing the behavior of the perpetrators. Repeatedly you refer discreetly to other possible behavior, without a superior attitude, without requiring heroism: just more than this unquestioning participation.[33]

For Cohen, Timm's book represents a more nuanced look at the perpetrators of the Holocaust, one that neither passes final judgment on them nor seeks to exculpate them but endeavors to gain some sort of understanding of what they believed they were doing. According to Michael Braun, in order to achieve this sort of understanding, Timm avoids the bitter struggle with his parents that occupies the more conventional father books:

---

[31] "Timm erarbeitet sich nämlich rückblickend den Vater. Dass das nur über den Umweg des Bruders funktioniert, macht das Büchlein so einzigartig" (Wutschke).

[32] "der eigentliche Kern der Auseinandersetzung" (Dattenberg).

[33] "Du gibst nicht die (erklärenden, d.h. beruhigenden) Antworte, sondern bürdest der Leserschaft und vor allem dir selbst dieses quälende Nichtverstehenkönnen auf, ohne dadurch das Verhalten der Täter zu fetischisieren. Mehrfach weist du behutsam auf ein mögliches anderes Verhalten hin, ohne Besserwisserei, ohne Heldisches zu verlangen: nun mehr als dieses fraglose Mitmachen" (Cohen, 8–9).

Uwe Timm writes no book of reckoning with the "father generation" as a "perpetrator generation," but rather a distressing story that already in its title demands an exemplary character. With the example of his brother and his family the silent taboo that descended upon the first postwar generation is broken and the much-quoted "inability to mourn" is examined. The conventional boundaries between the roles of perpetrator and victim, between fathers and their children become blurred and require new definition.[34]

In Braun's opinion, although *Am Beispiel meines Bruders* interrogates the disturbing past of both Timm's father and his brother, it does not seek the same sort of reckoning as do other texts of *Väterliteratur* and in this way represents a different sort of project. Rather than explicitly reproaching his parents, Timm attempts, from his own contemporary perspective, to introduce issues about which the parent generation simply refused to talk, and thus he highlights particular problems or contradictions in their narratives. Timm focuses on what Braun terms the silent taboo of the postwar generation, the ways in which German culpability was methodically erased from both public and private discourse. Timm terms this injunction on talking about German crimes "*deathly silence*" (*In My Brother's Shadow*, 96)[35] and cites Primo Levi's assertion that in such silence lay the Germans' deepest guilt. By bringing to light what was repressed in the postwar family sphere and integrating it into the German dialogue about the war years, Timm thus attempts to puncture this "deathly silence," the taboo that, like Bluebeard's dictum to his wife, kept him and his generation from opening the nation's closet and facing the horror that it housed.

The Impoverishment of Language

Timm's interest in the postwar discourse of the German family goes beyond the transgression of the silent taboo. Rather, Timm stresses that silent amnesia was only one form of discursive evasion in which the postwar generation engaged: "My father's generation, the generation of perpetrators, lived by either talking about it or saying nothing at all. There seemed to be only

---

[34] "Uwe Timm aber schreibt kein Buch der Abrechnung mit der 'Vätergeneration' als 'Tätergeneration,' sondern eine bedrängende Erzählung, die schon im Titel exemplarischen Charakter beansprucht. Am Beispiel seines Bruders und der Familie wird das Schweigetabu, das sich über die erste Nachkriegsgeneration gelegt hat, gebrochen, wird die vielzitierte 'Unfähigkeit zu trauern' hinterfragt. Die herkömmlichen Grenzen zwischen Täter- und Opferrollen, zwischen Vätern und ihren Kindern werden unscharf und damit aufs Neue definitionsbedürftig" (Braun, 86).

[35] "dieses *Totschweigen*" (Timm, *Am Beispiel meines Bruders*, 106).

those two options: either you kept discussing it or you never mentioned it" (*In My Brother's Shadow*, 93).[36] For this reason, in addition to exposing the silent taboo (that is, what was *not* said in his family), Timm takes a careful look at what his parents *did* say. He analyzes the language they employed to talk about Karl-Heinz and the war in order to understand how certain aspects of his brother's memory were perpetuated, how the value system of the Nazi period was reproduced in the postwar era, and how German crimes in the war and the Holocaust were justified and normalized. In short, Timm performs an extensive discourse analysis of the ways in which his family, especially his father, narrated its experience and communicated these stories with one another.

Timm notes how, in contrast to the contemporary image of Germans' complete repression of the war years, there was a great deal of talk about the past:

> These were the everyday stories told after the war, at work, in bars, at home, in dialect or in educated High German, and they ground down and wore away what had happened, and with it the guilt. And you could talk about it perfectly freely, something that seems unimaginable today. (*In My Brother's Shadow*, 120)[37]

Timm stresses that, far from remaining rigidly silent about the war years, his parents' generation often talked a great deal about their experiences during the Third Reich. However, their repetitive talk was not evidence of an open dialogue about the past. On the contrary, as Timm stresses, the more his parents (in particular, his father) and their friends talked about the past, the less they had to say, and their narratives began to take the form of guarded and ritualized litanies that carefully regulated the way in which the past could be represented. Every discussion between his parents about the past "always came around to the same subject" (*In My Brother's Shadow*, 67):[38] his brother's death, the family's losses in the war. In order to make their experience comprehensible, his parents developed a formulaic narrative that sought to explain their loss and at the same time avoid any questioning of

---

[36] "Die Vätergeneration, die Tätergeneration, lebte vom Erzählen oder vom Verschweigen. Nur diese zwei Möglichkeiten schien es zu geben, entweder ständig davon zu reden oder gar nicht" (Timm, *Am Beispiel meines Bruders,* 102).

[37] "Das waren die alltäglichen Geschichten, die nach dem Krieg erzählt wurden, in den Betrieben, den Kneipen, zu Hause, im Dialekt, im gepflegten Hochdeutsch, so wurde das Geschehene und mit ihm die Schuld kleingemahlen. Und man konnte davon — was man sich heute nicht mehr vorstellen kann — ganz frei erzählen" (Timm, *Am Beispiel meines Bruders,* 131–32).

[38] "kam [. . .] jedesmal wieder zu einem Gespräch desselben Inhalts" (Timm, *Am Beispiel meines Bruders,* 75).

causality or how the actions of the German leadership (with whom the father identified) contributed to their misfortune:

> My parents' set phrase for what had happened to them was *a blow dealt by fate*, a fate beyond the reach of personal influence. *Our boy and our home both lost:* it was the kind of remark that saved you having to think about the reasons. You felt that with that suffering you had done your bit for the general atonement. Everything was *dreadful* for the very reason that you had been a *victim* yourself, the victim of a collective and inexplicable fate. (*In My Brother's Shadow*, 82)[39]

In a spin on indirect discourse, Timm's use of italics here reproduces the exact language the parents used, signaling to the reader that Timm reports but does not endorse their euphemistic or uncritical use of terms like "victim" or "fate." He thus embeds their language in a critique that attempts to highlight the unstated assumptions and the avoidance of questioning that ground their remarks.

Throughout the narrative, Timm employs the technique of italicization to call attention to the ways his family's language reveals their world view and the sometimes subtle power relations between them. For example, beginning as early as on the second page and repeated several times throughout the book, he refers to himself as the "*afterthought*" (*In My Brother's Shadow*, 4).[40] This designation of his parents for him, the youngest child, reveals the centrality of Karl-Heinz, "*that brave boy*" (*In My Brother's Shadow*, 10),[41] in family memory and Timm's own feelings of marginalization as the younger son who could never live up to the myth of the brave older brother who died valiantly in battle. Timm describes these designations — both positive and negative — as "word-for-word statements of fact" (*In My Brother's Shadow*, 10)[42] that were accepted by all parties as valid and true, but his implied critique reveals the ways in which his family valorized the dead son while minimizing the importance of the living one.

Timm's critique of language in the family also concentrates on the influence of National Socialist language, with its dehumanizing euphemisms and

---

[39] "Die formelhafte Zusammenfassung der Eltern für das Geschehen war der *Schicksalsschlag*, ein Schicksal, worauf man persönlich keinen Einfluß hatte nehmen können. *Den Jungen verloren und das Heim*, das war einer der Sätze, mit denen man sich aus dem Nachdenken über die Gründe entzog. Man glaubte mit diesem Leid seinen Teil an der allgemeinen Sühne geleistet zu haben. *Fürchterlich* war eben alles, schon weil man selbst *Opfer* geworden war, Opfer eines unerklärlichen kollektiven Schicksals" (Timm, *Am Beispiel meines Bruders*, 91).

[40] "*Nachkömmling*" (Timm, *Am Beispiel meines Bruders*, 10).

[41] "*Der tapfere Junge*" (Timm, *Am Beispiel meines Bruders*, 16).

[42] "wörtliche Festlegungen" (Timm, *Am Beispiel meines Bruders*, 17).

normalization of violence. He notes the manipulation of language during the war that allowed both German soldiers and civilians to believe that the extreme measures being taken against others were justified:

> I have now read other diaries and letters of the time; some observe the suffering of the civilian population and express outrage, others speak of the killing of civilians — Jews and Russians alike — as the most natural thing in the world. The language they've been taught makes killing easier: inferior human beings, parasites, vermin whose lives are dirty, degenerate, brutish. (*In My Brother's Shadow*, 85)[43]

For Timm, whose concern with his family's memory of the past reveals at the same time an apprehension about the power of language, the violence of the war and the Holocaust was already immanent in the violence of language in the Third Reich. However, his main concern is not how language was abused during war, but rather how this language of murder and domination survived after the war and worked, on the one hand, to circumvent the war generation's frank acknowledgement of the actual crimes that the various euphemisms signify, and on the other, to force the second generation to observe the parents' language taboos and thus hinder any critique of the parent generation from taking form. Timm sees in the continued use of Nazi language in the postwar West German family "the impoverishment of language and linguistic repression alike" (*In My Brother's Shadow*, 90),[44] an indication that the everyday language of postwar Germans was stigmatized by Nazi crimes, despite their unwillingness to concede guilt for them. An extreme example of a euphemism that signifies for Timm the corruption of language both during the Holocaust and in the postwar period is *Endlösung* (Final Solution):

> There were solutions for that too: resettlement for the inferior Slavs, and *the final solution of the Jewish problem.* Final solution. A term that will be held in contempt forever and proof of the fact that even the German language has lost its innocence, innocence in the literal sense of freedom from guilt. In the same way, there were all those abbreviations, some of them branded on the language and unforgotten [...] — a subversion of the language that cast a shadow well into the postwar

---

[43] "Inzwischen habe ich andere Tagebücher und Briefe gelesen, solche, die durchaus die Leiden der Zivilbevölkerung wahrnehmen, die Empörung äußern, und andere, in denen mit größter Selbstverständlichkeit von der Tötung der Zivilisten, Juden wie Russen, berichtet wird. Es ist die angelernte Sprache, die das Töten erleichtert: Untermenschen, Parasiten, Ungeziefer, deren Leben schmutzig, verkommen, vertiert ist" (Timm, *Am Beispiel meines Bruders,* 94).

[44] "gleichermaßen Verrohung und Verdrängung in der Sprache" (Timm, *Am Beispiel meines Bruders,* 100).

period. Army terminology, linguistic mutilations that found their counterpart in physical injury: men limping, on crutches, an empty jacket sleeve fastened with a safety pin, trouser legs turned up, squeaking artificial limbs. (*In My Brother's Shadow*, 91–92)[45]

According to Timm, terms like *Endlösung*, which maintain the façade of benign banality but which actually signify the horror of the Nazis' carefully planned and executed murder of millions of European Jews, brand the German language indelibly as complicit with mass murder, just as Cain's mark signifies his crime of violence. However, the effects of this tainted language do not remain in the past; rather, this corrupted and stigmatized language casts its shadow in the future, corroding the language of the postwar generations and precluding their ability to develop any innocent relationship with language. This is what Timm means by the impoverishment of language (specifically the German language); for a writer such as Timm, who is sensible to the problematics of semiotics, it is not only the legacy of Germany's crimes in the war that is bequeathed to the second generation, but also a language that bears the traces of this violence. Timm's comparison of language with men who have been permanently injured by battle is instructive; like their bodies, which signify the effects of the violence the men experienced and thus function as visceral reminders of the war that disrupt postwar forgetting, so too language has been crippled by its own proximity to and complicity with violence.

With this interrogation of language, Timm thus exposes the ways in which his family (again, particularly his father) was complicit in the crimes of the Nazi period, the war, and the Holocaust, if not on the level of action (Timm never really learns if either his brother or father performed any atrocities beyond the "normal" and conventional participation as soldiers in battle), then on the level of linguistic endorsement — both during the war and afterward. Although Timm recognizes the critical difference between word and deed, between talking about a "Jewish problem" and attempting to "solve" it by means of genocidal violence, he is unable to downplay the violence contained in language as harmless or even as merely metaphorical.

---

[45] "Auch dafür gab es Lösungen: die *Umsiedlung* für die slawischen *Untermenschen* und die *Endlösung der Judenfrage*. Endlösung. Ein Wort, das für immer geächtet bleiben wird. Und ein Beleg dafür, daß auch die Sprache, die deutsche, ihre *Un-schuld* verloren hat. Wie auch all die Abkürzungen, einige sind wie ein Brandmal der deutschen Sprache aufgedrückt und bleiben unvergessen [. . .] — Wortverfinsterungen, die weit in die Nachkriegszeit hineinreichten. Die Kommißsprache, die Sprachverstümmelungen, die ihre Entsprechungen in körperlicher Versehrtheit fanden: die Hinkenden, an Krücken Gehenden, die mit einer Sicherheitsnadel hochgesteckten leeren Jackenärmel, die umgeschlagenen Hosenbeine, die quietschenden Prothesen" (Timm, *Am Beispiel meines Bruders*, 101).

Rather, he views the manipulation of language as prior to and inherent in any systematic deployment of violence. For this reason, he refuses to dismiss as meaningless talk the ways in which his family skirted Germany's wartime crimes against civilians and at the same time litanized their own losses. Moreover, and this is critical for Timm, although Germany's murderous violence against Jews and designated others ceased with the end of the war, the linguistic violence did not, even if the official discourse of the Federal Republic was purged of the more obvious traces. Thus, to a certain extent, the Third Reich and its war lived on in the language of the postwar family, which maintained a value system that extolled racism, nationalism, self-denial, obedience to authority, and conformity. Timm's contribution to *Väterliteratur* is therefore one in which the focus shifts from the father himself to the father's use of language, allowing, as Cohen claims, for a measure of understanding. *Am Beispiel meines Bruders* does not represent an Oedipal battle against brother and father, in which Timm exposes and condemns them as perpetrators; rather Timm struggles against the language that his parents bequeathed to him, whether consciously, in the form of admonitions toward obedience and self-denial, or unconsciously, in the reproduction of the language of the very system that was responsible for Karl-Heinz's death.

Väterliteratur and Wishful Thinking

Both Bernhard Schlink's *Der Vorleser* and Uwe Timm's *Am Beispiel meines Bruders*, as we have seen, are recent texts that participate in the project of *Väterliteratur* and at the same time complicate the ways in which the father novel represents how the legacy of the Holocaust is bequeathed to the German second generation. Schlink's novel figures the relationship between the generations as erotic attachment and calls into question the second generation's ability to distance itself from the crimes of the war generation. Michael's love for Hanna, a Holocaust perpetrator, is not one of a child for its parent, which, according to Michael, "is the only love for which we are not responsible" (*The Reader*, 170).[46] Rather, according to Michael, because he chose to have a relationship with Hanna (unlike his contemporaries, who were born into their relationships with perpetrators), he is implicated in her guilt and thus finds himself unable to judge her: "I had to point to Hanna. But the finger I pointed at her turned back to me. I had loved her" (*The Reader*, 170).[47] However, as we have seen, Michael's failure lies not in his inability

---

[46] "ist die einzige Liebe, für die man nicht verantwortlich ist" (Schlink, *Der Vorleser*, 162).

[47] "Ich mußte eigentlich auf Hanna zeigen. Aber der Fingerzeig auf Hanna wies auf mich zurück. Ich hatte sie geliebt" (Schlink, *Der Vorleser*, 162).

to sever his connection to Hanna or pronounce judgment against her, but in his zeal to exculpate her and restore the aura of innocence to her that she appeared to possess during their relationship. For, according to his logic, if she is guilty, then he is guilty by association. In order to free himself from her crime, he must pronounce her innocent.

Timm's narrative, on the other hand, largely avoids the dichotomy between condemnation and exculpation that plagues many of the father texts and Schlink's narrative as well. Timm avoids the one-on-one battle of the father texts and demonstrates instead how Nazism permeated the entire family in both conscious and unconscious ways. He attempts to determine whether his brother and father committed any crimes, and because he finds little evidence, he speculates on the possibility based on information from other texts. Importantly, he does not condemn them for actions he cannot prove they committed, but he also does not seek to exculpate them based on scant evidence. Moreover, rather than censuring them excessively for the actions he knows they performed, he focuses on imagining alternate ways in which they might have behaved, and thus is able to avoid the self-righteous stance that plagues some of the father texts. In contrast to Michael, he consciously avoids creating an elaborate explanation that would allay his fears and apprehensions: "[I] must be careful not to indulge in wishful thinking instead of describing what I actually remember" (*In My Brother's Shadow*, 71).[48] Above all, unlike Michael, who manipulates language to downplay Hanna's crimes and cover over his own failure to acknowledge them, Timm focuses on the complex linguistic games that allowed the Nazis to justify their crimes and his parents to obsess over their losses. By making language the center of his investigation and by showing how not only his family, but he as well, has been influenced by a corrupted language, he avoids Michael's monological denial of the past and creates a dialogical text that disrupts the one-way movement of *Väterliteratur*.

---

[48] "[Ich] muß mich davor hüten, aus der Beschreibung des Erinnerungsvorgangs in wunschgelenkte Mutmaßungen zu kommen" (Timm, *Am Beispiel meines Bruders*, 79).

Conclusion:
The "Glass Wall": Marked by an Invisible Divide

Memory connects us, memory divides us.
— Ruth Klüger, *weiter leben*[1]

IN HIS NOTORIOUS STATEMENT from *The Differend* (1998), the French philosopher Jean-François Lyotard likens the Holocaust to a powerful earthquake that has demolished not only the physical landscape but also the very instruments that can measure the earthquake, which, in the case of the Holocaust, include documentation that might help the historian analyze and reconstruct the event (56–58). Although Lyotard's analogy is widely known and quoted, scholars, in particular historians, have vehemently objected to it, for it appears to ignore the massive amount of data gathered on the events of the Nazi genocide of the European Jews, information that not only takes the form of facts and documents but also is expressed in testimony, historical reconstruction, and imaginative literature. Moreover, Lyotard's image of the earthquake, which Sidra DeKoven Ezrahi calls "a metaphor to beat all metaphors" (122), collides like all metaphors with the limits of its own ability to adequately contain the object it is meant to represent and thus dramatically demonstrates the danger inherent in the metaphorical process. For the Holocaust was *not* an earthquake, not a geological disaster. It was not the result of the unleashing of the powerful but disinterested forces of nature, but rather a series of events in which the German nation systematically identified, isolated, and murdered millions of Jews who were both its own countrymen and citizens of other, sovereign countries. With an earthquake, one may ethically use the passive voice: a building was destroyed. With the Holocaust, on the other hand, it cannot be forgotten that there were not only victims but perpetrators as well. Lyotard's characterization of the Holocaust as an earthquake, though evocative of the notion of disaster, threatens to perform the very sort of amnesia it laments, for it erases the agency of extermination that is essential to the crime.

Despite the problematic limitations of Lyotard's metaphor, it remains a powerful image of the cataclysmic destruction the Holocaust has wrought in

---

[1] "Erinnerung verbindet uns, Erinnerung trennt uns" (Klüger, 220).

the postwar world, not only immediately after the event but also into the present moment. Extending his metaphor a bit further, one could say that although the rubble of the earthquake has since been cleared and the destroyed structures largely rebuilt, the destruction continues to make itself known in powerful aftershocks that reverberate even today, reminding us that the effects of an event of the sheer magnitude of the Holocaust do not remain exclusively within the confines of the generation that experienced it. Rather, as an exponentially growing body of imaginative literature indicates, the aftermath of the Holocaust continues to resound powerfully in the post-Holocaust world, marking the lives not only of those who experienced it personally but also of those to whom the legacy of the Shoah is bequeathed.

In particular, Lyotard's image of the earthquake's rupture represents the position of the second generation, a group born after the Holocaust who finds itself by the nature of its family history bound to an event it did not experience. For, unlike the participants of the Holocaust, both survivors and perpetrators, the generation born after has no memory or experience of the seismic activity of those years of suffering and atrocity. It is divided from the catastrophe by the nature of the event itself, which cuts off any ties to the time before. Just as a person born after an earthquake knows that disastrous event only by the traces of physical trauma to the environment and the evidence of rebuilding on old foundations, the members of the post-Holocaust generation can only access the Holocaust by viewing the destruction left in its wake from their position on the other side of the divide. This generation stands at the edge of a debris-strewn rift and attempts to imagine the uncleaved landscape that existed there before. The chasm caused by the unknown event separates these writers from the other side, a time before the war, when European Jewish life still flourished and Germany had not yet become a nation that planned and executed genocide. As Melvin Jules Bukiet, the son of Holocaust survivors, characterizes this experience, "If an enormous chasm opened in the lives of Elie Wiesel et al., they could nonetheless sigh on the far side and recall the life before. There is no before for the second generation [. . . They] attempt to peer across the chasm, but they cannot see the other side." The second generation thus finds itself in a sort of epistemological state of exile, left stranded on the other side of a history it does not know by an event it did not experience, cut off from the essential knowledge of what happened to their parents or what their parents did.

Lyotard's earthquake is helpful to us in a further way, for not only is it useful for conceptualizing the epistemological dilemma of the second generation as a whole, but it also allows us to visualize the fault line that exists between two very different legacies of the Holocaust — that of perpetration and that of survival. For the existential rupture caused by the earthquake not only separates the second generation temporally from the parents' past but divides the children of perpetrators from the children of survivors as well, despite their parallel anxieties about their respective legacies. The descendants of those who perpetrated and those who suffered the Holocaust stand opposite one another and peer not only below, into the vast destruction of an incomprehensible event, but across the chasm at one another as well. As Eva Hoffman describes the connection, "There was a historical horror between us; but we were distinctly not enemies. Indeed, we were looking at the horror from a similar point of view — if from opposite ends of the telescope" (*After Such Knowledge*, 109). The children of perpetrators and those of survivors are both linked and separated by the Holocaust; they are structurally analogous to one another, but not identical. Robert Schindel highlights this dialectical tension between positional similarity and qualitative difference in *Gebürtig*, where we witness the convergence of two radically different second-generation positions. In the novel's opening scene, the Austrian children of survivors and perpetrators encounter each other in a Viennese café. Although the two groups interact, they are at the same time essentially divided: "This table breaks into two halves, as though a glass wall were erected between the two respective pairs, mute, invisible, hermetic."[2] Schindel's metaphor of the invisible glass wall that marks the encounters between Austrian Jews and non-Jews is fitting for the ways in which the legacies of survival and perpetration relate to each other, for in its illustration of the parallel perspectives of the two groups, the essential divide of experience that separates them and the possibility of mutual recognition, it exemplifies Dan Diner's notion of a "negative symbiosis" in which Germans and Jews are both bound together and at the same time separated by their common history. Schindel thus presents the reader with the dilemma that characterizes attempts by each second-generation group to remember, integrate, and represent its own familial history of the Holocaust and at the same time to acknowledge the radically different perspective of the other group, a relationship Hoffman characterizes as "contrapuntal" (*After Such Knowledge*, 118). The critical question is thus: can these two legacies ever contribute to a joint memory of the Holocaust, or will their views on the past always remain divided? Although by the end of Schindel's novel, in the retelling of the opening scene in the café, the glass wall is absent and the divide between Jews and non-Jews is bridged by the momentary solidarity between Mascha and Christiane, Schindel's novel leaves this question open.

Indeed, as *Gebürtig* further suggests, perhaps it is naïve to pose such a question — to expect that, one generation after the disaster, the two second-generation legacies can somehow heal the open wound of history and bridge

---

[2] "dieser Tisch in seine zwei Hälften auseinanderbricht, als baue sich zwischen den jeweils Zweien die gläserne Wand auf, stumm, unsichtbar, hermetisch" (Schindel, *Gebürtig*, 12).

the chasm that divides them. After all, such an expectation ignores the critical feature that characterizes trauma, namely, its belatedness and, as stressed by this study, its intergenerational transmission. As Marianne Hirsch argues, the trauma of the Holocaust really only manifests itself fully in its legacy: "Perhaps it is *only* in subsequent generations that trauma can be witnessed and worked through, by those who were not there to live it but who received its effects, belatedly, through the narratives, actions and symptoms of the previous generation" ("Surviving Images," 12). The power of the trauma thus spills over between generations, and the unresolved conflicts of the previous generation are left to be worked through by the subsequent one. Yet perhaps the trauma of the Holocaust is too powerful to be solved in the second generation, especially across the divide that separates the two legacies. If we accept Hirsch's claim, then it follows that not only does the trauma of the Holocaust not end with the survivor or the perpetrator, but it does not end with their children either. According to Vamik Volkan, the trauma of the Holocaust is rarely solved on the level of the second generation: "If the next generation cannot effectively fulfill their shared tasks — and this is usually the case — they will pass these tasks on to the third generation, and so on" (186). In this way, the task of resolving the divide between perpetration and victimization, if not bridged by the children of the survivors and perpetrators, is passed down the line to their children.

    I would therefore like to conclude this study with a brief glance at a third-generation text, Jonathan Safran Foer's *Everything is Illuminated,* a picaresque novel that chronicles the attempts of two third-generation protagonists to uncover their respective grandfathers' experiences in the war. Jonathan, a young American Jew, travels to Ukraine to find both his grandfather's shtetl, Trachimbrod, and the woman who, during the Holocaust, hid his grandfather, who died before Jonathan was born. Jonathan is escorted through the Ukrainian countryside by two tour guides: Alexander, a young Ukrainian translator (and, at least at the beginning, not a very good one), and a driver, Alexander's grandfather, an elderly depressed man. During their travels, both Jonathan and Alexander make important discoveries. For his part, Jonathan learns that his grandfather's shtetl has been completely effaced from both the landscape and Ukrainian memory, while Alexander discovers two important facts about his own grandfather: that he hails from Kolki, a town near Trachimbrod, and not from far-away Odessa, as he had long maintained; and that in the town of Kolki, during the war, he became an unwilling coperpetrator when he revealed to the Nazis that his best friend was a Jew. The two young men come to realize that they share legacies that, while radically different, are oddly parallel: the physical effacement of one grandfather's Trachimbrod is mirrored by the other grandfather's mnemonic effacement of Kolki, a repression that is further linked to both the Ukrainian collective forgetting of its once-thriving Jewish communities and the individual silence on the part of Alexander's grandfather about his forced betrayal of his best friend.

Although the novel begins with an account of Jonathan's journey, it is not Jonathan who narrates this investigation into the past, but Alexander, whom Jonathan charges with telling his story. The narrative complexity of the novel is enhanced by its division into three types of narrative that are woven together: Alexander's chronicle of their common journey to uncover the past; Alexander's letters to Jonathan about his task of writing the chronicle; and Jonathan's own fictional history of Trachimbrod, which he writes in a wildly fantastic magical realist style, beginning with the eighteenth century and ending with the war. On his end, Jonathan attempts to restore narratively the destroyed and forgotten shtetl, while Alexander, through his communications with Jonathan and his account of the journey, tries to come to terms with his beloved grandfather's difficult past and to gather the courage to separate himself and his young brother from their own abusive father. What begins as Jonathan's attempt to recover his grandfather's story thus gradually becomes a common endeavor, a joint project that connects the two young men: Alexander tells of the present and Jonathan imagines the past. In this way, the two men become partners in quest of the truth of their grandparents' respective experiences, seeking at the same time to understand what those violent events of over fifty years ago have meant for their families and continue to mean for themselves. Although each is firmly situated in his own familial legacy, Alexander and Jonathan conduct their review of these legacies together and thus attempt to bridge the chasm of historical experience that separates them. As Alexander concludes in one of his letters, by together creating this common space with which they can review the past, they are able to join their very disparate legacies to produce a shared narrative of both the Holocaust and the present: "With our writing, we are reminding each other of things. We are making one story, yes?" (144).

Works Cited

Anhalt, Irene. "Abschied von meinem Vater." In Heimannsberg and Schmidt, *Das kollektive Schweigen: Nationalsozialistische Vergangenheit und gebrochene Identität in der Psychotherapie*, 37–56. In English, "Farewell to My Father." In Heimannsberg and Schmidt, *The Collective Identity: German Identity and the Legacy of Shame*, 31–48.

Antze, Paul, and Michael Lambek. Introduction to *Tense Past: Cultural Essays in Trauma and Memory*. Edited by Paul Antze and Michael Lambek. New York: Routledge, 1996: xi–xxxviii.

Apel, Dora. *Memory Effects: The Holocaust and the Art of Secondary Witnessing*. New Brunswick, NJ: Rutgers UP, 2002.

Appelfeld, Aharon. *Beyond Despair: Three Lectures and a Conversation with Philip Roth*. Translated by Jeffrey M. Green. New York: Fromm International, 1994.

Auerhahn, Nanette C., and Dori Laub. "Intergenerational Memory of the Holocaust." In Danieli, *International Handbook of Multigenerational Legacies of Trauma*, 21–41.

Bagley, Petra M. "The Death of the Father — the Start of a Story: Bereavement in Elisabeth Plessen, Brigitte Schwaiger and Jutta Schutting." *New German Studies* 16, no. 1 (1990–91): 21–38.

Bar-On, Dan. "An Encounter between Children of Survivors and Children of Perpetrators of the Holocaust." In *The Uses and Abuses of Knowledge: Proceedings of the 23rd Annual Scholars' Conference on the Holocaust and the German Church Struggle*, edited by Henry F. Knight and Marcia Sachs Littell, 431–40. Lanham, MD: UP of America, 1997.

———. *Fear and Hope: Three Generations of the Holocaust*. Cambridge, MA: Harvard UP, 1995.

———. *The Indescribable and the Undiscussable: Reconstructing Human Discourse after Trauma*. Budapest: Central European UP, 1999.

———. *Legacy of Silence: Encounters with Children of the Third Reich*. Cambridge, MA: Harvard UP, 1989.

Behrens, Katja. "Arthur Mayer oder Das Schweigen." In *Salomo und die anderen*, 67–155. Frankfurt am Main: Fischer, 1993. In English, "Arthur Mayer, or The Silence." In *Contemporary Jewish Writing in Germany*, edited and translated by Leslie Morris and Karen Remmler, 33–78. Lincoln, NE: U of Nebraska P, 2002.

Berger, Alan L. *Children of Job: American Second-Generation Witnesses to the Holocaust*. Albany: State U of New York P, 1997.

Berger, Alan L., and Naomi Berger. *Second Generation Voices: Reflections by Children of Holocaust Survivors and Perpetrators*. Syracuse, NY: Syracuse UP, 2001.

Bergmann, Martin S., and Milton E. Jucovy. *Generations of the Holocaust*. New York: Basic, 1982.

Bosmajian, Hamida. "The Orphaned Voice in Art Spiegelman's *Maus I* & *II*. *Literature and Psychology* 44, no. 1–2 (1998): 1–21.

Brandstetter, Alois. "Prosaische Annäherung an die Väter: Zu einem Motiv-Boom." In *Der gemütliche Selbstmörder*, edited by Ludwig Legge and Wilhelm Solms, 35–45. Marburg: Hitzeroth, 1986.

Brasch, Thomas. "Wort und Totschlag." *konkret* 6 (1987): 77.

Braun, Michael. "Krieg und Literatur: Zu den neuen Romanen von Ulla Hahn, Klaus Modick und Uwe Timm." *Der Deutschunterricht* 3 (2004): 84–86.

Broder, Henryk M. "Diese Scheißbilder trage ich mit mir rum." *Der Spiegel* 28 (1987): 166–68.

Browning, Christopher R. *Ordinary Men: Reserve Police Battalion 101 and the Final Solution in Poland*. New York: HarperCollins, 1992.

Bukiet, Melvin Jules. "Unto the Next Generation." *The Washington Post*, 4 May 1997.

Bullivant, Keith. *Realism Today: Aspects of the Contemporary West German Novel*. Leamington Spa, UK: Berg, 1987.

Burgess, Gordon. "'Was da ist, das ist [nicht] mein': The Case of Peter Schneider." In *Literature on the Threshold: The German Novel in the 1980s*, edited by Arthur Williams, Stuart Parkes, and Roland Smith, 107–22. New York: Berg, 1990.

Burstein, Janet. "Traumatic Memory and American Jewish Writers: One Generation after the Holocaust." *Yiddish* 11, no. 3–4 (1999): 188–97.

Calhoun, Karen S., and Patricia A. Resick. "Post-Traumatic Stress Disorder." In *Clinical Handbook of Psychological Disorders*, edited by David H. Barlow, 48–98. New York: Guilford, 1993.

Caruth, Cathy. Introduction to *Trauma: Explorations in Memory*. Edited by Cathy Caruth. Baltimore, MD: Johns Hopkins UP, 1995, 3–12.

———. *Unclaimed Experience: Trauma, Narrative and History.* Baltimore, MD: Johns Hopkins UP, 1996.

Celan, Paul. *Die Hand voller Stunden: Gedichte.* Munich: Deutscher Taschenbuch Verlag, 1991.

———. *Selected Poems and Prose of Paul Celan.* Translated by John Felstiner. New York: W. W. Norton, 2000.

Cohen, Robert. "Brief an Uwe Timm über sein Buch *Am Beispiel meines Bruders.*" *Das Argument* 254 (2004): 8–9.

Danieli, Yael, ed. *International Handbook of Multigenerational Legacies of Trauma.* New York: Plenum, 1998.

Dattenberg, Simone. "Die verbotene Tür zum Grauenhaften." Review of *Am Beispiel meines Bruders,* by Uwe Timm. *Münchner Merkur,* 24 August 2003. http://www.merkur-online.de/nachrichten/kultur/kunstakt/art282,317303.html. Accessed 6 July 2005.

Diagnostic and Statistical Manual of Mental Disorders. 4th ed, text revision. Washington, DC: American Psychiatric Association, 2000.

Diner, Dan. "Negative Symbiose: Deutsche und Juden nach Auschwitz." In *Ist der Nationalsozialismus Geschichte? Zu Historisierung und Historikerstreit,* edited by Dan Diner, 185–97. Frankfurt am Main: Fischer, 1987. In English, "Negative Symbiosis: Germans and Jews after Auschwitz." In *Reworking the Past: Hitler, the Holocaust and the Historian's Debate,* edited by Peter Baldwin. Boston, MA: Beacon, 1990: 251–61.

Doherty, Thomas. "Art Spiegelman's *Maus:* Graphic Art and the Holocaust. *American Literature: A Journal of Literary History, Criticism and Bibliography* 68, no. 1 (1996): 69–84.

Donahue, William Collins. "Illusions of Subtlety: Bernhard Schlink's *Der Vorleser* and the Moral Limits of Holocaust Fiction." *German Life and Letters* 54, no. 1 (January 2001): 60–81.

Eckstaedt, Anita. *Nationalsozialismus in der "zweiten Generation": Psychoanalyse von Hörigkeitsverhältnissen.* Frankfurt am Main: Suhrkamp, 1989.

Epstein, Helen. *Children of the Holocaust.* New York: Penguin, 1979.

Erlanger, Steven. "Postwar German Writer a Bard of a Generation." *The New York Times,* 19 Jan. 2002: A4.

Ewert, Jeanne C. "Reading Visual Narrative: Art Spiegelman's *Maus.*" *Narrative* 8, no. 1 (2000): 87–103.

Ezrahi, Sidra DeKoven. "Representing Auschwitz." *History and Memory* 7, no. 2 (1996): 121–54.

Fiero, Petra S. "'Bis zur Vergasung': Katja Behrens' Kritik an der deutschen Sprache und Vergangenheitsbewältigung." *Germanic Notes and Reviews* 30, no. 1 (Spring 1999): 143–52.

Figge, Susan. "Fathers, Daughters, and the Nazi Past: Father Literature and Its (Resisting) Readers." In *Gender, Patriarchy and Fascism in the Third Reich: The Response of Women Writers,* edited by Elaine Martin, 274–302. Detroit: Wayne State UP, 1993.

Foer, Jonathan Safran. *Everything is Illuminated.* New York: Perennial, 2002.

Fölting, Anne. "Art Spiegelman: *Maus.* The Interaction of Pictorial Elements and the Narrative." Seminar paper written at the Universität Dortmund, April 1999.

Frank, Niklas. *Meine deutsche Mutter.* Munich: C. Bertelsmann, 2005.

———. *Der Vater: Eine Abrechnung.* Munich: Wilhelm Goldmann, 1993. In English, *In the Shadow of the Reich.* Translated by Arthur S. Wensinger and Carole Clew-Hoey. New York: Alfred A. Knopf, 1991.

Freeman, Thomas. "Jewish Identity and the Holocaust in Robert Schindel's *Gebürtig.*" *Modern Austrian Literature* 30, no. 1 (1997): 117–26.

Fresco, Nadine. "Remembering the Unknown." *International Review of Psycho-Analysis* 11, no. 4 (1984): 417–27.

Freud, Sigmund. *Beyond the Pleasure Principle.* Translated by James Strachey. New York: Liveright, 1950. Original German, "Jenseits des Lustprinzips." In *Gesammelte Werke,* vol. 13. Frankfurt am Main: S. Fischer, 1969.

Frieden, Sandra. *Autobiography: Self into Form.* Frankfurt am Main: Peter Lang, 1983.

Fröhlich, Hans J. "Väter und Söhne: Literarische Neuerscheinungen aus Herbst 79 und Frühjahr 80." *Jahresring* 1980–81: 205–21.

Frühwald, Wolfgang. "Vaterland — Muttersprache: Zur literarischen Tradition moderner Väterliteratur." In *Communication fidei: Festschrift für Eugen Biser zum 65. Geburtstag,* edited by Horst Bürkle and Gerold Becker, 343–55. Regensburg: Friedrich Pustet, 1983.

Gebürtig. Directed by Robert Schindel and Lukas Stepanik. Produced by Cult Film, Extrafilm, Dazu Film, Akson Studio. Life Size Entertainment, 2002.

Gehrke, Ralph. *Literarische Spurensuche: Elternbilder im Schatten der NS-Vergangenheit.* Opladen: Westdeutscher Verlag, 1992.

Genette, Gérard. *Narrative Discourse: An Essay in Method.* Translated by Jane E. Lewin. Ithaca, NY: Cornell UP, 1980.

Giordano, Ralph. *Die zweite Schuld oder von der Last, Deutscher zu sein.* Munich: Knaur, 1990.

———. Foreword to *Der Vater: Eine Abrechnung,* by Niklas Frank, 5–10.

Grimm, Reinhold. "Elternspuren, Kindheitsmuster: Lebensdarstellungen in der jüngsten deutschsprachigen Prosa." In *Vom anderen und vom Selbst: Beiträge zu Fragen der Biographie und Autobiographie,* edited by Grimm and Jost Hermand, 167–82. Königstein: Athenäum, 1982.

Grossman, David. *See Under: Love.* Translated by Betsy Rosenberg. New York: Noonday, 1989.

Hardtmann, Gertrud. "Children of Nazis: A Psychodynamic Perspective." In Danieli, *International Handbook of Multigenerational Legacies of Trauma,* 85–95.

Harrison, Keith. "Telling the Untellable: Spiegelman's *Maus.*" *Rendezvous* 34, no. 1 (1999): 59–73.

Hartman, Geoffrey. *The Longest Shadow: In the Aftermath of the Holocaust.* Bloomington, IN: Indiana UP, 1996.

———. "On Traumatic Knowledge and Literary Studies." *New Literary History* 26, no 3 (1995): 537–63.

Hass, Aaron. *In the Shadow of the Holocaust: The Second Generation.* Cambridge, MA: Cambridge UP, 1990.

Haubl, Rolf. "Das Gesetz des Vaters: Trauer und Magie in einigen stellvertretenden Biografien der späten siebziger Jahre." In *Die Sprache des Vaters im Körper der Mutter,* edited by Rolf Haubl, Eva Koch-Klenske, and Hans-Jürgen Linke, 10–65. Gießen: Anabas, 1984.

Heberer, Patricia. E-mail to the author. 25 Aug. 2005.

Heimannsberg, Barbara, and Christoph J. Schmidt, eds. *Das kollektive Schweigen: Nationalsozialistische Vergangenheit und gebrochene Identität in der Psychotherapie.* Cologne: Edition Humanistische Psychologie, 1992. In English, *The Collective Identity: German Identity and the Legacy of Shame.* Translated by Cynthia Oudejans Harris and Gordon Wheeler. San Francisco: Jossey-Bass, 1993.

Herman, David. *Story Logic: Problems and Possibilities of Narrative.* Lincoln: U of Nebraska P, 2002.

Hershman, Marcie. Review of *Elijah Visible,* by Thane Rosenbaum. *Ploughshares* 22, no. 2–3 (1996): 242–43.

Hewitt, Andrew. *Political Inversions: Homosexuality, Fascism, and the Modernist Imagination.* Stanford, CA: Stanford UP, 1996.

Hirsch, Marianne. "Family Pictures: *Maus,* Mourning and Post-Memory." *Discourse* 15, no. 2 (1992–93): 3–29.

———. "Surviving Images: Holocaust Photographs and the Work of Postmemory." *The Yale Journal of Criticism* 14, no. 1 (2001): 5–37.

Hoffman, Eva. *After Such Knowledge: Memory, History and the Legacy of the Holocaust.* New York: Public Affairs, 2004.

———. "The Uses of Illiteracy." Review of *The Reader,* by Bernhard Schlink. *The New Republic,* 23 Mar. 1998, 33–36.

Holy Bible. New International Version. Grand Rapids, MI: Zondervan, 1985.

Horowitz, Sara R. "Auto/Biography and Fiction after Auschwitz: Probing the Boundaries of Second-Generation Aesthetics." In *Breaking Crystal: Writing and Memory after Auschwitz,* edited by Efraim Sicher, 276–94. Urbana, IL: U of Illinois P, 1998.

Hulse, Michael. "Fathers and Mothers: Recent Works by Christoph Meckel, Brigitte Schwaiger, Jutta Schutting and Waltraud Anna Mitgutsch." *The Antigonish Review* 64 (1986): 133–41.

Huyssen, Andreas. "Von Mauschwitz in die Catskills und zurück: Art Spiegelmans Holocaust-Comic *Maus.* In *Bilder des Holocaust: Literatur-Film-Bildende Kunst,* edited by Manuel Köppen and Klaus R. Scherpe, 171–89. Cologne: Böhlau, 1997.

Iadonisi, Rick. "Bleeding History and Owning His [Father's] Story: *Maus* and Collaborative Autobiography." *The CEA Critic* 57, no. 1 (1994): 41–56.

Ian, Marcia. *Remembering the Phallic Mother: Psychoanalysis, Modernism, and the Fetish.* Ithaca, NY: Cornell UP, 1993.

Ingarden, Roman. *Vom Erkennen des literarischen Kunstwerks.* Tübingen: Max Niemeyer, 1968.

Jensen, Birgit A. "Peter Schneider's *Vati:* Contesting a German Taboo." *Critique* 43, no. 1 (2001): 84–92.

Kaiser, Konstantin. "Kühler Kopf und warme Füße: Robert Schindels Wintermärchen." Review of *Gebürtig,* by Robert Schindel. *Literatur und Kritik* 265/266 (1992): 99–102.

Kanes, Eveline L. "In Search of Fathers." *Denver Quarterly* 18, no. 1 (1983): 3–13.

Karpf, Anne. *The War After: Living with the Holocaust.* London: Heinemann, 1996.

Kaukoreit, Volker. "Robert Schindel." In *Kritisches Lexikon zur deutschsprachigen Gegenwartsliteratur,* edited by Heinz Ludwig Arnold, vol. 8. Munich: Edition Text+Kritik, 1995.

Kenkel, Konrad. "Der lange Weg nach innen: Väter-Romane der 70er und 80er Jahre." In *Der Deutsche Roman nach 1945,* edited by Manfred Brauneck, 167–87. Bamberg: Buchners, 1993.

Kernmeyer, Hildegard. "Gebürtig Ohneland. Robert Schindel: Auf der Suche nach der verlorenen Identität." *Modern Austrian Literature* 27, no. 3–4 (1994): 173–92.

Kirmayer, Laurence J. "Landscapes of Memory: Trauma, Narrative and Dissociation." In *Tense Past: Cultural Essays in Trauma and Memory,* edited by Paul Antze and Michael Lambek, 173–98. New York: Routledge, 1996.

Klages, Norgard. *Look Back in Anger: Mother-Daughter and Father-Daughter Relationships in Women's Autobiographical Writings of the 1970s and 1980s.* New York: Peter Lang, 1995.

Klüger, Ruth. *weiter leben: Eine Jugend*. Munich: Deutscher Taschenbuch Verlag, 1992.

Konzett, Matthias. "The Politics of Recognition in Contemporary Austrian Jewish Literature." *Monatshefte* 90, no. 1 (1998): 71–88.

Koonz, Claudia. *Mothers in the Fatherland: Women, the Family and Nazi Politics*. New York: St. Martin's, 1987.

Kreis, Gabriele. "'Ach Vati, deine Substantive.'" *konkret* 6 (1987): 66–67.

Kühner, Angela. *Kollektive Traumata — Annahmen, Argumente, Konzepte: Eine Bestandsaufnahme nach dem 11. September*. Berlin: Berghof Forschungszentrum für konstruktive Konfliktbearbeitung, 2002.

LaCapra. Dominick. *History and Memory after Auschwitz*. Ithaca, NY: Cornell UP, 1998.

———. "Representing the Holocaust: Reflections on the Historians' Debate." In *Probing the Limits of Representation: Nazism and the "Final Solution,"* edited by Saul Friedlander, 108–27. Cambridge, MA: Harvard UP, 1992.

———. "Trauma, Absence, Loss." *Critical Inquiry* 25 (Summer 1999): 696–727.

Laub, Dori, and Nanette C. Auerhahn. "Knowing and Not Knowing Massive Psychic Trauma: Forms of Traumatic Memory." *International Journal of Psycho-Analysis* 74 (1993): 287–302.

Levi, Primo. *The Drowned and the Saved*. Translated by Raymond Rosenthal. New York: Summit Books, 1988.

Linville, Susan E. *Feminism, Film, Fascism: Women's Auto/biographical Film in Postwar Germany*. Austin, TX: U of Texas P, 1998.

Lyotard, Jean-François. *The Differend: Phrases in Dispute*. Translated by Georges Van Den Abbeele. Minneapolis: U of Minnesota P, 1998.

Magnus, Uwe. "Die Einschaltquoten und Sehbeteilungen." In *Im Kreuzfeuer: Der Fernsehfilm Holocaust — eine Nation ist betroffen*, edited by Peter Märtesheimer and Ivo Frenzel, 221–24. Frankfurt am Main: Fischer, 1979.

Mahlendorf, Ursula R. "Trauma Narrated, Read and (Mis)understood: Bernhard Schlink's *The Reader*: '. . . irrevocably complicit in their crimes . . .'" *Monatshefte* 95, no. 3 (2003): 458–81.

Marcuse, Harold. "Generational Cohorts and the Shaping of Popular Attitudes towards the Holocaust." In *Remembering for the Future: The Holocaust in an Age of Genocide,* edited by John K. Roth and Elisabeth Maxwell, 3: 652–63. London: Palgrave, 2001.

Martin, Richard. "Art Spiegelman's *Maus*, or 'The Way it Really Happened.'" In *Historiographic Metafiction in Modern American and Canadian Literature*, edited by Bernd Engler and Kurt Müller, 373–82. Paderborn: Ferdinand Schöningh, 1994.

Massing, Almuth. "Auswirkungen anhaltender nationalsozialistischer Weltanschauungen in Familienschicksalen." In Heimannsberg and Schmidt, *Das kollektive Schweigen: Nationalsozialistische Vergangenheit und gebrochene Identität in der Psychotherapie*, 71–84. In English, "Effects of Lingering Nazi Worldviews in Family Life." In Heimannsberg and Schmidt, *The Collective Identity: German Identity and the Legacy of Shame*, 95–108.

Mayer, Hans. "Väter, Mütter, Töchter, Söhne." In *Die unerwünschte Literatur: Deutsche Schriftsteller und Bücher, 1968–1985*, 127–41. Berlin: Siedler, 1989.

McGlothlin, Erin. "Theorizing the Perpetrator in Bernhard Schlink's *The Reader* and Martin Amis's *Time's Arrow*," forthcoming in *After Representation?*, edited by R. Clifton Spargo and Robert Ehrenreich.

Meckel, Christoph. *Suchbild: Über meinen Vater*. Düsseldorf: Claasen, 1980.

Mellinkoff, Ruth. *The Mark of Cain*. Berkeley, CA: U of California P, 1981.

Metz, Joseph. "'Truth is a Woman': Post-Holocaust Narrative, Postmodernism, and the Gender of Fascism in Bernhard Schlink's *Der Vorleser*. *The German Quarterly* 77, no. 3 (Summer 2004): 300–323.

Meyers, Jeffrey, Jay Martin, and Conor Cruise O'Brien. "Session III: How to Recapture Selective Memories." *Partisan Review* 68, no. 1 (Winter 2001): 91–126.

Miller, Roger K. "A German Novelist Considers His Life." Review of *In My Brother's Shadow*, by Uwe Timm. *The Washington Times*, 3 Apr. 2005, B7.

Mitscherlich, Alexander. *Auf dem Weg zur vaterlosen Gesellschaft: Ideen zur Sozialpsychologie*. Munich: R. Piper, 1965. In English, *Society Without the Father: A Contribution to Social Psychology*. Translated by Eric Mosbacher. New York: Harcourt Brace and World, 1969.

Mitscherlich, Alexander, and Margarete Mitscherlich. *Die Unfähigkeit zu trauern: Grundlagen kollektiven Verhaltens*. Munich: R. Piper, 1967. In English, *The Inability to Mourn: Principles of Collective Behavior*. Translated by Beverley R. Placzek. New York: Grove P, 1975.

Modiano, Patrick. *Dora Bruder*. Paris: Gallimard, 1997. In English, *Dora Bruder*. Translated by Joanna Kilmartin. Berkeley, CA: U of California P, 1999.

———. *La Place de l'Étoile*. Paris: Gallimard, 1968.

Moffit, Gisela. *Bonds and Bondage: Daughter-Father Relationships in the Father Memoirs of German-Speaking Women Writers of the 1970s*. New York: Peter Lang, 1993.

Morgan, Peter. "The Sins of the Fathers: A Reappraisal of the Controversy about Peter Schneider's *Vati*." *German Life and Letters* 47, no. 1 (1994): 104–33.

Morris, Leslie, and Karen Remmler. *Contemporary Jewish Writing in Germany: An Anthology*. Lincoln, NE: U of Nebraska P, 2002.

Nabbe, Hildegard. "Die Enkelkinder des Doppeladlers: Einblendung von politischer Vergangenheit in den Alltag der Gegenwart in Robert Schindels *Gebürtig.*" *Modern Austrian Literature* 32, no. 2 (1999): 113–24.

Niven, Bill. *Facing the Nazi Past: United Germany and the Legacy of the Third Reich.* London: Routledge, 2002.

The Oxford Dictionary and Thesaurus. American Edition. Edited by Frank Abate. New York: Oxford UP, 1996.

Peitsch, Helmut. "Die Väter-Welle und die Literaturkritik." In *Subjektivität — Innerlichkeit — Abkehr vom Politischen? Tendenzen der deutschsprachigen Literatur der 70er Jahren,* edited by Keith Bullivant and Hans-Joachim Althof, 71–87. Bonn: DAAD, 1986.

Posthofen, Renate. "Erinnerte Geschichte(n): Robert Schindels Roman *Gebürtig.*" *Modern Austrian Literature* 27, no. 3–4 (1994): 193–211.

Prager, Emily. *Eve's Tattoo.* New York: Random House, 1991.

Prince, Robert M. *The Legacy of the Holocaust: Psychohistorical Themes in the Second Generation.* Ann Arbor, MI: UMI Research P, 1985.

Raczymow, Henri. "Memory Shot Through with Holes." Translated by Alan Astro. *Yale French Studies* 85 (1994): 98–105.

———. *Writing the Book of Esther.* Translated by Dori Katz. New York: Holmes and Meier, 1995.

Rehmann, Ruth. *Der Mann auf der Kanzel.* Munich: Hanser, 1979. In English, *The Man in the Pulpit.* Translated by Christoph Lohmann and Pamela Lohmann. Lincoln: U of Nebraska P, 1997.

Reynolds, Daniel. "A Portrait of Misreading: Bernhard Schlink's *Der Vorleser.*" *Seminar* 39, no. 3 (September 2003): 238–56.

Riordan, Colin. Introduction to *Vati,* by Peter Schneider. Edited by Riordan, 1–31. Manchester, UK: Manchester UP, 1993.

Roberts, Ulla. *Starke Mütter — ferne Väter: Töchter reflektieren ihre Kindheit im Nationalsozialismus und in der Nachkriegszeit.* Frankfurt am Main: Fischer, 1994.

Rosen, Alan. "The Language of Survival: English as Metaphor in Spiegelman's *Maus.*" *Prooftexts* 15, no. 3 (1995): 249–62.

Rosen, Norma. *Accidents of Influence: Writing as a Woman and a Jew in America.* Albany: State U of New York P, 1992.

Rosenbaum, Thane. *Elijah Visible.* New York: St. Martin's, 1996.

———. *The Golems of Gotham.* New York: HarperCollins, 2002.

———. *Second Hand Smoke.* New York: St. Martin's P, 1999.

Rosenfeld, Alvin H. *Imagining Hitler.* Bloomington, IN: Indiana UP, 1985.

Rosenthal, Gabriele, ed. *The Holocaust in Three Generations: Families of Victims and Perpetrators of the Nazi Regime*. London: Cassell, 1998.

Rossbacher, Brigitte. "Cultural Memory and Family Stories: Uwe Timm's *Am Beispiel meines Bruders*." *Gegenwartsliteratur* 4 (2005): 236–56.

Santner, Eric. *Stranded Objects: Mourning, Memory and Film in Postwar Germany*. Ithaca, NY: Cornell UP, 1990.

Schindel, Robert. *Gebürtig*. Frankfurt am Main: Suhrkamp, 1992. In English, *Born-Where*. Translated by Michael Roloff. Riverside, CA: Ariadne P, 1995.

Schlant, Ernestine. *The Language of Silence: West German Literature and the Holocaust*. New York: Routledge, 1991.

Schlink, Bernhard. *Der Vorleser*. Zürich: Diogenes, 1995. In English, *The Reader*. Translated by Carol Jane Janeway. New York: Vintage, 1997.

Schlipphacke, Heidi M. "Enlightenment, Reading, and the Female Body: Bernhard Schlink's *Der Vorleser*." *Gegenwartsliteratur* 1 (2002): 310–28.

Schmitz, Helmut. *On Their Own Terms: The Legacy of National Socialism in Post-1990 German Fiction*. Birmingham, UK: U of Birmingham P, 2004.

Schneider, Michael. "Väter und Söhne, posthum.: Das beschädigte Verhältnis zweier Generationen." In *Den Kopf vekehrt aufgesetzt oder Die melancholische Linke: Aspekte des Kulturzerfalls in den siebziger Jahren*, 8–64. Darmstadt: Luchterhand, 1981. In English, "Fathers and Sons, Retrospectively: The Damaged Relationship Between Two Generations." Translated by Jamie Owen Daniel. *New German Critique* 31 (1984): 3–51.

Schneider, Peter. "German Postwar Strategies of Coming to Terms with the Past." In *Legacies and Ambiguities: Postwar Fiction and Culture in West Germany and Japan*, edited by Ernestine Schlant and J. Thomas Rimer, 279–88. Washington, DC: The Woodrow Wilson Center P and The Johns Hopkins UP, 1991.

———. *Vati*. Darmstadt: Luchterhand, 1987.

Schönfeld, Gerda-Marie. "So eine Nachbarschaft." *Der Spiegel* 11 (9 March 1987): 216–19.

Schwaiger, Brigitte. *Lange Abwesenheit*. Vienna: Paul Zsolnay, 1980.

Schwarz, Gudrun. "'During Total War, We Girls Want to Be Where We Can Really Accomplish Something': What Women Do in Wartime." In *Crimes of War: Guilt and Denial in the Twentieth Century*, edited by Omer Bartov, Atina Grossmann, and Mary Nolan. New York: New Press, 2002: 121–37.

Sebald, W. G. *Luftkrieg und Literatur*. Munich: Carl Hanser, 1999. In English, *On the Natural History of Destruction*. Translated by Anthea Bell. New York: Random House, 2003.

Segebrecht, Wulf. "Christoph Meckels *Suchbild* unter anderen Vaterbildern." In *Christoph Meckel*, edited by Franz Loquai, 78–96. Eggingen, Germany: Isele, 1993.

Semel, Nava. "Intersoul Flanking: Writing about the Holocaust." In *Second Generation Voices: Reflections by Children of Holocaust Survivors and Perpetrators,* edited by Alan L. Berger and Naomi Berger, 66–71. Syracuse, NY: Syracuse UP, 2001:.

Sicher, Efraim, ed. *Breaking Crystal: Writing and Memory after Auschwitz.* Urbana, IL: U of Illinois P, 1998.

———. "In the Shadow of History: Second Generation Writers and Artists and the Shaping of Holocaust Memory in Israel and America." *Judaism: A Quarterly Journal of Jewish Life and Thought* 47, no. 2 (1998): 169–86.

Sichrovsky, Peter. *Schuldig geboren: Kinder aus Nazifamilien.* Cologne: Kiepenheuer & Witsch, 1987. In English, *Born Guilty: Children of Nazi Families.* Translated by Jean Steinberg. New York: Basic Books, 1988.

Šlibar, Neva. "Anschreiben gegen das Schweigen: Robert Schindel, Ruth Klüger, die Postmoderne und Vergangenheitsbewältigung." In *Jenseits des Diskurses: Literatur und Sprache in der Postmoderne,* edited by Albert Berger and Gerda Elisabeth Moser, 337–56. Vienna: Passagen, 1994.

Snyder Hook, Elizabeth. *Family Secrets and the Contemporary German Novel: Literary Explorations of the Aftermath of the Third Reich.* Rochester, NY: Camden House, 2001.

Sobol, Joshua, and Niklas Frank. "Der Vater: Eine blutige Komödie." *Zeitung, Schauspielhaus Bochum* 9 (1996): 123–64.

Spiegelman, Art. *The Complete Maus.* CD-ROM. New York: Voyager, 1994.

——— *Maus I: A Survivor's Tale: My Father Bleeds History.* New York: Pantheon, 1986.

——— *Maus II: A Survivor's Tale: And Here My Troubles Began.* New York: Pantheon, 1991.

Staub, Michael E. "The Shoah Goes On and On: Remembrance and Representation in Art Spiegelman's *Maus.*" *Melus* 20, no. 3 (1995): 33–46.

Stier, Oren Baruch. *Committed to Memory: Cultural Mediations of the Holocaust.* Amherst, MA: U of Massachusetts P, 2003.

Tabachnick, Stephen E. "Of *Maus* and Memory: The Structure of Art Spiegelman's Graphic Novel of the Holocaust." *Word and Image* 9, no. 2(1993): 154–62.

Taberner, Stuart. *German Literature of the 1990s and Beyond: Normalization and the Berlin Republic.* Rochester, NY: Camden House, 2005.

Theweleit, Klaus. *Männerphantasien.* Vol. 1. Frankfurt am Main: Roter Stern, 1977.

Timm, Uwe. *Am Beispiel meines Bruders.* Cologne: Kiepenheuer & Witsch, 2003. In English, *In My Brother's Shadow.* Translated by Anthea Bell. New York: Farrar, Straus & Giroux, 2005.

Der Vater. By Joshua Sobol and Niklas Frank. Directed by Uwe Dag Berlin. Schauspielhaus Bochum. 12 June 1997.

Volkan, Vamik. "Traumatized Societies and Psychological Care: Expanding the Concept of Preventative Medicine." *Mind and Human Interaction* 11, no. 3 (2000): 177–94.

Vormweg, Heinrich. "Ein kleineres Ensemble von Grabmälern: Die Väterbilder in der neueren Literatur." In *Sturz der Götter? Vaterbilder im 20. Jahrhundert*, edited by Werner Faulstich and Gunter E. Grimm, 213–28. Frankfurt am Main: Suhrkamp, 1989.

Wardi, Dina. *Memorial Candles: Children of the Holocaust.* Translated by Naomi Goldblum. London: Tavistock, 1992.

Webster's Encyclopedic Unabridged Dictionary of the English Language. New York: Gramercy Books, 1989.

Wehler, Hans-Ulrich. "Vergleichen — nicht moralisieren." Interview with Stephan Burgdorff and Christian Habbe. *Der Spiegel* 2 (2003): 51–52.

Weigel, Sigrid. "'Generation as a Symbolic Form: On the Genealogical Discourse of Memory since 1945.'" *The Germanic Review* 77, no. 4 (2002): 264–77.

———. *Die Stimme der Medusa: Schreibweisen in der Gegenwartsliteratur von Frauen.* Dülme-Hiddingsel, Germany: Tende, 1987.

———. "The Symptomatology of a Universalized Concept of Trauma: On the Failing of Freud's Reading of Tasso in the Trauma of History." *New German Critique* 90 (2003): 85–94.

———. "Télescopage im Unbewussten: Zum Verhältnis von Trauma, Geschichtsbegriff und Literatur." In *Bruchlinien: Tendenzen der Holocaustforschung*, edited by Getrud Koch, 255–79. Cologne: Böhlau, 1999.

Windaus-Walser, Karin. "Frauen im Nationalsozialismus: Eine Herausforderung für feministische Theoriebildung." In *Töchter-Fragen: NS-Frauen-Geschichte*, edited by Lerke Gravenhorst and Carmen Tatschmurat, 59–72. Freiburg: Kore, 1990.

Wittstock, Uwe. "Vatis Tod." *Frankfurter Allegemeine Zeitung*, 11 April 1987, 22.

Wutschke, Jürgen. "Er hält ihn fest in seinem Arm." Review of *Am Beispiel meines Bruders,* by Uwe Timm. *viewmag.de* 47 (2003). http://www.viewmag.de/kultur/03/47/timm.html. Accessed 19 Nov. 2003.

Young, James E. "The Holocaust as Vicarious Past: Art Spiegelman's *Maus* and the Afterimages of History." *Critical Inquiry* 24, no. 3 (1998): 666–700.

———. *Writing and Rewriting the Holocaust: Narrative and the Consequences of Interpretation.* Bloomington, IN: Indiana UP, 1988.

Zeitlin, Froma I. "New Soundings in Holocaust Literature: A Surplus of Memory." In *Catastrophe and Meaning: The Holocaust and the Twentieth Century,* edited by Moishe Postone and Eric Santner, 173–208. Chicago: U of Chicago P, 2003.

———. "The Vicarious Witness: Belated Memory and Authorial Presence in Recent Holocaust Literature." In *Shaping Losses: Cultural Memory and the Holocaust,* edited by Julia Epstein and Lori Hope Lekkovitz, 128–60. Urbana, IL: U of Illinois P, 2001.

Index

achrony. *See* timelessness
acting-out, 213–14
alienation effect. *See* Verfremdungseffekt
Améry, Jean, 215, 218
amnesia, 4, 9, 24, 55, 56, 60, 221, 228
Anhalt, Irene, 3
Anhalt, Irene, works by: "Abschied von meinem Vater" ("Farewell to My Father"), 3–5, 6, 7, 10, 12, 27, 181
anti-Semitism, 96, 98, 128, 130, 131, 135, 136, 179
Antze, Paul, 91
Apel, Dora, 23
Appelfeld, Aharon, 66
atlas, genre of, 133, 137–39
Auerhahn, Nanette C., 6, 7, 56
Auschwitz, 3, 21, 22, 32, 39, 49, 66, 68, 69, 71, 73, 76, 78–79, 84, 125, 125, 128, 129, 136, 139, 149, 204. *See also* Auschwitz tattoo
Auschwitz tattoo: assumption of in the second generation, 3, 23; meaning of, 3, 20, 21–23
Austria, 25; relationship between Jews and non-Jews in, 91, 93, 96, 97, 98–107, 114, 230
autobiography, 37–38, 138, 145–52, 156, 172–73, 180, 199–200, 202. *See also under* fiction

Bagley, Petra M., 145
Bar-On, Dan, 6, 13, 14, 174
Behrens, Katja, 33

Behrens, Katja, works by: "Arthur Mayer oder das Schweigen" ("Arthur Mayer or The Silence"), 33, 35, 36, 37, 39, 125–31, 133–36, 139
Berger, Alan L., 8, 11, 13, 16, 17, 37, 92, 113
Berger, Naomi, 13, 16, 92
Bergmann, Martin S., 6, 13, 14
Bible, The, 17, 18, 20, 24, 25, 26, 48, 144
Bildungsroman, 71, 76, 77
biography, 37–38, 127–28, 133–34, 139, 145–49
Bloch, Ernst, 197, 198
Bluebeard, Grimm story of, 216–19, 221
Bosmajian, Hamida, 70
branding. *See* marking, tropes of
Brandstetter, Alois, 145
Brasch, Thomas, 149
Braun, Michael, 220–21
Broder, Henryk M., 34, 183
Browning, Christopher R., 174, 215, 218
Bubis, Ignatz, 201
Bukiet, Melvin Jules, 229
Bullivant, Keith, 145, 200
Bunte Illustrierte, 38
Burgess, Gordon, 149, 150–51, 156, 172
Burstein, Janet, 46, 64

Cain, mark of, 26, 144, 159, 225
Calhoun, Karen S., 52
Caruth, Cathy, 52–53, 54
Celan, Paul, 113
Chaplin, Charlie, 193

248 ◆ INDEX

children: of Holocaust perpetrators, 3–5, 5–12, 14–16, 24–30, 91–93, 98–102, 145–49, 152–56, 174–78, 180–81, 187, 205–10, 212–15, 229–31; of Holocaust survivors, 1–3, 5–12, 14–16, 20–24, 27–28, 44–47, 53–54, 91–93, 98–102, 113, 127–28, 229–31. *See also* second generation
chronology. *See* narrative time
Cohen, Robert, 199, 220, 226
coming to terms with the past. *See Vergangenheitsbewältigung*

Dachau, 32, 85
Danieli, Yael, 6
Dattenberg, Simone, 220
denial, 30, 46, 96, 97, 137, 139, 172, 179, 214, 227
detective story, 126, 128
diegetic levels. *See* narrative levels
Diner, Dan, 14, 15, 230
discourse, narratological category of, 70–76, 86–89
displacement, 10, 19, 52, 93, 127–28, 136, 196
dissociation: in narrative, 57–61, 63, 64; as a symptom of trauma, 55–57
documentary project, 133–39
Doherty, Thomas, 69
Donahue, William Collins, 207–8, 211
Drancy, 126

earthquake, Lyotard's metaphor of, 228–29
Eckstaedt, Anita, 6, 14
Egoyan, Atom, 87
encyclopedia, genre of, 133, 139
Endlösung (Final Solution), 152–53, 156, 172, 224–25
epic narrative, 71, 76
Epstein, Helen, 13

Erbsünde (original sin), 25
Erlanger, Steven, 203
Ewert, Jeanne C., 72, 75
Ezrahi, Sidra DeKoven, 228

fathers. *See under Väterliteratur*
fiction, 37–38, 93, 136, 149–52, 156, 172, 193; distinction between autobiography and, 37–38, 148–52
Fiero, Petra S., 130
Figge, Susan, 19, 145, 146, 175–76, 180
Foer, Jonathan Safran, works by: *Everything is Illuminated*, 231–32
Fölting, Anne, 81
France: collaboration with Nazis in, 131–32; Holocaust memory in, 126–27, 131–33, 137–39
Frank, Hans, 34, 38, 94, 182, 186, 188
Frank, Niklas, 34, 94
Frank, Niklas, works by: *Meine Deutsche Mutter*, 183; *Der Vater: Eine Abrechnung* (*In the Shadow of the Reich*), 34, 36, 37, 38, 39, 182–86, 188, 198, 214. *See also Der Vater* (play co-authored with Joshua Sobol) *under* Sobol, Joshua
Freeman, Thomas, 94, 105, 108
Fresco, Nadine, 8, 9–10, 23, 43, 56–57, 64, 210
Freud, Sigmund, 7, 52, 53, 54, 175
Frieden, Sandra, 146
Fröhlich, Hans J., 145
Frühwald, Wolfgang, 145, 146, 181
fugue states. *See* dissociation
fuzzy temporality, 86–87

Gebirtig, Mordechai, 94
Gebürtig (film). *See under* Schindel, Robert

Gehrke, Ralph, 145, 146
gender: Nazi ideology of, 184, 190, 197–98; role of in relationships between Jews and non-Jews in Austria, 102–7. *See also under Väterliteratur;* women
generational conflict. *See under* Germany, relationship between postwar generations in
Genette, Gérard, 71, 73, 76, 86, 88
genre, 37, 71, 128, 133–34, 139, 145–52, 173–74, 175–76, 199–200, 202–3, 214, 216, 220. *See also* autobiography; fiction
Germany: discourse on German wartime suffering in, 201–2, 215–16, 219, 222–23, 226; discourse on Holocaust in, 4, 9, 19, 35, 128–31, 134–36, 145–46, 151, 194–95, 200–202, 212–15, 221–26; discourse on women in postwar period in, 177–81, 194–95; effacement of Jewish memory in, 9, 128–31, 134–36, 155, 210–11, 224–26; relationship between postwar generations in, 19, 145–47, 152–56, 174–75, 181, 187, 203–10, 212–14; student generation in, 152–56, 205–10, 212–14
Giordano, Ralph, 24, 182, 183
glass wall, metaphor of, 98, 102, 103, 104, 106, 230
Goldhagen, Daniel, 201
Grass, Günter, 202
Grimm, Reinhold, 145, 146, 148
Grossman, David, 22
guilt: assumption of by children of Holocaust perpetrators, 5, 24–27, 143–45, 156–63, 219, 224–27; of Holocaust perpetrators, 24, 186, 201, 203–4, 208, 214

Hamlet, figure of, 148
Hansen, Miriam, 172
Hardtmann, Gertrud, 6
Harrison, Keith, 69, 72, 74, 76
Hartman, Geoffrey, 12, 14, 17, 125, 126
Hass, Aaron, 13
Haubl, Rolf, 146
Heberer, Patricia, 207
Herman, David, 86–88
Hershman, Marcie, 45, 46, 60
Hewitt, Andrew, 97–98
Hirsch, Marianne, 10–11, 14, 17, 53–54, 55, 70, 72, 74, 76, 84, 127, 231
Historian's Debate, 200
Hitler, Adolf: figure of in literature, 186, 192–98
Hitler Youth, 18
Hoffman, Eva, 6, 7, 8, 9, 18, 32, 199, 230
Holocaust (television mini-series), 146
Horowitz, Sara, 38
Hulse, Michael, 177–78, 180, 181, 184, 194
Huyssen, Andreas, 72

Iadonisi, Rick, 75
Ian, Marcia, 192
iconography, Holocaust, 4, 20–24, 30
identification: with perpetrators of the Holocaust, 5, 28, 68, 81, 159, 172, 212, 214, 226–27; with victims of the Holocaust, 28, 30, 127, 155–56
images, 43–44, 66–69, 73, 80–85
imagination, role of in the second generation, 10–11, 14, 36–39, 65, 75, 127–28, 150–151
Ingarden, Roman, 60

Jensen, Birgit A., 149, 150, 159
Jewish mourning ritual, 23–24, 43
Jewishness, 18, 44, 46, 62–63, 83, 96, 98–107, 128–31, 134–36
Jucovy, Milton E., 6, 13, 14

kaddish. See Jewish mourning ritual
Kaiser, Konstantin, 93, 107, 109
Kanes, Eveline L., 176
Karpf, Anne, works by: *The War After: Living with the Holocaust*, 1–3, 4, 5, 6, 7, 10, 12, 22, 27–28, 30
Kaukoreit, Volker, 37, 93, 108, 109, 123
Kenkel, Konrad, 145, 146, 176–77, 180
keri'ah. See Jewish mourning ritual
Kernmeyer, Hildegard, 105–6, 107, 109, 110, 115, 123
Kirmayer, Laurence J., 55–56, 60–61
Klages, Norgard, 145
Klüger, Ruth, 228
Konzett, Matthias, 93, 109–10
Koonz, Claudia, 180
Kreis, Gabriele, 150
Kristallnacht, 18, 129, 200
Kühner, Angela, 15
Künstlerroman, 71, 76, 77

LaCapra, Dominick, 69, 72, 75, 76, 78, 213–14
Lambek, Michael, 91
Language. *See under Väterliteratur*
latent memory, 52
Laub, Dori, 6, 7, 56
League of German Girls, 18
Levi, Primo, 21, 215, 218, 221
lexicon, genre of, 133–36, 139
Linville, Susan E., 194–95

literature of the fathers. *See Väterliteratur*
Lyotard, Jean-François, 228–29

Magnus, Uwe, 146
Mahlendorf, Ursula R., 206–7, 210
maps. *See* atlas, genre of
Marcuse, Harold, 18
marking: Nazi methods of, 3, 20–21; tropes of: in the legacy of Holocaust perpetration, 2–7, 9, 24–30, 144–45, 157–59, 192–94, 216–19; in the legacy of Holocaust survival, 2–3, 5–7, 8–9, 20–24, 27–28, 30, 44, 68. *See also* Auschwitz tattoo; Cain, mark of
Martin, Richard, 74, 75
Massing, Almuth, 9
Mayer, Hans, 145
McGlothlin, Erin, 204
Meckel, Christoph, 144
melancholia, 195
Mellinkoff, Ruth, 26
memorial candles, 47, 51
Memorial to the Murdered Jews of Europe, 201
Mengele, Josef, 34, 38, 67, 68, 149, 150, 157
Mengele, Rolf, 149, 150
metonymy, 33, 104, 136, 168, 193
Metz, Joseph, 207
Miller, Roger K., 220
Mitscherlich, Alexander, 194–95
Mitscherlich, Margarete, 194–95
Modiano, Patrick, 33
Modiano, Patrick, works by: *Dora Bruder*, 33, 35, 36, 37, 38, 39, 126–28, 131–34, 137–39; *Le Place de l'Étoile*, 33
Moffit, Gisela, 19, 145, 146, 148
Morgan, Peter, 149, 150
Morris, Leslie, 125–26

mothers. *See under* phallic mother; *Väterliteratur;* women
mourning, 8, 23–24, 30, 43–44, 46, 83, 194–95, 218, 221–23

Nabbe, Hildegard, 105
naming, tropes of, 93–97, 134–36, 156–63
narrating, narratological category of, 70–71, 73–76, 86–90
narrative coherence, 56, 59, 61, 92–93
narrative continuity, 45–46, 51, 78, 92, 100, 110
narrative counterparts, 91–107, 113
narrative crisis, 110, 120, 122, 159
narrative levels, 70–78, 91–97, 107
narrative metalepses, 73
narrative time, 69–90, 107
narrative voice, 56, 59–60
narrator, role of, 70, 72–73, 107–24. *See also* split narrator
negative symbiosis, 230
Neue Innerlichkeit (New Inwardness), 199
Neue Sensibilität (New Sensibility), 199
Neue Subjektivität (New Subjectivity), 199, 200, 202
Niven, Bill, 200–201

Oedipal complex, 19, 174–75, 194–95, 207, 226
original sin. *See Erbsünde*
otherness, 5–7, 107, 123, 135, 144, 152, 156–63, 192, 198, 224

Peitsch, Helmut, 145
phallic mother, 192–98
phantom pain, metaphor of, 9–10, 56–57, 210

polychronic narration, 86–88
polychrony, 86–88
polyidentity, 44–47, 49, 51, 57, 59
polyvocality. *See* narrative voice
Posthofen, Renate, 93, 107, 109
postmemorial narrative, 133, 139
postmemory, 10–11, 14, 53–54, 55, 127–28
Post-Traumatic Stress Disorder, 52
Prager, Emily, 20
Prince, Robert M., 13
psychoanalysis, 52, 53, 183, 194

Raczymow, Henri, 1, 11, 24
Ravensbrück, 32
reading, trope of, 163–68
Reagan, Ronald, 200
Rehmann, Ruth, 175
Remmler, Karen, 125–26
repair, metaphors of, 11–12, 13, 47, 51, 65, 106–7, 123–24, 231–32
repetition-compulsion: in narrative, 61–65; as a symptom of trauma, 53, 54–55
representation, 10–13, 37–39, 55, 66–69, 73–76, 78–79, 81, 89–90, 91, 101, 127–28, 133–34, 147–49
repression, 12, 46, 52, 55–56, 58, 95, 97, 159, 177, 180, 195, 213, 221, 222, 224, 231
Resick, Patricia A., 52
Reynolds, Daniel, 206
Riordan, Colin, 38, 144, 145, 146, 149–50, 157, 172
Roberts, Ulla, 178–79, 180–81
Rosen, Alan, 70, 76
Rosen, Norma, 14
Rosenbaum, Thane, 31
Rosenbaum, Thane, works by: *Elijah Visible*, 31, 36, 37, 39, 43–51, 57–65; *The Golems of Gotham*, 31; *Secondhand Smoke*, 31

Rosenfeld, Alvin H., 193–94
Rosenthal, Gabriele, 6, 14
Rossbacher, Brigitte, 215–16
rupture, metaphors of, 10–12, 17, 23–24, 30, 47, 59, 61, 64–65, 69, 84, 101, 109–10, 228–30

Santner, Eric, 8, 14, 18–19
scapegoating, 21, 25, 195
scar, metaphor of. *See* marking, tropes of; wound, metaphor of
Schindel, Robert, 32
Schindel, Robert, works by: *Gebürtig* (film), 32; *Gebürtig* (novel), 32–33, 36, 37, 39, 91–124, 230
Schlant, Ernestine, 28, 145, 146, 155, 200, 202, 206, 210, 213
Schlink, Bernhard, 34
Schlink, Bernhard, works by: *Der Vorleser* (*The Reader*), 35–36, 37, 39, 199, 202–15, 226–27
Schlipphacke, Heidi M., 207
Schmitz, Helmut, 206
Schneider, Michael, 28, 145–49, 152, 153, 174–75, 176, 213
Schneider, Peter, 34, 145, 151, 182
Schneider, Peter, works by: *Vati*, 34, 37, 38, 39, 143–45, 149–73, 182
Schönfeld, Gerda-Marie, 150
Schwaiger, Brigitte, 175
Schwarz, Gudrun, 180
Sebald, W. G., 201
second generation: analysis of the term, 16–18, 19–20; in Austria, 91, 93; comparison between children of perpetrators and children of survivors, 5–12, 13, 15, 16, 19–20, 24, 30, 98–107, 146–47, 229–31; relationship with war generation, 8, 18–19, 28, 47–51, 65, 68, 82, 83–84, 145–47, 152–56, 174–75, 181, 187, 203–10, 212–14, 221–26. *See also* children, of Holocaust perpetrators; children, of Holocaust survivors
second-generation Holocaust literature, 8, 10–12, 13–16, 20–30, 31–39, 47, 127–28. *See also Väterliteratur*
second-generation witness, 17, 74, 113–24
Segebrecht, Wulf, 145, 146, 200
Seghers, Anna, 87
Semel, Nava, 11, 23
sewing, metaphor of, 11–12, 23
sexual alterity, 105–6
Shivah. *See* Jewish mourning ritual
Sicher, Efraim, 9, 10, 13–14, 17, 26, 38, 45–46
Sichrovsky, Peter, works by: *Schuldig geboren* (*Born Guilty*), 25–27, 29–30, 150
signification, 8–10, 12, 44, 91, 93, 144, 172, 192–98; crisis of, 10–13, 20, 23, 25, 27, 30, 39, 44, 156–63, 192
signifiers of gender and sex, 177, 188–90, 192–93, 196, 197, 198
Šlibar, Neva, 92, 93
Snyder Hook, Elizabeth, 145, 149
Sobol, Joshua, 34
Sobol, Joshua, works by: *Ghetto*, 191; *Der Vater: Eine blutige Komödie* (co-authored with Niklas Frank), 34–35, 36, 37, 38, 39, 183, 186–98
Spiegelman, Art, 70, 77; use of animal trope, 72, 74–75, 78–79, 81
Spiegelman, Art, works by: *Maus I & II*, 20, 31–32, 33, 36, 37, 38, 39, 66–90
Spielberg, Steven, 201
split narrator, 107–15

Staub, Michael E., 72, 81
Stepanik, Lukas, 32
Stern, 34, 182
Stier, Oren Baruch, 20
stigma (stigmata), 3, 4, 5–7, 8–10, 12, 20–30, 144–45, 155, 157, 185, 202, 224–25
story, narratological category of, 70–76, 86–89
storytelling, 105, 106
student generation. *See under* Germany
Sturm und Drang, 148
Stürmer, Der, 135
super-present, 76–78, 82, 85–89. *See also* narrative time
symbiosis, German-Jewish, 114, 135. *See also* negative symbiosis

Tabachnick, Stephen E., 71, 77
Taberner, Stuart, 220
Tasso, 53
Täterliteratur, 19
tattoo. *See* Auschwitz tattoo
temporality. *See* narrative time
Tendenzwende (change in trend), 199
testimony, 53, 70–73, 76, 86, 99, 113–14, 116, 123–24, 212, 228
theater. *See under Väterliteratur*
Theresienstadt, 95, 123
Theweleit, Klaus, 198
third generation, 18, 19, 231–32
Thomas, D. M., 87
tikkun (repair), 11
timelessness, 78, 86–88. *See also* narrative time
Timm, Uwe, 215
Timm, Uwe, works by:
 Am Beispiel meines Bruders (*In My Brother's Shadow*), 35, 36, 37, 39, 199, 202–3, 215–27
trauma: characteristics of, 6, 12, 52–57, 213–14, 231; of children of Holocaust perpetrators, 6, 15, 213–14, 231; of children of Holocaust survivors, 15, 46, 53–55, 231; inherited, 5, 7–10, 46, 53–55, 231. *See also* acting-out; denial; displacement; dissociation; repetition-compulsion; repression; working-through
traumatic knowledge, 7, 12
traumatic paralysis, 64–65

Väterliteratur (literature of the fathers): analysis of the term, 14, 16, 18–20, 147; critique of National Socialist language in, 152–53, 169–72, 185, 203, 221–26; fiction and, 148–52; generic qualities of, 145–49, 172–73, 174–76; position of mothers in, 176–81, 195; question of gender and, 19, 175–81, 207; question of generations and, 18–19, 174–76, 203–15; recent permutations of, 203–27; role in Germany of, 145–49, 174–75; theater as space of, 186–88, 198; time span of, 145–46, 199–203
Verfremdungseffekt (alienation effect), 37, 38, 187, 191
Vergangenheitsbewältigung (mastery over the past), 147, 156, 173, 175, 182, 187, 194, 195, 206, 213
Volkan, Vamik, 231
Vormweg, Heinrich, 145, 182

Waffen SS, 35, 203, 215, 219
Walser, Martin, 201
Wardi, Dina, 28, 47, 61. *See also* memorial candles
Wehler, Hans-Ulrich, 201–2
Wehrmachtsaustellung (*Wehrmacht* exhibit), 201

Weigel, Sigrid, 14, 17–18, 24, 28, 53, 145
Windaus-Walser, Karin, 179
witnessing, 14, 23, 53, 68, 70–76, 89, 104, 109, 113–24
Wittstock, Uwe, 150
women: discourse about in postwar Germany, 177–81, 194–95; role of in the Nazi period, 178–81, 207. *See also* gender; *under Väterliteratur*
working-through, 213–14
wound, metaphor of, 2–3, 4–5, 8–9, 11, 13, 26, 43–44, 52, 53, 57, 81, 137, 144, 216–19, 230
writing, trope of, 163–72
Wutschke, Jürgen, 219–20

Young, James E., 17, 18, 47, 69, 70, 71, 72, 76, 84

Zeitlin, Froma I., 14, 44, 206